Death,
Grief,
and Caring
Relationships
SECOND EDITION

Death, Grief, and Caring Relationships

SECOND EDITION

Richard A. Kalish

BROOKS/COLE PUBLISHING COMPANY
MONTEREY, CALIFORNIA

Brooks/Cole Publishing Company
A Division of Wadsworth, Inc.

Printed in the United States of America

10 9 8 7 6 5 4 3 2 1

Library of Congress Cataloging in Publication Data

Kalish, Richard A. [date]
   Death, grief, and caring relationships.

   Bibliography: p.
   Includes indexes.
   1. Death 2. Bereavement. 3. Grief. 4. Helping
behavior. I. Title.
HQ1073.K34 1984   155.9'37   84-14994
isbn 0-534-03630-9

Sponsoring Editor: *C. Deborah Laughton*
Editorial Assistant: *Mary Tudor*
Production Editor: *Candyce Cameron*
Manuscript Editor: *Rephah Berg*
Permissions Editor: *Carline Haga*
Interior and Cover Design: *Vernon T. Boes*
Cover Photo: *Jerry Takigawa*
Art Coordinator: *Judith Macdonald*
Interior Illustration: *Kevin East*
Typesetting: *Instant Type, Monterey, California*
Printing and Binding: *R. R. Donnelley & Sons Company, Crawfordsville, Indiana*

TO TONI, WHO, AS WIFE, COMPANION, COLLEAGUE, MAY BE FOUND IN THIS BOOK IN MANY PLACES. WITH LOVE.

About the Author

Social psychologist Richard A. Kalish has, in his own words, "grown to ripe middle age with Brooks/Cole." His first textbook was published in 1959 by Wadsworth, the parent company of Brooks/Cole. In the quarter century of the company's existence, Kalish, a Ph.D. from Case Western Reserve University, has written books on study methods, introductory psychology, aging, and death. In addition to textbooks, he has published more than 100 journal articles and book chapters and numerous book reviews, mostly in the area of aging and death/loss. He and wife wife, Toni, presently live in Santa Fe, New Mexico, where they are collaborating on a book about adult development and mental retardation.

◆

Preface

Reading a book about death and grief can be a little like taking your favorite porcupine for a walk: you want to be close enough to enjoy the walk but not close enough to feel frequent sharp pain. Although the metaphor is obviously absurd, the reality isn't. We can spend our entire lives without even seeing a porcupine and not be the worse for it, but to avoid contemplating death or experiencing grief is not possible, and attempting to do so is not advisable.

In many ways, the philosophy that has guided the writing of this book is the same philosophy that guided the writing of the earlier edition. Like the first edition, this is written for people who want one book to give them the most understanding of death, the process of dying, and grief. These may be individuals who work, or plan to work, with the dying in professional or volunteer settings; they may be students in a class on death and grief; they may be people in the community who have found death or grief to be an important part of their lives; or they may simply be those who wish to learn and understand more about death and grief.

The second edition of *Death, Grief, and Caring Relationships*, like the first edition, is intended for people who are just beginning their inquiry as well as for those who have extensive experience with death, the dying, and the grieving. I have tried to combine the academic, the philosophic, and the practical, and I have tried to do this through an integration of the observations of professionals and nonprofessionals, of research and speculation, of theory and data, and of what I have learned personally and professionally over the years.

And finally, as in the first edition, I have tried to integrate academic/professional issues with personal concerns. Each of the five parts opens with a very personal account. The chapters themselves emphasize academic and professional issues that have been blended with matters of personal concern to the reader.

There is logic, but no magic, in the way the chapters are presently arranged. Each instructor can make whatever adjustments work best to accommodate his or her course. Since many students are eager to move quickly to personal and emotional issues, especially those involved in caring relationships, and some instructors may want to be responsive to these concerns, I can suggest an alternative pathway through the chapters:

> Begin with Chapter 1 but then go directly to Part 5 ("Caring Relationships"), Chapter 14; return to Chapters 2 and 3, move on to Chapters 7, 8, 10, and 11, then to Chapters 15 and 16; end with Chapters 4, 5, 6, 9, 12, and 13.

This arrangement deals first with caring relationships, the dying process, and grief, as well as relevant programs, and postpones the more philosophical issues and the extensive literature on attitudes. The part openings should be assigned the first time a chapter from that part is to be read, but I believe that these essays are sufficiently compelling that many students will read all of them in the first few days that they own the book.

At this juncture, I would like to acknowledge all of those individuals who helped with the first edition and whose efforts are still felt in this edition. I also want to acknowledge two wonderful women who, fortunately for me, were excellent typists and skilled in the use of the english language—Kathy Sallee and Shelley Stoffer. Special acknowledgement goes to those who contributed to this edition, either by writing for it (Philip H. Deisher, Toni C. Mehler) or by reading and reviewing (Jeanne Benoliel, University of Washington; Jane Glover, Sinclair Community College; Thomas Gullotta, Rita S. Heberer, Belleville Area College; Dennis Klass, Webster University; and Abraham Levine, El Camino College). Finally, I would like to thank the staff at Brooks/Cole Publishing Company—my editors, C. Deborah Laughton, Candy Cameron, and Rephah Berg; and designer Vernon Boes.

Richard A. Kalish

Contents

Curiosity

may have killed the cat; more likely
the cat was just unlucky, or else
wanted to see what death was like.

Face it.
Only the curious have, if they live,
a tale worth telling at all.
Dogs say cats love too much,
are irresponsible, marry too many wives,
desert their children, chill all dinner tables
with tales of their nine lives.

Yet—
a cat minority of one
is all that can be counted on
to tell the truth. And what he has to tell
on each return from hell
is this:
that dying is what the living do
that dying is what the loving do
and that dead dogs are those who do not know
that dying is what, to live, each has to do.

Toni C. Mehler

THE
MEANING
OF
DEATH

"DEATH.
DYING.
DEAD."

The Horse on the Dining-Room Table

I struggled up the slope of Mount Evmandu to meet the famous guru of Nepsim, an ancient sage whose name I was forbidden to place in print. I was much younger then, but the long and arduous hike exhausted me, and despite the cold, I was perspiring heavily when I reached the plateau where he made his home. He viewed me with a patient, almost amused look, and I smiled wanly at him between attempts to gulp the thin air into my lungs. I made my way across the remaining hundred meters and slowly sat down on the ground—propping myself up against a large rock just outside his abode.

We were both silent for several minutes, and I felt the tension in me rise, then subside until I was calm. Perspiration prickled my skin, but the slight breeze was pleasantly cool, and soon I was relaxed. Finally I turned my head to look directly into the clear brown eyes, which were bright within his lined face. I realized that I would need to speak.

"Father," I said, "I need to understand something about what it means to die, before I can continue my studies." He continued to gaze at me with his open, bemused expression. "Father," I went on, "I want to know what a dying person feels when no one will speak with him, nor be open enough to permit him to speak, about his dying."

He was silent for three, perhaps four, minutes. I felt at peace because I knew he would answer. Finally, as though in the middle of a sentence, he said "It is the horse on the dining-room table." We continued to gaze at each other for several minutes. I began to feel sleepy after my long journey, and I must have dozed off. When I woke up, he was gone, and the only activity was my own breathing.

I retraced my steps down the mountain—still feeling calm, knowing that his answer made me feel good, but not knowing why. I returned to my studies and gave no further thought to the event, not wishing to dwell upon it, yet secure that someday I should understand.

Many years later I was invited to the home of a casual friend for dinner. It was a modest house in a typical California development. The eight or ten other guests, people I did not know well, and I sat in the living room—drinking Safeway Scotch and bourbon and dipping celery sticks and raw cauliflower into a watery cheese dip. The conversation, initially halting, became more animated as we got to know each other and developed points of contact. The drinks undoubtedly also affected us.

Eventually the hostess appeared and invited us into the dining room for a buffet dinner. As I entered the room, I noticed with astonishment that a brown horse was sitting quietly on the dining-room table. Although it was small for a horse, it filled much of the large table. I caught my breath but didn't say anything. I was the first one to enter, so I was able to turn to watch the other guests. They responded much as I did—they entered, saw the horse, gasped or stared, but said nothing.

The host was the last to enter. He let out a silent shriek—looking rapidly from the horse to each of his guests with a wild stare. His mouth formed soundless words. Then in a voice choked with confusion he invited us to fill our plates from the buffet. His wife, equally disconcerted by what was clearly an unexpected horse, pointed to the name cards, which indicated where each of us was to sit.

The hostess led me to the buffet and handed me a plate. Others lined up behind me—each of us quiet. I filled my plate with rice and chicken and sat in my place. The others followed suit.

It was cramped, sitting there, trying to avoid getting too close to the horse, while pretending that no horse was there. My dish overlapped the edge of the table. Others found other ways to avoid physical contact with the horse. The host and hostess seemed as ill at ease as the rest of us. The conversation lagged. Every once in a while, someone would say something in an attempt to revive the earlier pleasant and innocuous discussion, but the overwhelming presence of the horse so filled our thoughts that talk of taxes or politics or the lack of rain seemed inconsequential.

Dinner ended, and the hostess brought coffee. I can recall everything on my plate and yet have no memory of having eaten. We drank in silence—all of us trying not to look at the horse, yet unable to keep our eyes or thoughts anywhere else.

I thought several times of saying "Hey, there's a horse on the dining-room table." But I hardly knew the host, and I didn't wish to embarrass him by mentioning something that obviously discomforted him at least as much as it discomforted me. After all, it was his house. And what do you say to a man with a horse on his dining-room table? I could have said that I did not mind, but that was not true—its presence upset me so much that I enjoyed neither the dinner nor the company. I could have said that I knew how difficult it was to have a horse on your dining-room table, but that wasn't true either; I had no idea. I could have said something like "How do you feel about having a horse on your dining-room table?" but I didn't want to sound like a psychologist. Perhaps, I thought, if I ignore it, it will go away. Of course I knew that it wouldn't. It didn't.

I later learned that the host and hostess were hoping the dinner would be a success in spite of the horse. They felt that to mention it would make us so uncomfortable that we wouldn't enjoy our visit—of course we didn't enjoy the evening anyway. They were fearful that we would try to offer them sympathy, which they didn't want, or understanding, which they needed but could not accept. They wanted the party to be a success, so they decided to try to make the evening as enjoyable as possible. But it was apparent that they—like their guests—could think of little else than the horse.

I excused myself shortly after dinner and went home. The evening had been terrible. I never wanted to see the host and hostess again, although I was eager to seek out the other guests and learn what they felt about the occasion. I felt confused about what had happened and extremely tense. The evening had been grotesque. I was careful to avoid the host and hostess after that, and I did my best to stay away altogether from the neighborhood.

Recently I visited Nepsim again. I decided to seek out the guru once more.

He was still alive, although nearing death, and he would speak only to a few. I repeated my journey and eventually found myself sitting across from him.

Once again I asked "Father, I want to know what a dying person feels when no one will speak with him, nor be open enough to permit him to speak, about his dying."

The old man was quiet, and we sat without speaking for nearly an hour. Since he did not bid me leave, I remained. Although I was content, I feared he would not share his wisdom, but he finally spoke. The words came slowly.

"My son, it is the horse on the dining-room table. It is a horse that visits every house and sits on every dining-room table—the tables of the rich and of the poor, of the simple and of the wise. This horse just sits there, but its presence makes you wish to leave without speaking of it. If you leave, you will always fear the presence of the horse. When it sits on your table, you will wish to speak of it, but you may not be able to.

"However, if you speak about the horse, then you will find that others can also speak about the horse—most others, at least, if you are gentle and kind as you speak. The horse will remain on the dining-room table, but you will not be so distraught. You will enjoy your repast, and you will enjoy the company of the host and hostess. Or, if it is your table, you will enjoy the presence of your guests. You cannot make magic to have the horse disappear, but you can speak of the horse and thereby render it less powerful."

The old man then rose and, motioning me to follow, walked slowly to his hut. "Now we shall eat," he said quietly. I entered the hut and had difficulty adjusting to the dark. The guru walked to a cupboard in the corner and took out some bread and some cheese, which he placed on a mat. He motioned to me to sit and share his food. I saw a small horse sitting quietly in the center of the mat. He noticed this and said "That horse need not disturb us." I thoroughly enjoyed the meal. Our discussion lasted far into the night, while the horse sat there quietly throughout our time together.

Richard Kalish

CHAPTER ONE

Becoming Aware

Dying. Death. Dead. Three words so easy to pronounce and so difficult to say. And because they are so difficult to say, we often say them in very strange ways. Sometimes we use euphemisms: passed on, terminal, gone west, no longer here, expired, in heaven, in a better place, beyond help, with the angels. Sometimes we restrict our thinking to large numbers: 2 million deaths a year, over 50,000 killed annually in automobile accidents, 1000 dead in Chilean earthquake. Sometimes we fall back on platitudes: it's better that way; she's at peace now; we all have to go sometime; he was old anyway.

Death is the ultimate touchstone for human endeavors. It is the ultimate organizer of time. It is the ultimate enemy of self. It is the ultimate leveler of all persons. It is the ultimate uncertainty and the ultimate certainty, the ultimate chance event, the ultimate negator of passions and plans and power and personal growth.

We are the only members of the animal kingdom able to anticipate personal death and potential extinction, although other animals obviously fight for survival, and some appear to know when death is impending. Nonetheless, only we can plan our lives and our individual actions with our future deaths as one determinant. This very ability to anticipate death is a source of anxiety, planning, denial, love, achievement and lack of achievement, and feelings of meaningfulness and meaninglessness. Awareness of death leads to poetry and visual art and music, to building and conquest, as well as to deceit and whining and pain and pettiness.

The significance of personal death is so immense, so overwhelming, that in order to escape its contemplation we use many devices: humor, alcohol and drugs, denial and overt anger. We immerse ourselves in activities in order to avoid thinking of death and risk our lives in order to challenge and symbolically overcome death. Even reading a book on death or taking a course—or writing a book or teaching a course—may be a device to shift death and dying from the personal into the academic, from the emotional to the intellectualized.

There are times when we want to talk about dying or death or the dead; the words form in our minds and on our tongues, but they will not come out of our mouths, so we just giggle or pass on to another topic or pluck a euphemism from the air.

La Rochefoucauld, a philosopher writing over 300 years ago, said that "the human mind is as little capable to contemplate death for any length of time as the eye is able to look at the sun" (Choron, 1964, p. 107). When we need to or wish to look at the sun, we wear special smoked glasses and protect ourselves from danger and pain; when we need to or want to look at death, we also find ways to protect ourselves from danger and pain.

In the past decade, people have begun to "look at the sun" in increasing numbers. The words—*dying, death, dead*—are becoming easier to say, at least for many people. Your foremost concern may be with your own eventual death, with the death of one other person, with the deaths of many people, with the deaths of innumerable others whom you presently don't know—or with all of these. Whatever your individual circumstances, you are now reading this book and, therefore, "looking at the sun." I obviously don't agree with La Rochefoucauld—I wouldn't or couldn't have written this book if I did. I do fully believe that by the time you have read about 100 pages, you will find yourself able to look at the sun. Doing so will not make you a hero or mean you are supernaturally strong. It will indicate that you live in an era when looking at the sun has been made somewhat easier.

For a few people, the sun will still be painfully blinding, and I would encourage them to find some way to avoid the sun. Even those of us who have been studying, writing about, talking about, and working with death and the dying for many years find there are times when it shines too brightly, and we retreat for a while. You too may find such times. Or you may find that you need to retreat completely. If so, please do. This book should be read for enlightenment, learning, ideas, perhaps enjoyment; reading it is not an endurance test or a mark of personal worth.

THE HORSE ON THE DINING-ROOM TABLE

Recall the parable about a horse on the dining-room table. When the guests came in for dinner, there it was, quietly sitting and munching. The host, not wishing to upset his guests, made no reference to the horse; the guests, not wishing to upset the host, made no reference to the horse. Consequently, they ate their dinner in silence—so overwhelmed by the presence of the horse that they could neither carry on a conversation nor enjoy the dinner and so imbued with their notion of politeness that they dared not mention the horse. The horse, of course, was death.

We do not have the luxury of ignoring the horse on the dining-room table. Death makes an impact on all of us. Some of us encounter death through our academic programs; some of us meet death in our work; all of us experience death and its multiple meanings in our personal lives and day-to-day actions.

Academic Programs

One might assume that only student funeral directors deal with death in their academic programs, but this definitely is not the case. The subject matter of many academic fields includes death. Medicine, nursing, anthropology, history, religion and theology, philosophy, criminal justice and law, and demography are only the most obvious examples.

The fact that death and dying are part of an academic program says little about their treatment in the program. Although death often guides the course of history, historians rarely become emotional about deaths; although anthropologists and archeologists study funeral rituals, tombs and burial sites, and death-related practices, they seldom become personally concerned about the death of one individual; and not only demographers, who study death rates, but medical students, who study the etiology and treatment of death-causing diseases, frequently become more involved in numbers or in tissues than in people.

This does not mean that student historians, anthropologists, and physicians ought to mourn each death they read about—only that colleges and universities have long taught about death and dying in contexts that often depersonalized this extremely personal event.

Death-Related Vocations

For centuries, a special caste in Japan, the *eta*, was discriminated against because its members slaughtered animals for food and leather. The caste was hereditary; outsiders were reluctant to marry into the *eta* or otherwise join a group that was ostracized from most of the rest of society (Dore, 1958). Although the strict sanctions of decades ago no longer prevail, the *eta* today remain victims of discrimination.

Work with the dying and dead has also been taboo in much of modern-day Western culture. Funeral directors, for example, serve as the butts of jokes and as lightning rods for guilt and anger. Gravediggers and other cemetery workers, though avoiding the attacks made on funeral directors, are frequently considered persons to be avoided. Deputy coroners also feel that they share this taboo by virtue of their work in investigating causes of death. The wife of one deputy coroner told friends that her husband "worked for the county," in order to be vague about the kind of work he did; many deputy coroners admit that they prefer to socialize with each other to avoid the embarrassment of discussing their vocations with outsiders who would not understand (Reynolds & Kalish, 1976). This sounds a great deal like the plight of the *eta* in Japan today—not officially segregated or isolated, but kept apart by the responses of others and their own discomfort.

Not all vocations concerned with death and dying elicit avoidance. Physicians and nurses are constantly involved with death, and the association does not appear to affect their social status; of course, only a small portion of their work is with the dying, and virtually none is with the dead. Other hospital workers also encounter death: licensed vocational nurses, aides, orderlies, social workers, administrators, recordkeepers—even the janitorial staff and volunteers occasionally find themselves relating to the dying, the dead, or the survivors.

Consider some of the other vocations that lead to working with the dying, the dead, or matters concerned with death and dying:

- Florists, a large proportion of whose business depends on funerals and cemetery visits.
- Police officers, who rarely kill—or even shoot—anyone, but who often arrive at the scene of a death, decide what to do with a body, and inform family members of the death.
- Life insurance salespersons, who, if properly named, would be called "death insurance salespersons" because they spend their time persuading people to hedge their bets on living and to bet on dying. That is, the sooner a person dies, the more the insurance company has to pay off; if a person lives a long time, the payoff is much less.
- Estate planners, who, like life insurance salespersons, are involved mainly with people who are concerned that after their own deaths their money, property, children, spouses, and/or businesses will be properly cared for.
- Politicians, whose legislation in the areas of crime punishment, health funding, wars, and the physical and psychological environments frequently determines who lives and who dies.
- Actuaries and demographers, who predict and tabulate deaths by the tens, hundreds, thousands, and millions.
- The military and military planners, who are sometimes ordered to kill and at other times required to decide how many millions of deaths a particular country can suffer and still have a military capability.
- The neophyte journalists who write the obituaries.
- The chemists who provide the embalming fluids, makeup, and other chemicals for the funeral industry; the hair stylists and makeup artists who work on those bodies that will have open-casket ceremonies or otherwise be viewed; the casket manufacturers; the automotive industry that manufactures hearses.
- The clergy: those who have congregations, those who serve as chaplains in hospitals and nursing homes, those who provide pastoral counseling.
- Writers, artists, and musicians who are sufficiently moved by death, dying, and suffering to create words or visual representations or music to communicate their insights and feelings.
- Psychotherapists and counselors, who provide help and support to people who are coping with concerns that involve death, dying, and grief.

There are others you may wish to mention: judges, ambulance drivers, and firefighters, for example. Some of the professions in our list allow their practitioners to remain isolated from the emotional impact of actual dying and death. Actuaries and chemists, for example, never have any contact in their work with individuals who are dying. Their professional relationships with the dying are impersonal, and they seldom—from what we know—even think very much about individual deaths, except when their personal circumstances evoke such thoughts.

Others cannot remain so isolated. Life insurance salespersons often must call on the survivors; police officers may find themselves leading a funeral procession along a freeway or informing a young woman that her husband has been killed in an automobile accident; clergy and health professionals frequently minister to the dying and their survivors, although both their areas of specialization and personal preferences determine how frequent and how extensive this care is.

It would be reasonable to assume that persons in these last-named vocations might have background training in the meaning of death and in working in the death-related setting. As is often the case, however, the reasonable course is not the one followed. Only recently have health professionals and clergy begun to develop educational programs that focus on the dying; only in very unusual settings will police officers or life insurance salespersons attend any formal program on death and dying. If my personal observations are accurate, nurses, clergy, and funeral directors have done more than other vocational groups to advance their knowledge of how to care for dying persons and their survivors; however, even their training sometimes consists of no more than a brief one-day program every two or three years. In the final analysis, of course, it is personal reactions and social attitudes, not vocational identity, that matter most, and many people, using just common sense and intuition, do very well without training or experience.

Death and Dying in Personal Experiences

For a very few people, death and dying are a significant, even a major, part of their vocation, and they must confront these events on a personal level every day; for many more people, death and dying are a modest or minor part of their vocation, and they confront these phenomena on occasion or at considerable psychological distance.

What about you?

You are alive and over the age of 10. Therefore, the event of death most likely has or will soon become part of your experience; perhaps the event has already occurred. A grandparent, a neighbor, a family friend, sometimes a pet dies. Each of us faces about five or six major deaths in our lifetimes. Maybe you were first on the scene after a fatal traffic accident or a neighbor's heart attack. The person who died might have been someone to whom you were very much attached or perhaps someone you never saw. The deaths of John and Robert Kennedy and Martin Luther King affected millions of people as strongly as deaths of friends or family members.

If you are under 30, it is possible—not probable but possible—that you have not yet encountered a death that has seriously affected you. You never really knew your two grandparents who died recently, and the other two died before you were 18 months old; you were out of town when the man who lived in the apartment below you died, and you never had much to do with him anyway; you were attached to your dog, but it was really much more your brother's pet than yours.

If you are over 40, it is very likely that you have lost someone close through death. Even if you did a good job of anticipatory bereavement—that is, worked through your feelings about an impending death before the death occurred—or you disengaged from a strong attachment some time before the person died, the impact of the death would not have disappeared altogether.

And then there is your confrontation with your own death. On the basis of what people have told me over the years, I would estimate that the odds are about one in five or one in six that you have already experienced a situation in which you expected to die: you almost drowned; you were in a serious automobile accident; you were lying in a hospital bed when you overheard the physician tell someone that you were not likely to pull through; you were trapped by a forest fire. The older you are and the more risks you like to take with your life, the more probable it is that you have had such an experience.

There is another kind of death confrontation, one that can happen to anyone at any time. For example: one morning, as you were driving to work, the automobile radio announced the death of a close friend in a motorcycle accident. While you were stuck in traffic, you began to think about this death, and your thoughts drifted to your own eventual death. Suddenly it struck you: Someday I'm going to die. Me. *I* am going to die. This too shall pass—and I am part of *this. I* will be a statistic, an obituary in the newspaper, a death notice, a body prettified in a casket around which those I love will weep, a decaying body in the desert/on a snow-covered mountain/in the ocean. . . .

You came several degrees closer to acknowledging your own mortality, your own finitude, your own humanness. You experienced your own death in fantasy, and the experience was distressingly real.

Death and dying are not at all foreign to your experience. You encounter reminders of your death in your aging process. You have read about death, seen dying portrayed in the media, visited people who were dying or who had recently lost someone they loved through death, spent several minutes studying a crucifix, wondered about the meaning of "Now I lay me down to sleep," which you first heard as a child, spent several seconds watching a heavy truck coming straight at your VW at 45 miles per hour. You have done these things, and you have survived, sometimes a little worse for the experience, more often a little better for it. This may or may not be the first book you have ever read about death and dying, but it is most definitely not your first significant experience with these notions.

The Words Are There

Maybe you are young or fortunate enough not to have lost anyone close. Or perhaps, although the death of others has been part of your life from time to time, you feel that these events have never played a meaningful role in what you do or what you think about. Although you may have been untouched in either way, perhaps you still find that death and dying are on your mind, indirectly or symbolically, much of the time. How close death and dying are to our consciousnesses is shown by the extent to which death-related words and expressions appear in everyday vocabulary. For example:

- dead serious
- sudden-death overtime
- talk a subject to death
- drop dead
- a dead issue
- dead right
- dead ahead
- dead ringer
- scared to death
- dead reckoning
- deadhead
- dead from the neck up

- dead weight
- graveyard shift
- killing time
- dead personality
- crucified a speaker
- killed legislation
- political suicide
- deadbeat
- dead end
- dying to meet you
- dying gasp

None of these words and idioms refers to literal death, but—with two or three exceptions—you have little difficulty in knowing what is meant, even if you have never heard the expressions before. And with relatively little effort, you could add another six or eight phrases yourself in a few minutes.

Many of these expressions have become so much a part of normal conversation that their reference to death is not even noticed. So have some other kinds of language:

> Ring around the rosy,
> Pockets full of posy,
> Ashes, ashes,
> All fall down.

A familiar rhyme. Children holding hands, moving in a circle, then sprawling in many directions with many poses. Did you ever wonder what the familar rhyme originally meant? Probably not—I never did until someone called it to my attention.

"*Ring around the rosy*": The infections of bubonic plague, which devastated Europe during the Middle Ages, erupted as a rose-colored pox with a ring around each.

"*Pockets full of posy*": Death was so common that people carried flowers with them to cover the stench; flowers for the dead were also carried.

"*Ashes, ashes*": Cremation was necessary to get rid of the bodies that no one wished to touch.

"*All fall down*": Often "All fall dead" is substituted.

Children in one century developed a rhyme game to cope with death—a rhyme that children in a later century continue to find fun. Although today's children are not aware of the original meaning of the rhyme, it appears that in some unconscious fashion they respond with excitement to its message—perhaps as a way of handling their own death anxieties.

And the Words Are Not There

Sometimes just the opposite happens. We use the words *death* and *dead* when we mean something else, but we use other words to talk about death and the dead. A number of years ago I spent well over an hour with a lawyer discussing my will and the disposition of my estate. Underlying all that we were talking about was the *fact*—not the assumption or premise or hypothesis, but the fact—that I was eventually going to die. Yet at no point in the conversation did the lawyer ever use the words that referred most directly to what we were discussing.

What did he say? "When you are no longer here . . ." "After you've gone . . ." "In the event of your inability to provide . . ." Finally I asked him where I was going to be "when I was no longer here," but the question so disconcerted him that I decided to leave the issue alone.

The number of euphemisms for death-related words is legion: passed over, went west, across the Great Divide, expired, is with God, went to her Maker, is sleeping with the angels, gone to a well-deserved rest, went to his reward, and so on. There are some situations in which we can easily say "He died" or "How do you feel about dying?" In other situations, the words stick—they just won't come out—and so we shift to other words that have the same meaning but express it in ways that seem gentler. What makes these words "gentler" is that they mask the painful reality of what has occurred.

Thus, although our vocabulary is filled with *dead* and *die* and *death*, the literal meanings of these words are often not used and frequently are avoided. And the closer the reality of death is to us or to those we are talking with, the less likely we are to use the words.

DEATH AND DYING: FROM FAD TO BUREAUCRACY

As long ago as the 1920s and 1930s, a handful of psychologists, sociologists, and psychiatrists were writing about death, dying, and grief (for example, Bromberg & Schilder, 1933; Eliot, 1933; Hall, 1915), but their work was essentially ignored by their contemporaries and had no apparent impact on the delivery of health or social services to the dying and the bereaved. In the late 1950s and throughout the 1960s, the numbers of serious research studies and the community's interest in providing effective services grew slowly, with considerable impetus from Herman Feifel's collection of articles *The Meaning of Death* (1959). Then, just before the end of the 1960s, a popular magazine carried a photographic story of a young psychiatrist struggling to help the dying live out the remainder of their lives in greater comfort. The article appeared just at the time when many people, both health professionals and others, were ready to consider the meaning of their own deaths and the deaths of others and to encourage better treatment for the dying and care for the bereaved.

In 1969 the same young psychiatrist wrote a book that discussed both her experiences and her model of the stages of dying, and the death-awareness movement began to come to national attention. So did the psychiatrist, Dr. Elisabeth Kübler-Ross.

Factors Underlying the Initiation of the Death-Awareness Movement

Well before Dr. Kübler-Ross wrote her book, health and behavioral scientists and practitioners were writing articles, holding meetings, publishing books, and even writing and circulating a newsletter, edited by Robert Kastenbaum and Richard Kalish, that later became the journal *Omega.* And—or at least so it seemed—every book or article began by commenting that death and dying were taboo topics.

What were the factors underlying the surge of interest in these concerns that permitted their emergence from taboo topic to popular fashion? Several factors could be viewed as contributing to the development of the **death-awareness movement** during the late 1960s through the mid-1970s. However, all of these are highly speculative and impressionistic.

First, during the 1960s, there was what seemed to be a search for under-serviced, underprivileged persons. Initially this search focused on ethnic minority communities, but as these communities strengthened and became more self-sufficient, the younger and middle-class activists needed to turn elsewhere to find people for whom to work and serve as advocates. Among the groups they found were the elderly and the dying. An added advantage to serving these people was that, in contrast to the ethnic movements or the women's movement, they were more likely to encourage the young activists rather than take over the movement themselves.

Second, the rapid increase in gerontological research and services inevitably required a more careful look at the concerns of the dying and the bereaved.

Third, the potential for complete and total destruction through nuclear war was emphasized during the 1960s. "The atomic bomb does not merely destroy; it destroys the boundaries of destruction" (Lifton & Olson, 1974, p. 8). When asked whether they had "ever seriously considered that all human life might be eliminated from the earth," nearly 60% of an adult sample said they had, most of them indicating that nuclear explosions would be the cause (Kalish & Reynolds, 1981).

Fourth, advances in medical and biomedical technology and research brought attention both to the possibility of a quantum leap in life expectancy and to the increased length and discomfort of the dying process. This caused more interest in the right to die and to reject the prolongation of what some saw as meaningless life, as well as the ethics of extended impersonal institutional care.

Fifth, during the early 1970s, people came to see the limits of social activism, and many had become cynical owing to the outcome of the Vietnam War and the events leading to the resignation of President Nixon. At the same time, they were distressed by the failure of the gods of science and technology to effect the good life and to alleviate poverty. They thus moved from seeking satisfaction in changing the world outside themselves to seeking fulfillment within themselves; through their contemplation and, often, meditation, the meaning of life and death became more important.

Bureaucratization of the Death-Awareness Movement

By the late 1970s, death and dying were no longer taboo topics. Books, articles, educational films, newspaper and magazine coverage, community programs—all were examining death, dying, and grief. The hospice movement was recognized; two academic journals, the original *Omega* and the later *Death Education*, were being published quarterly; over 1000 college and university courses were offered on death each year (Knott, 1979); the Forum for Death Education and Counseling had been established and was holding annual meetings and providing other educational forums; and health agencies, religious institutions, and other community groups were putting on what undoubtedly amounted to thousands of seminars, workshops, lectures, discussion groups, planning sessions, and so forth each year.

As might be expected, the emphasis was no longer on the exploration of new ideas but, rather, on how to provide better services and how to help individuals deal with the eventuality of their own deaths and the deaths of others. The need to provide services brought up issues of program administration, cost-effectiveness analysis, and Medicare/Medicaid funding. Death and dying became referred to, on occasion, as "d'n'd."

In the process, bureaucratization seems to have taken place. What had been exciting new ideas and programs have become routine. Hospices are spending immense time and effort on third-party payments, cost effectiveness, reducing health costs, and institutional linkages: all necessary, to be sure, but with little focus on the individual needs of the individual dying person or that person's family members. Universities schedule courses on death and researchers write articles for scholarly journals on death, but the uproar, the controversy of a dozen years ago, is missing.

Early advocates of the death-awareness movement placed strong emphasis on the need to deal effectively with the extreme tendency of many people to deny the reality, the emotional power, of death. Now we face the possibility that a new form of **death denial** is occurring, encouraged by some of the people whose work with the dying places them in important opinion-influencing positions. A well-known theorist could write that "No life event can stir more emotionally directed thinking in the individual and more emotional reactiveness in those about him" (Bowen, 1978, p. 322). Yet hospices and college courses and academic studies can all serve the purpose of denying the emotionality of death, dying, and grief by placing them in neat, regulated cubbyholes in hospital or university bureaucracies (Kastenbaum, 1982).

It is very difficult for any of us to develop an accurate picture of the meaning of social trends that we are personally experiencing; so you, as reader, need to view the previous paragraphs with some skepticism. They are based on my own observations and speculations. You will be reading these lines many months after I have written them, and you may by then have a more accurate perspective.

SOURCES OF INFORMATION

Learning about death, dying, and grief, like learning about most matters, can combine personal experiences with the knowledge, insights, and reported experiences of others. These others include not only behavioral and health scientists, whose writings form the basis for most of this book, but also philosophers, artists, historians, and those individuals who are most experienced in being with and working with the dying, the dead, and the bereaved.

Death and grief are difficult to study because they represent experiences that are deeply personal and strongly colored by powerful emotions and deeply held and deeply defended values and beliefs. Consequently, each source of information has its strengths and its limitations. By integrating the various resources, we eventually develop a reasonable picture of what is going on. The sources most frequently used in this volume include personal observations, clinical cases, controlled observations, interviews and questionnaires, experiments, program evaluations, ethnographic and participant-observer approaches, and demographic data.

Personal Observations

"I once knew a woman who . . ." "Last year a student of mine . . ." "A friend telephoned me just the other day to . . ." "When my uncle died, I . . ." "At the funeral in Minneapolis, the minister . . ."

Part of learning in life is to make effective use of personal observations; it is also part of learning to avoid making too much of these observations. Sometimes a personal observation rings so true and seems to typify so many other experiences that it remains vivid. For example, some 20 years ago, a student told me that when his mother was dying, the physician and his father and sister would talk about his mother's condition in whispers at the foot of the bed, then come to the head of the bed and tell her how well she looked. His mother finally said to him "They must think I'm either stupid or deaf not to know what they're talking about."

Personal observations can alert you to kinds of behavior and situations of which you may not previously have been aware, and then you can determine whether subsequent observations confirm your impressions or indicate that they were atypical. Also, when you observe or are told that the same event has happened to different people in various settings, you obviously begin to develop a principle from your observations.

There are serious limitations to placing too much faith in personal observations. First, because you bring your own feelings and biases to a situation, you are likely to attend to and recall only what fits them. A negative bias toward physicians or clergy may lead to your focusing on stories in which such persons are unfeeling or inept. Second, your life brings you into contact with a limited range of people; what they tell you represents, for example, primarily college graduates or primarily people who have joined a church or primarily young couples in a suburban community. Third, most of us don't have very many experiences from which to draw, so that one or two observations may lead us to our conclusions, or else a particularly dramatic event may cause us to ignore a larger number of contrary events.

However, a lack of objectivity should not lead you to reject information altogether. It is rare that a personal observation or experience can prove that something is true, but such examples provide excellent illustrations that permit a better understanding of the significance of an issue. In the same fashion, I would encourage you to draw from your own experiences and observations to increase your depth of understanding.

Clinical Cases

Physicians, psychotherapists, lawyers, and other professionals who have intensive interaction with a number of individuals sharing specified characteristics are able to report their observations and document them with case descriptions. Sometimes they will report on one case in depth. At other times these people will review and draw generalizations from a series of cases.

The limitations of small numbers of reported cases as a source of information are the same as those just described for personal observations, with the exception that a person collecting cases is likely to be more accurate and objective than a person making unsystematic observations, screened through personal feelings, of what is taking place.

Controlled Observations

Similar to clinical cases, controlled observations involve the perceptions that a trained person reports of the behavior of other individuals. The recorder might be looking for interpersonal interactions between nursing staff and patients on an **oncology** (cancer) ward, and he or she might record a large number of such interactions, perhaps through a shorthand device, and then tally the number of times the patient took the initiative, the number of times the nurse took the initiative, the reason for the interaction, the behavior of each party, and the final outcome of the interaction. The final data analysis might require counting how often a particular kind of behavior occurred and how often each of several responses to this behavior occurred, or it might be a more subjective, less statistical analysis.

Interviews and Questionnaires

The academic journals are filled with studies based on interviews and questionnaires and concerned with death anxiety or fear of death or of dying. A recent critical review by sociologist Victor Marshall (1982) outlines and evaluates many of the instruments. Although matters have improved since an earlier review (Lester, 1967), there is still a long way to go. Developing a reliable and valid measure of feelings about death is extremely difficult, and it might be argued that all the measures available fall short of adequacy. One difficulty is that many studies are conducted with college students exclusively, who represent only a small segment of the population.

Of course, not all studies utilizing interviews and questionnaires are conducted on college campuses. Other groups that have been studied over the years include the elderly, children and adolescents, mental hospital patients, the physically ill, cancer patients, physicians and nurses, widows and widowers, and the dying themselves. Nor have all such investigations been limited to specially defined groups; a few have been conducted in the community at large. These studies operate in a variety of ways. Some ask open-ended questions that encourage participants to talk about anything that comes to mind; others employ questionnaires that require one-word or multiple-choice answers. Some questionnaires are sent through the mail; others are distributed door to door; and still others are handed out in school—for example, at the beginning of the first class meeting and again at the end of the last class meeting.

Not only the procedures but the kinds of information elicited also vary. Although questionnaires typically ask for attitudes, beliefs, and values, they may also request information about experiences, expectations, and knowledge. (See Chapters 5 and 6 for a more complete discussion.)

Neither interviews nor questionnaires are restricted to direct questions with direct answers. More subtle approaches, such as projective techniques, can be used. People can be asked to tell stories from cards depicting scenes that have some relation to death or to complete sentence fragments involving the theme of death. It is even possible to use the technique of word association. All these methods are less susceptible to conscious or unconscious faking and distortion, but their responses are more difficult to interpret, and conflicting interpretations are common.

Although studying attitudes toward death through interviews and questionnaires has limitations, I will frequently use information obtained through these methods. It is important to recognize the limitations of a procedure, but it is equally important to recognize the insights to which the procedure can lead.

Experiments

Although initially the idea of conducting an "experiment" about death might seem strange or even somewhat macabre, none of the experiments with which I am familiar has partaken of those qualities. Probably the best-known series of studies (and among the very earliest) was conducted by Professor Irving Alexander. Working mostly with young people, Alexander and his associates in one study selected 27 words that had previously been shown to be similar in frequency of usage in English. Eighteen words were considered neutral in meaning, but the remaining nine were equally divided among "sex" words, "school" words, and "death" words. A student was presented with each word separately and asked to respond with the first word that came to mind; at the same time, the student's galvanic skin response (perspiration change usually measured on the palm and assumed to be an indication of stress) was also measured. It took students significantly longer to respond to death-related words than to neutral words; similarly, death-related words produced a much greater change in galvanic skin response than neutral words. However, there was no difference between the death-related words and either the sex or school words (Alexander, Colley, & Adlerstein, 1957).

A more recent version compared the responses to death-related stimuli of two groups: graduate students in psychology and religion, and nonstudents who were either Zen meditators or users of hallucinogenic drugs. The graduate students showed not only greater galvanic-skin-response rates but also higher heart-rate responses. However, when the responses of the two pairs of groups were compared on the basis of stimuli not related to death or on a questionnaire asking about fear of death, the differences were minimal or nonexistent (Garfield, 1977). Perhaps the training of the nonstudent groups, or perhaps the qualities that drew people to these groups initially, did enable them to cope with death with less fear.

You can probably think of other kinds of experiments that would shed light on death and loss. For example, the effects of marijuana and LSD on the dying have been examined (Grof & Halifax, 1977; Pahnke, 1969). So has the willingness of senior-center participants to volunteer to spend time with a dying cancer patient (Smith, Sherman, & Sherman, 1982–83).

Program Evaluation

Programs related to death, dying, and loss are becoming increasingly familiar—the hospice movement, counseling the dying, widow-to-widow outreach, and death education, for example. As these programs are planned, developed, and conducted, the people involved have the opportunity to learn a great deal about death and dying. Sometimes, through either the requirements of funding organizations or the wishes of program directors, the programs are evaluated in written reports.

This is the place not to debate the pros and cons of program evaluation but to underscore the fact that a good evaluation report can provide a variety of kinds of valuable information. These include (1) a description of the program itself—its purposes and goals, its procedures, and the people it serves, (2) the outcome of the program—the ways in which it was successful or not and the reasons for both, and (3) ideas and recommendations for similar programs in other communities.

Ethnographic and Participant-Observer Methods

Living with people—becoming immersed in their social milieu and their daily lives—is a very important method for learning about them. Although this approach has traditionally been used by anthropologists to study foreign cultures, today others have applied this method to various problems of social research. For example, one anthropologist, posing as a depressed, suicidal patient, entered a psychiatric hospital. Before entering, he used sophisticated psychological procedures that enabled him to feel depressed and highly suicidal, so that he was not acting or pretending so much as functioning as an actual participant (Reynolds & Farberow, 1976).

Many studies of funeral rituals and other ceremonies have been written by people who were active participants (for example, Rodabough, 1981–82). An additional example comes from the work of a sociologist who, some 20 years ago, studied the role of death and the process of dying in two hospitals. By spending an immense amount of time observing death-related events, talking to hospital staff and patients, and carefully recording what he observed, he provided some excellent ethnographic data. For example, he described how bodies are prepared for removal from the bed where the person died: "The body is generally handled nonreverently by aides and orderlies. In turning it around to wrap the sheet, it is grabbed roughly and rolled over with none of the gentility which one observes in the rolling of live persons" (Sudnow, 1967, p. 72). And "one aide, in demonstrating how bodies are wrapped to a new employee, took the young girl into a room where a patient had just been wrapped, and as she pointed to those features of the completed product which marked a good job, she made a point of ostensively showing what she meant, almost hitting the body at each point to demonstrate how tightly the sheet fit" (p. 22).

Although this method lacks the statistical analysis and, sometimes, the objectivity that can be obtained in the more familiar questionnaire or experimental studies, it has the advantage of probing a topic in greater depth and with a much fuller view of the total context and the more subtle dynamics.

Demographic Data

Who dies each year and of what causes? What percentage of all deaths are of children between the ages of 6 and 10? What percentage of children between 6 and 10 die each year? What percentage of women over the age of 75 are in nursing homes or other long-term-care institutions when they die? What percentage of men are married when they die? What percentage of women? What percentage of all deaths are from some form of cancer? What percentage of all deaths of persons under 45 years of age are from cancer? What were the comparable figures in 1930? in 1870?

Statistics like these provide help in planning social programs, in understanding what is occurring in a community, in preparing for future trends, and in interpreting observations. For example, many more men than women die at home—most probably because husbands are older than their wives, have a briefer life expectancy, and are cared for at home by their wives. The fact that widows are more numerous and generally younger than widowers has implications for program planning and development and for understanding the marriage role of the surviving spouse.

Other Procedures

Numerous other procedures have been used to study death, dying, and loss. One study asked people to describe what "death" looks like as a person (Kastenbaum & Aisenberg, 1972). A second analyzed the content of dreams about death (Coolidge & Fish, 1983–84). A third studied death-related writings from 12th- through 15th-century England, with emphasis on the death of King Richard the Lionhearted (Jankofsky, 1981–82).

No one method is without flaws, nor is any method lacking in value. One in-depth interview conducted by a skilled and knowledgeable interviewer can offer insights that 500 questionnaires cannot uncover; conversely, 500 well-constructed questionnaires, administered to a carefully selected sample of individuals, can provide an understanding of diverse views and feelings that one or a handful of in-depth interviews cannot reveal.

Myths and the Arts

Two additional ways of gaining in understanding of death, dying, and grief are through myths and through the various arts, such as fiction, drama, poetry, paintings, and music. A third approach, which will not be discussed in this book but which deserves your attention, is through changes in the meaning of death through history (see Ariès, 1981; Choron, 1963, 1964).

Myths.   A myth is not simply a story; it is a legend that describes and explains, in symbolic form, the significant philosophic and religious practices, beliefs, and meanings that have evolved in a culture. Some people will take a myth literally and will believe that the events occurred just as described; others will view it as legend, perhaps true and perhaps not; still others see a myth as a fantasy that symbolically represents what a people believe.

How did death come to be in the first place? Each society has its own myths about the origins of death, just as it does about the origins of life.

> God, who made the first man and woman, allowed them to live forever as long as they would not pick the fruit of the tahu tree. When the woman became big with child, she decided that she must eat that fruit. . . . Her husband warned her that God had forbidden them to eat the fruit, but the woman argued, cried, and screamed. In desperation . . . the husband picked the fruit, and they ate it together . . . God . . . became angry and punished both by condemning them to hard work, illness, and ultimate death. He punished the woman even more for initiating the problem and gave her the pain of childbirth [Corcos & Krupka, 1983–84, p. 188].

This myth, which may sound familiar to you although it describes the legend of an African pygmy tribe, embodies one of several themes described in myths of the origins of death, that of the "forbidden fruit." A second theme, the "delayed or garbled message," is represented by a legend in which the word of God that confers immortality is lost, forgotten, delayed, confused, or not believed, and therefore the people are doomed to die (Corcos & Krupka, 1983–84). A third theme is that death came to the world in order to prevent overpopulation (Corcos & Krupka, 1983–84). These mythic themes are only a few among many that have existed around the world.

The arts.   All the arts have something to say about death and the process of dying. The most immediately obvious, perhaps, are those that use language: fiction, drama, poetry, film, and the lyrics of songs. The novel of James Agee, *A Death in the Family*, expresses the anguish of a dying person and his survivors more vividly than any lecture on the topic. In the novel *Cancer Ward*, Alexander Solzhenitsyn uses death as both reality and metaphor. The death of Don Quixote in Cervantes' novel is accompanied by his decision to halt his bizarre behavior. *Memento Mori*, by Muriel Spark, is a profound novel of older persons' encounters with death. And Tolstoy's famous short story, *The Death of Ivan Illych*, is probably the best-known piece of fiction that describes the feelings of a man who is condemned to death by illness. The list is endless.

In some plays of Shakespeare, such as *Hamlet*, *Macbeth*, *King Lear*, and *Romeo and Juliet*, death is eloquently examined through plot, character, and language. Willy Loman, the salesman in Arthur Miller's *Death of a Salesman*, represents many feelings about the meaning of life and about leaving life. Thornton Wilder's *Our Town* has a poignant scene in which a young woman who has died is permitted to relive one day of her life—but the pain of how much the living take life for granted is too great, and she begs for an early return to the grave.

We have become so deeply concerned about the role of media like television and comic books in portraying death to children that we tend to ignore the importance the theme has always had in children's "media." In *Snow White and the Seven Dwarfs* and *Sleeping Beauty*, the apparently dead return to life; in *Jack and the Beanstalk* and *The Wizard of Oz*, good children kill the perpetrators of evil; in the tales of *King Arthur* and *Robin Hood*, the villains die, but the heroes also eventually die. And most of the deaths in these stories are violent.

Movies, of course, often have death themes. Two such films, one from the early 1970s and the other more recent, are frequently brought back to local theaters: *Harold and Maude* and *All That Jazz*.

Death and dying are not always presented literally in the arts. For example, in the lovely "September Song," the lyrics tell us that it's a long time from May to December, while the days grow short on reaching September. It may help to know that in *Knickerbocker Holiday*, the musical comedy that this song comes from, the singer was a middle-aged man in love with a young woman. May represents her age; September represents his age; December represents death.

Popular songs, including rock, country-and-Western, and musical show tunes, often have messages about death; their lyrics frequently describe the death of a beloved person. Although I need not enumerate how often death figures in operas, even comic strips and television shows occasionally touch on the serious side of life through a comment on death.

Paintings and other graphic art forms often depict either scenes or symbols of death. Sometimes, of course, the scene is obvious: a man before a firing squad, a battlefield strewn with corpses, a family surrounding a sick woman. Visual symbols frequently include an hourglass or some other timepiece (Ingmar Bergman's films have also used this device), a scythe, a skull, bones, a closed book (in some contexts), coffins, a figure representing death, knives, guns, the ruins of buildings, a cemetery (Gottlieb, 1959). Both the content and the mood are relevant in examining the message of the artist.

Through the centuries artists have also applied their talent to "designing for death." As British artist Barbara Jones examines in her excellent book, artists have designed coffins, gravestones, cemeteries, memorial monuments, and death announcements (Jones, 1967).

Because music is abstract, the theme of death may be harder to identify in this art. Nevertheless, some music has been composed specifically for death: traditional and Black funeral marches, requiems, and spirituals, for example. Other music has death and dying as its theme: think of Richard Strauss' *Death and Transfiguration* and Saint-Saëns' *Danse Macabre.*

This topic deserves far more attention than is given here. The arts are the expression of our deepest feelings—frequently of feelings and experiences of which we are only partly, or not at all, aware. Even during the time when death and dying were not much discussed around hospitals and homes, creative artists continued to represent their feelings in their work. Observations of children have shown that, even at an early age, they can both respond to death themes in the arts, especially fiction and paintings, and create their own artistic productions for comfort and insight (Bertman, 1979–80).

The vocabulary of death is always around us, and the themes of death and dying permeate our folk history and legends. Their symbolic, mythic treatment of death allows us to experience our death-related anxieties in such a way that we remain defended against feeling too much anxiety.

THE REST OF THE BOOK

A book on death, the dying process, grief, and caring relationships can have any of several goals or any combination of the same goals. Those that come immediately to mind are—

- To help people think more about death so that they can better prepare for their own deaths.
- To help people know more about the dying process so that their own may be less distressing.
- To help people understand their feelings about the deaths of others so that they can be both more effective in relating to others who are dying and more capable of doing their own grieving later.
- To help people who wish to work in a professional or paraprofessional capacity with the dying and the bereaved.
- To help people who work in the innumerable fields that touch on death, dying, or grief to know a little more and think a little more about their roles.
- To help people grapple with one of the major philosophical problems— the meaning of death.

The remainder of this book aims to accomplish all these goals—some directly and some indirectly. I hope to open up many ideas for thought, provide some basic information on the theme, present occasional personal views on the matter, and then leave the final resolution to you.

Since death and the process of dying are studied by more than one discipline, this book is both multidisciplinary and interdisciplinary. Since I am both teacher and human being, this book will move from a teaching stance to a human and personal stance. Your reading will, therefore, take you from the reporting of research data to intense personal experiences, from the psychological to the sociological to the theological to the medical and then back to the psychological, from attempts to get you to examine your own values and feelings to attempts to have you look at the topic from an impersonal distance.

In some instances, the information provided is based on research, clinical observations and experience, or rigorously developed theory. In other instances it is speculative and impressionistic. You can easily determine when each of these modes occurs and adjust your reading accordingly.

These 16 chapters are divided into five parts. The first part introduces the field and explores the meanings of death, people's attitudes and feelings about death, and beliefs concerned with transcending death.

Part 2 begins with the process of dying and the needs of the dying and then discusses some specific ways in which people die—suicide, homicide, accidents, disasters, and unexplainable deaths. Part 3, which studies grief and bereavement, explores both the grieving process for individuals and the social roles and institutions that surround mourning and bereavement.

The fourth part provides a life-span perspective on death, dying, and grief. Much research and many services involving these issues are related to age, and one chapter on childhood and adolescence is included, as well as one on adulthood. And the final part describes caring relationships, caring people, and some of the programs available for the dying and their survivors.

CHAPTER TWO

What Is Death?

You know what death is, of course. Well, what is it?

It's a biological event that occurs naturally to all living things. It's a passage from this existence into the next. It's the transition from somethingness to nothingness. It's a consequence of original sin. It's the absence of life. It's an evolutionary necessity to keep the earth from overflowing with whatever form of life is under discussion. It's a transition into wholeness—becoming one with God. And there are other possibilities, each of which describes someone's definition.

A simple way to define death is "the transition from the state of being alive to the state of being dead" (Kass, 1971, p. 699). Although that definition differentiates *death* from *dying* and from *being dead*, it doesn't help with the broader, more philosophic, and more personal understandings of the meaning of death. For the moment, let's examine the simpler and more limited definition; we will explore the more profound meanings at a later time.

If **death** is a transition and being **dead** is a state, we can describe **dying** as a process, and we can assume that it is dying that we are observing, although we cannot be absolutely certain that we are watching dying until death has occurred. We may be watching apparent-dying or not-quite-dying instead.

A MORE CAREFUL LOOK

Do you strongly agree, agree, feel uncertain, disagree, or strongly disagree with this statement: I am afraid of death.

Think about the statement and mark your answer down in some way. More people would indicate that they disagree or strongly disagree than that they agree or strongly agree—a phenomenon discussed in a later chapter. What I want to know right now is, when you responded to the question, exactly what was it that you were afraid of or unafraid of or uncertain about? What were you conceptualizing as *death?* What images did you develop? Were you really thinking of the process of dying rather than of death—of leaving your family, of being in a hospital, of being helpless and in pain, of losing your ability to experience? Were you thinking of *being dead—* that is, for example, of existing in a nirvana-like state, of being in heaven or hell, of your relationship with a Supreme Being (however you conceptualize that), of total extinction? Or were you thinking of *death*, that moment of transition when you will finally know what death means—or, if death is extinction, when you will know nothing at all ever again?

It's possible that you had a fairly clear idea of what death meant when you answered the question, but it is also very possible that you had only the haziest idea. Perhaps you combined the concepts of death, the process of dying, and being dead and then reacted to a vague concept, which produced feelings of unease and discomfort, rather than to a sharp image that you could readily define. The more we look at these three concepts, the more obvious it becomes that they cannot be given precise, nonoverlapping definitions, but we can develop some basic distinctions.

Dying

When do you begin to die? The simplest answer is "When you are born." Although I've used that response also, it strikes me as a glib and essentially meaningless explanation. Why not consider it the moment of conception or the time when your parents decided to conceive you or the moment when your parents were conceived? By saying that living is dying, we imply that there is no separation between living and dying. That may be poetically true, but it also seems irrelevant. Although it is important to keep in mind that everything that lives also dies, I find it more useful to view the process of dying as only one phase of living.

People are certainly not in full agreement on when dying begins. Some, like Feigenberg (1980), would propose that dying requires that the individual experience the threat of death at an emotional level; others would extend the beginning of the dying process to the moment at which an imaginary qualified person with all the necessary facts available could say, in effect, that the individual was going to die of conditions that presently existed within his or her body. Similarly, some would say that dying exists only if death is the outcome; others would contend that a person might be defined as dying when all information overwhelmingly indicates that death was to be the result but that on occasion a person can change status from dying to nondying.

Perhaps it isn't possible or even important to agree on when dying begins or on the exact definition of dying. Lack of such agreement has not led to confusion in significant ways, and the practical applications of such definitions are limited. In fact, the more practical concern may well be the extent to which a person is suffering from a life-threatening condition and whether it is possible to modify the extent to which the condition is life-threatening.

It is possible, nonetheless, to refer to the process of dying in three ways that are related but still distinct: as it is perceived by the person who is dying, as it is perceived by other concerned persons, and as it would be perceived by some objective qualified person who was privy to all knowable information.

Objectively, therefore, *my* dying begins when the condition that will cause my death becomes obvious enough to be noticed by someone who has access to all relevant data. Subjectively, for *me*, my dying begins when *I* learn that I have a condition that will eventually cause my death. Subjectively, for *you*, my dying begins when *you* learn that I have this condition.

For example, I consider myself healthy until one day when I have a routine physical examination. Concerned with symptoms that I described, my physician requests additional tests, which reveal that I have advanced stomach cancer. Now, instead of assuming that I will live at least 10 or 20 or 30 years more, I can assume I have only one or two years; I can also assume that I am most likely to die from the stomach cancer. I must confront "the crisis of knowledge of death" and enter what Pattison (1977) calls the **"living-dying interval."**

If, instead of dying from stomach cancer, I die from drowning, the crisis of knowledge of death may never arrive, or it may last only a minute or two before I die. The objective dying period is then very brief, and the subjective living-dying interval lasts only a moment or does not exist at all.

When Pattison uses the expression *living-dying interval*, he is making an extremely significant point: we are alive until we are dead; we are living until we die. Obvious as that may seem, it is often forgotten or ignored. As soon as I am categorized as dying, people begin to respond to me differently. It is almost as though I were already dead. I become a nonperson, as others not only plan what remains of my life—often without including me in the planning—but also begin to plan both the present and the future for themselves as though I were not still among them.

This disengagement need not and, of course, does not always happen, but it can occur very easily. Many years ago, having decided to leave one teaching position for another, I announced my resignation several months before the end of the year, and my replacement was appointed about six weeks later. Shortly after his appointment, I noticed that people who had previously consulted with me were telephoning him, that plans not only for the following year, when I would be gone, but for the academic year when I was still there were being developed without me. My colleagues remained cordial and seemed truly sorry that I was leaving, but they had already begun the process of disengaging from me and reengaging with my replacement.

A similar process of disengagement occurs with a dying person; unfortunately, he or she is much less capable of coping with it than I was. For my departure, leaving was equated with having left; for the dying person, dying is thought to equal dead. We need to remain aware that, during the living-dying interval, an individual is *living*—although under different conditions than before.

Being Dead

We can all agree on some aspects of the nature of being dead: the body ceases to function and begins to decay. Not only has the body ceased to function, but the various body parts and organs also cease to function and begin to decay, not necessarily immediately and not necessarily at the same moment, but within a very short period. Being dead must, by definition, follow the process of dying and the transitional moment of death. Perhaps you believe in an eventual resurrection that permits the spirit to reassume bodily form, perhaps through reconstituting the original body, but more probably in a "body of a new order, the perfect instrument of the spirit" (Cross, 1958, p. 1158). Or you may believe that the body becomes dust and will never be reconstituted.

What happens to *you* when you are dead? At this point the disagreements will increase rapidly. By *you*, I mean that unique and never-again-to-be-found entity that is locked within your body (and even that statement may be debated). It is what you mean when you say "I." What happens to that *you* when your body—every part of it—ceases to function?

Do *you* cease completely? Are you extinguished? Annihilated? Nevermore? Do *you* inhabit another physical body? A person? Another animal form? A vegetable or mineral? Do *you* exist in nonphysical form? In heaven? In nirvana? As a ghost?

What dying is *not*/what being dead is *not*. Aging does *not* equal dying; aging does *not* equal being dead. To the extent that aging produces decrement (and much aging produces gains, not losses), it is a process that makes us more susceptible to a variety of conditions that can cause our death. With age, our resistance to disease and our ability to recover from illnesses and accidents diminish. Newborn infants share with the elderly a low resistance to disease and a slow recovery rate from some illnesses and accidents, and their death rate is quite high, compared with that of older infants and children, though much lower than it was a century ago. But being old is not dying any more than being newborn is dying.

What is unique about dying? What is unique about being dead? The only quality in the dying process that is unique is its eventual end in death. When you imagine dying, you are likely to think about physical pain, psychological stress, discomfort, the loss of other people, unpleasant medical and hospital (or at-home) routines, and the arrangements necessary for after your death. But none of these circumstances is unique to the dying process.

People suffer pain on many occasions, and the pain of the dying process depends on the cause of your dying, the medical treatments you receive, the psychological care you get, and probably your own attitudes as well. Similarly, you can suffer discomfort and psychological stress on many occasions; you can encounter unpleasant medical and hospital routines without being a dying person; you can suffer the loss of others or arrange for what will occur after your death at almost any time in your life.

But after you die, you will be dead. That situation is very different from others you may have faced. First, being dead, actually dead, is irreversible. (See Chapter 4 for an alternative position.) Furthermore, we have no empirical evidence of what being dead is. You may feel you have various kinds of evidence about the nature of being dead—from religious teachings, from logic, from other kinds of experiences, from feeling "it has to be like this"—but very few people would contend that this evidence is empirical (gathered from observable facts or experiences). Therefore, being dead is a state with empirically unknown (and probably unknowable) characteristics, and this is unique. Third, being dead is forever; at the very least, your present body and earthly existence will be dead forever. Nothing else is forever.

For many people, however, the most significant unique quality about being dead is that they will be unable to experience—unable to think or perceive or behave or have feelings. Obviously those who believe that there is another existence after this one in which they will be able to think, perceive, and have feelings will not share this view. For them, the most significant unique feature of being dead may be the opportunity to experience the presence or wholeness of God and/or Jesus Christ, Buddha, or Mohammed personally, to experience another body, to bask in the loving oneness of the universe, or to have their being recreated in another body, in keeping with their karma, or deeds, from this life, while their essences (for example, body, thought, feelings) cease.

Death

Earlier, death was defined as the period of transition between the process of dying and the state of being dead. The transition may last a moment or a few minutes, but the determination of that period has immense practical and philosophical consequences. Why? After all, we talk about people being "more dead than alive," about people being "as good as dead," about the possibility of returning to life after death. Why is it important to define the moment of death?

The answer is simple: because a train of events follows death, and this train of events does not follow "being more dead than alive" or "being as good as dead." Nor can it occur if the dead person is going to return to life. When *I* die, if it is in a hospital, I will be encased in sheets and removed by a gurney or cart to the hospital morgue, where eventually the funeral-home vehicle will pick me (is it "me"?) up for delivery to the mortuary, where, depending on whether I am to be buried or cremated, I may undergo further processing. If I am not dead, this will not happen.

My survivors will contact insurance companies, the Social Security office, and the office that handles my retirement program, and a variety of business procedures will be set in motion that will eventually lead to payments to my heirs. The funeral home will call either a cemetery or a crematorium and set another process in operation (Veatch, 1976).

Close family members will contact distant family members, who will need to decide whether they will make the trip to attend the funeral; the clergy may be contacted to officiate at the funeral; local relatives will prepare both for the funeral and for the visits of out-of-town family members. The local newspaper will be notified, and some friends may decide to miss a few hours of work to attend the funeral, offer condolences to my survivors, and probably eat and drink a little. I will be buried or, perhaps, cremated—but only if I am dead.

There may be some form of religious ritual; close family members and friends will mourn—each in his or her own fashion. These people will now plan a future that is somewhat different from what they had planned before I died—even though each of them had undoubtedly already begun to anticipate my death and plan for that contingency. (A sudden and unexpected death, of course, gives rise to somewhat different dynamics.)

None of these things can happen until I am dead. Not as good as dead, not more dead than alive, not dead but capable of returning, but *dead!* As Veatch puts it, "Most types of death behavior (religious ritual, will reading, succession to the presidency) either happen or they do not. A point must be established at which the individual is no longer treated as living" (1976, p. 29). For many reasons, we require accurate knowledge of when (and whether) death occurs.

KINDS OF DEATH

What constitutes the end of life is apparently seen quite differently by different people. (Table 2-1 offers an example.) One approach to the determination of death, and thereby the determination of life, delineates three levels of existence (or nonexistence): physical, further divided into biological and clinical; psychological, the state of self-awareness; and social, further divided into self-perceived and other-perceived.

TABLE 2-1.
Percentage* of Students Selecting Various Responses to the Question "When Is a Person Dead?" (Kalish, 1966)

Condition	% (N = 105)
When the heart stops beating	52
When person loses self-awareness	35
When person wishes to die or gives up	35
Entering hospital or nursing home, knowing he/she will never leave alive	14
Learning of a terminal diagnosis	4
Becoming senile	4
People never die or don't die at time of physical death	18

*Adds up to more than 100% because some respondents proposed more than one possible definition.

Physical Life/Physical Death

Physical life refers to both the existence of functioning organs and the existence of a functioning organism. In the former case, each organ can have a somewhat independent existence; at the same time, the body as an entirety can live or die independently of individual organs. The former has been termed **biological life** and the latter **clinical life.** Each has a beginning, an existence, and an ending, and although these two periods are closely related to each other, they are not necessarily identical.

Clinical life and clinical death, for example, are all-or-none propositions: the organism is either functioning or it is not functioning; it is either clinically alive or clinically dead. When clinical death occurs, the death certificate can be signed.

Persons suffer **biological deaths** as each organ dies, but the individual himself or herself does not necessarily die. The heart may cease to function at a different moment from the lungs, liver, kidneys, or stomach. The brain may cease to function, or cease certain of its functions, while the heart is still reasonably healthy. The beginnings of biological life also do not necessarily mean that the individual qua individual is living. Most of the organs begin to function during the fetal period, and we have fairly accurate information about when each develops.

The initiation of clinical life is a matter of definition, and the theologian, the philosopher, the physician, you, and I all have an equal right to an opinion. Do we begin our lives at conception? At birth? When we are viable, or capable of continued existence outside our mother's womb? How much biological life must there be before we can say of an individual "That person is alive"? How much biological death must occur before we can say "That person is now dead"?

When these questions were asked of public health professionals, 43% answered that human life begins at conception; another 26% selected some time after conception but before birth; 9% believed life began at birth itelf; and 22% thought it was some time after birth (Knutson, 1967). Obviously there is room for disagreement even among those who are most concerned professionally. Your belief about when clinical life begins will influence your feelings about the rights of an unborn child, the prerogative of a pregnant woman to select abortion over childbirth, or the nature of a crime committed against a fetus.

My tooth dies (biological death) as a part of me when it is pulled from my body; so does my leg if it is amputated, although the skin, blood, tissue, bones, and nerves in the leg do not all die at the moment the leg is severed. As a matter of fact, animal tissues "have been preserved outside the living organism—far exceeding the life-span of the organism from which they were taken" (Choron, 1964, p. 4).

So some parts of me may far outlast "that which is me" and some parts of me will die before "that which is me" dies. We don't disagree much about those parts; what we disagree about is when the "me" dies. For this to happen, the organism that is "me" must cease to function as an organism, and given our present state of knowledge, the cessation must be irreversible. When this event occurs, the legal definition of death has been met, and the death certificate can be signed.

Psychological Life/Psychological Death

Psychological life refers to being aware of self or the world around; **psychological death** occurs when this awareness ceases. Deciding the beginning of psychological life is difficult, but it would occur very early—perhaps at the time of the earliest cognitive acts in which purpose is involved. When an infant cries to gain parental attention or makes a conscious effort to move in order to avoid discomfort, that would indicate the earliest phases of psychological life. Or it might be viewed as beginning at or even before birth.

Psychological death, when it occurs, most often affects those who are very old or who have suffered some severe losses in brain function, perhaps through an accident but more commonly through Alzheimer's disease or a similar condition. It is normally not an all-or-none occurrence, since most people move in and out of awareness or function with some level of hazy awareness. Total psychological death comes, most often, at the time of physical death but in some instances takes place earlier.

A happily married woman in her mid-fifties suddenly lost her husband through an unexpected heart attack. Her grieving was intense, and within a few months after her husband's death, she began to notice that her memory lapses, which had been slightly bothersome for some years, were becoming more frequent and for more important matters. When she broached the concern to a close friend and later to her son, they both responded by telling her that older people frequently forgot things and that the stress from her husband's death might have exacerbated the condition. Her physician told her, in effect, the same thing.

The memory lapses came more and more often, however, and she scheduled a visit to a neurologist for further evaluation. The evening before the appointment, she read a magazine article that described Alzheimer's disease, a serious health condition with symptoms very much like hers. Reading more of the article was extremely disturbing, since Alzheimer's disease has no cure, is progressive at an irregular rate, and leaves the victim with very limited intellectual capacity, eventually culminating in a state of total loss of memory.

With her husband dead and her son and his wife struggling to support three young children, the woman became fearful and depressed. She faced the prospect of increasing dependency on others until she would need institutionalization. "Who will I be," she asked herself, "when I have no memory of who I was?" She canceled the appointment with the neurologist the next morning and spent the day drinking vodka straight and crying.

People who are psychologically dead not only do not know who they are—they do not know *that* they are. This circumstance is obviously very distressing to family members. You often hear comments like "That isn't really my father—my father died weeks ago" or "I don't know her, and she doesn't know me. Why doesn't her body die also?"

Physical death is irreversible. What about psychological death? We seldom know for certain. An elderly, apparently disoriented woman suddenly regains a semblance of psychological life when her daughter visits, improves further when she sees her grandchildren, and then lapses into confusion when the family leaves. Psychological death can be accelerated by a hostile or an empty environment or by medications that leave a person semistuporous. It can be postponed by a warm, embracing environment, by sensory stimulation, by avoiding use of such medications as long as possible, and perhaps by a strong desire to remain psychologically alive.

It is this very possibility of reversibility that adds a significant moral issue to the human and health treatment of persons who are psychologically dying. If we treat such people like nonpersons by ignoring them, by talking about them in their presence as though they were not there, by depriving them of social or sensory stimulation, we may very well be increasing their confusion. In so doing, we may actually be hurrying their physical deaths as well. Since these people are sometimes seen as being "as good as dead," the tendency is to treat them as though they were already dead, and family members and health caretakers all withdraw psychologically. The possibility that the condition is reversible, at least in part, is never tested. This means that these people are deprived of whatever remaining psychological life they might otherwise have had.

But ministering to people who are in this condition is not easy for most family members or health professionals. A substantial effort is frequently required to effect relatively little change in responsiveness (although sudden and extreme changes do occur). For the family member, the process is difficult and painful; for the health professional, the process is frustrating and often regarded as not worth the effort.

Social Life/Social Death

Although you can be **socially alive** or **dead** to yourself as well as to others, the term more frequently refers to the ways you are perceived by others. When a person perceives you, for all practical purposes, as dead or nonexistent, you are socially dead for that person. For example, your mother enters a nursing home, where the only concrete evidence of her existence is her monthly bills and occasional cards; her role as your mother has ceased, and you and she have not substituted new roles. She may be socially dead to you and to others in your family in varying degrees: totally dead to one sister who lives near the nursing home but never sees her and rarely mentions her, still alive to a brother who lives some distance away but retains his concern and involvement.

Is she socially dead to herself also? That depends, of course, on how she sees herself. If her self-image now is of someone who is as good as dead or, for all practical purposes, dead, then she is socially dead to herself; if she perceives herself as still having at least the vestige of vitality, she is not socially dead to herself.

Social death can lead to psychological and physical death. If your family perceive you as socially dead (although they might feel some anxiety or guilt about so doing), they are likely to isolate themselves from you. You would find this depressing and stressful; if you were elderly, somewhat confused, and in an institution, the depression and stress might well have significant effects on your interest in living and on your daily habits of eating, exercising, and remaining stimulated. Your physical and social environments would become less stimulating, and, consequently, psychological death might occur more readily.

Being written off as socially dead can lead to feelings of hopelessness. Your need for the strength and supportiveness of others is not met, and your present situation does not permit you to function effectively without these supports.

He had been a farmer and a good husband and father in Laos, working the land that his ancestors had worked for generations, but the war overtook him, and he considered himself fortunate to be one of those who escaped and made their way to the United States. He was eventually settled in Southern California, near Long Beach, with his wife, their two sons, and one infant grandson.

Though only 49 years old, he looked to Americans like a man of 60. He had a heart condition, high blood pressure, and a moderate hearing loss. Once provided with housing in Orange County, the two sons quickly took it on themselves to look for work, while simultaneously learning English. Their mother found work cleaning houses, which left the father at home taking care of his grandson, whose mother had died during their escape from Laos.

Within two years, everyone had learned English, except for the father. Then first one son, then the other, relocated to New Mexico, where their rapidly acquired computer skills, recently acquired English skills, and knowledge of farming found them jobs. The father of the infant remarried and had his son sent to live with him.

A year later, the father had a stroke, which incapacitated his left side and destroyed most of his remaining hearing. His wife was unable to lift him, and he had to be placed in a nursing home only eight miles from the family home but lacking access by public transportation. And no one else in the home spoke his dialect.

The farmer, not yet 53 years old, was isolated from everyone who knew him. His children and grandchildren were hundreds of miles away and lacked the money to visit or even to telephone except on special occasions. His wife lived close by but had no telephone and was seldom able to visit the home. The functional roles that he had enjoyed in Laos—husband, father, worker, local-community leader—had all disappeared, along with the other roles that supported him, such as brother, grandfather, and father-in-law. And no desirable new roles seemed to develop. In fact, given his stroke, from which he recovered only partially and very slowly, and his hearing loss, his ability to learn English was extremely limited. Even watching television, which occupied most of his waking hours, provided little more than the opportunity to watch moving figures (and he had never learned to read in his home country).

In this instance, the farmer was not socially dead, since his remaining family members loved him and thought about him a great deal. However, their contacts with him were minimal, and the others in the nursing home ignored him except when absolutely necessary. Since they had trouble pronouncing his name, they called him "Hank," which further diminished him as a functioning human being. He was socially dead to most people in his life, barely socially alive to others, and only marginally socially alive to himself.

We find a powerful interaction between psychological death and social death. An elderly person's confusion and disorientation will predispose others to withdraw; when others withdraw, the potential for becoming confused and disoriented increases. And although rigorous experimental evidence is lacking, these factors most probably work together to hasten physical death.

A Legal Definition

In spite of the complexities discussed in the previous pages, the definition of death that makes the most difference is its legal definition. **Legal death,** of course, is based on a medical statement and refers to the death of the entire organism, not of a particular organ. But even here the definition is not precise—there is a gray area of uncertainty.

If death is the boundary between a body containing the essential qualities of humanness and a body not containing these qualities, then for death to have occurred, these qualities must be lacking. Veatch (1979) suggests four elements that have historically satisfied this criterion: irreversible loss of flow of vital fluids, irreversible loss of the soul from the body, irreversible loss of the capacity for bodily integration, and irreversible loss of the capacity for social interaction.

Veatch himself opts for the fourth of these qualities, since he views the essential characteristic of being human as the capacity to have social interactions, however minimal these might be. In this definition, we don't need to debate whether death occurs when the heart ceases to function or whether the brain ceases to function, since it is the death of the entire person that concerns us (Veatch, 1979). Veatch then goes further, pointing out that there are various definitions of legal death and that different hospitals follow different policies in this regard; therefore, each individual should be able to die according to his or her own definition of death, as confirmed by a medical authority and as limited by generally acceptable definitions. In effect, he is saying that I should not be declared dead by your philosophic beliefs about what death is (Veatch, 1979).

Another concern is that social and economic pressures to declare a person dead can take precedence over policies unless the policies are carefully devised to prevent this. An example: a legal case some years ago involved a heart transplant that occurred when the donor appeared to be fully functioning, except for total lack of brain activity. A respirator was maintaining his heart, and other organs were functioning. He was taken off the respirator, declared dead, and then hooked up again to machines to keep his organs in adequate condition for the transplant (Veatch, 1979). The issue in this instance is not whether the lack of brain activity was sufficient to have the man declared dead but that he might not have been declared dead had his heart not been needed for the transplant. Financial needs, such as the costs of maintaining a psychologically dead person in a hospital for a long period, may also influence the determination of death. Again, the issue here is not whether these criteria are appropriate but that they are used differently for different people, often without the knowledge of the individual himself or herself (since that person is unable to make such decisions at that point) or even of the next of kin.

A committee formed at Harvard Medical School attempted to respond to the concerns of defining death that have emerged because the advances of medical technology now permit the body's organs to function long after all cognitive activity has ceased. This committee proposed four criteria, all of which must be met for death to be declared: (1) unreceptivity and unresponsivity, (2) no movements or breathing, (3) no reflexes, and (4) flat electroencephalogram. Furthermore, these tests must be made again, 24 hours later, to confirm what has been found (cited in Veatch, 1976).

Many feel that these criteria are too conservative, because they would permit people to continue to exist long after any meaningful life had ceased. Others claim that only the very most conservative determinations of death should be applied, because any alternative might deprive some people of a portion of their life—even if a brief portion—and because it can never be known with absolute certainty in advance exactly how much life might be added.

To try to grasp the complexities of these decisions, ask yourself a few questions. Would you sign a paper that would require your physician to cease all medical treatment and care if you were defined dead by the Harvard Medical School criteria—even though your heart and other organs could be kept operative by hospital machinery? Would you require your physician to cease all medical treatment and care if you were defined dead because you would never regain consciousness, although movements, breathing, and reflexes were continuing? Would you wish your physician (or someone else) to hasten your clinical death if you would never again regain consciousness? And finally, think of the person whom you love best in this world: how would you answer the previous three questions if you had to make decisions for that person's life?

EXTENDING LIFE

Contemplating the various kinds of death brings up the possibility that the time at which each kind of death occurs may be postponed for a significant duration, that life expectancy can be extended. We know that this is possible, since life expectancy in the United States has been increased by many years since the turn of the century. This has occurred through disease control, improved sanitation, better public health, more knowledge of and adherence to good health practices, modern medical advances, better nutrition, and other developments. As we become more informed and more willing to pursue healthful life styles, life expectancy is likely to continue to increase.

Reports of Long-Lived Societies

From time to time, a newspaper or magazine article will report on a society in which amazingly large numbers of people live to be very old. The three societies that have received the most attention in the past 15 years or so are the Vilcabamba in Ecuador, the Georgians in Russia, and the Hunza in the Indian province of Kashmir (Leaf, 1973). Unfortunately for those who believe that following the practices of one of these groups would increase their own healthy life and life expectancy, careful examination of these communities suggests that their residents don't live nearly as long as claimed. For example, a more recent study of the Vilcabamba concentrated only on official records and discussions with the residents of the area. The researchers found a "systematic age exaggeration beginning at about 70 years" (Mazess & Forman, 1979, p. 97). One man who claimed to be 97 years old in 1970 was recorded as 140 when he died in 1971; another was 61 years old in 1944 but claimed to be 70 at that time and to be 80 in 1949, then 127 in 1974. The Russian data are similarly suspect (Medvedev, 1974).

It is not that these people are lying or falsifying information but that being accurate about their age is simply not important to them. Early researchers often took age claims at face value and misinterpreted church birth records because they failed to understand that many people in these societies have the same or similar names. In Russia some of the exaggeration was the result of young men having falsified their age, many years earlier, in order to avoid being drafted (Medvedev, 1974).

Currently Available Means of Life Extension

But dispelling the fantasies of extremely long life does not mean that you, as an individual, cannot extend your own life by appropriate physical, social, and emotional behavior. Proper use of preventive health care procedures, good diet, appropriate exercise, avoiding tobacco and excessive alcohol, caution in all drug use, and learning effective methods of coping with stress are all life-enhancing. At a societal level, we can work to reduce harmful pollutants in the air, water, and soil as well as in food additives, and we can serve as advocates for improved industrial safety, traffic and vehicle safety, and other forms of safety. And although it may seem a platitude, life expectancy will be increased when people drive more carefully, reduce interpersonal violence such as child abuse, reduce the use of guns and other weapons, and so forth.

Of course, you already know all of the above. Yet it seems fascinating that people will seek to increase their life expectancy through strange diets or dubious health programs while ignoring the obvious and time-tested ways to good health and longer life.

There may be an outer limit to normal life expectancy—perhaps around 90 or 100 years—but eliminating disease as well as accidents, war, homicide, and suicide would permit most of us to live up to this outer limit. The ultimate fantasy of this approach is that we all live a healthy life until we arrive at the age of 97 years, two months, and seven days, at which point we immediately drop dead of a cause we might term *life-running-out.*

Extending Life by Intervening in the Aging Process

Intervening in the aging process, which some biologists say may well occur sometime during the next 50 years (for example, Comfort, 1969), would have a very different effect. It may be possible to slow down the entire aging process, so that the physical conditions that are typical of age 30 today would then come at age 60, and the normal life expectancy might become 140 years instead of 70 years.

This intervention would require some kind of treatment—perhaps a pill or an injection—and might also include changes in living and health habits. Some interesting speculations develop about this treatment: (1) who would control it, (2) would there be enough to go around or only enough for some people, (3) what would the cost of this program be and who—governments or individuals—would pay for it, (4) would it have side effects, (5) would it be a one-time treatment or an ongoing one, and (6) would it help those who were already middle-aged or elderly or only those who were young?

Any program that successfully increased life expectancy might introduce a host of problems:

- Would changes occur so rapidly that great dislocations in populations would result (for example, all of a sudden we would have a doubling of people over age 70, without time to plan for it)?
- How would the resulting population explosion affect the world's food supply and amount of empty land space?
- What kinds of relationships would occur when six-generation families were common? What happens to inheritances?
- How would people feel about the possibility of working for 100 years or being married for 100 years?
- How would we accommodate workers and people in general to living through so many different eras and changes in social values and technologies? Will people remain in supervisory positions for 80 years? Or, will it take 80 years to become a supervisor?
- Could our educational institutions adapt to all these changing demands?

One concern that is frequently voiced is whether scientists have the moral right to work to extend life by interfering with the aging process—especially since the social problems that will emerge are obviously going to be considerable. Not only will laws and customs require altering, but the difficulties of handling the population increase that is expected with increased life expectancy are tremendous. How much longer would you want to live? How much longer would you want those whom you love to live? How much, in money and effort, would you be willing to pay for extra years?

A final issue that develops from these speculations is how a substantial life extension will alter our perceptions of death. If the boundary of death is first pushed back 20 years, will we then press to push it back another 20 and another and another? Will death be seen as more distressing when it does come early (which may be at age 80), because we assume a life of 140 years? Or will people become so bored with a long life—even a healthy life—that death will not be unwelcome?

Many kinds of death exist—of that there is little doubt. You will occasionally hear someone refer to a "living death"—usually a reference to being in prison, holding a despised job, residing in a community he or she hates, being constantly in severe pain, or being in an intolerable marriage or family situation. You may have called someone "dead from the neck up" to imply that his or her ideas and feelings were stultified and routinized. To each kind of death, certain reactions are appropriate. It seems important to have a clear idea of exactly what kind of death we are confronting so that our reactions are appropriate to the situation. We would not, therefore, respond to a social death as though it were a psychological death or to a psychological death as though it were a clinical death.

Death means different things to different people under different conditions. The term is used literally and metaphorically. It is used in an absolute sense to describe what most of us would agree death is and in relative senses to describe partial deaths or deaths of parts. The more we probe into the meanings of death, the more complex we find the situation.

You know what death is, of course. Well, what is it? Those two sentences opened this chapter. They seem appropriate to close the chapter as well.

CHAPTER THREE

The Meanings of Death

We all confront the possibility of death—our own and that of others—at all times. The only difference between you and the 90-year-old man or woman severely ill in a hospital whose predicted death is an hour away is that the statistical odds are immensely high that your death will come later. The odds are not 100%; indeed, the only time the odds become 100% is when you're betting that you will die eventually.

In other eras, this life was regarded as a brief respite between birth and death, between being conceived and entering the kingdom of heaven. "The man of the late Middle Ages was very acutely conscious that he had merely been granted a stay of execution, that this delay would be a brief one, and that death was always present within him" (Ariès, 1974, p. 44). Or, as the Yaqui mystic Don Juan tells Carlos Castaneda, "The man also realizes that death is the irreplaceable partner that sits next to him on the mat" (Castaneda, 1972, p. 150).

Was this awareness of the proximity of death so distressing that no enjoyment of life was possible? Not according to the French social historian Ariès: "That man felt a love of life which we today can scarcely understand, perhaps because of our increased longevity" (p. 45). Not according to Castaneda, who wrote of Don Juan: "He knows his death is talking to him and won't give him time to cling to anything, so he tries, without craving, all of everything" (p. 151). And certainly not according to the major religious faiths of the world.

Life is precious because it isn't forever, because we don't have more than we want. Thus, in its own strange way, the knowledge of the certainty of eventual death and of the possibility of immediate death enhances the richness of life—at least for those willing to live life in the face of what some have termed the absurdity of death.

WHOSE DEATH?

The meaning for me of facing my own death is quite different from the meaning for me when I face your death or the notion of death in general. The meaning for me in facing death now is quite different from the meaning for me of facing death at a later specific time or indefinitely far off in time.

In the event of your death, I—as an observer—still remain. I can view your death from outside—no matter how much you are a part of my life. If you are my client, patient, parishioner, customer, then I have learned to come close to death and yet to get up and walk away when all is said and done; my world is not untouched by you, but with rare exceptions it remains very much intact. If you are a casual friend, an acquaintance, a neighbor, my world is touched, perhaps somewhat moved, but except for a brief time the effect of your death on me is slight. If you are someone very close, my world may be disrupted by your death, but at least I remain. My own death "means the total disintegration and dissolution of [my] personal world" (Koestenbaum, 1971, p. 6). For all practical purposes, then, when I die, the world ceases to exist.

This doesn't necessarily mean that I prefer your death to mine, although that may well be the case. I may actually prefer that you outlive me, since the loss of you through death might be more difficult for me to face than my own death. The death of a loved one is often perceived as worse than the death of oneself (Geer, 1965).

Sometimes we look at our own death as though we were looking at the death of someone else. Not only do we plan our funeral and visualize it occurring; we see the sadness of our friends and family members. The truth, of course, is that we can see these scenes only in fantasy, since with our death our ability to experience ceases also.

BUT FIRST, MEANINGS IN LIFE

Death is one boundary of life. Conception or birth is another. You may see death as a permeable boundary, through which you will move to another form of existence, or you may see death as an inflexible boundary at which you will cease. In either event, the meaning of death is intimately bound up with the meaning of life. "Since death . . . belongs to life as obviously as the border belongs to a country . . . , the only way to inquire about death is obviously to inquire about life" (Thielicke, 1970, p. 8).

Before moving ahead, we need to distinguish two concepts that are so intertwined they may initially appear identical. The first—the **meaning *of* life**—implies the existence of some ultimate meaning that explains why people exist in the first place. The second—**meaning *in* life**—is a totally different matter. Meaning *in* life is what is so important to you that it gives purpose to your life.

Choron (1964), a foremost philosopher on death-related issues, proposes that meaning *of* life be considered as follows: (1) whether each individual life is part of a unified plan or process that can be understood as such, (2) whether life can be understood as the expression of a pervasive world spirit, and (3) whether life is a symbol of something else that is "above" or "beyond" an individual life.

Although these significant questions are far beyond the scope of this book, how people feel about them does affect their view of death. If, for example, you feel that your life is part of a universal plan, then you are likely to believe that your death is also part of that plan. Rather than being absurd and meaningless, your death will fit into something much grander than you yourself. Does this make your own death easier for you to accept? We certainly don't have any good evidence about that question, but it might well do so.

Meaning or purpose *in* life need not have any significance broader than your own pleasure. Give some thought to what makes your own life meaningful. It need not also make your life meaningful in the future, but it must be something that you would feel very empty without right now.

Is work what gives purpose to your life? Perhaps your present work and your career goals make your life meaningful. (Mandatory retirement is extremely unpopular among some elderly people not only because of loss of income or social contacts but because of loss of participation in the work itself.) Or is it achievement in general that gives your life meaning: the number of books you write, the number of insurance policies you sell, the number of patients you help, the number of awards you receive, the number of people you enable to become better people? What about status and recognition? Is one of your purposes to win awards or to have people know your name—to attain fame (and, if possible, fortune)?

How about personal growth? Is your main purpose in being alive the opportunity to become "the best *you* that you can possibly become?" Is it to grow in understanding of yourself and of others, to mature in wisdom and knowledge, to make the most of the abilities that you have?

Or do loving and being loved give your life meaning? Do you wish more than anything else to leave your mark by developing loving human relationships? Or even relationships with nature?

What about a cause? Is there a cause to which you are so dedicated that it forms a significant—even the most significant—purpose in your life? The cause might be political or religious or social or creative; it might have a formal organization, an informal organization, or no organization; it might be finite in nature—for example, the next political campaign—or almost infinite in nature—for example, the espousal of world peace.

Does serving God offer you most of what you wish? Perhaps you see both life and death "as part of the gift of being that is given by God, whose love sustains and gives meaning and value to life, while dying is part of the wholeness of life" (John Evans, personal communication). Then do you wish to live in relationship to God? Is this the traditional God of Western religions? Is it some other god?

All of the above offer purposes in living, but none—except possibly the service or adoration of God—explains the meaning of life. Furthermore, each of the purposes ends with death—either your death or the deaths of persons you have influenced. These are human purposes, and like all else that is human, they are finite.

How difficult is it for you to consider the transitory nature of what you have accepted as the most significant meanings in your life? For one friend of mine, it was the source of immense sadness. Fifteen years earlier he had written an extremely fine book, which was more widely quoted and more widely used as a textbook than any other on the topic. He had expected that this book, this achievement, would still be important 10 and 20 years later; he had wanted this achievement to live because only in that way could this accomplishment continue as a source of meaning in his life. Then, a year from retirement, past the point of desire to write another book, he realized that more recent students had not even heard of him. He became depressed at the transient quality of his accomplishment and came to feel that his life had been without meaning. Had he been able to accept the time-bound character of his achievement, he might have been satisfied that he had contributed to the knowledge of tens of thousands of people over a 10-year period, but because of the kind of person he was, he needed to extend that contribution to many more tens of thousands of people over a 30- or 40-year period, or, by implication, forever.

To return to our original concern: because death is a boundary to life, it annihilates meaning *in* life for most of us. Your work, your achievements, your status and recognition, your personal growth, your capabilities for loving and being loved, your contribution to causes are all negated by your death or, if not by your death, then eventually by the deaths of others.

MEANINGS OF DEATH

I've just said that one meaning of death is that it negates most meanings *in* life; it does not need to negate meanings *of* life. For example, if life is perceived as part of God's gift—as it is in traditional Judaism and Christianity—death is also understood as part of the same gift. The German theologian Thielicke (1970) believes death is an expression of God's will that human beings not forget that they are human and not God. Since God is infinite and people are finite, people cannot effectively aspire to be God.

If death is God's will, as the Old Testament states in Job 1:21, then death has meaning—although any particular death may still be painful for both the dying person and the survivors. Death may also be part of an evolutionary plan that does not depend on a traditional God. For example, death may be perceived as an evolutionary necessity. Older things and people die to make room for the younger, while the selective reproducing processes promote the adaptation of the organism to a changing environment. If all the old of a species lived, the world would soon be overrun with that organism. At the same time, the species would not change, since the old would also continue to reproduce. Only because some individuals die before reproducing can the species change genetically. Evolution can be seen as another kind of plan—except that we don't need to assume that God has developed it.

Being part of an evolutionary or religious plan may offer some consolation, but it seems a dubious argument to invoke with someone facing a very intimate and personal event. I'm dying and you want to talk about some absolutes that are never going to affect me in the least. This is much too abstract and impersonal, and it leaves me emotionally untouched.

In both the divine plan and the evolutionary plan, death is seen as necessary—perhaps good, perhaps evil, but necessary. Death may not be so much part of a plan as simply a part of life. If it is part of life, a natural and inevitable part, then there should be no reason to fear death—or so one familiar argument goes. Unfortunately, it may not be very persuasive. "Disease, injury, congenital defects are also a part of life, and as well murder, rapine, and pillage" (Ramsey, 1975, p. 82). True, these other events may be preventable in part, but they are certainly part of life today. It is unlikely you would tell an automobile-accident victim "That's too bad, but—well—it's part of life." The same explanation may well be equally unsatisfying to someone who is dying.

When we contemplate the nature of death and of being dead, we often develop conflicting beliefs. For example, we might view death simultaneously as absurd and meaningful, as beautiful and ugly, as extinction and as transition, as punishment and as reward. These apparent contradictions need not be real contradictions, however; for example, an event may partake of both beauty and ugliness. Sometimes one aspect is more in evidence and sometimes the other.

Death Destroys Meaning/Death as Meaning

Consider this apparent conflict. First, because death makes life transient and because anything that does not exist is without meaning, death destroys the meaning of life by destroying the possibility of further life. Second, since death provides an end to life and since the end of life means that time is finite, people are forced into making irreversible decisions concerning the use of time (because once time is spent, it can never be retrieved), and these decisions reflect the meaning people impose on life.

In the former case, death has no meaning in and of itself. It merely *is*. Death occurs without logic or inspiration; it has been built into a genetic program, which each generation inevitably passes down to its successors. This view proposes that death robs life of meaning.

A modification of this position is that it is not death itself, but fear of death, that robs life of meaning. People who lead the lives they wish to lead will feel fulfilled as they approach their later years and death; they will have little fear of death, and therefore the meaning of death will not be so strongly negative. For those who have not lived as they had wanted, death puts an end to all possibilities of changing their circumstances. Therefore, as they age and confront the imminence of their own death, death is frightening and has a strongly negative valence (Lepp, 1968).

The well-known psychoanalyst and philosopher C. G. Jung was deeply concerned about the relationship between death and meaning. In translating his words from the German, Choron (1964) quotes Jung as writing that "never does the question of life's meaning and value arise more urgently and painfully than when we see the last breath leave a body that was alive only a moment ago" (p. 160). Jung viewed such issues as aging, religion, and death and the fear of death as major influences on people from their midthirties on, a position that contrasted with those of most of his contemporaries in psychology and psychoanalysis.

In the view of Frankl and many others as well, death gives life the potential for meaning. Several centuries ago, the predominant view was that death was a trial conducted by God to determine the worthiness of each dying person (Ariès, 1974). Your ability to avoid temptation and die courageously was, in large part, a measure of your entire life. In the extreme case, if you died well, it did not matter how you had lived.

For entirely different reasons, some contemporary writers assign death a meaning. They believe that the knowledge that you will die challenges you to do something with the life you have and that the passage of time—the death of each moment—challenges you to do something with each moment (Bulka, 1974; Frankl, 1963).

A further point can be made: the mystery and power of death can be a creative force. "The highest spiritual values of life can originate from the thought and study of death" (Kübler-Ross, 1975, p. 1). Because death is such a basic matter in both religions and myths, it gives rise to serious thought and creative endeavors. Michelangelo is quoted as stating "No thought exists in me which death has not carved with his chisel" (Kübler-Ross, 1975, p. 2). It is not that death should be welcomed but that there is in death a constructive as well as a destructive force (Kübler-Ross, 1975)—death both obliterates meaning and creates meaning.

Death Is Beautiful and Tranquil/Death Is Ugly and Fierce

> Come lovely and soothing death,
> Undulate round the world, serenely arriving, arriving,
> In the day, in the night, to all, to each,
> Sooner or later, delicate death.
> —*Walt Whitman, "When Lilacs Last in the Dooryard Bloom'd"*

> The last enemy that shall be destroyed is death.
> —*I Corinthians 15:26*

> Cry woe, destruction, ruin, loss, decay;
> The worst is death, and death will have his day.
> —*Shakespeare, Richard II, III, ii, 102–103*

Is death lovely and soothing? Or is it an enemy to be destroyed? In one of its familiar images in our culture, death is compared to a pastoral scene, where all is calm and contented. After the pain and toil of life, death offers peace and love or else peace and nothingness. The view of the 19th century was that death and even the bodies of the dead were beautiful, comforting, and exalting (Ariès, 1981).

One experienced death counselor has described how he encourages dying people to "let go"—to permit themselves to die, to relax and "be taken by death." He paints a picture for them of how easy it is to die and how good it will be to be dead. This technique is used only for individuals who, though near death, hold on to one thread of life because of some unfinished business or fear of dying.

This view of death is supported by reports from people who claim to have died and then returned to life (for example, Moody, 1976). Their descriptions of what it is like to be dead almost always include warm reunions with loving family members or some other very positive experience.

Many years ago I read a science fiction story—I can't recall either the author or the title—in which a man found the secret to truly long life and made himself impervious to death for several hundred years. Then, through an ironic turn, he was incarcerated, and the prison was unexpectedly abandoned. The story ends with his realization that he is doomed to be totally alone—without any human contact or sources of pleasure—for hundreds of years. The Struldburgs in *Gulliver's Travels* suffer a similar fate: they continue to age and to endure the problems of aging while unable to die. At first Gulliver believes them the most blessed of people, but he later realizes the horrors of their lives.

Death can be a welcome relief for people who are weary or ill or who see themselves as burdensome to others and useless to themselves. Pneumonia was once called "the old man's friend" because it caused death for many elderly people who were suffering greatly from other illnesses.

A number of years ago, a psychologist asked people to personify death and describe their personifications. What does death look like? What would death be like? The responses were categorized, and one of the most frequently mentioned categories was termed "the gentle comforter." According to one woman, a registered nurse, "Death would be calm, soothing, and comforting. . . . He would be kind and understanding and yet be very firm and sure of his actions and attitude" (Kastenbaum & Aisenberg, 1972, p. 157). This seems remarkably like the views expressed in Whitman's poem quoted at the beginning of this section and certainly represents a significant theme on the nature of death.

The unpleasant side of death, called "the macabre" in the research, was also represented in the study. "An extremely thin and emaciated form, scarred, burned, contorted, about twelve feet tall." "The personality is a coldness, hollowness, absolute nothingness." "He's grouchy, cranky, sullen, sarcastic, cynical, mean, evil, disgusting, obnoxious, and nauseating" (Kastenbaum & Aisenberg, 1972, p. 156). These quotations, the responses of three undergraduate students, remind one of Shakespeare's description of death as comparable to woe, destruction, ruin, loss, and decay—and yet still worse than any of these.

Which is death really: beautiful and tranquil or ugly and fierce? The answer, of course, is in the eye of the beholder. The answer also depends on what kind of dying process is occurring *and* whether we are considering that dying process or its end point, for the process could be fierce and death itself serene.

Shneidman (1971b) takes a particularly strong position on the question whether death is beautiful or ugly. He discusses the need to deromanticize death. "Psychologically, our current attitudes toward death are unconsciously sentimental" (p. 11). Since consciousness is all that we have, its loss is the worst thing that could occur. Rather than consider death to be a serene and natural ending to life, Shneidman calls it the "curse to end all curses" (p. 12). He argues that it is about as loving as kidnapping or rape, since, like those two acts, it violently takes its unwilling victims.

Although these words need to be heeded, they give rise to a serious dilemma. On the one hand, if we advocate that death is beautiful, we may be guilty of trying to avoid dealing with the real emotional difficulties faced by dying persons; we offer them a sedative when what they require is the emotional support to face their own pain. On the other hand, if the romanticization of death seems so widespread and so important in the coping processes of many persons, an iconoclastic, myth-destroying position may be less a matter of being honest than of displaying our own power and self-righteousness.

It seems that a strong case could be made to support the idea that viewing death as beautiful is a way to avoid the confrontation with the ugliness and unpleasant passions that often accompany death and dying. It may even be a more sophisticated way to deny the reality of death, or at least the unpleasant realities of death. In the final analysis, death robs me of me, and although I recognize that the time may come when life will be so painful that I will welcome death as an alternative, death can easily be seen as cruel and unfair.

Perhaps the entire debate, which has become intense at times, could be settled by a suggestion by theologian Dennis Klass (personal communication, 1983). Klass proposes that one can simultaneously affirm the position that there is beauty *in* death but that death is not beautiful. Following this position, we might remark that a particular death occurred in a beautiful fashion or that the strength and spiritual qualities of a dying, now dead, person were beautiful or that someone we love looks beautiful in death. None of this contends that death itself is beautiful.

Then, if that isn't sufficient to assuage both camps, Klass (personal communication, 1983) proposes that death is neither beautiful nor ugly. Perhaps the continuum isn't even relevant for the concept. So we have the possibilities that death is beautiful or ugly, beautiful and ugly, neither beautiful nor ugly. Settling the matter may be impossible, but becoming aware of its many manifestations is important.

Death as Extinction/Death as Transition

Is it possible to think of yourself as being in a state of nothingness? A void? Extinction? Nonbeing? Perhaps this is impossible; perhaps we can think of others as no longer existing but not of ourselves as such. I can conceptualize a world that exists without me, but I cannot conceptualize a "me" that exists without the world—that is, without consciousness. Certainly the perception of death as the total, irreversible, permanent cessation of consciousness is one of the most familiar ideas of what does occur at the time of clinical death, regardless of the difficulties of applying it to our own consciousness. "It is the prospect of not being any more that makes most men abhor death" (Choron, 1964, p. 10).

Which does death mean to you: extinction or transition? What happens to your consciousness? After clinical death, is there anywhere and any way in which any thing knows it is still you? Will this whatever-it-is continue to know that it is you for only moments or for years or for centuries or forever? If so, death is a transition, a **passage** from existence in bodily form in this world, either to existence in another form in this world or to existence in some form in another setting. If, however, you believe that clinical death marks the complete cessation of all consciousness or you-ness forever, then for you death is **extinction.**

Two separate issues enter into a decision about whether death is passage or extinction: first, what you believe and, second, what you would like to believe. It is not unusual for someone to believe that death is extinction yet want his or her own soul or existence to continue in some fashion. Many people have forcefully expressed their need to believe in continuation. For example, Bismarck, the great 19th-century German leader, said: "Without the hope of an afterlife, this life is not even worth the effort of getting dressed in the morning." Franz Kafka wrote: "Man cannot live without a continuous confidence in something indestructible within himself." According to Emerson, "The blazing evidence of immortality is our dissatisfaction with any other solution."

Statistical evidence supports these quotations. When David Reynolds and I asked 434 adults in Los Angeles whether they believed they would live on in some form after death, just over half responded affirmatively. When we returned to the issue with the question "Regardless of your *belief* about life after death, what is your *wish* about it?," fully 70% said they wished there were life after death, while 1 respondent in 8 wished there were not (Kalish & Reynolds, 1981).

It is difficult to accept the idea that all consciousness ends forever with clinical death. Indeed, one psychiatrist has claimed that the fear of death and anxiety over being finite is *the* major factor in schizophrenia (Searles, 1961). The schizophrenic symptoms provide an escape from dealing with the anguish of knowing we are not "forever." People diagnosed as schizophrenic sometimes experience themselves as already dead—perhaps the ultimate symptom in avoiding a realistic death encounter. If I am already dead, then I can't be made dead. Even though this is a highly speculative and probably untestable idea, it opens up a provocative area of thought.

Extinction and passage are not, however, the only possibilities. A third is an intermediate state following clinical death and prior to either extinction or passage. Thus, a number of African societies recognize a *Sasa* period during which an individual continues to exist after his or her clinical death. It lasts as long as some living person still recalls the dead person and his or her name from personal contact. The person remains in a *living-dead* state and can continue to appear among the living and be recognized and acknowledged by them. When no one who knew the dead person is still alive, he or she enters a state of *collective immortality*, which is a kind of permanent limbo for spirits or shades of the dead. The dead person may, however, be forced into nonexistence, and this is seen as the worst possible happening (Mbiti, 1970).

In a variation of this, a Melanesian tribe sees the 100 days following death as existing between life and afterlife; the dead person can be seen in nature, as a flash of light or a butterfly, or be heard as in a birdcall. The person is "dead but not gone." In cases of unexplainable deaths, this period is used to determine the cause of death (Rodman & Rodman, 1983–84).

Many people maintain a strange ambivalence concerning extinction and passage. Although they claim to believe in extinction, in nothingness, and assert that their views coincide with their preferences, they maintain a number of values that contradict their verbalized position. Just ask such people how they would feel if their bodies were chopped up and ground down the disposal. A grotesque image? Not if there is no symbolic value to the body. I recall one friend who, after passionately declaring his aversion to any kind of life after death, asked that his ashes be scattered at the top of a mountain he had had great pleasure in conquering. I suspect he maintained, at some level of consciousness, an image of himself peering out through his ashes with 20/20 vision at the surrounding countryside.

Death as Punishment/Death as Reward

The idea of death as punishment is deeply ingrained in Western culture. In the Old Testament Adam and Eve are punished for their sins by expulsion from the Garden of Eden, where they could have remained immortal (Choron, 1963). Because of their sin, known as original sin, they fell from grace and lost God's gift of immortality for themselves and for all their descendants. Consequently, we are all condemned to die. "Once death appeared, the only thing God could do for man was to prolong his life, as a reward for obedience to His Law" (Choron, 163, p. 82).

Some people believe that the sins they perpetrate as individuals will also shorten their lives. A long life, then, would be one reward for appropriate behavior. Death occurring to large numbers of people may also be seen as a punishment for the sins of a society. God flooded the world—destroying everyone except Noah and his family—in retribution for humankind's evil ways. Through the centuries, people have attempted to propitiate various gods with prayers and gifts in order to avoid catastrophes, and some victims and nonvictims of disasters view them as punishments for individual or societal behavior (Wolfenstein, 1977). When a calamity strikes some person, group, organization, or country that you dislike, you assume it is a punishment for the victims' "sins" (or whatever term you might prefer using); when a comparable calamity befalls you or your group, organization, or country, however, you are more likely to ask "Why me?"

Many cultures share the view that one's own sins contribute to a briefer life. The Hopi believed that kindness, good thoughts, and peace of mind led to a long life; according to the Berber, deceit was punished by a shorter life (Simmons, 1945). Among the general population of the United States, over one-third of 434 respondents to a questionnaire agreed with the statement "Most people who live to be 90 years old or older must have been morally good people" (Kalish & Reynolds, 1981); the implication, of course, is that they view long life as a reward for good behavior. Nonetheless, the same people may also believe that "the good die young"—the implication in this statement is that the good are protected in this fashion from the evils of this world—and that the deaths of the elderly are not punishments. These latter deaths are frequently seen as appropriate—these people had lived out their allotted years, and it was time for them to die.

Frequently, when someone who isn't old dies, we seek an explanation for the early death in the person's behavior. At one level, we may look to heavy drinking or smoking, to poor health and eating habits, to working too hard because of greed as reasons for having died "before one's time." Then we can think "Of course that man had a heart attack—smoking two packs a day, drinking like a fish, and working 12 hours a day to pile up the dollars; he was just asking for it." He has been punished for his secular sins, and since we don't smoke, drink, or work as he did, we won't have to die. Indeed, it even appears that people who survive a heart attack feel morally and psychologically superior to those who have died (Appleton, 1975). If we can blame the dead person for having died, we can escape both our own mortality and our own responsibility.

At a second level, we may literally see "the hand of God" reach out and cause individuals' deaths because they were "bad" people. Nearly two-thirds of the respondents in the Los Angeles study mentioned in the preceding section agreed with the essentially fundamentalist position that "accidental deaths show the hand of God working among men" (Kalish & Reynolds, 1981).

Death can also be seen as a reward. We have earlier noted some of the positive aspects of death—the ideas that it gives meaning to life, that it challenges people to do their best, that it is part of a divine plan or of evolutionary necessity, and that it is a release from suffering.

DEATH AS LOSS

Stop and think for a moment. What will *you* lose when you are dying? What will *you* have lost when you are dead? Loss is a constant theme in writings on death and dying. For many people, death is the ultimate loss because it is the loss of consciousness, which, as Shneidman has said, is really all we have.

Of the many losses that accompany the dying process and death, I will discuss only a few here: the loss of experiencing, the loss of people, the loss of control and competence, the loss of the capacity to complete projects and plans, the loss of body, and the loss of the dream.

Loss of Experiencing

Although the loss of the capacity to experience anything seems to strike many philosophers and writers as the most important of all losses, respondents to several questionnaires appeared to feel otherwise. Given seven possible losses caused by death, several hundred to several thousand respondents in each of three studies ranked the loss of the ability to experience first, fourth, and sixth.

Although the differences among the studies initially seemed confusing, they eventually developed into a very sensible picture. The respondents in the study ranking highest concern for this loss were primarily young, introspective, and intellectually sophisticated (Shneidman, 1971a); the study in which the loss of experiencing ranked near the bottom was based on participants who were older, more likely to be parents or grandparents, and more likely to believe in traditional religious and social values (Kalish & Reynolds, 1981); the third study was more heterogeneous in its population (Diggory & Rothman, 1961). Furthermore, in both of the latter studies, it was shown that older people were less likely to be concerned with loss of this ability than were younger people; the remaining study did not provide information on age differences.

We will assume for the present that death will lead to the loss of capacity to experience, but what about the process of dying? In some serious and terminal illnesses there is a tendency to become confused (loss of capacity to experience accurately and, perhaps, meaningfully) and to sleep a great deal or to lose consciousness. Moreover, medication for pain often produces drowsiness and other kinds of loss of consciousness. Therefore, most dying persons experience more than usual loss of consciousness and capacity for experiencing during their last hours, days, and weeks.

Loss of People

When I die, I will lose you. You will lose me. I will lose me. And I will empathize with your losing me. The loss of others begins during the dying process. As my energy diminishes, I cease being willing to make the effort to see people who don't matter a great deal to me. Increasingly as time goes on, I restrict myself to two groups who mean the most to me: first, to those family members and very close friends whom I care for the most and who are themselves capable of being with me in my present state and, second, to the health professionals and hospital staff, who may be very instrumental in keeping me comfortable, free from pain, and in a good mood; who, in effect, have power over my life; and whom I often have come to care for (or despise) with great intensity.

When time becomes very short, I can only bother with those whom I consider highest priority. Even if this means I will hurt a few people's feelings, I can't help it. I really know my priorities now and must serve my own needs, rather than the needs of others. There may be some to whom I am very close whose presence disturbs me—perhaps because I am upset by their grief or because they play games, irritate me, or talk too much. I can try to get my message across to them because I do want to see them, but I may not have the time for such messages or the energy to figure out how to deliver them.

I also know that when I am dead, I will have lost these people. Therefore, my anticipation of my impending loss forces me to adjust, to cope with what is to come before it has come. I may try to push these losses away from my awareness, but that is almost impossible. Nor do I need to have begun the living-dying process to be upset by knowing these losses will occur. Merely being alive and over the age of 9 or 10 may be sufficient, and young children do sometimes fantasize the loss of parents.

I also know that you will grieve for me and mourn my death, and that both pleases me and further saddens me. I would hate not being missed, since I want to feel that others care for me; at the same time, I dislike being the source of your upset and sadness. I know how sad I am at losing you, and I assume you are also sad at losing me. Of course, you will—well, you *may*—eventually get over losing me and will—well, *may*—find a replacement, but I will be dead and therefore . . . .

How upset is a dying person that his or her survivors will be bereaved? Apparently it is extremely important, and dying people often go to great lengths to protect their friends and relatives during the dying process. The Los Angeles survey (Kalish & Reynolds, 1981) found that "my death would cause grief to my relatives and friends" was the most important of the seven losses or effects of death listed; the other study involving many older and married participants also had it ranked first (Diggory & Rothman, 1961).

Anticipation of death does not give rise only to thoughts of the loss of others. It may also bring about the exact opposite: hopes for reunion with others. This theme, familiar in Western culture, has recently reemerged in conjunction with the search for proof of an afterlife. Numerous books appearing in the mid-1970s detailed reunion experiences of people about to die and of those who had presumably been declared dead and subsequently returned to life (Moody, 1976; Osis & Haraldsson, 1977). The literature on suicide also discusses the fantasy many people have that their deaths will reunite them with loved ones who have already died (Perlin & Schmidt, 1975). Once again we find apparent opposite meanings in death: loss of others and reunion with others.

Loss of Control and Competence

As I sit at the typewriter and write these paragraphs, I am in full or reasonable control of much of my life. Within limits, I can eat when and what I want; I can go to bed and get up when I want (work, telephone, and children permitting); I can stay at home or leave the house, turn the television on or leave it off, and walk slowly or run quickly when and if I wish. My body does what I want it to—again within reason. Except for an occasional yawn when I am trying to appear alert, my body follows my conscious and unconscious orders.

What kind of control will I have when I am dead? I know that I will lose some control during the dying process, but I don't know what will happen to me when I am actually dead. In this existence, I have at least some control, some influence, over what happens to me and what goes on around me. But will any of that remain when I am dead? Some people value control greatly. It is important to them that they not appear foolish to others, that they not become so involved in a relationship that the "power" is turned over to someone else, that they always appear to know what they are doing on the job. Knowing what is happening and what is going to happen next are ways of having at least some control. In death, we don't know what our control, our power, will be. And this can be extremely disturbing to many people.

Competence also matters a great deal. We are presumably rewarded in some fashion on earth for our competence, but what about in death? Death, as Kastenbaum (1981) says, is the great leveler. Just as guns became known as equalizers, because they permitted a weak person to be as powerful as a strong person, death levels or equalizes the rich and the poor, the powerful and the powerless, the creative and the pedestrian, the competent and the incompetent, the religious and the irreligious.

Death completes the leveling process. Although a grand monument may be built for you and a small stone plaque placed flat on the ground for me, these symbols acknowledge memories of you and me, not an actually existing you and me. This ancient awareness was well expressed over 2000 years ago by a contemporary moralist, Publius Syrus, who said "As men, we are all equal in the presence of death." Your power and riches may help you live a little longer, but you and I share the eventual losses of competence and control that are part of death.

Loss of Capacity to Complete Projects and Plans

Right this moment, as I am writing these sentences, I have innumerable projects and plans that I wish to complete. Most immediately obvious is my wish to finish this book; I also want to see my children grown and independent—not because they need me to accomplish that but because I want to see it. And there are many places I want to visit. You may have comparable projects still incomplete—perhaps some academic program or a sales campaign or a fund-raising drive for your favorite political or charitable cause.

If you learned that you were going to die before these projects could be finished, you would undoubtedly feel frustrated and angry. One of the first things people do when they begin to realize that they will die fairly soon is try to figure out how to get their projects finished. Sometimes it is possible to complete the project before death occurs; sometimes it is necessary to compromise or permit someone else to help; sometimes it is necessary to realize that the project will never be finished.

Your unfinished business may be less concrete than a sales campaign. Perhaps you had an argument seven years ago with your brother, and you haven't spoken to him since; perhaps you cheated a friend some years ago and you have been meaning to admit your guilt; perhaps you had been postponing a backpacking vacation in the Rockies until you had more time. Often the projects and plans that are uncompleted at the time of our deaths are tasks that have been unfinished for a long time.

Loss of Things

Death negates all the wonderful things that materialism offers. You have saved for a color television set, a sports car, an expensive stereo with tape recorder, and a vacation home. If only you could live forever, you could continue to accumulate more and more things. Or you could accumulate friends or experiences or store up trips to foreign countries. When you are young, it seems that if you wish hard enough and work hard enough, you could eventually earn all the good things.

There's an old expression, You can't take it with you. And to that, one person responded "If I can't take it with me, I ain't going." What is the use of having all those expensive things if you can't have them forever? Death certainly puts earning money in a different light. Perhaps the despair that Erikson (1963) discusses in his characterization of the stage conflict that occurs in old age derives to some extent from the realization that life will end and, therefore, will not permit the unending acquisition of things, of people, of places, of experiences.

Since you can't take it with you, what is it that is important to have or to have done by the time you die? On what would you like to look back when you are 65 or 70? Can you live today in a manner that allows you to have that kind of life and those kinds of things to look back on?

Loss of Body

What happens to your body when you are dead? Perhaps you believe that it really doesn't matter. All right, but try to imagine yourself without your body. It's very difficult. In spite of the changes in our bodies, in spite of whatever unhappinesses we may have with our bodies, the truth is that we see ourselves in terms of our bodies. With death, the body—at least for some people—becomes a shell that no longer has any meaningful relationship with the essence or spirit of the individual who inhabited it; for others, the body disappears physically but remains in some sort of psychic state in which it waits for a resurrection; for still others, the corporeal body ceases to exist, but its symbolic representation is generated in heaven or in some other kind of existence after death.

As was mentioned earlier, even if we insist that we don't care about our bodies, our behavior often implies that we really do care—very much. Many people respond with horror to the image of *their* body (or, to make it worse, the body of someone they love) devoured by worms underground, or burned or cremated, or buried without the protection of a casket. The virtual terror that is expressed at the thought of desecration or deterioration of the body strongly suggests that people in fact find the body very important.

The theme of mutilation is powerful and familiar in myths, fantasies, and fears of death. In part, death is seen as a mutilation or the process of dying is seen as (often justifiably) a mutilating process. This means that dying and death lead to a loss of body integrity or physical wholeness. Not infrequently the medical treatment required to keep people alive—or alive longer—is also harmful to the body (for example, cobalt treatment for cancer or some form of surgery). People then must face mutilation of the body in order to live several months longer, and some prefer more rapid death.

Thus, in the dying process, mutilation may be caused by the disease or accident or by the treatment. Mutilation through decay occurs to the body after the death occurs. And symbolically the entire process of dying-death-dead may be seen as desecration and mutilation. Part of the mortician's task in the United States and Canada is to restore the appearance of the body to eliminate the appearance of mutilation.

Loss of the Dream

As your future becomes your present and then your past, it can no longer be altered, nor can the time be used for anything other than what it was used for already. "The moving hand, having writ, moves on," as the adage goes. We can compensate for, but not undo, what has been done. And we cannot regain the time that has been spent. As we get older and closer to our own death, this concern becomes greater, since the duration of probable future life decreases, and with this decrease, the chances of the dreams of earlier days coming true decrease as well.

Throughout our lives, we all have dreams: accomplishments, fame, success, money, wonderful marriage, brilliant and happy children, and so forth. The prospect of death produces the awareness that certain of these are impossible dreams. As death comes closer, bargains are struck with oneself concerning which dreams may still be accomplished (see Chapter 7 for discussion of Kübler-Ross' stages of dying) or the extent to which dreams must be modified. Death is the negator of all these dreams.

DEATH AS AN ORGANIZER OF TIME

It was mentioned earlier that death provides a boundary to life. Without this boundary, it would rarely be necessary to do anything today—it could usually be done as well tomorrow, and we would never run out of tomorrows. In fact, death brings not one but two boundaries: the certainty of eventual death and the uncertainty of the time when it will arrive. Death might appear in five years or five days or five minutes.

Each of us must find a way to balance these two boundaries. How would you live the next five years if you knew five years were all the time you had? How about the next five days? How about living until you are 90? Each of these is possible, and each individual, either by plan or by negligence, develops his or her own life plan. Some bet more on a brief life and give little thought to long-term plans; others bet on long life and expend their time and energy in "building today for a better tomorrow"; some few are fortunate and can do both simultaneously. Most of us develop some kind of balance, and this balance changes as we grow older, marry or establish comparable relationships, assume family responsibilities, and see our friends and relatives die or become seriously ill.

Death places a particularly severe time boundary on the dying. They now must allocate their remaining time, a relatively scarce commodity, among the many things they wish to do. Often the difficulties caused by this—as well as by poor health—prevent the dying from using their time in satisfying ways. This is one of the reasons to shy away from the expression "death with dignity" and try to focus on "living with dignity until death."

The notion of death as a boundary lacks some reality for the person who is not yet in the living-dying period. Nonetheless, all of us can contemplate what we would do with a finite, predictable amount of life ahead. Knowing that you are going to die in the foreseeable future shares many characteristics with leaving a home or community. Many people wish to take in as much as possible of life in the time they have left; others prefer to withdraw quickly. When basically healthy people were asked "If you were told that you had a terminal disease and six months to live, how would you want to spend your time until you died?," the largest category of people responded that they wanted no change in what they were doing (see Table 3-1). However, almost as many people indicated that they would show their concern for other people by being with them, expressing their love for them, and doing things for them; large numbers also stated that they would withdraw and focus on their inner lives or that they would change their lives markedly (Kalish & Reynolds, 1981).

TABLE 3-1.
Responses of 434 Adults of Four Ethnic Communities in Los Angeles to the Question "If You Were Told That You Had a Terminal Disease and Six Months to Live, How Would You Want to Spend Your Time until You Died?" (Percentages)

Response category	Age			Sex	
	20–39	40–59	60+	Male	Female
Marked change	24%	15%	9%	23%	11%
Withdraw/inner life	14	14	37	17	24
Concern with others	29	25	12	16	29
Complete project	11	10	3	9	8
No change	17	29	31	28	24
Other	5	6	8	7	6

Note: Coding was done by interviewers for responses to open-ended questions (Kalish & Reynolds, 1981).
From *Death and Ethnicity: A Psychocultural Study,* By R. A. Kalish and D. K. Reynolds. Copyright © 1981. Reprinted by permission.

Note the correlation of sex and age with different responses. Some of the reasons for differences are structural; for example, the elderly, who generally have fewer projects they are working on, are less likely to have projects to complete; similarly, they have fewer people they love who are still alive and in need of their attention. Sex differences seem to reflect traditional role-perception differences of men and women.

Statistics, obviously, can present only one part of the picture. The comment made by a middle-aged woman to a similar question deserves, I feel, to become immortal. "If I knew I only had a brief time to live? I'd just buy a better brand of cologne." She went on to explain that she wouldn't change her lifestyle, but she would afford herself a few luxuries of "the simple things in life." And another statement, perhaps one that epitomizes death for so many people, was made by a 13-year-old who was dying from an accident: "I didn't have time to . . ." The statement was never finished (from the notes of Amy Schenone).

RELIGION AND THE MEANING OF DEATH

One significant task for almost any religion is to enable its adherents to cope with their own deaths and with the deaths of others. Another significant task for almost any religion is to ascertain that its adherents are behaving in accordance with the tenets of the religion. Given the immense power of death and of the hope of an existence after death, we could hypothesize that many organized religions use people's beliefs in their capacity to determine what happens after death to control the behavior of people in life. This is not to suggest that a group of religious leaders sat down to discuss this issue, then decided to do so; rather, these values developed, virtually inevitably, through the histories of religions.

Therefore, if you behave well in this life (however your faith defines proper behavior), your next life will be a reward. If you behave badly in this life, your next life will be (1) hell, (2) lack of oneness with God, lack of eternal peace and love, or limbo, (3) a return to earth in another, and less desirable, form, (4) more accumulated bad karma.

Informal interviews with a number of physicians, nurses, and hospital chaplains found that one of the three most important factors contributing to an "appropriate death" was finding meaning in the life that had been lived, as well as finding meaning in the relatively brief life that was to come. This meaning was often expressed in terms of religion, relatedness to God, and a sense of continuity or immortality (Augustine & Kalish, 1975).

Before discussing the relationship among religion, meaning, and death, we need to have a common understanding of the definition of religiousness. **Religion** can be defined in terms of denominational affiliation, church attendance, or the performance of prayers and other rituals; it can be understood as adherence to a set of beliefs or having had feelings or experiences that people will agree are "religious"; knowing about religion and behaving according to religious principles are other ways of determining whether an individual "has" religion (Glock & Stark, 1965).

To understand the effect of religion on a person's feelings about death and dying, we need to learn how to help people communicate these religious feelings; for when this communication is possible, the essence of the feelings and experiences is communicated, not merely broad empty symbols. That is, if you and I have experienced the death of someone we loved deeply, and if we have both been open to the full force of the experience and haven't diluted it with meaningless words, then we have shared a religious experience and we can understand, within limits, each other's feelings. There is deep meaning in what we have experienced and shared, and our religiousness has been expanded by grasping this meaning.

For all of us, then, death has many meanings. The meanings vary with our age, sex, religious affiliation, and ethnicity. More important, they vary with life circumstances, such as health and available support systems, our personality characteristics such as coping abilities and ego strength, and our personal histories and experiences. Developing a coherent concept of what death means can be very useful but is often not possible. We are entitled to be inconsistent about what death means to us at any given time, since it is so immense and so complex that its meanings are often in flux—changing at the very moments that we try to grasp them. But we continue to think, feel, and behave on the basis of what we assume the meanings of life and death to be.

CHAPTER FOUR

Transcending Death:
Religion and Immortality

"If immortality be untrue, it matters little whether anything else be
true or not."
—*Henry Thomas Buckle* (1821–1862)

"Without the hope of an afterlife, this life is not even worth the
effort of getting dressed in the morning."
—*Prince Otto von Bismarck*

"Man cannot live without a continuous confidence in something
indestructible within himself."
—*Franz Kafka*

"As for a future life, every man must judge for himself between
conflicting vague possibilities."
—*Charles Darwin*

"Neither can I believe that the individual survives through death of
his body, although feeble souls harbor such thoughts through fear
or ridiculous egotism."
—*Albert Einstein*

The title of this chapter is "Transcending Death." What does it mean, to
transcend something? The dictionary defines it as going beyond the usual
limits or as going beyond or being outside of what is perceived or available in
experience. Another definition is that transcending means being above
material existence or apart from the universe. But Robert Bellah, a contemporary sociologist and student of religion, puts the concept in more appropriate perspective: "It still seems essential to appreciate there is a reality
independent of ourselves, our societies, or our cultures" (1970, pp. 196–197).

The notion of transcending death, then, is that there is something outside our experience, perhaps outside our possible experience, even outside what we know to be reality, that permits us to go beyond the assumed limits imposed by what we observe as death. Death, as we see it, is *the end.* However, we may transcend that, or go beyond death as the end.

TO NOT BE OR TO NOT NOT BE

Religious and cultural belief systems, dating back to prehistoric times, have supported the view that clinical death is not the end of existence for the individual. Evidence for the antiquity of this view has accrued from numerous sources, such as early myths and legends and Scripture and other written accounts. Another source has been burial sites and tombs, where gifts and personal possessions were buried with the body, presumably to make things easier in the next life. Usually the body would be accompanied by eating vessels and jewelry, but for the extremely rich and powerful, servants and wives occasionally joined their "lord and master" in death.

Although the general principle of belief in immortality or the capacity of the person to transcend this life is well accepted, the specific mechanism through which such transcendence is thought to occur differs greatly from culture to culture and from person to person within some cultures. The subsequent existence may be aware that it had an earlier existence or it may be aware only of its own existence, or it may have no self-awareness at all. It may take a physical form, recognizable to others, or it may have no physical form. It may be a return to earth in some form that represents the fruits of the past existence (reincarnation) or it may never return to earth again. There may be no judgment, reflecting the behavior of the past existence, or there may be judgment.

The fact that most people since the beginning of humankind have believed in some form of existence after death, however, is not proof that there is in actuality such an existence. This is not a matter on which a majority vote can establish truth. What one person accepts as fully adequate evidence for an afterlife may be seen as absurd by another person. In the final analysis, each person needs to evaluate the evidence that he or she finds acceptable and make a decision based on that evidence.

When all is said and done, it remains indisputable that the weight of opinion supports the existence of an **afterlife** and, for those who are uncertain, that there *should* be one. And what one believes about the unknowable can affect behavior, feelings, and various attitudes just as much as what one believes about knowable issues. Choron, from whose book earlier quotations were selected, states "There is no doubt that the denial of the finality of death appears to most people as the most satisfying solution to the problems of death" (1964, p. 14). It seems as though people who have not had a satisfying life look toward subsequent existence as a way of compensating for what did not occur on earth, while those who have found life pleasurable seek for some kind of continuation of consciousness.

Studies confirm the assumption that most people believe in life after death. Thus, a national survey in 1936 found that nearly 2 out of every 3 adults believed in life after death; this increased in 1944 to 76% and has remained near that figure at least through the early 1970s (Argyle & Beit-Hallahmi, 1975). While most people believe in an existence of some sort after death, an even larger number desire that such an option exist (Kalish & Reynolds, 1981).

Nevertheless, conflicting opinions coexist. For example, a well-conducted national study found that over half this country's adults believed that death was like a long sleep (Riley, 1970). This suggests a kind of nonaware existence, and it seems to contradict the more common notion that death leads to a "life of abiding union with ... Christ" (Cross, 1958, p. 682). I suspect the truth is that many people have vague and inconsistent images of an afterlife and that this occurs regardless of a person's religious affiliation. There seem to be several reasons for not wanting any kind of life after death. First, some individuals undoubtedly fear either divine punishment for what they have done during their lives or some other hellish afterlife—their notions of hell ranging from the physical tortures Dante wrote of to the psychological tortures described by Sartre. A second reason for wanting no afterlife would be a simple preference for extinction, for nothingness, for a permanent leavetaking of everything. And third, people may not believe in an afterlife because they find it impossible to conceptualize such an existence.

TRANSCENDING DEATH

I am very attached to me. I don't want me to leave everywhere forever. If I must die—and I suppose that I must—it seems unfair for death to mean that nothing more continues. I can accept the thought that I wasn't here before I was born—although you may not share that view—but I have considerable difficulty in coping with the idea that my being is temporary.

Are we really temporary? After all, to believe in life after death or in some kind of immortality is to assume that some part of our existence continues beyond clinical death. Perhaps only life on earth is temporary, while existence is forever. In Chapter 2, I discussed three kinds of death—physical death, psychological death, and social death—and I alluded to other forms of death, such as legal death. Here I would like to return to these themes again in a discussion of life after death.

Physical Immortality

Physical death has two subcategories: biological death and clinical death. Since we die biologically when parts of us die, we can live on biologically when some physical part of us continues after "we" die. Perhaps this is why having children is so important to many people. Each child carries something physical of each parent. In a very real way, the parent continues through the child, the grandchild, and so on ad infinitum. As long as your descendants continue to have children and as long as humanity exists, some part of you continues and you attain **biological immortality.** This mystique that a biological part of the parent exists in the child is probably one reason that many people resist adopting children.

If your children are biological extensions of you, then you are similarly a biological extension of your parents. In recent years people have tried to look back across generations in order to find their origins, their "roots." Similarly, many adopted children have sought their biological parents. Both trends appear to represent an attempt to connect with one's past. To some extent this also means seeking a physical preexistence: who was I before I was born?

Our present life thus becomes one existence in a series of existences, and we are part of a series rather than simply an isolated life. The series stretches far back in time and also will stretch far forward in time. Lifton points out that this kind of immortality is more than just biological and that people can express it through symbolic connections with "one's group, tribe, organization, people, nation, or even species" (1977, p. 278).

In contrast to biological death, clinical death describes the death of the organism. **Clinical immortality,** therefore, means that the body does not really die, or, to state it more cautiously, it means the body does not really cease to be. The history of the world contains many examples of the belief in clinical immortality—ghosts are one—in which the physical body continues to exist though in altered form. That physical body, as I will discuss later, must be inhabited by a "self" or a "soul." Keep in mind the story of Dracula and the other characters on the midnight television horror films. Their bodies, altered perhaps by longer teeth and fingernails, continue to exist, but they are inhabited either by a totally new personality or by the old personality in altered form.

Clinical immortality, to be meaningful, must also involve psychological immortality (see below). Otherwise the body is possessed and becomes, for example, a zombie or the vehicle for creatures from outer space—the stuff of science fiction. Although most people in our culture probably believe that the body becomes an empty shell after clinical death, what happens to that body is still important to them. Many elderly people living alone, for example, are greatly concerned that their bodies may not be found for several days after their death. Funeral establishments sell airtight and watertight vaults to encase airtight and watertight caskets that encase carefully embalmed bodies. Our behavior and our feelings certainly indicate that many of us retain a strong psychological attachment to our bodies.

Psychological Immortality

Psychological death is the cessation of self-awareness or consciousness, and it affects relatively few people in this society. **Psychological immortality,** which is the continuation of consciousness after death, provides the basis for the traditional Christian concept of afterlife as an existence in which the individual retains awareness of self and experiencing after suffering clinical death. Those who do not accept this form of immortality are faced either with total extinction at the time of death or with some form of "being at one with God" or "being unified with the universe," which implicitly, but not explicitly, signifies the loss of self-awareness and conscious experiencing.

Although most people would probably agree that "it is the prospect of not being anymore that makes most men abhor death" (Choron, 1964, p. 10), some would favor the idea that even extinction is "reassuring and more logical than a concept of afterlife that includes perception without organs, memory without brain, and existence without matter" (C. M. Parkes, personal communication, 1967).

To become more personally involved, try this fantasy: think of yourself as a body without a brain; then think of yourself as a brain without a body. Under which condition are you more likely to perceive yourself as no longer you?

If you do remain psychologically immortal, what can this mean? First, it might be manifest through an afterlife that replicates much of what exists in this life. That is, you might be with family and friends and perhaps even meet new friends; you might eat and sleep and play; you might even experience challenges and tensions, successes and failures. This is the notion that children seem to develop, along with the presence (or sometimes absence) of a Supreme Being.

Second, psychological immortality may mean that your experiencing is limited to a sense of oneness with a Supreme Being, with nature, or with the universe. Rather than offering the anthropomorphic appeal of the first alternative, this possibility suggests a kind of eternal peace and love, the "peace that surpasses all understanding."

Third, you could remain immortal by staying on earth but not being perceivable by any living persons. You would be a ghost. You couldn't interact with any of the living, except under unique circumstances, but you could observe them and perhaps influence their lives in limited ways.

Fourth, you might be reincarnated into another body, but to have psychological immortality this new body with "you" residing in it must be aware that "you" once resided in another body. This is not the Eastern religious concept of transmigration of souls, which assumes that the new entity has no memory of previous existences; it is believed, however, by some persons in the West. The famous case of Bridey Murphy, a 19th-century Irish woman who purportedly was a previous existence for a 20th-century American woman, is an example. Awareness of the prior life occurred to the American woman under hypnosis, and she showed a remarkable, though inconsistent, knowledge of 19th-century Ireland. It later turned out that as a child the American woman had had an Irish housemaid who had regaled her with stories and descriptions of Ireland; so this evidence in support of reincarnation is dubious.

A fifth possibility, once again cut from the cloth of science fiction: it is conceivable (perhaps you think it inconceivable) that our consciousness and personality could be transplanted either to another body or to a form that was not like a human body. This would be an earthly immortality and could last at least until science, customs, and natural disasters obliterated the new form.

Spiritual Immortality

One kind of immortality has no counterpart in the kinds of death discussed in Chapter 2. Some individuals regard life on earth as a lower or less adequate form of life than existence after death. Life on earth requires struggle, pain, upsets, emotions, stress, decay; life after death is filled with peace, love, fulfillment, and a sense of harmony. Leading a spiritual life brings one to this kind of immortality, which signifies that one is "in harmony with a principle extending beyond the limited biological life span" (Lifton, 1977, p. 278).

One example of **spiritual immortality** is **nirvana;** this is a state that is undefinable, immeasurable, and infinite and not a state of annihilation (Watts, 1957). In nirvana one is released from the pains of going through continuous incarnations and lives. The issue of consciousness seems to be resolved by the implicit assumption that self-consciousness ceases when nirvana is achieved.

The Western counterpart to the Buddhist nirvana is often expressed as "being at one" with God or with nature or with the universe or with humanity. It is not clearly specified and defined, because it defies specification and definition. The belief generally includes negation of the meaning of time as well as of the meaning of matter. That is, all time is now; all matter is matter and is unity or one single whole. And psychological life ceases. If these ideas strike you as strange or even ridiculous, you have a lot of company. However, if you can grasp what the words mean—if something in you is attuned to their meaning—you also have a lot of company.

Social Immortality

When others perceive you as living, you are socially alive; when others perceive you as dead, you are socially dead. **Social immortality** is probably as familiar and perhaps as important as psychological immortality. After your clinical death, you will continue to exist for others in symbolic ways. This doesn't mean that *you* will exist clinically or psychologically; rather, many symbols of you will exist, and people will relate to these symbols to some extent in the way that they had related to you. Consider some of the kinds of social immortality (Lifton, 1977):

- In memories. Other people will remember you—the kind of person you were, the things you did with them, the meanings you had for them. For example, your grandfather, who died when you were very young, still lives in your memory.
- In oral tradition. We tend to associate the oral tradition with societies that lacked writing or printing, but we all have a kind of oral tradition. The stories that your mother told you about her grandparents are part of your oral tradition. These days we have two useful alternatives to the old form of oral tradition: writing and taping. (Capture your own oral or

written tradition for yourself and your descendants by interviewing your parents and grandparents.) These extend the duration of social immortality beyond the lifetimes of the persons with the actual memories.

- In groups to which you have belonged. Almost all of us have been part of many groups: family, friendship, school, church, social club, work, political party. Our impact on each of these groups often extends beyond the time of our membership in the groups, and it can even extend beyond our own lifetime.
- In your family name. In many traditions maintaining and honoring the family name is significant. The family name provides a kind of continuity for the parents—especially for the male members of the family.
- In ancestor recognition. In some cultures ancestors are acknowledged in rituals and ceremonies long after their deaths and even long after they have been forgotten as individuals.
- In creating or achieving something that will continue to live. In addition to being a form of biological immortality, children are a means of social immortality. In planting and tending a garden one also creates something living. Helen Burke, a Seattle woman whose integrity and toughness bought her several years of life that her physicians had not expected, planted a garden shortly after she learned that she was terminally ill with cancer. "I wanted something of me to grow after I had died," she said. You can also gain social immortality by developing a business, writing a book, patenting an invention, playing college football, acting in theater productions, or having your name on a tombstone. Your name is already immortalized with insurance companies, schools, colleges and universities, Social Security, the Internal Revenue Service, hospitals, and other such institutions.
- In entering history books or record books. Those men and women who have expended great effort, perhaps even lost their lives, for a cause that was recognized by history have gained a type of social immortality. Many individuals expend immense effort to get their names in the *Guinness Book of World Records* for the same reason. Politicians and other well-known figures often become deeply concerned with the ways history will record their deeds.

Legal and Economic Immortality

Also symbolic, but still different from social immortality, is the extension of self that we can attain through control of property after our death. Through estates, trusts, and wills, the very wealthy achieve **economic immortality** by endowing universities and museums, maintaining businesses, and establishing foundations, all of which carry their names for years, even centuries, after their deaths.

There are cultures in which the possessions of the dead are buried with them (Shaffer & Rodes, 1977); each new generation begins over with the acquisition of material goods. This is definitely not true of the United States. In spite of inheritance taxes, it is possible to continue to provide support and to control the nature of this support beyond the limits of your own lifetime. Through legal actions, such as creating a will and a trust or estate, you can attain **legal immortality** and determine what your children will have money for—college and medical care but not vacations, for example. You can punish or reward your children by respectively giving a large portion of your money to other relatives or to charity or bestowing a large proportion of your estate on one child.

You can also set conditions on the dispersal of money: one child will receive a portion of your estate only if she completes college within four years after your death; another child will lose her share if she marries the man with whom she has been living. In practice, the courts may strike down your conditions, but even then you have had a substantial impact after you died—though perhaps not the impact you wished.

And you can will or give material possessions to others that will enhance their memories of you and place a symbolic part of you in their homes and lives. There are many ways you can exert control after your death.

The Limits of Immortality

Some immortality is more immortal than others. Obviously, this is a ridiculous statement, but my previous uses of the term *immortality* have not been consistently appropriate. In fact, I have used *immortal* when I should have used a more modest term. *Immortal* means both "escape from death" and "lasting fame." Except for spiritual immortality and infinite psychological immortality, the other examples are temporary.

Let me use myself as an example again.

I have three children. Through them I will gain both biological immortality and social immortality. I have made a substantial impact on the lives of some other people, and they will carry me in their memories. I have an estate and some material possessions, which I shall give to others and thus attain some legal/economic immortality. I have written books and articles, which are in individual and public libraries, including the Library of Congress; my name is in many indexes, abstracts, and library cards. My father was a sculptor, and as a result I have my image at ages 6 months and 18 months in bronze and marble. And the records: birth, school, college, draft, medical, insurance, credit, Social Security, investments, businesses, home ownership, marriage and on and on.

But such immortality is not full immortality. Eventually no one left alive will remember me or will remember hearing anyone talking about me. My children will die, and the family name will disappear or change. My material goods will wear out, fall apart, mildew, burn, or get lost. The libraries will crumble—if the books and index cards don't disintegrate first—and the innumerable records will eventually turn to dust. Someday, 500 years from now, an archeologist or farmer will turn up the bronze statue of a small infant, and my social immortality will be in a museum as an anonymous infant of the 20th century.

Unless you believe in spiritual or psychological immortality, your immortality is likely to be temporary and, therefore, only of limited meaning. Your ways of transcending death will do so only for finite periods of time, not infinitely. Intrinsic religious belief systems traditionally provided the basis for a belief in immortality, but as one psychiatrist has suggested, lack of faith has undercut a belief in immortality for a large proportion of the population. It may be that modern-day despair has been caused by this lack of faith (Lifton, 1977).

The potential for total annihilation of all human life, which is part of the nuclear age, presents some complications for all concepts of immortality. First and most obvious is the fact that if the world is destroyed, all forms of secular immortality become impossible (Choron, 1964). That is, there will be no libraries, people with memories, descendants, investments, tombstones, computers, or ghosts on earth to establish immortality. Second, if the earth and humanity cease to exist, the religious concept of the resurrection must change, and virtually all concepts of immortality except spiritual immortality become meaningless or, at the very least, require considerable reconceptualizing (Lifton & Olson, 1974).

The development of the nuclear age may have required that people reevaluate their traditional views of religion and of the nature of being human. However, the extent to which people are constantly aware, even unconsciously, of the potential for such complete destruction of the world is uncertain. Interviews with substantial numbers of persons suggested that the potential effects of nuclear destruction did not appear to affect their views of immortality, although the effects may be lurking in their unconscious thoughts and feelings (Schmitt, 1982–83).

What Does It Mean?

You may have found the previous few pages extremely abstract. What implications do the various kinds of immortality have for human behavior? What is your idea of what will happen to you after your clinical death? Perhaps you have several contradictory ideas: (1) there is only extinction, (2) you will exist in some form with God or with some universal spirit, and (3) you will be able to watch those on earth whom you love. Believing such contradictory ideas is not unique. The mixture of your views will, of course, affect how you feel about your own death, how you respond to your grandmother when you talk about her dying, and what you feel when you read that a casual friend of yours has committed suicide.

If your vocational interests draw you toward working with the dying, the concept of immortality becomes more immediate and relevant for you, since dying persons often talk about what, if anything, they will be after clinical death. You might evaluate your own social immortality, as I did mine above, and in some instances you might encourage others to do the same.

Even if you don't especially wish to work with dying people, you will inevitably find yourself, if you enter any of the helping professions, in contact with people for whom death and dying are significant, pressing matters. As these people face their own deaths or the deaths of others, their concepts of immortality will become part of their patterns of coping. The more you understand in advance your own concepts and those of others, the more effective you are likely to be in your work.

MOVEMENTS THAT TRANSCEND DEATH

Undoubtedly the most significant movement that encourages belief in immortality is organized religion. Christians are encouraged to believe that they can overcome death through some combination of belief and appropriate behavior; Moslems, Hindus, and Buddhists can achieve the same goal by practicing their religions; for Jews and Confucians, the possibilities of transcending death are more obscure, but as individuals, many persons from both religions do believe in some form of existence after death.

Do these religions, then, represent a denial of death? In one sense they do. But it is very important not to evaluate an entire belief system because one segment of it may be interpreted as a denial of death. First and most important, even if we could establish beyond a shadow of a doubt that a belief system was death-denying, we would not thereby be saying anything about the larger truth or validity of that system. Second, by applying knowledge of psychology to explain the needs of people to accept certain beliefs, we are showing only why people believe as they do, not whether their beliefs are true. In fact, one could make a strong case for religious transcendence of death as healthy acceptance rather than denial.

People who have religious views that enable them to transcend death are sometimes criticized. The tone of the criticism often suggests that the religious person is a kind of intellectual sissy who doesn't have the strength or integrity to know *the* truth: that death is extinction. This criticism overlooks two important facts. Although for some people a belief in overcoming death is comforting, for others a belief in extinction after death is comforting. And whether or not a particular belief is comforting is certainly not a test of its truth.

There are other movements that propose that people can overcome death. For some of these our present bodies would be immortal. One movement, for example, first suggests that the duration of life can be extended by proper health practices and then jumps to the assumption that if we only used *the* really proper health practices and had *the* really proper beliefs, we could remain alive almost indefinitely. Similarly, some persons who have discovered the importance of the emotions and of motivation in overcoming physical ailments leap to the conclusion that if our emotions and beliefs were totally what they should be, we could live forever.

There seems to be good reason to be skeptical about these ideas. Not only are they likely inaccurate, but it also seems possible that they will both exacerbate the guilt that sick people already feel and encourage others to avoid those who are sick. The logic of those ideas appears to add up to: If you are sick because you lived improperly or thought improper thoughts, then it is your fault that you're ill, and I don't need to take any responsibility for what you're going through. After all, according to these ideas, being sick doesn't just happen by itself—it happens only when you want it to happen or when you deserve it.

The evidence, it seems, is just the opposite. Certainly few people doubt that health can be drastically changed, for better or for worse, by beliefs, emotions, and health practices. Nonetheless, it still appears obvious that sickness and death remain in everyone's future and that there is a limit on the extent to which beliefs, emotions, and health practices can be improved to extend life. Although research will undoubtedly continue to find ways to enable people to live longer, it is questionable whether a major breakthrough in life extension will occur.

Death is transcended in numerous other ways, one of which deserves special attention. The Church of Jesus Christ of Latter-Day Saints, often called the Mormon church, encourages its members to identify their ancestors and thus provide these ancestors with the grace of the church itself, even though they are long since dead. This has the interesting effect of giving the dead ancestors a kind of spiritual immortality through the church rituals and a kind of social immortality by virtue of becoming, at least in a way, real to their Mormon descendants. It appears, then, that residing in someone's memory does not require that you have had personal contact with that person or even that you have existed for the person prior to the person's search into his or her genealogy.

Another movement that suggests we don't really die at all is **cryogenics.** The cryogenicists arrange to freeze bodies just at the moment of death—to do so earlier might be considered homicide—and then to maintain these bodies in a state of limbo. When the cures for the causes of death of these people are found, they are to be revived and treated, and consequently they will have overcome death (Ettinger, 1966). In the event that the freezing process doesn't work, then the individual is indeed dead, which is no worse than he or she would have been anyway. Although all this sounds like science fiction, a number of people have in fact been frozen in the hope of later revival.

The cryogenics movement raises a number of problems that also sound like science fiction. For example, cryogenicists usually assume that the world in which the frozen people will be revived will be a better one. But what if it is worse? What if the revived people are kept captive and used only for strange kinds of medical research? Further, consider the problems of 20th-century Rip Van Winkles: How would they adjust to the new world? What kinds of work could they do? What would happen to family relationships? There are some highly practical problems also. Can the estates of these people be given to their heirs? Should insurance companies pay the beneficiaries?

ENCOUNTERING THOSE WHO HAVE DIED
AND RETURNED

Virtually all preindustrial societies believed in ghosts (Simmons, 1945). In fact, becoming a ghost or spirit was in many ways considered compensation for being dead, since "the life of a spirit could be, under favorable conditions, more noble and desirable than an earthly existence which had already become burdensome at best" (Simmons, 1945, p. 224). Being a ghost was not at all bad: you could have power over the living and receive deference from them, in the form of services and sacrifices. Ghosts were appeased, since the living wanted their support and feared their anger, through gifts, food, rituals, prayers, lavish funerals, and other means (Blauner, 1966; Simmons, 1945). In exchange, ghosts expected to be called on to help their survivors by protecting them against enemies, by intervening with other supernatural forces, and by watching over them.

Assumptions about ghosts vary, of course, from community to community. In one culture, they are viewed as evil, and it is believed that the dead will behave like pigs unless properly propitiated (Van Arsdale & Radetsky, 1983–84). In other cultures, the name of the dead person is given to a newborn infant so that the soul of the dead can continue in the new body (DeSpelder & Strickland, 1983); in such instances, it is extremely important to select the name of a person whose qualities you wish to have in your own child, although family and community pressures may restrict your choice.

Nor do all ghosts from any given community return in similar fashion. Blauner (1966) has suggested that the ghosts of people who were the most involved with their community at the time of death are the ghosts to be most feared: they have so much unfinished business that they will be restless, unhappy, and even punitive. We also find that, on occasion, persons who were able to demand more sacrifices from others when they were alive can continue to demand more sacrifices after their death; their good will can be gained only by dint of more than the usual number of prayers, offerings, gifts, or other demonstrations of obedience.

Among the Anggor, a tribe in New Guinea, death is seen as the final separation of two components of the individual: the *vital spirit* and the consciousness or personality. In life, the personality dominates, but when the person dies, the life spirit takes control. Since the powers of the vital spirit are great and since such spirits do not behave rationally, they can harm the community, and the Anggor will call on their guardian spirits for help (Huber, 1972). There are certainly historical parallels in our society; for example, why do we use such heavy tombstones, and what is the meaning of *rest in peace?*

A common fear about ghosts was that the spirits would retaliate. If you feel guilty about your behavior toward someone who has died—especially if you at all think that your actions may have contributed to the person's death—you may express your guilt through fantasies of retaliation. Conversely, have you ever fantasized that you died and returned with increased powers to reward your friends and punish your detractors?

Like preindustrial societies, highly developed nations also have a tradition involving ghosts and returned spirits—although the latter communities do not officially accept their tradition. In fact, one kind of event that might be viewed as involving ghosts is very familiar in this country and in Western Europe. In a national survey of a few years ago, 27% of the respondents admitted to having felt sometime that they were in touch with someone who had died (Greeley, 1975). In my own work with David Reynolds (1981), over 40% of those interviewed answered yes to the question "Have you ever experienced or felt the presence of someone after he had died?" As many younger people as older people had had this experience. When asked to describe the nature of their experience with the dead person, a large number of respondents explained it in such terms as "Well, it was like in a dream, but I knew that it wasn't really a dream, because I was awake. I know it sounds crazy, but I'm not crazy."

> He knew that Judith was 2500 miles away and that she was presumably healthy and safe, but the night was spent in restless turning and tossing. Toward morning, shortly before twilight, he opened his eyes and saw Judith standing by the bed, smiling at him, not saying anything. He stared through half-opened eyes for perhaps four or five seconds, but there was no doubt that he was able to see Judith and also to see, directly through her, to the dresser and door and walls of his room, which looked as they always did. He forced himself to full wakefulness, and as he did so, Judith disappeared, although all else in the room remained exactly the same. The next day he learned that Judith had been killed in an auto accident as she drove home from her late shift at the hospital, probably about five hours before the specter appeared to him.

Many of these encounters occur with someone who has died fairly recently. Nearly all of 22 young and middle-aged widows reported experiencing the presence of their dead husbands in some way (Parkes, 1972). "It was like a dream, but it wasn't really a dream" is a typical description of one of these encounters. A familiar statement is "That is the chair that he sat in, every day when he came home from work, and he smoked his pipe and read. I still see him in that chair, and I smell the pipe tobacco, although I know he isn't really there." Or "My grandfather. I will feel the room [get] cold, and I'll feel his presence near me."

Experiencing the presence of someone who has just died has been compared to the phantom-limb phenomenon, in which a person whose leg or arm has been amputated still feels its presence. "The brain undoubtedly contains a 'working model' of each limb. . . . It is therefore no surprise to find that the amputation of a limb does not abolish our 'working model' of that limb" (Parkes, 1972, p. 348). Perhaps the strong sense of attachment to the person who has died, like attachment to the limb that has been lost, maintains the previous "working model" for a period of time. Because of the intimacy of the relationship, the person who has died has become like a part of the survivor. After the death, the image representing that part continues to exist.

Mystical and transpersonal experiences are frequently reported, but people are often reluctant to discuss them except with trusted friends. Encountering the dead, having an out-of-body experience, and perceiving different realities are all very different kinds of experiences, but they share the problem of being interpreted by others as a sign that you are a "little crazy." Our fiction is filled with such occurrences, some frightening and some comforting *(Hamlet, Carousel, A Christmas Carol, Macbeth, Wuthering Heights)*, which often represent actual, desired, or feared experiences.

Although relatively few encounters with the dead are frightening (Kalish & Reynolds, 1981; Moody, 1976), one kind of experience is—that of being **possessed.** A play of some decades ago depicted the possession of the body of a young girl by a *dybbuk,* a legendary figure in Jewish lore who had some business on earth he wished to transact. In exorcising the dybbuk, the girl was also killed. Much more recent were the extremely popular novel *The Exorcist* and the film based on the novel. Again a young girl was inhabited by the spirit of the devil. Supposedly based on factual events, *The Exorcist* confronts us with several questions: first, did these events really occur, and, second, if they did not really occur, what are the psychological dynamics that produce the behavior that appears to be caused by the devil? Further, why does the concept continue to reemerge in both fiction and reported fact? Is it fear or guilt or attachment that leads to such possession? Is it another way to express the "sickness of the soul"? Is it a manifestation of paranoid schizophrenia? Or is it the acceptance of particular myths within one's culture that makes possession acceptable? No explanation appears entirely satisfactory.

Despite the claims of some people that they have proof of communications with the dead, the reality of those events may well forever remain an unsolved mystery. As stated before, whether you believe in the possibility of such communication depends largely on what you require as evidence. And the significance of this phenomenon is twofold—both what it means if such communication does occur and, perhaps, can be made to occur with greater frequency *and* what the entire issue implies for our views of death and the transcendence of death.

NEAR-DEATH EXPERIENCES

Some people face their own deaths, fully believing that they are going to die, and then either recover or find out that the situation has changed and that death has been postponed. During the intervening period, perhaps seconds or perhaps weeks, they may prepare for death, confront death, and in some instances experience what seems like dying and then returning to the living.

The term **near-death experience,** sometimes abbreviated to **NDE,** is used in two overlapping ways. The first describes all persons who fit the criteria described above; the second is limited to persons who also recall mystical, transpersonal, or transcendent experiences as part of their NDE. In this volume, we will use the first of the definitions.

The Experience Itself

In one study of 323 near-death experiences (Kalish, 1969), the largest number were caused by physical illness and often occurred during surgery, although childbirth was the basis for some. The next-largest categories were motor-vehicle accidents, drownings, and—perhaps because of the age of the people interviewed and the date of the study—war-related events. When subjects were asked about their reactions during the experience, the most frequent responses involved fear or panic and concern about their survivors, although anger, prayer, resignation, calmness, recollection of past experiences, and the wish to escape and continue living were each also brought up on at least several occasions.

Although fear was the most frequently mentioned reaction, it was stated by only about 20% of those responding to the question. One possible explanation for the relative lack of fear is that the respondents had forgotten or repressed their actual feelings, but it is more likely that fear during death encounters is not as common as normally believed. Supporting this supposition are several studies based on interviews with persons who had had near-death experiences (Moody, 1976; Noyes & Kletti, 1976; Osis & Haraldsson, 1977). It has been proposed that a kind of depersonalization occurring in the face of life-threatening dangers separates one's conscious awareness from the distressing reality of one's impending death; this detachment even permits people to watch themselves dying—at least in some circumstances (Noyes & Kletti, 1976).

> Just as we veered toward shore, a large freak swell toppled us over, and I found myself in the water, nearly a mile from shore, my body aching and exhausted from prolonged strenuous physical activity. I have always been a poor swimmer, but I found a floating life preserver and put it on. However, my body began to go numb, my strokes became slow and weighted. In the midst of this, I had the thought "I wonder if this means I won't have tomorrow's anthropology asignment in?" In a moment I became aware of the absurdity of my concern and began laughing uproariously while swimming. I felt free and opened [from the notes of Stan Friedman].

In a more recent study, which used greater methodological sophistication (Noyes & Slymen, 1978–79), nearly 200 people who had survived life-threatening experiences completed a 40-item questionnaire of possible reactions. Statistical analysis showed that the items fell into three constellations: mystical (sense of harmony and unity, colors or vision, feeling of great understanding), depersonalization (loss of emotion, detached from body, altered passage of time), and hyperalertness (thoughts sharp or vivid, thoughts speeded up). The cause of anticipated death influenced the nature of the experience: feeling detached from one's body was almost twice as common in falling accidents as in drowning accidents; persons with serious illnesses were much more likely than accident victims to report feelings of great understanding (see Table 4-1).

TABLE 4-1.

Constellations of Items in Reports of Near-Death Experiences, Based on Factor Analysis

Factor I.	*Factor II.*	*Factor III.*
Mystical	**Depersonalization**	**Hyperalertness**
Feeling of great understanding	Loss of emotion	Thoughts sharp and vivid
Images sharp or vivid	Body apart from self	Thoughts speeded
Revival of memories	Self strange or unreal	Vision, hearing sharper
Sense of harmony, unity	Objects small, far away	Altered passage of time
Feeling of joy	Detached from body	Thoughts and movements mechanical
Revelation	World strange or unreal	
Controlled by outside force	Wall between self and emotions	
Colors or visions	Detached from world	
Strange bodily sensations	Body changed in shape or size	
	Strange sounds	
	Altered passage of time	

From "The subjective response to life-threatening danger: An interpretation," by R. Noyes and D. J. Slymen. In *Omega*, 1978–79, 9. Reprinted by permission.

Interestingly, even persons who survived suicide jumps off the Golden Gate and San Francisco Bay bridges were all found to have had transcendent experiences that resulted in increased religious and spiritual feelings. All of the seven persons interviewed were grateful to have survived, and only one subsequently attempted suicide. Several reported feeling they had died and been reborn (Rosen, 1975); this sense of rebirth was described by many of the people interviewed by Raymond Moody (1976) after near-death experiences and also by dying persons who had been given LSD under careful supervision (Grof & Halifax, 1977).

During the fall I experienced absolutely no unpleasant feeling. I clearly recall that I somersaulted in the air three or four times; that made me worry that I might lose the pocketknife that my father had given me as a present. In spite of the severe brain-rattling and several skin cuts, I . . . had not the slightest unpleasant, painful, or anxious feeling. I did not feel the impact at all since already well before that I had become completely unconscious (following a 72-foot fall) [Noyes & Kletti, 1972, p. 49].

The frequency with which mystical or transcendent experiences occur depends on the group of people asked. One prominent investigator reports that about half of NDEs result in such experiences (Ring & Franklin, 1981–82), while another found such occurrences in 21% of the terminally ill cancer patients with whom he worked (Garfield, 1979).

Early reports of near-death experiences were, for the most part, satisfied with establishing their existence and, subsequently, their nature and long-term influences, but in a descriptive fashion. More recently, investigators have approached these issues more critically. For example, psychologist

Kenneth Ring has developed a scale on which a near-death experience can be evaluated to determine whether it appears to fit the criteria for the well-known transcendent experience. Among the most common elements are—

- Feeling of peace and/or well-being
- Having an out-of-body experience
- Entering into a darkness or haze
- Seeing a white or golden light
- Encountering a "presence"
- Experiencing a life review
- Making a life decision or being told to return to life
- Awareness of "another world"
- Communicating with "spirits" of loved ones
- Hearing beautiful music (Ring & Franklin, 1981–82)

> A few years ago, I guess I was about 63 or 64 years old, I had undergone surgery for cancer, and my physician later told me that he figured my chances of surviving for more than a few days were about 50/50. One evening—it must have been a day or two after I returned to my room from intensive care—I noticed that someone was standing by my bed. I was hazy in most of my thinking at that time, but I tried to focus and was able to make out the form of a very close friend of mine, a woman about my age who had been part of a group to which I belonged that was studying mysticism and transpersonal experiences. She must have known how weary I was, because she held my hand and didn't say anything. Just before she left, she said "Bill, you will need to decide which reality you wish to enter—the present reality or the next reality." Then she departed. I knew exactly what she meant, and I thought long and carefully for the next few hours as to whether I wanted to live or not. Toward dawn, I decided I wasn't ready to leave this reality, that there was still some purpose for me here, and I opted to stay. I later learned that it was that morning that I was taken off the critical list and that my health began to improve.

The **out-of-body experience** often elicits both curiosity and skepticism from others. However, two Florida investigators interviewed some 50 patients who had suffered documented near-death experiences, during which they had become unconscious. Of these, seven had "definite recollections, while unconscious, either of viewing their bodies from a detached position of height several feet above the ground . . . or of 'traveling' into another region or dimension" (Sabom & Kreutziger, 1977, p. 196). None of these persons had a psychiatric history, nor did they have religious views that would predispose them to such accounts. The causes of the experiences, however, are still very much open to speculation.

> During the operation, I felt that I was awake and leaving my body. Then I realized that I was watching the surgeon operating on me, except that I was above the surgeon, looking down on the whole action. I moved around the room a little, but essentially I was intrigued with the operation, since its success would deter-

mine whether I would live or die. As the surgeon came near the end of his operation, I reentered my body and lost consciousness.

Sometimes the out-of-body experience takes the person far from the location of his or her physical body; the person may "visit" a friend or loved one or view a scene taking place at that moment or in the past. On occasion, the dying person, once revived, is reported to have learned something that couldn't have been known under "normal" conditions. Or the friend or relative visited also reports a strange and eerie feeling or a comforting sense of communication and awareness at the same time that the dying person recalls having visited.

So far only one person has studied these altered states of consciousness by talking with a large number of dying persons and determining their experiences (Garfield, 1979). All other researchers have simply followed up on claims of persons who have reported the experience after it occurred—frequently many months or years after its occurrence. Garfield worked with 173 cancer patients who subsequently died of their illness; he spent an average of three to four hours a week with each patient over a time span ranging from a few weeks to nearly two years. Of these persons, 21% mentioned altered-state experiences, and these could be classified in four categories:

1. In the first category were people who perceived a powerful white light and heard celestial music; they also encountered either a significant religious figure or a relative who had died previously. These individuals invariably described their experiences as "real, peaceful, and beautiful."
2. The second category of persons reported encountering demonic figures; their experiences also occurred with great clarity and reality.
3. A third group described dreamlike images that were blissful, terrifying, or both. Their images, however, were not nearly as vivid as those of the first two groups.
4. The fourth group of persons experienced a void or a tunnel or both. In their experiences they drifted in either an uncontrolled or a limited space, or they fluctuated beween the two.

Long-Term Influences

The immediate reactions to these experiences are certainly dramatic. What about the long-term effects? Does a near-death experience impose a handicap, or is it enriching? In one study mentioned above (Kalish, 1969), about 1 in 3 persons mentioned increased caution, fear, or avoidance of the cause of near death. However, no one described ongoing emotional problems, major somatic changes, or permanently increased anxiety levels, and only a handful indicated any long-term negative consequences. Much more frequent were claims that the experience had led to greater optimism and the living of each day as it came, to feeling better about life, and to appreciating the opportunity to live. Many people expressed an increased concern for other individuals and for humanity in general and an increased interest in religion (Kalish, 1969).

A recent study (Noyes, 1982–83) involved 215 mostly young persons with NDEs. When they were asked how the experience had affected their attitudes toward life and death, the responses were overwhelmingly favorable. The most common kinds of changes were (1) a reduced fear of death, (2) a sense of relative invulnerability, (3) a feeling of special importance or destiny, (4) a belief in having received the special favor of God or fate, and (5) a strengthened belief in continued existence.

Confrontations with death, especially through transcendent near-death experiences, seem to give more meaning to life. Many people have told me, consistent with the research findings, that after their near-death experiences they were able to live and enjoy each day as it came, that they appreciated life much more than they had before, that their various pursuits in life fell into truer perspective. Plato, in the *Apology*, stated that "the life which is unexamined is not worth living." Others have insisted that people cannot fully enjoy and appreciate life until they have confronted the reality of their own death. Ariès (1974) contended that life was enjoyed more when there was the chance that death could occur at any time, rather than when people felt assured of a high probability of long life, because enjoyment had to be taken immediately or else be forfeited forever. Near-death experiences cause life to be examined, increase one's feeling of being related both spiritually to the world and personally to others, and can enhance the richness of life.

You may be aware that many of the events reported as part of near-death experiences also occur under other circumstances: women in childbirth, believers during a religious experience, meditators, people taking mood-enhancing drugs. Therefore, the obvious question is "Did these events really happen?"

Your answer will depend on your personal and religious beliefs and on what you accept as evidence. Have you, or has someone you trust, had a NDE? Are you able to suspend your assumptions about normal reality, as defined by empirical psychology, and become open to kinds of reality that do not fulfill the criteria established by most psychologists? Do you seek to explain these events as products of fever, lack of oxygen, stress, anesthetic, drugs, fear? Do you chalk it all up to imagination or a kind of hallucination?

Whatever your views, it is important to know that these events are frequently reported and are not in any sense a necessary sign of pathology. It is equally important to recognize that people who have these experiences are going to be strongly affected by them—certainly in their view of death and probably in other ways as well.

The relationship among religious beliefs and practices, beliefs concerning immortality, and feelings about death is a complex one that has not yet been effectively integrated and understood. It would appear that both the content of a system of beliefs and the extent to which an individual incorporates these beliefs influence the person's perceptions of death. Unfortunately, there is relatively little evidence that a coordinated effort has been made by religious scholars and behavioral and social scientists to work on this task and even less evidence that individuals who combine knowledge of both areas are pursuing these matters.

CHAPTER FIVE

Experiences, Thoughts, and Attitudes

The experience of death must be as ancient as the experience of life. From the moment some human being was able to conceptualize the notion "I live," that same person was going to conceptualize "I die." The meaning of death was undoubtedly different at that moment than it is today, since death was viewed as a transition to another form of life, one very similar to the present form. The practices of burying the dead person in a fetal position and staining the body with red coloring, both very common in ancient cultures, suggest preparation for rebirth; the position of the body and the use of the color of blood indicate a new existence (DeSpelder & Strickland, 1983). But the experience was, nonetheless, of a death.

The history of humanity is also the history of explaining death and of integrating the way death is experienced with theology, cultural values and practices, and even political and financial issues. And throughout this history, people have been told how to experience death "for their own good." At various times and in varying degrees, people have been admonished to be brave in the face of death, to accept death, to fight and rail against death, and to welcome death.

What should your attitudes toward death be? That depends on you: on your personality and needs, on your values, on your experiences, on the ways in which you best cope with pain and with stress, and on other factors. It also depends on your present life circumstances, since you may find that in your dying process your attitudes toward death change. (Keep in mind that we are not discussing attitudes toward the dying process, which has overlapping but very different meanings.)

EXPERIENCE WITH DEATH

Whatever else the burial rituals of prehistoric peoples meant, they obviously show that those peoples considered death extremely significant. We also know that they experienced death much more frequently than we do today. One sociologist has pointed out that whereas the modern urban citizen might average one day per *decade* participating in funerals, a member of a preliterate society could have spent as much as 100 days per year (Robert Blauner, personal communication). If these data are accurate, our present funeral attendance is 0.1% that of our distant ancestors.

What has been your personal experience with death? How often have you spent time with someone who you knew would die soon? How many funerals have you attended? Have any of your friends committed suicide or been a homicide or accident victim? Have you ever been at a gathering—a party, a political rally, a church affair—where someone unexpectedly died?

If you are typical of people in this society, your answers to these questions will be evidence that your contacts with death have been minimal. This does not refer to knowing people who have died but to experiencing the dying process and the deaths of others. A century ago, the chances were that your experiences with death would have been considerably more numerous. Today, death occurs primarily to the elderly; death occurs in the hospital; the physical site of the dying process is off limits to the young by regulation and custom. All these factors conspire to limit your experience with death. Even if your vocation brings you into frequent contact with death and dying, you have probably developed very different categories for deaths encountered professionally and deaths encountered personally.

In the Los Angeles study, people were asked "How many persons who were dying did you visit or talk with during the past two years?" Over 60% of the people we interviewed hadn't talked to or visited a dying person during that time period; 72% of those under 40 responded in that fashion, compared with only 55% of those 60 and over (Kalish & Reynolds, 1981). Actually, this isn't a great difference. Although the older persons undoubtedly had accumulated a much greater lifetime experience than the younger, the experiences didn't vary much during a two-year time interval.

Corresponding to our expectations, younger persons (20 to 39 years old) were much more likely than older persons (60 and over) to have experienced no deaths among their friends or family (25% versus 10%); conversely, nearly three times as many people in the older group had known eight or more persons who had died during that two-year interval (22% versus 8%) (Kalish & Reynolds, 1981).

Some evidence exists that people in our society are becoming more willing to face dying and death again. There is a movement to permit people to die at home, and there is some indication that hospitals now provide greater flexibility in the regulations that prohibit children and young people from visiting their relatives, especially dying relatives. But as long as it is older people who die and as long as older people live independently from their children and grandchildren and die in hospitals, our contacts with death will remain minimal.

For many people, especially younger people, experience with death and the dying process is indirect rather than direct. Death is in the newspapers, on television, in conversations, perhaps even in college courses or workshops, and certainly in religious teachings and scriptures. But death is not fully real.

You know that you could die any moment. But that is an intellectual awareness, and it seldom becomes an emotional reality, except in the face of the imminence of your own death or the death of someone else. If you are not old, not suffering from a life-threatening illness, and not connected either through work or through personal life to someone who is old or is suffering a life-threatening illness, your death may rarely or never appear as a reality.

Try to gain some empathy for people who lived in societies in which death was truly always possible, in which death was *not* highly predictable as a function of age, in which life-threatening illnesses were familiar at all ages. Consider what it must have been like to know that the infant death rate was enormously high, that many women would die in childbirth, that plagues were likely to wipe out entire communities, that contagious diseases—tuberculosis, pneumonia, cholera, scarlet fever, and the ever-present small-pox—could infect people and cause their death at any time, no matter how healthy and youthful they were.

Sometimes an experience that can be shared is useful. If you were at least 5 or 6 years old in 1963, you can probably recall what you were doing on November 22 of that year—the day President Kennedy was assassinated. Whether you were 5, 15, or 45 years old at that time, his death most probably had a significant impact on you. You may well have thought about your own finitude, your own human impermanence. You may have felt very weak and vulnerable, frightened, uncertain of what would happen next. If a powerful, charismatic, protected leader can be struck down, so can any one of us. It's difficult to recall, over two decades later, the feelings and fears that we had at that time; nonetheless, it is amazing how much most people can recall. Ask your friends what they felt and how they spent that day.

Some people have had more experience with death than the average person their age, while others have had virtually no experience at all. Consider some of the possible outcomes of lack of experience.

First, we tend to be ignorant in the face of death, dying, and relevant rituals. We don't know what to say when we are with a dying person because we have no prior experience; we are uncomfortable at funerals because we have gone to so very few; we don't know how to approach mourners—whether to cry with them or exhort them to be brave—because we have so seldom been with mourners and almost never mourned ourselves.

Second, we end up turning to experts to learn what to do. The experts have traditionally been older family members and friends, the clergy, and, more recently, the funeral director. Often there is still an older person around who has experienced death often enough to know what to do. Recently, we can also read a book or attend a workshop or get in touch with the local death educator, but the books, workshops, and educators are more likely to help us with our feelings than to teach us appropriate behavior and ritual. They can make it easier to speak with a dying person, but they rarely direct their efforts at helping us know what to do at a funeral.

Third, we may feel awkward in the situation, and when we feel awkward, we normally wish to get away. So we find reasons to avoid funerals, to postpone visits to the dying, to leave a wake quickly, to mumble something vague to the surviving spouse or child or parent. (There are many other bases for our discomfort in these situations, and lack of experience makes a difficult situation much more difficult.)

Fourth, we lack the reminders of the finitude of life. Ministers have, in past generations, used funerals—especially the funerals of the nonelderly—to remind their parishioners that life is fleeting and that faith, charitable works, love, and whatever else they were promulgating had to be expressed without delay. Death could come quickly and unexpectedly, and it was important to be prepared. When we encounter death and death rituals only on rare occasions, we can go for extended periods without stopping to consider our own mortality.

THINKING ABOUT DEATH

You probably have trouble recalling what happened November 22, 1973, or November 22 of last year, but it is likely that you do spend some time, perhaps only a little time, thinking about death on November 22. And on Easter, Veterans Day, and Yom Kippur (if you are Jewish or live in a community with many Jewish people). You may not think of your own death, but you do think about death and its meanings.

How often do you think about death? That's an extremely difficult question to answer, in part because you aren't certain whether it means all kinds of death (my death, my dying, your death, and so forth) or just death in the abstract; nor do you know whether it includes, for example, reading about a homicide in the newspaper or seeing a killing in a television police drama. Furthermore, you aren't exactly certain how often *often* is: if you brood about your own death one hour every six weeks, are you thinking about death occasionally or a great deal?

Despite these problems, however, if you were asked that question, you would probably give a quick answer that would at least represent your view of how often you think about death. An 1896 article, probably the first to report statistical survey data on this matter, indicated that only 7% of 226 adults never "dwelt on death or suicide," while 60% obviously had given at least moderate thought to the matter (Scott, 1896).

Other studies have reported varying data. One national study with excellent sampling found that almost equal thirds answered "often," "occasionally," and "hardly ever/never" when asked how often they thought about death (Riley, 1970). Another national sample that included more younger and better-educated persons asked the question in more concrete fashion. Just over one-fifth of the thousands of respondents said they never thought about their own death, while 5% did so daily (Shneidman, 1971a).

Two later studies, conducted in Los Angeles, used personal interviews with multiethnic samples. In one study, a third of the participants answered that they thought about their death "not at all," and only 9% did so "frequently" (Bengtson, Cuellar, & Ragan, 1977); in the other study, nearly 60% said they never or hardly ever thought about their own death, while 17% had such thoughts every day (Kalish & Reynolds, 1981).

What can we make of this hodgepodge of results? First, some trends run through the data: most people say they don't think of their own death more than occasionally; relatively few people think of their death every day. Second, we need to expect differing results in response to questions that are worded differently or offer different response categories; for example, "never or hardly ever" is not the same as "not at all." Third, we need to expect differing results from different populations of respondents; if one study focuses on older persons and another emphasizes minority-group respondents, we should not expect identical kinds of responses, since there is good evidence that the elderly think of their death much more frequently than younger people (Jeffers & Verwoerdt, 1970). And finally, perhaps the above numbers are close enough, despite their disparities, so that we can draw some general conclusions that are sufficient for our purposes.

Perhaps we empathize with Freud, who admitted to thinking of death every day; his biographer believed that he was preoccupied by thoughts of death (Jones, 1952). Or perhaps we agree with the person who commented "One does think of death, but one doesn't remember how often." That's really a very valuable point. For example, although I had been sitting at this typewriter and working on this section for nearly one hour, I hadn't contemplated *my* own death until I wrote the above quotation. At what point in reading this chapter did you contemplate your own death? Was it just a few moments ago?

So it seems that I can think a great deal about death—your death, death in the abstract, death of all those people over there—without ever thinking seriously of *my* death. That's probably fortunate, since a steady diet of thinking of *my* death is likely to be as counterproductive as a careful vigil to avoid thinking of my death.

What does it mean to think a lot about death in general or about your own death in particular? First and foremost, it means that for some combination of reasons death has a high degree of salience or relevance in your life. Death might be important because of something taking place in your environment—for example, the recent death of a close friend who was several years younger than you, a letter from your physician asking you to come in for extensive blood tests, or your mother's recent diagnosis of breast cancer. Reading this book, participating in an academic program about death, or attending a workshop on death might also increase your awareness of death in general and of your own death.

You might be thinking about death because of disturbing occurrences inside your body. Perhaps the other evening you had an excruciating pain running down the left side of your body; maybe there's a patch on your face that seems to be spreading; or perhaps you've had your first serious asthma attack since childhood (an asthma attack is not going to cause your death, but by keeping you from breathing, it may well lead you to think about death).

Or perhaps your thoughts focus on death because of earlier experiences that have made death salient for you over the years. Your mother died when you were 8; you were in an iron lung as a child; your uncle, whom you loved very much, died in a car accident on his way to visit you; your grandmother shared a home with your parents, and they cared for her during the two years when she was slowly dying of cancer. If death caused a significant threat or disruption in your early life—even if your parents and other adults assumed that you were too young to be aware of its significance at the time—you might find thoughts of death persevering in your adult years. Not really having understood the meaning of death at the time (if, indeed, we ever truly understand the meaning of death), you never adequately dealt with the feelings the early experiences elicited in you. Or even if you were old enough to understand something about death, you did not work through the fears and anxieties that the experience evoked. Now, as an adult, thoughts of death seem to press upon you—perhaps representing your unconscious attempts to come to terms with the experiences and feelings of many years earlier.

In fact, your earlier experiences did not necessarily have to be directly with death. Childhood fears of being abandoned or of being mutilated can translate into fears of death. Nor is it necessary for the experiences to have occurred during childhood. Recent experiences, such as the death of a close friend, may have the same effect. One 40-year-old man found himself constantly thinking of death after reading a vivid account of the horrors perpetrated by the Nazis in a German concentration camp.

Finally, death may frequently invade your thoughts as self-inflicted punishment for some real or imagined "sins" you have committed, because you feel immense anger with someone else and have a fantasied fear of retribution for your anger, or because you associate death with an escape from a world that you frequently find very painful.

There are obviously many reasons for death to be salient for you or for any other person. Whether these reasons imply a favorable or a negative reaction to death in general or to your own death, the overall significance is that death is important to you and that you are capable of dealing with thoughts of your own death. (You may not report thinking about death because you are repressing such thoughts, but that is another issue, which will be discussed later.) According to one study, people seem to think about death "under three deeply personal circumstances: an accident or 'near-miss,' a serious illness, or the death of someone significant to them" (Riley, 1970, p. 35). Although it was not mentioned in this study, it is probable that people also would think more about death as they grow older. Of course, because older persons are more likely to encounter serious illness and the deaths of others, they have both situational cues to death thoughts and life-circumstance cues as well.

We have very little information about how much dying people themselves think about their own deaths, although I would assume that most of them do a great deal of thinking, wondering, and fantasizing about what is happening to them. One study provides some information. In his hospital experiences in Great Britain, psychiatrist John Hinton (1972) examined the correlation between various aspects of a person's background and his or her willingness to talk about dying. He found only one correlation that occurred with even moderate consistency: dying persons with young children were more likely to talk of the fact that they might be dying.

Is thinking about death valuable? Or is it detrimental? Those questions cannot be answered in the abstract. Ignace Lepp, a French priest and psychotherapist, has suggested: "Constant meditation on death is paralyzing for both action and life. On the other hand, nothing is accomplished by repressing the thought of death or trying to drown it in a sea of distractions" (1968, p. 134).

THE DENIAL OF DEATH

The term **denial** is used so often and with so many meanings in discussions of dying and death that it deserves some explication. First, the definition: the defense mechanism or process, operating outside of awareness, that involves the refusal to acknowledge reality-based impressions or perceptions as emotionally meaningful. It is characterized by the isolation of those parts of self that would otherwise be capable of responding to the stimuli being avoided.

Denial is, therefore, different from avoidance. People may decide to avoid talking about death and dying; they may decide not to visit a cemetery; they may decide not to take a course about death or to read this book. To use the psychological definition, they are not *denying* death; they are avoiding it. Their actions are conscious, and denial is unconscious.

Another distinction is also important. Denying one's own dying is very different from denying death or denying extinction. The denial of death is the denial that I *can* die; the denial of dying is the denial that I am (or you are or he or she is) dying. Though related, the two are very different.

The individual denies death in many ways. One of these is through participation in activities in which death has a high probability of occurring. A friend of mine who had been seriously injured when his sports car went off the side of the road told me recently "It's just impossible that I should die from a car accident, and I still don't believe it can happen." Although he had used a larger car and driven more carefully for two or three years after his accident, he finally purchased another sports car and resumed his previous driving style.

Still other people—including many accountants and estate planners—express denial of death by not planning for it; for example, they don't make wills, because they feel that as long as they don't acknowledge the inevitability of their death by planning for it, they logically won't die. However, sometimes it's difficult to evaluate whether an individual who doesn't make out a will because "I'm just not concerned about death" is, in fact, strongly denying death or basically accepting of it.

Much of our behavior suggests that we believe we will live forever. The major compromises with good health habits that many of us make in our daily living imply that "it doesn't really matter." Just as significantly, we tend to use time as though we had all the time in the world, rather than a finite—and unknown—amount of time.

The previous paragraphs describe the denial of one's own death, but this is not the only form of death denial. We can also deny the death of someone else. The following paragraphs are taken from a paper that I wrote over a dozen years ago, in response to the death of a friend. Strangely enough, he wasn't even a close friend, although I knew him fairly well and respected him greatly. Perhaps it was the suddenness of his death or the fact that we shared many interests or my awareness that he was so young that led to my own denial. However, I assure you that everything described in the following passage is exactly as it happened. And even as the events were occurring, I was not only involved in them but also sitting slightly apart from me, watching what was going on. This kind of "split" response is experienced by many people. In fact, one noted philosopher commented that as his father was dying, he (the philosopher) was fully aware of the drama of the scene in which he was also a major player.

Perhaps those of us who study death in an academic setting or who spend our time compiling statistics and seeking psychosocial insights are trying to cope more effectively with our own finite nature. If this is our goal, I don't think we will succeed. We seem subject to the same confusions, upsets, and protections that we describe in others.

I was telephoned a few hours following Don Kent's death by Tom Hickey, who understood that I would wish to know about Don—and perhaps to share his own sorrow. There is no way I can describe my immediate feelings—nor should there be any need to.

A few things happened to me, however, that I had not anticipated. My first reaction after hanging up, and after a few moments of being with myself, was to send Don's wife a note. Somehow I could not do it—an overwhelming feeling kept pressing me to acknowledge that, perhaps, a mistake had been made, and that such a note would only bring embarrassment or confusion. It took me a week to write the note. My next feeling was that I should send Don a note, telling him how sorry I was about ... I wasn't sure about what. My selves watched each other struggle with this impossible thought, with only a thrust of reality that kept me from composing, "Dear Don, I am sorry to hear that ... but you will, of course, be ... if there is anything ... please ..." This feeling remained for several days.

Soon after Tom's call, within a couple of hours, I felt I wanted to contact someone who knew Don, to pass the word on. Was this to share my sorrow? Was it to verify what was still unreal? Was it the less pleasant motive of wanting the prestige accompanying the bearer of sad tidings? This feeling held me throughout the next day and the day after that. I called no one.

Then the arithmetic. If Don is 55 and I am . . ., then my youngest child will be . . . when I am 55, which means . . ., while my oldest will be . . . or about ready to . . ., and the middle one . . .

And finally the attempts to pull back from the view of my own termination. What had Don done to deserve to die? What was he doing that I was not doing, so that his death did not mean I was also mortal? Did he elicit the wrath of God? Did he violate the laws of good health? Perhaps he neglected an annual physical or consumed too much butter or bourbon or bacon or . . .

I cried a little, for us both, Don who died and I who will die. This was two weeks ago tonight. I continue to grieve a little, but I don't really think he is dead. Perhaps I mourn myself a little, having once again glimpsed the blinding light of finitude.

This is my memorial to Don. I have to write it. Please do not tell me whether you like it or not. It does not really matter [Kalish, 1972, p. 324].

Denial is a matter not only of my denying death or my death or your death, but also of the use of denial in cultural norms. For example, in the United States, coffins are called caskets and are not displayed openly, whereas in many other countries, funeral homes are located on shopping streets and place their coffins/caskets in the window. We no longer wear the black weeds of mourning or, with rare exceptions, even a black armband, in part because it seems unnecessary to commemorate the death in that fashion and in part because it feels unseemly to expose oneself to the world as a mourner.

Many authors, myself included, believe that the extent to which the United States is a death-denying culture is often exaggerated (Parsons & Lidz, 1967). Although we do use euphemisms, keep children from knowledge of death, and remove dead patients from their hospital rooms without telling their roommates why, we nonetheless accept death in other instances. For example, cemeteries are kept open to public view, and newspapers run obituaries and death notices.

Why does denial occur? Because—for some persons and under some conditions—death is too stressful to contemplate. Since we can't fully obliterate the knowledge that death is real, we unconsciously find ways to insulate ourselves from the emotional impact of this knowledge, and these may require us to avoid contact with or mention of death. If I don't talk about it or read it, then it isn't there, and it can't happen to me.

DEATH AS TABOO

A variation on the assumption that death is denied is the notion that death is a taboo topic. Being **taboo** means that a matter is dangerous, forbidden, profane, or unclean, often with sacred implications. Gorer, a British anthropologist, has carried this idea even further by writing about death as the new pornography (1967). He points out that, today, children are encouraged to think openly about sex but are still closed off from honest discussions of death and dying.

Certainly, when Feifel wrote on death as a taboo topic in 1961 (published in

1963), the case was easy to make. Is death still a taboo topic? The case can be made either pro or con: Assume that a close friend of yours was extremely ill. Would you telephone her to ask how she was feeling? Probably. What if she told you that she was feeling terrible and that she was "doubtful about the outcome of her illness"—the implication being, of course, that she might die? Would you ask her whether she meant that she might die? You probably would not, but you might ask someone else, another close friend, a relative, perhaps even someone who knew her medical condition. Somehow, it would feel like a violation of her personal world or a crude intrusion to ask the possibly dying woman whether she was dying. Or you might have assumed that she didn't want to discuss her prognosis. However, it would not have the same implications to ask someone else about her. Now assume that your friend has fully recovered from her illness. It is likely that you will be able to talk with her freely about her close call with death, but you may never feel able to ask her how her mother died, since you are under the impression that the death was caused by suicide.

Let's shift from this friend to some other friends. Consider, for example, a close friend whose husband just left her for another woman, or another friend whose business went bankrupt, or a friend whose parents were just sentenced to prison for fraud, or one whose child recently flunked out of college, or someone you have just learned is impotent and desperately wants to become a father. Would you be likely to telephone any one of these individuals to ask about their predicaments? In the event that you did call, would you say something like "I'm sorry to hear that your husband left you" or "That was too bad about your going bankrupt" or "How about getting together to talk about your impotence—I'm really a good listener"?

It is not death alone that is taboo—any more than marriage or business or imprisonment or education or sex is taboo. In our society we are uncomfortable in the face of certain kinds of failure, certain kinds of intimacy, certain kinds of loss, and we are led to believe that others are similarly uncomfortable. Therefore, we avoid topics that we feel would bring discomfort to them or to ourselves. Our attitudes toward death are such that, in certain contexts, we perceive it as failure, as intimacy, and as loss.

Fortunately, the taboo nature of death and dying does appear to have abated somewhat. Does this also mean that people are less afraid of death, less anxious in the face of death? Probably not, although the increased openness concerning death very likely permits us to handle our fears and anxieties better.

AN INITIAL LOOK AT ATTITUDES

What is an "attitude toward death"? One definition of *attitude* is "a relatively enduring tendency to think, feel, and behave in a consistently favorable or unfavorable fashion toward a concrete or abstract thing (including person) or idea." Thus, I may be expressing an attitude when I have unpleasant images of what my own dying will be like, when I feel that your death would create immense problems for me, and when I tell a friend that I will not accompany him to his brother's funeral.

The concepts of *attitude* and *feelings* overlap so much that it is virtually impossible to discuss one without the other. This chapter will discuss the feelings and attitudes of what we call the general population—that is, of all of us. (We will focus on the feelings and attitudes of persons who are themselves dying in Chapter 8, on those who care for the dying in Chapter 14, and on the bereaved in Chapter 10. Elsewhere in this book we will describe the death-related experiences of particular groups of people, such as children, churchgoers, the bereaved, and death-related professionals.)

Feelings and attitudes toward death, like all feelings and attitudes, vary considerably from person to person—even among individuals who have extremely similar backgrounds. Even if two persons share views about some aspects of death—perhaps the importance of funerals—they may well differ on other death-related matters, such as the propriety of allowing children at funerals. When we discuss the death views of "our society," we must keep firmly in mind that we are generalizing and are constantly running the risk of overgeneralizing.

Death attitudes not only vary among individuals or among societies; they also vary across time for a given individual or for a society. Consider yourself for a moment—only yourself. Are your views of death and its various components the same today as they were five years ago? Will they be the same five years from now? The evidence suggests that, depending on your mood, your experiences, and your immediate physical and social environments, they will vary from year to year and even perhaps from day to day or from moment to moment. Similarly, the views of our society or of groups within the society change over the years. For example, the death-awareness movement has represented social change in the ways we relate to persons who are dying.

Since death and dying mean many things, we cannot talk about *an* attitude toward death. I may have very different feelings about (1) my dying eventually, (2) my dying in the next few days or weeks, (3) your dying eventually, (4) your dying in the next few days or weeks, (5) my being dead, (6) your being dead, and (7) the abstract concept of death. The factors that determine my feelings include (1) what the relationship of the person concerned is to me, (2) how imminent death is, and (3) whether it is the process of dying or the state of being dead that is involved.

Of the several studies made of the relationship of these factors, two are especially important. In one, two psychologists devised four separate scales: fear of death of self, fear of death of others, fear of dying of self, and fear of dying of others (see Figure 5-1). These scales were then administered to two groups of undergraduate women, and the scores were intercorrelated. There was virtually no relationship between fear of death of others and fear of dying of self; similarly, the correlation between fear of death of self and fear of dying of others in the reciprocal relationship was erratic. However, there were significant correlations within the remaining sets of factors—the

Fear of own death   Fear of own dying

	Fear of own death	Fear of own dying
Fear of death of others	Moderately high relationship	Very low relationship
Fear of dying of others	Ambiguous relationship	Highest relationship

Figure 5-1. Relationships between selected death-attitude variables. (After Collett & Lester, 1969.)

strongest relationship being between one's own dying and the dying of others (Collett & Lester, 1969). Apparently, two separate concepts developed: death versus dying and self versus others. Relationships within either concept were significant; relationships between factors not tied together by one of the concepts were weak. Because the number of people in each study was only 25, only women were included, and the age and education ranges were limited, generalizing from these data must be done cautiously.

However, another study, discussed more fully in the next chapter, found four factors involved in death anxiety; these are death avoidance, death fear, death denial, and reluctance to interact with the dying (Nelson & Nelson, 1975). The two studies do not contradict each other, and no one to my knowledge has conducted research to integrate the two. It certainly appears that people differentiate between death and dying and that they recognize several bases for death fear and anxiety. We are mistaken when we describe *the* death attitudes of our society or of an individual as though there were only one set.

What Feelings and Attitudes toward Death Are Possible?

Frequently researchers consider "attitudes toward death" and "fear of death" synonymous. Not being afraid of death, accepting death, being open to one's feelings concerning death, and other possible attitudes toward death, many of which are at the opposite end of the continuum from fear of death, have been relatively ignored in research as well as clinical and theoretical writings (for a thorough discussion see Marshall, 1980).

A person may feel awe and wonder in the face of death. Death is so powerful, so overwhelming, so inevitable, so imposing, so permanent, that it can induce such feelings. The awesomeness and wonder may, in turn, lead to feelings of terror or feelings of peacefulness.

Or someone may be curious about death. What does it mean? Where does it lead? Is it really irreversible? How does it feel? Or does it feel at all?

One pair of authors investigated how people cope with imminent death, and since coping processes suggest underlying attitudes and feelings, it seems appropriate to consider the four styles they examined: confrontation, acceptance, resignation, and avoidance (Feifel & Nagy, in preparation). These styles suggest: I'm going to continue to try to do something about this;

I might as well stop fighting and make the best of it; I give up—I feel so sad I don't have any spirit left; and I'll ignore it as long as I can.

Perhaps the most ignored attitude toward death is *dislike*. If I like to be healthy and sickness keeps me from being healthy, I will dislike sickness; if I like being wealthy and high taxes keep me from being wealthy, I will dislike high taxes; and if I like being alive and death is going to keep me from being alive, I will dislike death. My dislike may be so intense as to be described as hate.

Strangely, relatively little has been written in the academic and professional literature about disliking or hating death, although there are numerous references to anger about one's own dying or the death of a loved one. One exception is an early study (Bromberg & Schilder, 1933) that concluded that people are more likely to express sadness, dislike, and regret in considering their own deaths than to express fear or anxiety.

Freud contended that we cannot imagine our own deaths, "and whenever we make the attempt to imagine it we can perceive that we really survive as spectators" (Freud, 1915/1959a, p. 305). Although we can consciously talk about our own death, "our unconscious does not believe in its own death; it behaves as if immortal" (Freud, 1915/1959a, p. 313). This, Freud speculates, might be the secret of heroism: that unconsciously we don't believe we will die and, therefore, again unconsciously, heroic and high-risk actions don't lead to fear of death. We do, of course, recognize the reality of the deaths of others, and Freud suggests that the origins of psychology itself might be in the concurrent emotional pain and sense of triumph that we feel at the death of a loved one (Freud, 1917/1959b).

Although we need to recognize Freud's wisdom when he says that we inevitably see ourselves as surviving our own deaths when we think about death, we don't need to agree with his assumption that we maintain an unconscious belief that we will never die. Each individual will need to decide this controversial issue for himself or herself.

The Effects of Unconscious Death Attitudes

What we tell others we believe about our death attitudes, what we tell ourselves, and what we may actually believe or feel without awareness represent three different positions. To a large extent, these positions are positively related, but for some individuals, the relationship is negative; that is, there are people who claim to have a very low concern about death or to have thoughts of death on rare occasions, if at all, whose level of concern is actually very high.

The conflict between conscious and unconscious death attitudes is apparent in our daily observations. A good friend of mine laughs at me for my interest in death, says that I must really be afraid of death to spend so much time worrying about it, then subsequently casually mentions that he is so unafraid of death that he hasn't even bothered to make out a will. (I make the opposite assumption—that a man with three children rapidly approaching college age who hasn't made out a will is avoiding the idea of death.)

Why is it, then, that people who say they aren't afraid of dying or of their own death show they are indeed afraid when we measure or observe their fears and anxieties indirectly? One obvious answer is that people are reluctant to admit death fears to others; they may feel it makes them appear weak or unduly vulnerable. An alternative explanation is that people don't normally think about death, and so their almost automatic response when asked is to reply in the negative without giving the matter serious thought—perhaps upset just enough by the question to avoid giving it serious thought.

A third possibility is that people are not aware of how fearful and anxious they are about death. When they say they aren't afraid, they are totally sincere, but their voice or their sweat glands or their eyes say otherwise.

There is a fourth alternative, which is frequently overlooked. When I ask you, whether in a research interview or in a casual conversation, whether you are afraid of death, you think of the abstraction, death, rather than the reality, death. Even if I ask you about *your* death, your response is the same.

If you were encouraged for two or three minutes to dwell on what it means to die or to be dead, the responses might be quite different. If I asked you to think of those you were going to leave behind or of facing the possibility of nothingness, of extinction, then you might become more fearful or anxious. The full impact of the meaning of *your* death to *you* probably cannot be absorbed in response to a simple question. While you are saying that you aren't afraid of dying or of death, you give evidence of general arousal and concern by the increase in the time it takes you to respond, by the change in your tone of voice, by the alterations in the biochemical responses of your body. The habit of displacing this fear and anxiety was instrumental for many decades in keeping Western psychology from recognizing death anxiety as a significant influence on human behavior.

Over the years, a handful of investigators have conducted research into the possibility that many death attitudes are held unconsciously, and they have also probed into possible inconsistencies between conscious and unconscious death attitudes. One important series of studies was initiated some three decades ago. In one study, with the title "Is Death a Matter of Indifference?" (Alexander, Colley, & Adlerstein, 1957), the authors concluded that it definitely was not. First, they asked a small number (N = 31) of college students how they felt about death; the students responded with a high level of indifference. Next, they showed the students a series of words flashed briefly on a screen, and, using the word-association technique, they asked for the first word that came to mind. The stimulus words fell into four categories: neutral, sex, school, and death. The time it took to respond to the words was measured, as was the students' galvanic skin response (a measure of stress and anxiety usually based on increase in palm perspiration). The results were very clear. Despite the claims of indifference, both measures of response to death-related words showed highly emotional patterns—like the responses to the school and sex words—and were very different from the responses to the neutral terms.

More recently, one of the major investigators in the field of death research,

Herman Feifel, has been pursuing the issue of conscious versus unconscious death attitudes. He and his colleagues have been studying reactions to death at the conscious, fantasy, and below-the-level-of-awareness levels. In spite of some understandable difficulty in determining the latter two levels, Feifel has made some highly important findings—for example, that "the dominant conscious response to fear of death is one of repudiation (of the *fear*); that of the fantasy . . . level, one of ambivalence; and at the nonconscious level, one of outright negativity" (Feifel & Branscomb, 1973, p. 286). The implications are apparent: the deeper we probe into the unconscious, the more death fear and anxiety we find. The consequences of this finding for our day-to-day behavior are more difficult to determine.

A later study (Feifel & Nagy, 1981) confirmed the importance of the fantasy-level measurement but did not show effects for the nonconscious measurement. Whether this result is due to the inadequacy of the investigators' nonconscious-measurement instrument or whether it has implications for unconscious/nonconscious reactions to death is uncertain.

Among the numerous reactions to death and dying, the category that has received by far the greatest amount of attention is fear of death, or death anxiety, or dread. And this is the topic of the next chapter.

CHAPTER SIX

Fear and Anxiety

"The thing of which I have most fear is fear."
—*Montaigne*, in 1580

"Nothing is so much to be feared as fear."
—*Thoreau*, in 1851

"The only thing we have to fear is fear itself."
—*Franklin Roosevelt*, in 1933

"We seem to fear the fear of death."
—*Kastenbaum & Aisenberg*, in 1972

No, the statement by Kastenbaum and Aisenberg is not in agreement with the previous three. In fact, its meaning is just the opposite—that we have an inordinate fear of death, that we go to unnecessary lengths to help (or even require) people to overcome their fear of death, that we are made so uncomfortable by the fear of death that one might question why we protest so much. Kastenbaum and Aisenberg seem to be saying that it is all right, perhaps even desirable, to have some fear of death. As one research participant said, "You are *nuts* if you aren't afraid of death" (Kalish & Reynolds, 1981).

However, there is a danger in putting too much faith in comments like those above: we begin to assume that fear of death is inevitable and, thereupon, exclude any basis for contradictory information. So when people admit to fearing death and their deaths, we surmise that they really fear death. But if other people insist that they do not fear death or their deaths, we surmise that they are denying their fear of death and really have this fear nonetheless. We know best because our theory tells us so—it doesn't matter what anyone else says. In fact, we may be correct. Perhaps individuals who

93

contend that they have no fear of death are unconsciously or consciously covering for a considerable fear. But the evidence is not yet in, and we are probably well advised to accept what people say at face value rather than assume we can be mindreaders.

There is little doubt that the death attitude that receives the most attention—and deservedly so—is the fear of death. The term **fear** is usually used when there is a specific, identifiable source of the fear; **anxiety** refers to feelings of apprehension and discomfort, similar to those felt in fear, but without a known identifiable source. It is difficult to know, when we consider death, whether the source is known or not, and so *death fear* and *death anxiety* are used almost interchangeably. We also use such terms as *terror* and *dread*.

What causes the fear and anxiety? As early as 1915, G. Stanley Hall stated "We long to be just as well, strong, happy, and vital as possible, and strive against everything that impedes this wish or will. . . . We love life supremely and cannot have too much of it . . . while we dread all that interferes with it" (p. 569). So we dread and, therefore, fear that which deprives us of what we love.

But death has other consequences that we fear—the many losses: loved ones, achievements, purposefulness, the possibility of experiencing, the physical body, control. For many people, the fear of death is the dread of extinction—of becoming nothing, of annihilation and obliteration—while for others it is the dread of entering the unknown and facing the possibility of judgment, punishment, and retribution. It may also involve the fear of separation and abandonment—separation from people, from places, from all that one has ever known. In addition to our fear of our own deaths, we fear and are anxious about our dying processes and the deaths and dying processes of those whom we love.

Fear of death has at least two positive outcomes. First, if we did not fear death, we would not exert nearly so much effort in avoiding it. And if that were the case, many, perhaps most, of us would die at an early age. This would have the effect of eliminating the human species. The fear of death, or at least a death avoidance, might even be the outcome of evolution, since presumably those species that did not fear death ceased to exist, and those individuals in our species who did not fear death did not live to reproduce.

The second positive outcome of death fear is less certain. There has been a great deal of speculation that fear of death has led to great creativity (for example, Becker, 1973). Those who hold this view believe that many artists have attempted to express their fear of death through their art; sometimes they express it directly by depicting death and sometimes indirectly by pouring their fear and anxiety into a variety of kinds of artistic endeavors.

LEARNING TO FEAR DEATH

A group of infants are removed to a desert island where they are cared for by effectively programmed robots that provide them with survival care, physical affection, and emotional support. Indeed, the robots do all the "right" parenting, but they know nothing about death, and their programming does not permit them to react in any way to the concept. The children develop their own method for communicating and their own social order. They will eventually experience the death of others on the island and the death of animals and plants. Now: do they develop a fear of death? Given 100 such islands, would individuals on all 100 develop a fear of death?

Several hypotheses are possible:

1. Everyone (or almost everyone) is born with a fear of death.
2. Everyone (or almost everyone) is born with no tendency to fear death, but living in this world makes it inevitable to fear death.
3. Everyone (or almost everyone) has an inevitable tendency to fear death, but this tendency can be overcome by appropriate love and learning.
4. We have no more tendency to fear death than to fear telephone poles, but many of us receive faulty early learning and develop this fear; then it becomes difficult, perhaps impossible, to overcome.

Bases for Development of Death Fears and Anxieties

Death fears and anxieties can develop in many ways. A few of these are early socialization, separation, anger and fear of retribution, and entering the unknown.

Early socialization.   Young children are given ample reinforcement for developing fear of death. Parents and others who socialize them are constantly reminding them when they are in danger or when they do something that might harm their health. They hear death spoken about in hushed voices, tinged with dread. They are often told very directly that certain behavior is expected of them so that they won't die. Fairy tales describe the deaths of evil people as punishment for their evil, while good people live happily every after. The constant message, both direct and indirect, is that "death is bad." This message is pervasive; it comes from family, friends, school, church, and the media.

The message to the young child actually goes beyond "death is bad." It includes "death is scary" and "death hurts" and "dead people can hurt you." What message is communicated by "Now I lay me down to sleep ..."? Implicit, and often explicit, statements of this sort are common.

Separation.   The young child has learned that the absence of his or her mother or other significant figure means the absence of the biological and the social support so necessary for well-being. Initially the infant is totally dependent on others for survival and satisfaction. The absence of mother (or father) means no food, no cuddling, no warm blanket, no clean diaper. Separation is always painful and difficult for the infant, especially as it challenges his or her sense of powerfulness and invulnerability—of virtual omnipotence (Becker, 1973).

As the child matures, he or she learns that death is a significant separation—perhaps the ultimate separation—from mother, father, and all significant persons. Given the anxiety and fear elicited by even brief separations, the child finds the possibility of this separation too great to bear. The separation of death is feared as the ultimate separation and the ultimate cause of vulnerability and helplessness. The death of someone else arouses these feelings, while contemplating the death of oneself does so even more dramatically.

Some people see the connection between infant and parent as even more powerful. They believe that the infant is not yet differentiated from the parent, so that the parent is viewed as an extension of self. In the words of one woman who, at the age of about six months, was separated from her mother for some months, ". . . recovery of memories has revealed that, at one early stage of this separation, I thought a part of me was actually missing, so that I feared I was disappearing or about to disappear, that time had stopped, and that there was no future. (I am, of course, translating my memory into adult vocabulary.) I now believe that an infant's periodic reunions with its primary caretaker provide a sense of continuity through time, and the expectation of *future* such reunions gives the child a sense of having a future, aside from whatever physical comforts the caretaker provides." This is another perspective that requires careful consideration.

Anger and fear of retribution. No relationship is perfect, and this is probably truer of intimate relationships than of more distant ones. No matter how good a parent/child relationship is, there will be ample cause for anger and hostility. Therefore, "no child escapes forming hostile death wishes toward his socializers" (Wahl, 1959, p. 24). However, the world of children is magical (after all, to get fed all they have to do is cry or demand or just be there), and the knowledge that they wish death (which may be understood as *removal*) for their parents suggests to them that their parents might have comparable reciprocal wishes. Furthermore, a parent definitely does have the power to put such wishes into effect, so if the child directs anger toward the parent, the parent might indeed respond with comparable anger and bring about either death or abandonment. This greatly enhances children's sense of vulnerability, since neither their power nor their magic is as great as that of their parents (Becker, 1973). Consequently, children, fearing the parent's anger and ability to abandon them, fear death, which is associated with these actions.

Entering the unknown. You may feel you "know" what happens after you die, so that death does not lead to anything unknown. If you believe this, you are probably in a minority. Most people have beliefs or assumptions or desires about what happens after death, but they don't claim to "know." Moving to a new community, entering a new college, or traveling abroad by yourself can all be exciting, but they can also be frightening. Sailing on uncharted seas—entering the unknown that is death—can be much more frightening because it is so completely unknown.

What are the possibilities? Perhaps there is no unknown, just nothingness.

Perhaps there is heaven and hell as described by authors of the Renaissance. Perhaps there is "peace and love everlasting." Perhaps there is judgment. Perhaps there is something that we cannot now possibly imagine. This is the place not to discuss what is after death but to acknowledge that knowing that the future is unknown and perhaps unknowable can make that future very frightening.

There are, of course, other ways in which we learn to fear death—for example, by learning to fear the losses that death causes: of experiencing, of loved ones, of projects, of things.

"Healthy-Minded," "Morbid-Minded"

If death fears and anxieties arise primarily or completely from the sources mentioned above, we should be able to overcome a large portion of those fears. We would take care to avoid destructive early socialization, to eschew unhappy separation fears, to help children work through their anger and fear of retribution, and to provide an understandable picture of what death is. This is the position that Becker (1973) describes as the "healthy-minded" argument. Given healthy family relationships, security, love, help with anger, and support in the face of the unknown, children need not develop a fear of death. Rather, they will later come to recognize death as a normal part of the life span.

Becker then posits the other side of the coin: the "morbid-minded" argument. In taking this position, he accepts the idea that the social environment and family relationships can modify the fear of death, but he posits that it cannot be altogether eliminated: "The fear of death is natural and is present in everyone, . . . it is the basic fear that influences all others, a fear from which no one is immune, no matter how disguised it may be" (1973, p. 15). In establishing his point, Becker argues that the fear of retribution occurs inevitably. Since this experience cannot be avoided, the fear of death cannot be avoided.

It is difficult to know whether Becker's healthy-minded position has more or less merit than his morbid-minded position. Both recognize the importance of early learning and later experience. Both allow family relationships and a sense of security to play a significant role. Both take into account the notion of unpredictability and vulnerability; that is, people may feel helpless both in protecting themselves against a punitive attack and in coping with unknown forces. This helplessness reminds them of their mortality, of their vulnerability to death. However, neither takes adequate note of anthropological studies. The difference is that the morbid-minded stance presupposes that some death fear, even terror, will remain no matter how "healthy" the social environment has been.

Some people contend that since death is normal and inevitable, fear and even avoidance of death are inappropriate. I would question this position. We might say "Cancer is merely a normal part of life; it is natural. What we need are courses, even in elementary school, to help people overcome their fear of cancer, so that when cancer comes, they recognize it as part of the natural flow of life and learn to accept it." Replace *cancer* with *stroke* and reread the sentence. Now try *rabid-dog bite*. Finally, use the word *death*. You probably realized why the passage sounded so familiar: you have seen it before.

This is not to deprecate attempts to reduce the fear individuals have of death. Such attempts are normally beneficial. However, my own views are that reasonable fear of death is just as normal as death itself, that such fears are adaptive, and that they need not be viewed as pathological unless they interfere in some significant way with the life of the individual. Indeed, as stated earlier, fear of death has evolutionary value, since if no one feared death, most people would die quite young, before they reproduced, and the human species would have ceased to exist long ago. This position does not require the existence of a survival or self-preservation instinct; it can arise from the second of the hypotheses presented earlier—namely, that people are not born with a fear of death but that inevitable life experiences teach them such fears.

EXPRESSING THE FEAR OF DEATH

When you are frightened or anxious, how does your behavior change? How does your internal state change? The obvious response is that there are a variety of possibilities and these depend on the circumstances. A similar response can be given in reference to death fears and anxieties.

Avoidance

We often avoid what frightens us, sometimes consciously and sometimes without awareness. The person who says "I am not going to that funeral because funerals depress me" is displaying a conscious avoidance of a symbol of death. The same person may well avoid a hospital visit to a dying friend for the same reason. Society provides many specific safeguards to permit us to avoid contact with death and dying. It provides institutions for the dying, encourages the use of euphemisms in discussing death, makes certain that the death-related aspects of funeral homes are not conspicuously displayed either in advertising or on the building exteriors, and socializes us to be uncomfortable in asking people how they feel about the death of a friend or family member.

Unconscious avoidance of death-related matters is also familiar. Rather than stating explicitly that funerals make us uncomfortable, we may find ourselves "too busy" to attend; rather than admitting that we don't wish to visit a dying friend, we may decide that she already has ample visitors or is probably too ill to appreciate our visit. If the topic of death or dying arises at a social gathering, some people are likely to drift away from the conversation fairly quickly, not necessarily from lack of interest (although that can be a motive also) but from strong feelings of vague discomfort (that is, of anxiety).

Another unconscious dynamic to avoid death anxiety is perceptual defense. This is the unconscious use of defense mechanisms so that matters concerning death and dying are not perceived and processed in the ways we usually perceive and process information. Early studies showed that death words took longer to recognize than neutral words (Alexander & Adlerstein, 1960; Golding, Atwood, & Goodman, 1966). Although not all studies consistently show these results, there is some evidence that people take longer to perceive signs and symbols of death in their social environments; a likely interpretation is that the delay is a perceptual defense. People who become sensitized to their environment as a defense mechanism are more likely to express a conscious fear of death than those who use repression. The repressors, on the other hand, display more unconscious fear than the sensitizers (Rosenheim & Muchnik, 1984–85). Thus, differences in defense styles may account for inconsistency in earlier research.

A very different way of avoiding death is to channel so much energy and time into other activities that there is nothing left for death. So people throw themselves into work, pleasure, the pursuit of fame, study, meditation, or travel, for example. Given this intense involvement, they are too busy when awake and too exhausted when ready for sleep to give thought to death. Their anxieties, however, appear in dreams or are expressed in somatic or psychological symptoms, since not even extreme activity and extreme exhaustion are sufficient to keep such anxiety from awareness forever.

When, for whatever reasons, death anxieties do produce too much discomfort as they press into awareness, there are still ways to avoid the feelings of tension. One familiar means is the use of certain mood-changing drugs or alcohol. It isn't unusual for heavy drinkers to admit that they want to drink themselves into oblivion (Lepp, 1968). Sleep is another way to avoid the pain of anxiety. Like drugs and alcohol, it serves as a retreat from the world. Sleep, in fact, is closely related to death in many ways: it is often a euphemism for death and was regarded by the ancient Greeks as the twin brother of death (Kastenbaum, 1981). Recall, also, the role of sleep or trance in *The Sleeping Beauty* and *Snow White*. Both characters had died, although they seemed as though they were asleep, and both were returned to life through love.

Changing Lifestyles

In our generation, the advice of the health professional is more likely to be heeded than that of any other professional, and health professionals fill us with advice about how we might postpone the time of our deaths. You are familiar with the advice: eat properly; avoid high-cholesterol foods; watch your weight; take vitamins; exercise properly; jog (or don't jog); swim; play tennis (but not too strenuously); follow a yoga regimen; sleep properly; avoid stress; avoid smog; avoid tobacco altogether and avoid abuse of coffee, liquor, and drugs.

There is nothing wrong with the advice. In fact, much of it is useful. The point here is that following such advice is an attempt to remain both healthy and alive. This seems to be one way of expressing a fear, or at least an unrealistic avoidance, of death.

Not everyone accepts health professionals' advice as the ultimate authority. Many people still believe that proper moral behavior will be rewarded with long life. This view is not restricted to those following traditional religious philosophies; it is also held by adherents of the holistic health movement, who talk about spiritual well-being, personal growth, and the importance of the whole person. So although one group espouses belief in a traditional God and another group encourages personal growth and self-actualization, both groups are assuming that their notion of holding to proper values will lead to a longer and healthier life.

> When Jerry passed his 50th birthday, what I had called his "creeping fear of death" ceased to creep and began to gallop. He had always been concerned about physical fitness and diet, but keeping fit became a major preoccupation. He read not only the popular diet books but the academic journals on nutrition and health. He ate certain foods (primarily fruits and vegetables) and avoided other foods (red meat, sweets of any kind, carbohydrates except for brown rice); foods like chicken and peanut butter confused him, since some findings encouraged including them in the diet and others rejected them. He jogged until he read in the orthopedic literature that jogging at his age could affect his spine, so he switched to swimming. He took megavitamins daily. And, of course, no liquor other than wine, no tranquilizers, no tobacco in any form (however, marijuana use was frequent, and cocaine was all right on occasion also). He lived, for the most part, a very healthy life. To complete the task of convincing himself that he was forever immune to death, he colored his hair as it grayed and had treatments to reduce the signs of aging in his face.

> When we talked, he would joke about how all this was going to enable him to live forever, but underneath his attempts at humor was a very strong endeavor to avoid, probably to deny, death. He even attended church and prayed in an explicit attempt to "get on His right side, just in case."

> Just before his 58th birthday, Jerry learned that he had cancer of the liver and would likely not live out the year. His immediate response was to intensify his health regimen, albeit more drastically and with numerous additional food supplements, and to become a born-again Christian. But he was also understandably furious with everything and everybody.

> He died 10 months later.

Jerry had good cause to be furious. He was successful at his work, had a good marriage and two grown children whom he loved deeply, and was basically enjoying life. But his fury exceeded that kind of response. He reacted as though he had entered into a binding contract to live a long and healthy life, almost to live indefinitely. He had maintained his part of the contract, but the nebulous forces with whom he had made the agreement had violated their promises. In talking with him, I could see that he even felt singled out for unfair treatment, and he continued to seek ways to reestablish the contract (Kübler-Ross, 1969, describes the stage of *bargaining* in the dying process) by offering more and better health practices and prayer.

Dreams and Death

Dreams are a representation of our feelings and thoughts in visual form. Some dreams represent feelings and thoughts of which we are not consciously aware; they occur at night, when our psychological guard is down and we are less defended. These dreams may symbolize wishes, fears, anxieties, needs that are unacceptable to the "critical me" that keeps such notions out of awareness during wakefulness. Other dreams may just represent feelings and thoughts that are impinging so strongly on our minds that they appear during sleep.

Since death fears and anxieties are both powerful and kept from consciousness most of the time, they do appear in various guises in dreams. Sometimes they produce nightmares; other times, a death dream will not be at all disturbing. One early study found that students who report more concern about death also report more frequent nightmares (Feldman & Hersen, 1967). As is true of all dreaming, death dreaming is usually symbolic and indirect. If you had a dream of yourself lying in a box, you might quickly recognize the box to be a coffin and the dream to be about your death. However, the dream might also be about your feeling restricted or isolated or peaceful or, if you pun in your dreams, boxed in or even being a boxer. Dreams are tricky, but if you find an interpretation that both fits the dream and "feels right," it is likely to be accurate.

How often do people dream about their own deaths? In the Los Angeles study of death attitudes, about one-fourth of the 434 respondents admitted to having dreamed of their deaths on at least one occasion. The older the individual, the more often this experience was reported (Kalish & Reynolds, 1981). Of course, these results have some limitations: most death dreams are not obviously about death, and most dreams in general are not recalled the next morning. Therefore, we need to take these responses with a grain of salt and recognize, first, that only a small minority of persons will acknowledge dreams of their own death and, second, that the fact that this number is small is in itself significant.

When the dreams of terminally ill cancer patients were compared with the dreams of older persons (Coolidge & Fish, 1983–84), the cancer patients were found to have more death themes, more themes of aggression, more highly emotional content, and more themes of the loss of resources. Since the cancer patients were, on the average, almost 30 years younger than the control group of elderly people, the fact that they had more aggressive dreams might be seen as a function of age differences. However, the remaining differences could not be attributed to age.

Also interesting was that, in spite of the numerous dreams about death experienced by the 14 cancer patients in the study, only one had a dream about his or her own death. The other dreams involved deaths that had been projected onto other people:

> I went to an outside all-night movie and I was standing in the middle of the street when this car pulled up and dumped out a young pregnant dead woman. . . . I ran over . . . and I was looking at me on the floor but the girl didn't look like me. (Told by

a 27-year-old woman 12 months before her death) [Coolidge & Fish, 1983–84, p. 3].

When people are very sick, perhaps dying, their dreams, reflecting their fears and anxieties, often differ from those of persons who are not facing their own imminent death. Frequently a dying person will describe a dream to a friend, family member, or member of a hospital staff in an attempt not only to understand what the dream meant but also to involve the listener in the dreamer's feelings and fears. The dying person is using the dream to make a statement that he or she hopes the listener will interpret correctly and respond to with support and understanding. One dream took place under very dramatic circumstances:

I had been driving through the desert on a seldom-traveled road when my car just stopped running, and my little knowledge of mechanics could not get it started again. I was already hot and thirsty, and my work on the car made me feel worse. I decided to try to walk to the main road and had the frustration of being passed by two cars that responded to my signals to flag them down by waving cheerfully back at me. I was still at least a few miles from the main road when I just couldn't walk any more and I sat down against a small shrub, waiting for the next car . . . if one came.

I obviously dozed off, and in my dream, I saw a man in black walking toward me, coming from some distance away. As soon as he was within about 20 feet of me, I pulled my head away and stared in another direction. And in a moment, I saw the same man dressed in the same fashion walking toward me. I did this several times, each time becoming slightly more afraid, until I felt myself being shaken. I shouted out, certain that the man in black had reached me, and indeed it was a man in black: a New Mexico state patrolman. (*Thanks to Kevin for providing this experience.*)

Are dreams of someone else's death ever accurate predictions? Is it possible to dream of someone dying, then to learn several days later that the individual did indeed die at that time? These are controversial issues, which you must answer according to your own experiences and beliefs.

Fear of death is also manifested in fantasies. Perhaps you have had death fantasies as you drove along a country road at twilight, when the calm beauty and slight boredom of the drive took your mind from your driving to your inner feelings. You may also have fantasies of death when you are drifting off to sleep at night. Did you ever fantasize being at your own funeral? Tom Sawyer and his friends had this fantasy come true: they were at their own funeral, where they listened to people cry over their deaths and extol their virtues. Have you ever said, either aloud or to yourself, "You'll be sorry when I'm dead?"

Death fantasies, like all fantasies, may be under conscious control or may occur when your thoughts appear to go wherever they wish. In either case, it is perfectly normal to have fantasies, including death fantasies, and sometimes fantasies—like dreams—appear frightening, grotesque, and distorted.

There are many other ways an individual can express fear of death, such as talking a great deal about death, associating with a group that believes death doesn't really occur, or writing poetry that contains death symbols.

OVERCOMING THE FEAR OF DEATH

Although fear of death is often appropriate, it can become powerful enough to be disruptive and to interfere with regular life tasks. Even when it is not disruptive, however, it is painful. Since most of us wish to reduce the pain we suffer, it is appropriate to work toward overcoming such fear—even though death fear is normal and even perhaps useful and adaptive.

A great many arguments have been advanced by philosophers and others over the centuries as antidotes to the fear of death. For example, Robert Burton in the 17th century urged us to divert our thoughts to other matters; Machiavelli suggested escape in study; Spinoza exhorted us to love God; Montaigne advised that we immerse ourselves in thinking and talking about death; in the second century, Marcus Aurelius argued that when death occurs we will have no sensation and therefore no awareness that death has in fact occurred (Choron, 1964). It has even been pointed out that since we don't fear our nonexistence prior to our births, we should not fear nonexistence after our deaths (Choron, 1964).

Each of the above arguments is used today to help people overcome their fear of death, and each helps some persons. However, the arguments tend to appeal to the intellect, and fear of death is a feeling that is often not influenced by such appeals.

If intellectual arguments are not particularly useful in overcoming death fear, how do people cope with such fears? Neither throwing oneself into involvements—pleasure, work, fame, sex, or study—to avoid thoughts of death nor challenging death directly will work indefinitely. The fears of death will manifest themselves in some fashion.

Living Life Fully

In my own experience and certainly in the experience of many others, the people who fear death the least are those who love life the most. This initially seems to be a contradiction, since one kind of logic suggests that you are best able to lose what you like least. We can apply another kind of logic. People who are not living as they want to live have not been able to get what they want from life. Their lives remain incomplete, and they seek for meaning and completion. It is not just that they find life boring; it is, rather, that although they wish to live life fully, they are not fully living life. When faced with their death, they are frightened. They have less adequate senses of self and are, therefore, generally more readily frightened. More important, however, they are frightened because they realize that now they will never have the chance to be *really* alive. In a way, their lives will be over before they begin.

Those who live their lives fully have enjoyed what they have had. They may feel cheated and angry, especially if they have unfinished tasks, but they are less afraid, since they have taken from life as much as they were able to take. These individuals still have some fears of death, but these fears don't interfere with their enjoyment of life. They are able to use each day well. Thus, if they die today, they do not regret having spent yesterday as they did.

In a way, they "realize that [they] might die at any moment, and yet live as though [they] were never going to die" (Lepp, 1968, p. 77).

This chapter has returned to the theme of the meaning of life, which was discussed first in Chapter 3. In talking about people who are serene when they face old age and death, Lepp writes "Conscious of having lived for something and having been fulfilled in life, they are capable of spontaneously conferring meaning on that ultimate act of their lives which is death" (1968, p. 142). Lepp has no trouble acknowledging that these persons still have some anxiety about death—he points out that even "Christ . . . knew the terrors of agony" (p. 142)—but the meaningfulness of their lives has made their deaths more acceptable to them.

Challenging Death

Another way to cope with fear of death is to challenge death constantly—and win. The lives of persons who do this resemble a constant game of Russian roulette, except that they express their challenge through dangerous activities (parachute-jumping, hang-gliding, car racing) or through dangerous work (combat soldiering, firefighting, transporting explosives). Of course, not all persons who participate in these activities or jobs are challenging death, and some who do so claim they are indifferent to death. Are they really indifferent? Are they so in love with death they want to die? Or do they fear death so much that they must continually risk their lives to prove to themselves that they can vanquish death? Perhaps all of the above are valid descriptions of some persons. We have little understanding of this phenomenon.

One study of risk (Kastenbaum & Briscoe, 1975) has some intriguing implications, however. Investigators positioned themselves at a busy thoroughfare crossing in Detroit and observed how people crossed the street. They evaluated the crossing behavior of 125 people on the basis of the risks they took. For example, at one end of their continuum was the Type A pedestrian, who stood on the curb until the light changed in his or her favor, glanced briefly at oncoming traffic, immediately entered the crosswalk, moved across at a moderate-to-brisk pace, and exhibited no erratic behavior. At the other end of the continuum was the type E pedestrian, who stepped out from some location other than the corner—for example, from between parked cars—and crossed against the traffic light without looking in either direction.

The researchers, who then interviewed the pedestrians, found that the more cautious street crossers both expected to and wanted to live longer than the high-risk crossers (even when age was controlled, since the high-risk crossers tended to be younger than the more cautious crossers); the low-risk crossers also reported less stressful lives than the high-risk crossers. Perhaps, then, people who challenge death do so to handle stress with the knowledge that their challenge may cost them their lives. Possibly death has a certain amount of fascination for them. This is a highly speculative interpretation, but the study opens up a variety of possibilities, among which are thoughts of creative kinds of research methodologies.

Finally, another way of challenging death may be by becoming a physician or other health professional. Although such persons eventually lose to death, they are instrumental in postponing the success of death for others and, perhaps symbolically, for themselves.

A list of ways to express fear and anxiety about death could continue almost endlessly. For example:

- Resorting to defensive humor—gallows humor—to make fun of death and thus establish superiority to death.
- Displacing fears of death onto other matters, such as work or sexuality, which in the long run are less distressing than death.
- Becoming death-related professionals, such as death counselors or educators, and perhaps writing books about death (like this one).
- Expressing feelings creatively in paintings, musical compositions, poetry.
- Expressing the anxiety through physical changes in the body—for example, through backaches, stomachaches, headaches, shallow breathing, perspiring.

Gaining Relevant Experiences

It seems possible that having some experience with death and the process of dying might diminish death fears and anxieties. However, such an effect would depend both on the nature of the experience and on the readiness of the person having the experience. For many people, then, taking a course or a workshop, reading a book on death, talking to people about death, attending funerals, or visiting the dying would serve to reduce death anxieties. For others, these acts would have a contrary effect.

Establishing Continuity of Life

An obvious way to overcome the fear of death is to believe that although physical death may destroy the body, it cannot destroy the spirit, soul, or existence of the individual. This belief permits clinical death to be a rite of passage to another form of existence rather than an extinction of existence. But this issue deserves a chapter of its own, and you may wish to review parts of Chapter 4 for this purpose.

WHAT IS DEATH ANXIETY AND HOW DO WE KNOW?

Death anxiety was just defined a few pages ago, so it might seem strange that the question in the heading above has been posed. Nonetheless, although it is easy to give a simple definition of death anxiety, and no doubt this definition is useful, there are still several important unanswered questions. First, is there really such a thing as death anxiety, or is it simply a manifestation of general anxiety? Second, is death anxiety one single factor, or is it best understood as a composite of different factors? And third, how good a job do we do of determining the extent to which a person or a group of people is anxious or fearful of death?

Death Anxiety and General Anxiety

When we are anxious about something, we feel apprehension and discomfort without being able to pinpoint the source. For someone to have a high level of death anxiety, he or she would need to become uncomfortable when death-related issues emerge in a conversation or at the thought of going to a funeral or perhaps when entering a hospital ward where seriously ill people are housed. The individual might be aware of the feelings and might even be aware that the feelings had something to do with death but would not know what it was about death that was causing concern, or he or she might deny that the issue of death was even related to what was being felt.

The question that arises is whether people who are anxious about death are also more anxious in general than those who are not. Can people display death anxiety but have a low level of anxiety regarding other matters?

The research literature is quite consistent in answering this question: there is definitely a strong relationship between death-anxiety measures and general-anxiety measures. This is true whether the respondents are undergraduates, nursing-home staff members, or staff members of agencies that work with the elderly (Pinder & Hayslip, 1981); it is also true of hospice workers (Amenta & Weiner, 1981) and of graduate students and the elderly themselves (Conte, Weiner, & Plutchik, 1982).

One group of investigators (Conte et al., 1982) carried the matter a step further than usual: they developed a scale to measure death anxiety and then correlated this scale with two other well-known scales of death anxiety and with the Taylor Manifest Anxiety Scale, which is probably the most widely used paper-and-pencil test of general anxiety available. The correlations with the other death-anxiety scales were 0.51 and 0.58, and the correlation with the general-anxiety scale was 0.53. These findings support the position that death anxiety is simply a form of general anxiety.

The implications for working with people having high death anxiety are considerable. If death anxiety is closely related to general anxiety, it is possible that the best way to reduce death anxiety is to work with whatever is causing general anxiety. In fact, it is conceivable that alleviating death anxiety by itself is not possible, since it is too tied in with the person's other fears and anxieties. If death anxiety is a separate matter, then it needs to receive separate attention.

Factors of Death Anxiety

When we use the term *death anxiety,* we appear to be discussing a number of interrelated components, rather than just one simple factor. This came up previously when we outlined four factors: fear of own dying, fear of dying of others, fear of own death, fear of death of others (Collett & Lester, 1969); it came up again in considering fear of death at the conscious, preconscious, and below-the-level-of-awareness levels (Feifel & Branscomb, 1973). There is still one more approach that calls for our attention: factor analysis.

This is not the place to discuss factor analysis, other than stating that it is a statistical method that extracts factors when numerous measures are all correlated with one another. Some of the factor analyses performed on measures of death anxieties or death attitudes in general have involved correlating test scores with one another; others have correlated responses to individual items; sometimes demographic variables are included.

Numerous articles have reported the results of such factor analyses. At this point, the findings of three factor-analytic studies will be integrated in an attempt to abstract the factors from these investigations (Durlak & Kass, 1981–1982; Nehrke et al., 1981; Nelson & Nelson, 1975). The major factors appear to be

- Death fear and anxiety
- Desire to avoid death and reminders of death
- Denial of reality of death and of possibility of own death
- Reluctance to interact with dying persons
- Preoccupation with thoughts of dying
- Negative reaction to pain
- Concern for afterlife

If you were performing the same task, you might have selected different studies to begin with, or you might have viewed the same studies but come up with somewhat different factors. Nonetheless, these appear representative.

Measuring Death Fears and Anxieties

Initially the items for scales measuring death fears and anxieties were developed by investigators who interviewed a number of people informally, did some reading, and then sat down and wrote out the statements that they believed represented the most important kinds of reactions to death. Some of the scales would then be submitted to a rigorous testing period; others were immediately put into use. (See Marshall, 1982, for the best available discussion of scales, including reproduction of several instruments.) Later researchers used factor analysis or sought measures of unconscious feelings. What have they learned, and what are the limitations of the use of such scales?

Probably the most familiar finding is that, in response to direct questions, people seldom indicate a fear of death. In the only national sample ever asked this question, Riley reports that only 4% "gave evidence of fear or emotional anxiety in connection with death" (Riley, 1968, p. 332). When asked in a later study what the "worst things" were about being old, less than 1 person in 10 cited fear of death (National Council on the Aging, 1975). However, slightly over one-fourth of the multiethnic respondents whom Dave Reynolds and I queried admitted that they were afraid of death (Kalish & Reynolds, 1981). Roughly 20% of the Black and "Anglo" respondents acknowledged fear, while slightly over 30% of the Japanese Americans and Mexican Americans did. The Kalish and Reynolds study may have found a higher proportion of fear because the question was asked in the middle of a one-hour personal interview on death and bereavement; the respondents may have felt freer to admit their fears, or they may have had previously unknown fears stirred into consciousness by the interview process.

The validity of the results of death-anxiety studies has been called into question. Do the findings actually represent what people are thinking and feeling? The truth is that we don't know. We can probably assume that the answers people give are what they *believe* that they believe, although some conscious distortion undoubtedly occurs. But we know neither how much unaware distortion occurs nor how often we ask so sophisticated a question that the respondent, never having given serious thought to the matter, answers with the first thing that comes to mind. (Of course, the first thing that comes to mind may be the best and most honest response anyway.)

Some other methodological and measurement limitations have come up earlier in this book:

- The difficulty of knowing what is meant when someone checks "4" on a 5-point scale, from Strongly Agree to Strongly Disagree, in response to the question "Are you afraid of death?"
- Not knowing what unconscious feelings might underlie the explicit statements.
- Confusing fear and anxiety, own death and death of others, and death and dying.
- Assuming that death fear or death anxiety is a single factor rather than several distinct, though interrelated, factors.
- Uncertainty of the relationship between death anxiety and general anxiety.

The many limitations to our measures of death fears and anxieties do not mean, however, that the studies should be ignored. In each study it is important to consider (1) the nature of the measuring instrument, (2) the characteristics of the group being questioned, and (3) the conditions under which the study was conducted. If you know these three things, you can evaluate the applicability of the research findings to what you want to know.

PREDICTING THE FEAR OF DEATH

As might be expected, since so many studies have investigated death fear and anxiety, the literature includes innumerable research reports describing demographic, personality, and other factors that appear to be predictive of the extent to which individuals exhibit death fear and/or anxiety. In the final analysis, of course, it is dubious to judge any single individual in terms of characteristics determined by research on groups, but the information can still provide some important clues. The factors to be considered include experiences with death and the dying, gender, cultural and ethnic differences, personality characteristics, and religious views and affiliations. There is also a substantial literature on the relationship between age and various responses to death, and this will be discussed in some detail in Chapters 12 and 13 of this book.

Experiences with Death and the Dying

It is reasonable to believe that personal experiences with death and dying will reduce death fears and anxieties. It is also reasonable to believe just the opposite. The available research evidence sheds a little light on this issue.

A study conducted in Germany defines "death experience" in a global fashion, such as attending funerals and seeing a friend or relative die. This study of late-middle-aged adults found no relationship at all between the measure of death experience and several measures of reactions to and fear of death (Wittkowski, 1981). Another study (Hoelter & Hoelter, 1980–81) was more helpful, although the respondents were limited to college undergraduates. Here the authors used eight scales, each measuring a different death-related fear (for example, fear of dying, fear for body after death, fear of the dead) and asked the students about their general exposure to death during the preceding five years and their specific loss of a member of their immediate families. Those who had been exposed to death in general ways during the previous five years showed somewhat higher fears on several of the scales than those who had not had that exposure; however, those who had lost a member of their immediate families through death showed a significantly lower level of death fear on all eight scales than those who hadn't had such a loss. Explaining these results is difficult, but one possibility is that people who have to cope with the death of someone very close learn that they can survive a major loss; they give thought to their own mortality and become capable of handling it. People who have been exposed to death, but not in an intimate way, do not go through an equivalent learning process.

Gender Differences in Death Fears and Anxieties

There is only moderate consistency among the numerous studies of differences between men and women in death fears and anxieties. Some studies have found no gender differences (for example, Dickstein, 1972; Handal, 1969), while many others show women to be more fearful (for example, Aday, 1984–85; Templer, Ruff, & Frank, 1971). Even studies limited to the elderly show the same inconsistency: some find older women displaying more anxiety than older men (for example, Wass & Sisler, 1978), and others find no differences (for example, Nehrke, Bellucci, & Gabriel, 1977–78).

As the research designs have become more sophisticated and as death fear and anxiety is viewed as a complex, rather than a unitary, factor, some explanations begin to emerge. Thus, Wittkowski (1981) found that women scored higher than men on both fear of death and dying *and* acceptance of death, while Keith's (1979) study of 600 older men and women showed that women were more likely to be favorably disposed toward death than men. It appears possible that women find the prospect of their own death to be more fear-arousing than men do but that they simultaneously are more accepting of their own deaths than men are. A study of Israeli teenagers showed that girls are more fearful of loss of identity and of personal annihilation, while boys are more afraid of the impact on their families and also of their fate in the hereafter (Florian & Har-Even, 1983–84). The authors interpret their findings in terms of social roles.

So it seems that we need to look carefully at the age and sociocultural backgrounds of the persons participating in the study, as well as at the specific nature of the testing instrument, in order to develop trends in gender differences.

Ethnic Differences

A handful of research has looked at differences in death fears among ethnic groups. In the largest of these studies (Kalish & Reynolds, 1981), 100 or more persons in each of four ethnic groups (Black, Japanese American, Mexican American, and "Anglo") were interviewed for over an hour each. Inevitably in a study of this nature, many differences among ethnic groups were found. In summarizing our results, we pointed out that the major theme underlying differences in response was that the Japanese Americans and Mexican Americans displayed a stronger concern for the role of the family, while the Blacks and "Anglos" were more focused on the individual. Nonetheless, in spite of this theme, each of the groups differed in the way this familistic attitude was expressed. For example, the Japanese Americans responded in terms of social sensitivity and community cohesiveness, such as protection of others, not disturbing others, and providing mutually supportive pursuits, while the Mexican Americans displayed more concern for cohesiveness within the family group.

However, as is so often true, inconsistent results are also found. In one study, Black Americans indicated lower fear of death than three other ethnic groups (Kalish & Reynolds, 1981), while in another study, elderly Blacks showed a higher level of death fear than elderly Whites (Myers, Wass, & Murphey, 1980). Again we find it difficult to draw conclusions, because investigators do not use the same instruments or comparable respondent groups.

Personality and Death Fears and Anxieties

Logic suggests that a number of personality variables will be related to death anxiety. For example, since dying implies losing control, people who are fearful of death might be expected to be fearful of loss of control. Similarly, people with high needs for achievement might fear death more than the average person, since their deaths would eliminate all possibilities for achievement. People who feel competent in general or who have been successful in self-actualizing might be able to face death with less fear.

These assumptions are not fully supported by the data. Two reviews of relevant studies emphasize that results are inconsistent but that most findings indicate that relationships fall far short of statistical significance (Pollak, 1979–80; Schulz, 1978). This could arise from inadequate instruments or faulty assumptions.

Not all studies, however, have inconclusive results. Thus, research has shown that among nursing students greater self-acceptance is related to considerably less fear of death (Vargo & Batsel, 1981); among a group of college students, death anxiety was lower for those with higher self-esteem (Aronow, Rauchway, Peller, & DeVito, 1980–81).

Several studies have also reported a relationship between meaning in life and death anxiety. The more an individual felt that life had no meaning for her or him, the greater the reported feelings of death anxiety (Blazer, 1973; Durlak, 1972, 1973).

Numerous studies have investigated the relationships between fear of death, variously measured, and personality difficulties. One respected interpretation of Freud (Fenichel, 1945) proposed that death is likely to arouse anxiety because it reproduces earlier anxiety-causing events, such as separation from mother. Other early theorists, contrary to Freud, believed that death fears were basic and important fears in their own right, not simply diverted expressions of other fears (Jung, 1934/1959; Klein, 1948; Stekel, 1949).

Given this background, it would logically follow that persons who feared death more would also display various kinds of emotional distress to a greater extent. In fact, one brief review indicates that there is a small but consistent relationship between various measures of emotional upset and neuroticism and various measures of death fears and anxieties (Schulz, 1978). And as might be expected, people who are depressed are more fearful about death (Jeffers, Nichols, & Eisdorfer, 1961; Rhudick & Dibner, 1961).

New studies dealing with death anxiety and personality variables are being conducted and published all the time, and presumably someone will develop a research methodology that will avoid the kinds of distortion that the present measures allow. Paper-and-pencil questionnaires have their place, but the measurement of death anxiety may be too complex to be accomplished adequately in this fashion.

Studies of Religion and Death

The debate about whether religious beliefs and affiliations increase or diminish fear of death goes on. One side claims that the punitive aspect of religion, encouraging fears of hell and judgment, is so strong that belonging to and believing in one of the major organized religions would increase death anxiety. Or, approached differently: since religious beliefs help people cope with death, those individuals who are more afraid of dying are more likely to become religious (Feifel, 1959). The opposite side states that religion comforts the dying by making them feel loved by God and certain they will experience life after death. Religion, therefore, reduces fear of death.

Unfortunately, the studies of religion and death ignore sophisticated kinds of definitions. Instead, religiousness is frequently measured by a combination of belief in God, church attendance, and fear of hell. Nevertheless, some studies have yielded interesting results.

The available research does appear to show that maintaining an *intrinsic* religious belief system diminishes the fear of death, although we might assume that it would not have this effect if the belief system itself were to promote specific death-anxious feelings. Numerous studies have shown that the more religious a person is, the less fear of death that person shows (for example, Jeffers et al., 1961; Martin & Wrightsman, 1965; Swenson, 1961; Templer, 1972). One investigation indicated that highly religious people showed less fear of death than less religious persons regardless of whether religiousness was defined as self-reported religiousness, intrinsic religiousness, belief in God, importance of religion in everyday life, or belief in life after death (Feifel & Nagy, 1981).

Other research has approached the task in a less usual fashion. Although the particular questionnaires and definition were not the same in all these studies, the findings were: all found that fear of death was least strong among *both* those who adhered most closely to traditional religious beliefs and those who rejected traditional beliefs most completely; persons intermediate or undecided showed the greatest anxiety (Aday, 1984–85; Gorer, 1967; Hinton, 1963; Kalish, 1963; McMordie, 1981; Nelson & Nelson, 1973).

However, in a study of Israeli high school students, those who were more religious showed greater death fears on several measures of attitudes toward death and showed lower death fear on none (Florian & Har-Even, 1983–84). This finding suggests that we can't assume that the religious views commonly found in the United States and England, where the other studies were conducted, will have the same effects on people as will the religious views in other societies.

The overall situation has been well presented by Elisabeth Kübler-Ross: Truly religious persons "have been helped by their faith and are best comparable with those patients who were true atheists. The majority of patients were in between, with some form of religious belief but not enough to relieve them of conflict and fear" (1969, p. 237). Kübler-Ross emphasizes the difficulty of knowing who is "truly religious" and who not.

Although much more could be said about religion, meaning, and death, one point seems particularly important to make. It is not religion itself—not simply going to church or claiming to believe in God—that influences death anxieties and fears. Rather, it is the particular beliefs that one holds and the intensity with which they are held that have significance. Persons with strong inner beliefs—in a traditional God and afterlife or not—most probably find more meaning in life. Whether they see their death as occurring because of divine or natural causes, whether their meaning comes from traditional religion or personal philosophy, whether death means continuity or annihilation, these people are secure in their beliefs and can better contend with death.

One excellent example of the influence of religious beliefs in conjunction with supportive family and community is found among the Amish people, a community of conservative Protestants living mostly in Indiana, Pennsylvania, Ohio, and neighboring states. These people believe strongly in their religious teachings, which include the concepts that death is a natural part of life that is itself temporary and that only eternal life with God transcends this life. Both preparing for one's own death and caring for those who are dying seem to be comfortably accepted. "One Amish woman related that each month her aged grandmother carefully washed, starched, and ironed her own funeral clothing so that it would be in readiness for her death" (Bryer, 1979, p. 257). Another woman described her appreciation for being able to help care for both her parents and her husband's parents in their dying processes. "In their intensive caring they had the opportunity to work through their grief. . . . In the same process, they were moving toward the personal reorganization . . . needed . . . to return to the tasks of living that follow the death of a loved one" (Bryer, 1979, p. 258).

As the Amish's religious beliefs encourage acceptance of death and the dying process, their close and supportive families and communities provide personal care that is often unavailable in less cohesive communities. Communication among family members about an impending death is common and not especially tense; a dying person is provided with as much autonomy as possible, which may include encouragement to make plans for his or her own death and death ceremonies; and both a dying person and the bereaved are given effective community and family support (Bryer, 1979).

Because Bryer's study focuses attention on the relationships among religious beliefs, personal interactions among community members, and the social structure of the family and the community, it's impossible to determine how much of the effectiveness of the Amish approach comes directly from religious beliefs and how much from personal relationships or community and family structure. However, community studies of this sort can do a great deal to shed light on the meaning of both religion and community in death and the process of dying.

The relationships among religious beliefs and practices, beliefs concerning immortality, and feelings about death are complex and have not yet been effectively integrated and understood. It would appear that both the content of religious beliefs and the extent to which these beliefs are intrinsic—that is, personally and meaningfully maintained—will influence the individual's perceptions of death. Unfortunately, it does not seem that religious scholars and behavioral and social scientists have coordinated their efforts effectively in working on this task.

This is the end of the section on death and its many meanings. Death is part of life throughout the entire span of life. In the next sections, we will examine the process of dying and the nature of grief. These concerns affect us more episodically; when we are influenced by dying or by grief, we are frequently deeply emotionally involved, often very painfully so, but usually for finite periods. When it is our own dying or grieving, the experience is often overwhelming; when it is someone else's dying or grieving, our response is more varied.

P A R T

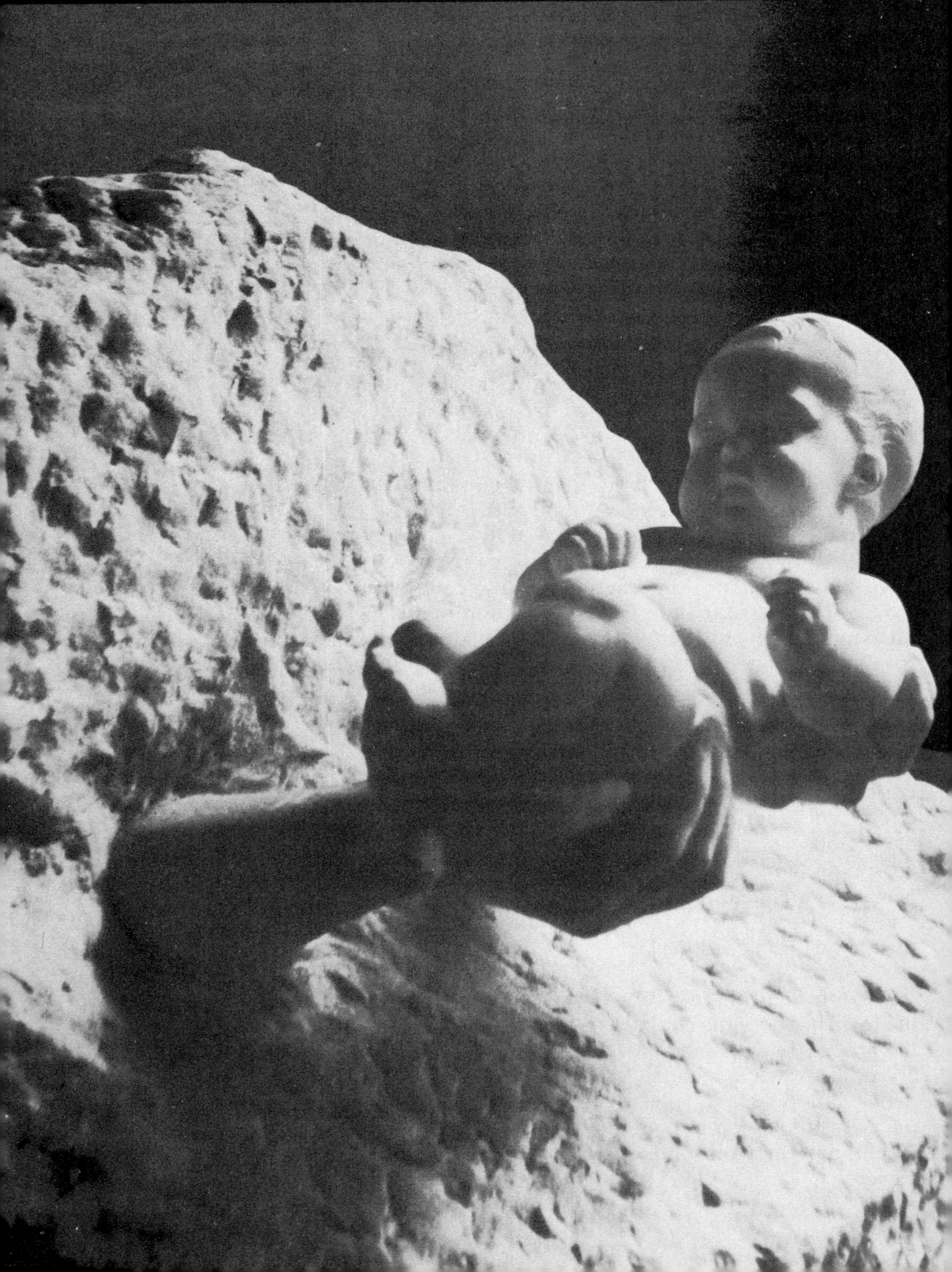

THE
PROCESS
OF
DYING

"WE ARE ENTITLED
TO ONE LIFE
AND ONE DEATH."

How I Live Now

1.

In my room I dwell with:
a stepladder behind the door
where my robe and nightgown hang,
a needlepoint frame in the corner,
a bed with a blanket I knitted
three years ago
while I sat on the sofa watching TV
waiting   waiting
for what would come next.

I live with a white armchair whose stuffing
is coming out of the arms under the cover,
the cover covered with a wool scarf I bought
on Christmas in a hippie house that smelled
of marijuana and popping corn.

I work on a yellow desk covered with
papers and books, a mirror, some masking
       tape;
I have a filing cabinet, portfolios, folders,
writing paper, two bottles of pills;
and a plastic container that serves as a
       wigstand.

I live with an oak coffee table
beside my bed where
my silver-framed clock ticks hard
through the night
like my cat when she purrs.

And there is a radio on the table
where I put my glasses; a scarf,
a bottle of lotion
and also in my room, two lamps.

I live now not as I lived before
I saw the dark disc as a shadow just under
my gracefully curving clavicle
on a sheet of film on the doctor's viewing
       box.

Perhaps it was not mine?
I never questioned it. I could
feel it bear on a nerve in my neck.

I knew kneading clay did not produce
    that pain.
I memorized the contour of that tumor
in a moment.
Later, it shrank.

How I live now is not
as I lived before
pictures showed another disc
far in the interior of my brain
a tiny thing in a silent place
as alien as a fleet of spaceships
bearing on earth from the sky.

I do not live as I lived before
the weeks I lay once a day
on a shining steel table
gazing into the eye of an electron
    accelerator
surely I was set alight and glowed
with a blue halo in the darkness.

Nights my mind raced to the stars and back
I watched from the morning star in the
    Eastern sky
and wept in myself as the sun rose—
for loves to be given up, for innocence, for
    my life.

Those nights were warm.
When they grew colder
I covered myself with my blanket
as I watched the sky.
The trees behind my house
turned orange and amber and gold
a-blazing against the day's blue.
Autumn storms tore down the leaves
and I trod on them in the street,
feeling the falling, the dying,
the death of the year, and I wept.

Now in December at Christmas
the temperature is ten below zero
and every window is covered with
frost, with crystals, lines, mysterious
scratchings from the arctic.
The dense air seeps through the cracks
around the windows and steals
under the edge of my blanket.

2.

I wake every morning
hating it
with my stomach jumping
before I've had a chance to think
of anything I awake non-thinking and I am
like a small animal backed into the corner
of a cage to escape from the hand
clutching,
reaching through the wire door
I feel the power of the hand's grasp
and fear it
without knowing what the power is.

Waking, I test my body
part of it I know
part I do not know
how has it changed in the night?
My body acts in ways that
indicate a stranger is in me
a different stranger every day.

I fear that stranger,
with its allusions to change,
to death.
I feel uncertain of whom I am,
for sure; not in the existential sense
of the shifting abstraction of *I*,
but because in concrete fact my body has
     changed,
my cells displaced by thoughtless strangers
     who
move at will, rob me of food and function,
who with their appetites,
can replace me. The me that can
see and talk and move and be a *person:*
replaced by masses of cells
taking up their stations and eating from me.

I feel the difference. I question the
     admission
of new sensations, without thinking. I know
when the stranger knocks at the door.

As a child of ten in my bath
I saw the first bristles of hair
and pretended I did not
saw the enlarged nipples
and pretended I did not

and then the blood flowed
and I could no longer deny
womanhood.

With time, I learned that the breasts,
the hair, the blood and the source itself
were me and so
now shall I admit the stranger
at the door the angel when
it lifts the knocker
now must I learn to become one with
    death?

Katherine Lesses
Cambridge, Massachusetts

CHAPTER SEVEN

Dying: Causes, Trajectories, and Stages

We can become philosophical about death and being dead. It is more difficult to become philosophical about the process of dying, because for so many people the process involves pain, extreme discomfort, and often feelings of hopelessness and depression. But as in everything else, there are immense individual differences in the way people die. Men die sooner than women, but not in all societies; the poor die sooner than the wealthy, but not in all instances; those who smoke die sooner than those who abstain, but not in all cases. We are all entitled to one life—and one death. When we die, what we die from, and how we die vary; what is invariable is that we die.

WHAT CAUSES DEATH?

What influences your life expectancy? Is it your genetic inheritance? Your mother's health and nutritional habits when she was carrying you *in utero?* Your own early and subsequent health and nutrition? The psychological stresses that you encounter and your methods of coping with them? Your medical care? Your inclination to overeat and put on weight? To smoke? To drink heavily? To lead a sedentary life with minimal exercise? Is it the air and water contaminants where you live? The risks required of you in your work? The risks in the leisure activities you pursue? Your use of preventive medical resources? Your exposure to unsanitary conditions? Your access to and utilization of a good health care system? Chance factors?

All of the above—and more than the above—contribute to the determination of how long you will live. To some extent, you can affect how long you will live. You can make certain decisions about your diet, your health care, the risks you take when you work or drive or play, your visits to physicians. You can make important changes in your life: reduce your stress at work by changing jobs, move out of a community where air pollution is high. But to some extent, you have nothing to say about how long you live: your genetic inheritance and your mother's health during her pregnancy, for example, are beyond your control.

Although most people would agree that the conditions listed above influence life expectancy, other influences are considerably more controversial. Would good behavior lengthen your life or evil behavior shorten it? Would a hex placed on you shorten your life? Even if you didn't know about it? If so, by whom? Your own psychological forces or some outside entity?

In some cultures today, it is believed that disease occurs because of the ill wishes of enemies and that cure must be brought about either by propitiating those enemies or by rallying one's own gods on one's behalf. Among Africans "the commonest cause [of death] is believed to be magic, sorcery, and witchcraft" (Mbiti, 1970, pp. 203–204). Among 47 cultures for which Simmons (1945) could find data, 17 regarded death as unnatural (for example, the result of hexes, witchcraft, supernatural interventions), and 26 others only partially accepted the idea that death was a natural event.

For example, the Anggor tribe of New Guinea perceive death *only* as resulting from active aggression of particular persons. An anthropologist investigating 177 deaths in this area found that 72% were unequivocally attributed to sorcery; another 15% were attributed to homicide, which is interpreted there as a kind of sorcery; the remaining deaths were considered to result from epidemics, intervention of spirits, and old age, which is itself believed to be the result of a kind of sorcery (Huber, 1972). Similarly, the Squamish, a Native American tribe, believed that each human being served as host to a spirit and that, if not treated well or sometimes for other reasons, the spirit might decide to punish its host by being violent and sometimes causing death (Ryan, 1983–84). Other cultures, such as those living in Vanuatu, also assume that spirits can cause death, although they, like the Squamish, were Christianized a long time ago (Rodman & Rodman, 1983–84).

Nor are we, in North America, immune to this kind of thinking. Some individuals today see length of life as caused in part by rewards or punishments for good or evil behavior. When asked whether "most people who live to be 90 years old or older must have been morally good people," just over one-third of a carefully selected mixed ethnic sample answered affirmatively (Kalish & Reynolds, 1981).

Your beliefs about what factors influence your life expectancy are going to influence your behavior, and your willingness to alter your behavior in directions that will increase your life expectancy says a great deal about how much you value long life in comparison with other satisfactions.

Death Rates and Causes Here, There, and Then

The life expectancy of a girl who was born in 1982 is over 78 years; her male counterpart has a 50/50 chance of living until just under the age of 71. At the other end of the life spectrum, a 65-year-old woman is likely to live another 19 years, and a 65-year-old man another 14½ years. If you are Black or other non-White, your life expectancy at birth is four or five years less, but if you are Black or other non-White and 75 years old, your life expectancy is a few months longer (*Statistical Bulletin*, Metropolitan Life Foundation, January–June, 1983).

All the above figures are substantially higher than the 51 years for new-born girls and 48 years for newborn boys reported for 1900. Not only has general life expectancy increased greatly over this period but the differential between males and females has also increased. Much of the increase in life expectancy, however, has occurred because of reductions in infant mortality, childhood deaths, and maternal deaths in childbirth. Thus, the increase in life expectancy during the same period for White men age 40 has been around 6 years, and for 40-year-old White women nearly 11. In other words, in 1900 a 40-year-old White man could expect to live until he was about 68; by 1979 this had increased only to 74. For White women, the comparable figure went from 69 to slightly over 80 (*Statistical Bulletin*, Metropolitan Life Foundation, July–September 1979 and January–June 1983).

If we continue back as far as prehistoric times, we find that the best estimate of life expectancy is about 18 years, with many and perhaps most deaths caused by violence (Dublin, 1951). In early Greece and Rome, people probably lived into their early twenties; by the Middle Ages this had extended in England into the early thirties (Lerner, 1970). As the age of expected death changed and as the common causes of death changed, the meaning of death and the appropriate care of the dying also changed.

The reduction in infant mortality has been considerable. In the United States, the death rate for White infants, those under 1 year of age, declined by nearly 75% during a 40-year period, from over 43 per 1000 live births in 1940 to just over 11 per 1000 live births in 1979 (*Statistical Abstracts*, 1982–83). The large number of infant deaths in earlier times is one reason women had many more pregnancies then than today. The typical married couple who lived to their early forties were very likely to have lost at least one child by epidemic, accident, or illness, and the deaths of two or three children were not at all unusual. This means that very few people reached adulthood without having lost a brother or sister. Most certainly the exposure to death at a personal level was immensely greater than today.

There is considerable variation in death rates among countries: the statistics of less developed nations today are comparable to those of other countries at the turn of the century. Rates and causes of death are influenced by climate, health care availability, public health practices, food supply, sewage facilities, and so forth.

Social class also influences death rates. Among low-income persons, deaths occur more commonly during infancy, childhood, and the young adult years; many of these deaths are caused by gastrointestinal disease, the communicable diseases of childhood, influenza, and pneumonia—even though these illnesses have been virtually eliminated among persons with higher incomes (Lerner, 1970). Lack of access to health services and lack of awareness of preventive measures probably contribute to these data. However, members of the more affluent middle class are more susceptible to deaths from heart attack, stroke, and cancer in their middle and late years.

The blue-collar working class appears to escape both the early deaths of the low-income groups and the midlife deaths of the higher-income groups. Overall, it has the best mortality record (Lerner, 1970).

Just as death rates have changed with the decades, so has the predominancy of causes of death. In 1900, influenza and pneumonia were the major causes of death (just under 12% of all deaths), followed by tuberculosis (11%), gastritis and related diseases (8%), and heart disease (8%). Cancer was ranked eighth, with under 4%. By 1979, however, heart disease accounted for 38% of all deaths, and all major cardiovascular causes of death combined accounted for nearly half of all deaths; cancer was causing 21% of deaths, but pneumonia and influenza were causing fewer than 2½% of deaths, and tuberculosis caused just 1 death in 1000 (*Statistical Abstracts*, 1982–83).

As health problems are eliminated by medical research and treatment and improved care, life expectancy increases and the major causes of death change in nature. Thus, cancer was not a major cause of death a century ago because cancer is largely an illness of the elderly, and most people didn't live long enough to be susceptible to cancer—they died earlier from smallpox or tuberculosis or pneumonia. At the same time, there were probably fewer carcinogens created by human endeavors a century ago, although we do not know that for certain. This brings up an intriguing speculation: what will people die from when cancer and cardiovascular disease are eliminated?

Heavy smoking, working in a high-stress job, or living in a smoggy city is never listed as a cause of death, although numerous studies have investigated their effect on life expectancy (see Woodruff, 1977, for review). The destructive effects of long-term exposure to low levels of radiation are not attributed to "human error" or "mechanical error" but are hidden away among the tens of thousands of cancer deaths. Obviously, what we consider to be a recordable cause of death is the result of our cultural values; we tend, for example, to look to an illness or medical model.

Beneath the Statistics

Beneath each statistic on causes of death are real people who have died in real ways. Somehow large numbers of deaths can turn the human reality of death into an abstraction. One death of one person, especially of one person who has made some impact on your own life, is very real.

Similarly, the vast arrays of numbers about causes of death can also become very real if we give some thought to what each cause of death means to the person who is dying, to that person's family and friends, and to those who are caring for the dying person.

First, the cause of death says a great deal about the extent to which dying is accompanied by pain and suffering. This is not simply a matter of sudden death versus nonsudden death. It is a question of what hurts and how much it hurts, of what discomforts there may be—such as difficulty in breathing, reduced ability to walk or talk, incontinence—and how long and with what intensity these discomforts endure.

Second, the probable health care program develops directly from the cause of death. What kinds of medications are necessary, and what kinds are encouraged? What side effects, both physical and psychological, do these medications have? What kinds of care can occur at home, and what kinds require hospitalization?

Third, what is the person capable of doing during the living-dying interval? With some terminal illnesses, the individual can pursue normal tasks for a long time. With other conditions, normal tasks slowly or, sometimes, suddenly become impossible to accomplish.

Fourth, the dying person's self-concept depends to an appreciable extent on the nature of the terminal condition. With some kinds of treatment, secondary effects, such as loss of hair, chronic fatigue, or vomiting and extreme stomach upset, are common. Besides affecting behavior in the obvious ways, these affect a person's self-concept—for example, the willingness to enter into social activities and the ability to continue to view oneself as a normal person with normal difficulties.

Fifth, the cause of death influences the ways in which others perceive the dying person. Some people, because of their health, are immediately recognized as being very sick; others can be very sick but not have their sickness visible. Some forms of death are frightening to others: cancer is still perceived, though not always consciously, as contagious, and many people will avoid cancer patients; stroke victims who cannot speak or whose bodies are no longer under their control are also distressing to their friends and family.

And, of course, there is great variability in what happens within any single cause of death. There are many kinds of cancer, each with its own range of possible medical and psychological occurrences. The same can be said of each kind of illness or other death-causing condition.

Thus, all deaths, regardless of cause, have certain qualities in common; deaths from the same cause have additional qualities in common. And at the same time, among persons dying from a particular cause, there is a great range of possible health-related and behavioral kinds of responses, feelings, and events.

Causes of Death and How We Live

"While we can readily claim that dying is a process that is fully as complicated as living, because it *is* a part of living, to say that people die as they have lived is from a psychological viewpoint wholly meaningless" (Weisman, 1972, p. 122). Throughout our lives, our behavior shows reasonable consistency, so that it is moderately predictable; and throughout our lives, our behavior shows reasonable inconsistency, so that it is moderately unpredictable. Like any kind of behavior, our dying process is both consistent and inconsistent with our previous behavior.

One factor that influences how we die is often ignored, although it is overwhelmingly important: what we die from. Death can occur through a lengthy illness or a sudden illness, through a condition that enables us to continue to function or one that reduces our functioning greatly, through so-called natural causes or through accidents or suicide, through a painful condition or through a relatively painless condition. I might fare amazingly well after a sudden coronary—pick up the pieces of my life when I leave the hospital and reengage in my previous activities until a subsequent heart attack causes my death two years later—but I might fall apart in the face of a disease that is progressively crippling. You, in contrast, perhaps show tremendous spirit with your crippling illness, but you could not handle the anxiety of knowing that a sudden second heart attack could strike without warning. The truth is, perhaps surprisingly, that we have almost no information on how or even whether different kinds of people cope with some kinds of deaths better or less well than with other kinds. However, there are numerous writings concerning the psychosocial factors that surround the specific conditions that cause death. These range from a description of the 14th-century plague, the Black Death, that wiped out at least one-fourth of the population of Europe (Langer, 1964) to a brief paper describing the conditions under which 51 infants were dying from hyaline membrane disease (Morgan, Buchanan, & Abram, 1976) to a sophisticated study on the psychosocial components of cancer deaths (Weisman & Worden, 1975).

THE DYING TRAJECTORY

Claudia Teder was diagnosed as having terminal cancer when she was 48 years old; her prognosis, assuming that she underwent radiation treatment, was for a probable life expectancy of eight to ten months, and she was told that she would probably spend the last three or four weeks in the hospital. After two treatments, she decided to discontinue the program; she returned to work, remained home with her husband and son, and was found dead one Sunday morning after a party about a year later.

Ed Briscoe had a heart attack at 41 and another at 51; following each of these, he returned to almost full activity. His third attack, at age 58, came without additional warning, and he died before the ambulance arrived.

Harvey Muller, a 33-year-old policeman, was called to break up a fight between a husband and wife. As he arrived at the scene, the wife yelled at him to leave; he didn't, and she shot him through the head. He died immediately.

Laurene Marks reached her 80th birthday in good health, but shortly thereafter she complained about not feeling well. The subsequent diagnosis was cancer; because of her age, she and the physician agreed not to attempt an operation. She then accepted a modified treatment program. Her health deteriorated very slowly, and she remained active for two more years, then housebound for another six months. Finally, just before her 83rd birthday, she died in the hospital.

The dying process of each of these four persons could be charted across time. Set up a graph with *time* along the horizontal axis and *nearness to death* along the vertical axis. Then chart the condition of each of these persons across time. This curve is known as the **dying trajectory** (Glaser & Strauss, 1968).

The purpose of understanding the dying trajectory is most certainly not to play statistical games with people's lives. Glaser and Strauss point out that people who are dying, their family members and friends, and the relevant health professionals anticipate the dying trajectory of the ill and make their plans around it. Work associates, political supporters, or more casual friends might also wish to understand the death trajectory: how long will the dying person remain alive, in reasonable health, able to care for himself or herself; how is the death most likely to occur; how probable is the death to occur as predicted?

When the trajectory is as anticipated, the various participants in the process are prepared, both psychologically and in terms of providing care, for what occurs. When the assumed trajectory does not take place, people, left unprepared, experience additional dismay and stress—even though the dying person might be living a longer and healthier life than was expected (Glaser & Strauss, 1968). There is also the possibility that either a patient's acceptance of a physician's projected dying trajectory or a patient's own fantasized trajectory will become a self-fulfilling prophecy. The expectations that others have of us are powerful forces in molding our behavior and attitudes; perhaps these expectations can influence the duration of the living-dying interval as well.

Sometimes, of course, the dying person and those in her or his environment will anticipate differing trajectories. For example, the terminal patient may assume that death will come in about two or three years after a lengthy period of mild discomfort; the medical staff may believe that death is much more imminent and that the discomfort will be much more acute. These differing perceptions can lead to a range of problems: the patient may be unwilling to follow a particular treatment program, or he or she may feel betrayed by and angry with the health professionals when (and if) they are found to be correct. Ironically, when the patient far outlives the prognosis of the physicians, it is not unusual for the latter to be upset, irritated, or embarrassed, even though they may be pleased for the patient's sake. After all, none of us likes to be in substantial error in matters that involve our presumed competence.

Since most deaths in the United States and Canada are caused not by those respiratory ailments that used to affect people of all ages but by chronic degenerative diseases that affect mainly the elderly, the nature of the dying process and, therefore, the care of the dying have changed over the decades. For example, some forms of cancer lead to a living-dying interval of several years, during much of which time the patient can go about his or her everyday tasks as before; dying from a stroke may also permit a lengthy living-dying interval, although many stroke deaths occur very quickly. However, dying from influenza or pneumonia normally means a dying trajectory of two or three weeks to six or eight weeks, during which time the patient remains too sick to participate in normal activities.

Deaths Sudden and Not Sudden, Expected and Not Expected

The commonly accepted ideal death, if there is one, would be a healthy 85-year-old's dying suddenly of a heart attack that has occurred without causing pain. The trajectory is like half a rectangle: a straight line across time drops immediately to the baseline at age 85. When asked which was more tragic, a sudden death or a slow death, half again as many people thought the latter was worse, although the differences diminished greatly with the increasing age of the respondent (Kalish & Reynolds, 1981).

Believing that a sudden death is preferable is based partly on the assumption that there is less pain in a sudden death. Moreover, because sudden deaths are often unexpected, a person is spared most of the anxiety and stress that develop from anticipating death. Even when sudden death can be anticipated—for example, by a coronary patient—the elimination of a long living-dying interval is often desired.

Deaths that are slow need not also be painful, either for the dying person or for family members. Sometimes, of course, the pain, both physical and emotional, is immense, and there is no real escape. "There is the slow, inexorable debilitation of a chronic illness or traumatic injury.... [The process] is worsened by . . . being forced to watch the disintegration and loss of the image of the loved one as he slowly dies" (Paulay, 1977–78, p. 173). This is the kind of death that we all fear.

The sudden-death trajectory, however, has many problems that are often ignored. It may be a cruel death for the survivors. Although they are spared the anguish of caring for the dying person, they are also prevented from preparing themselves for the death. The shock can be immense, since there has been no opportunity to become accustomed to the idea that the person is going to die. Denial is probably greater for the survivors of a sudden, unexpected death.

In addition, frequently there is unfinished business, especially if the dead person is not yet elderly. Perhaps arrangements for dying have not been made: there is no will; no one knows where the key to the safe-deposit box is; bankbooks are scattered about the house and office; many tasks related to business or family or household matters are still up in the air. And even more important, there is often unfinished personal business: goodbyes are not possible, old angers cannot be salved, unexpressed feelings can never be expressed. The survivors also have been cut off from doing the things they had planned to do and saying the things they had always planned to say.

Deaths from accidents, suicides, homicides, and natural disasters are often sudden and unexpected, although sometimes the victim holds onto life for weeks, months, or even longer. Although these deaths are usually sudden, they are often regarded as particularly tragic or unpleasant for several reasons: they are mutilating; they often occur to people who are young or who are seen as dying prematurely; and they are often seemingly unnecessary or absurd.

The family members of these victims are frequently concerned with the possibility that they have some kind of responsibility for the death. "I knew she was depressed, but I didn't think she would do this!" "I tried to tell him not to drive home when he was so tired." "I did my best to keep him away from those people." "I just had the feeling that she shouldn't have gone to work—there was something in the air."

Influencing the Trajectory

Many factors besides the nature of the health condition itself influence the course of the dying trajectory. Moreover, even the "nature" of the health condition itself isn't inevitable and unchangeable—a condition forced on a passive organism by some all-powerful external source.

Some of the influences are obvious: the previous health of the individual, the extent of medical care, the nutrition—the usual considerations that facilitate good health in some individuals and less adequate health in others. In addition, misdiagnosis and inappropriate health care and personal care can shorten life expectancy and, therefore, change the shape of the trajectory.

Undoubtedly the will to live and the will to die also influence the dying trajectory:

> One young man, recently a father, was explicitly told that his physical condition offered no hope of living more than a few additional months. Ten years and many operations later, he explained his pulling through as due to his intense desire to know his child.

Sometimes the will to live may be successful only for a brief period:

> The mother of a law student had an extremely serious heart attack two weeks before her daughter was to take the bar exam; the young woman telephoned the hospital (it was in a city 1500 miles away) each day to learn that her mother was still alive and would apparently live another day. The woman took the exam, then flew to see her mother, who died the day she arrived. When she was telling me about the experience, the lawyer felt certain that her mother willed herself to stay alive until the exam was over—knowing that, had she died sooner, her daughter would have come to her funeral rather than have taken the bar exam.

There's no way, with our present knowledge, to "prove" that the young man lived because he wanted to know his child or that the older woman held on to help her daughter through the exam period. After all, others have had equal reason to continue to live but haven't succeeded. Nonetheless, many of us find that we do believe these accounts—perhaps because we want to believe them.

Some evidence suggests that the extent to which people are in control of their environments and their selves is a major factor in their will to live and in how long they live. Recall that hopelessness and helplessness are often proposed as the feelings that precipitate suicide. It would seem quite possible that the same feelings would lead to premature death, which can be interpreted as a kind of suicide or self-destructiveness.

The term **learned helplessness** is used to refer to an emotion and related behavior that occur when people believe there is nothing they can do to avoid punishment or to obtain satisfaction. Such individuals anticipate that, no matter what they do, the situation will not change. This condition can readily lead to depression (Seligman, 1975). Robert Kastenbaum, a highly creative scholar whose work on death dates back over 25 years, and his wife

Beatrice (1971), have suggested the concept of learned *hopelessness*, in which people come to have little faith in the possibility of the system ever changing. It is to avoid these feelings of helplessness and hopelessness that some physicians prefer that their patients not learn that they are terminally ill. They believe that after hope dies, the patient dies.

How can learned helplessness and hopelessness be reversed? One likely possibility is that these feelings develop not from a lack of knowledge that we will die but from an inability to make relevant decisions or remain in control of our behavior and functioning. Therefore, it would seem very possible that an accurate knowledge of the significance of our health condition would enable us to feel less helpless, especially if we are brought into the decision-making process.

Also influencing the dying trajectory are the individual's personality and social relationships. One very significant and sophisticated study developed an approach, based on careful analysis of the patient's health in relation to the extensive statistics available on cancer patients, to determine the probable life expectancy of different cancer patients (Weisman & Worden, 1975). The authors then monitored the patients to see whether they lived longer or died sooner than expected. Their conclusions were intriguing:

> *Longer survivals* are associated with patients who have good relationships with others and who manage to preserve a reasonable degree of intimacy with family and friends until the very last. They ask for and receive much medical and emotional support. As a rule, they accept the reality of serious illness, but still do not believe that death is inevitable. . . . They are seldom deeply depressed but may voice resentment about various aspects of their treatment and illness. Whatever anger is displayed . . . does not alienate others but commands their attention. They may be afraid of dying alone and untended, so they refuse to let others pull away without taking care of their needs.
>
> *Shorter survivals* occur in patients who report poor social relationships, starting with early separations from their family of origin and continuing throughout life. Sometimes they have diagnosed psychiatric disorders, but almost as often talk about repeated mutually destructive relationships with people through the years. At times, they have considered suicide. Now, when treatment fails, depression deepens, and they become highly pessimistic. . . . They want to die—a finding that often reflects more conflict than acceptance [p. 71].

One article began by describing numerous cancer studies that seemed to show a connection between expressing anger "toward not only their disease but their doctors" (Holden, 1978, p. 1364) and living longer, as well as between denial, despair, and limited supportive relationships and living more briefly. The author presented alternative physiological and biochemical explanations of how these correlations might be produced—giving full consideration to the possibility of the placebo effect. She also explored the alternative that the research was faulty and that in fact there are no psychological or social predictors of cancer or cancer deaths. Her overall evidence, however, appeared to support the idea that life expectancy is affected by these psychosocial variables.

Another study of women dying of breast cancer confirmed these results. Those who lived longest not only were more demanding of their physicians and less satisfied with their treatment but also were rated as less well adjusted, more anxious, and more hostile (Derogatis, Abeloff, & Melisaratos, 1979).

Leo Durocher, the well-known baseball player and manager, once stated that "nice guys finish last." Apparently "nice guys" die first, since those who live longer appear to be able to ask for help, to make demands, and to express resentment, *but* they do it in a way that "does not alienate others but commands their attention." Most probably, people who are too "nice" don't make the demands on others that they really require to have their health needs satisfied; at the same time, some people who seem "nice" are probably depressed and suppressing their underlying anger.

Labeled "Dying"

At some point in the dying trajectory, the individual is regarded as "dying." The label does not necessarily get applied all at once, nor do all important persons use it at the same time. Sometimes, for example, people don't agree on a prognosis, or one or more individuals retain hope of recovery long after the others have given up. But eventually everyone concerned applies the label.

By the time this occurs, the dying person may welcome it as an opportunity to stop fighting for life, to eliminate some of the discomforting and exhausting treatments, to fall back into passivity. Frequently the individual is both tired and weak, does not feel well, and may be ready to die. It is not unheard of for someone to remain alive not because he or she truly wishes to but because some member of the family is not ready for death to occur.

In addition, once a person is labeled dying, certain freedoms are granted. In some hospitals, visiting hours become more flexible, and occasionally children, who are otherwise forbidden to see the patient, are spirited up back staircases. Patients' complaints may be responded to and their irritability ignored. Family and friends become more solicitous; people from the past, especially close relatives who live some distance away, make a significant effort to visit. If not in a hospital, recently forbidden foods, tobacco, alcoholic beverages may be returned, since "it doesn't make much difference now."

Along with the prerogatives, however, come some intensified problems. There is a definite tendency for us, the not-yet-dying, to isolate ourselves from the imminently dying. Their dying impinges on our consciousness, cuts through our denial, and is often painful in many ways, the more so if we love them. Therefore, many dying persons receive fewer visits from friends and family after the label is applied.

Health professionals may also reduce their visits, partly for the same reasons as family members and partly because they view their own skills as best utilized for patients who can still recover. Despite pronouncements to the contrary, medical training focuses on cure more than on care, and

physicians often underestimate the importance of their presence for someone even after the label of dying has been applied.

THE DYING AS NONPERSONS AND THEIR SOCIAL VALUE

The labeling process can transform the dying person into a nonperson—not
officially, of course, but in the eyes of the hospital staff and even, to some
extent, in the eyes of family and friends. You can discuss nonpersons even
while they are present, because nonpersons are incapable of hearing. Not
that these things are done on purpose or with malice; they just happen.

Besides, nonpersons don't remind us as much of our own eventual fate.
The dying process and death of another inevitably remind us that we are also
mortal. Becker (1973) has described the powerful fear of decay and vulnerability that each of us feels, and it is felt especially in the face of death. If we
can only depersonalize the dying person, then we are less likely to have to
deal with the obvious: the state that person is in is the state I will be in
eventually. I don't want to be helpless or hopeless, vulnerable or at the mercy
of powers beyond my control—like this dying person. By making the dying
person a nonperson, I don't need to contemplate such terrible possibilities At
least, I can postpone them a little longer. Even if Becker's theories exaggerate
what most people actually experience, some of the process commonly
occurs.

What makes a particular life valuable? Of course, the rhetoric is that all
lives are valuable, probably equally valuable, but is that true for you? Is it
true for most people? Probably not. Most of us place a higher value on those
persons who represent certain valued characteristics. What are some of
these values?

First, people in our society place a great deal of emphasis on the future; we
believe in deferring present gratifications for the future—in planning for the
future and not simply living in the moment. As part of this future-centered-
ness, we value those who appear likely to make a substantial future contribution to the society and, to some extent, to themselves.

Second, we value people who are presently productive and achieving. The
productivity may be financial or creative, or it may involve the production of
useful services. Although we also respect past productivity, we seem to place
much more emphasis on present and future achievements.

Third, we respect people who are liked by others, who have many friends.

Fourth, we respond to physical attractiveness and sexuality, which are
personified by the young and the healthy.

Fifth, we admire knowledge, and we may be especially responsive to
scientific and technological knowledge.

Sixth, influence and power certainly receive respect.

Seventh, we like people who can enjoy life, if their enjoyment does not
violate our sense of ethics and morality.

Eighth, we like people who make us feel good, who don't make us feel
guilty.

Ninth, we value persons who do the "right things" in life, however we may define those. Certainly people who get into knife fights, who drive while drunk, who attempt suicide, are not people we value. We may understand the psychological or social dynamics that made them who they are, but they aren't people we normally respect.

Examine these nine criteria, or whatever other criteria you wish to include, with an individual who is dying in mind. There isn't much about the dying person to be valued; if the dying person is elderly, his or her social value has probably been low for some time.

The death of a highly valued person makes a greater impression on the health caretakers than that of someone with little value. An elderly wino, who has been in and out of the hospital for various causes for several years, is brought in dead; he has no known family. His death is not likely to upset the hospital staff. But the 25-year-old mother who has fought a valiant battle with leukemia and finally succumbs will cause grief for everyone (Glaser & Strauss, 1964). Unlike the elderly man, the young mother is at least valued for being productive (being a mother), for the physical attractiveness and sexuality of youth, and for having done the "right" things in life.

STAGES OF DYING

- A middle-aged man walks into the hospital clutching a paperback book; tomorrow morning he will have exploratory surgery for a possible cancer.
- A young poet, knowing he is to die within approximately two years, arranges for his remaining time to be filmed; in the film, he comments bitterly that his anger about dying was discounted by a nurse who told him that he was "in the *anger* stage."
- In a small California resort town, 3000 people jam the local auditorium to hear a psychiatrist talk about dying.

There is little doubt that the most familiar name associated with death and dying is that of the Swiss-born psychiatrist Elisabeth Kübler-Ross. Her book *On Death and Dying* and her innumerable lectures, workshops, and films have been a powerful force to raise the general consciousness of people about the meaning of death and the concerns of the dying. Kübler-Ross' major theoretical contribution has been the development of five stages of dying, and these deserve careful examination.

Her first stage in the dying process is **denial and isolation.** Almost all patients, she points out, make use of denial both early in their awareness of their dying and from time to time later. It is not only a familiar but frequently a healthy response to a highly stressful situation; it acts as a temporary buffer to protect the individual from the shock of what is to be faced.

Later in the dying process, people may use the defense mechanism of isolation, which refers to the elimination of the emotional aspects of thoughts or experiences, while retaining memory of the occurrence. Though a kind of denial, isolation permits the patient to "talk about his health and his illness, his mortality and his immortality as if they were twin brothers permitted to exist side by side, thus facing death and still maintaining hope" (Kübler-Ross, 1969, p. 37).

Following denial and isolation, the dying person arrives at the stage of **anger,** which includes rage, envy, and resentment. If denial said "It can't be me," anger asks "Why me?" Family members and health caretakers find the stage of anger very difficult, since the anger is likely to flare up for a variety of reasons, not all of them overtly associated with the person's health.

Sometimes the anger is expressed directly through shouting; other times its expression is indirect, through complaints about the care; still other times its expression takes the form of bitterness about not being around to enjoy next summer or about having been abandoned by God. Since hospital staff prefer to operate a smooth-running institution, they may resent anger and either ignore the patient or respond in punitive or defensive ways. Although this resentment is understandable, the reasons for the dying person's anger are also understandable, and after all, it isn't the staff person who is going to die shortly.

Bargaining is the third stage. The patient attempts to postpone the death or reduce the pain or gain some extra strength. "Most bargains are made with God and are usually kept a secret" (Kübler-Ross, 1969, p. 74). When I was an undergraduate, a professor told us that he had been drowning and had promised God that if he lived, he would become a devout Catholic; he was saved, and he fulfilled his part of the bargain. Extremely few individuals, of course, find their offer to bargain so readily accepted.

When it becomes obvious that bargaining is not going to work, the dying person enters the stage of **depression.** Denial is no longer possible to sustain; anger has dissipated; bargaining has failed. Death is recognized to be inevitable, and the feelings of loss become overwhelming. Depression has been defined as an emotional state that involves sadness, gloominess, pessimism regarding the future, and often feelings of guilt and personal worthlessness. We have all experienced some degree of sadness or depression when losses have occurred. We feel heavy, lack the desire to be involved, wish to avoid activity, often feel sorry for ourselves. Even though we know that our "down" mood won't last, we may feel too lethargic to do very much.

Depression doesn't last forever; eventually the dying person works through the acute sense of loss, finishes mourning for himself or herself, and arrives at the stage of **acceptance.** Acceptance need not be a happy stage: Kübler-Ross describes it as being "almost void of feelings" (1969, p. 100). The dying person has now become extensively disengaged from most of what goes on in the world. Now is not the time to be stirred up—it is the time to be left alone. Energy may be low, and only a few persons are still welcome visitors. Like the person about to retire who has lost interest in the job while finding increasing interest in retirement activities, the dying person is losing interest in this world and may find increasing interest in the existence still to come—however that existence is defined. For those who do not believe in a future existence, the new engagement can be with sleep and rest, with cessation of pain, or with reminiscence.

The person who has accepted death is no longer fearful; time can now be used for whatever is both possible and desired, since the anxiety of handling denial, anger, or depression is no longer incapacitating. This stage, according to Kübler-Ross (1969), is the desired goal of dying persons.

Significance of Kübler-Ross' Stages

Kübler-Ross' book appeared at just the right time. People, especially those who had been caring for the dying, were ready to read something about death and dying—especially something that would help them make sense of the process. *On Death and Dying* did just that: "Many people have felt remarkably better after becoming acquainted with the stage theory of dying. Anxiety and lack of cognitive structure are replaced by the security of knowledge" (Kastenbaum, 1975, p. 40).

Her book also appeared at the time that people were expressing displeasure about the impersonality of health services and care and the apparent victory of technology, especially medical technology, over humanistic concern. Kübler-Ross very clearly came down on the side of humanistic involvement and in opposition to impersonal efficiency and extensive use of medical technology (Klass, 1981–82).

This was also an era in which there was considerable discussion of "masculine" sides and "feminine" sides of people and of the need to permit the feminine side to emerge more fully, in both men and women. Kübler-Ross emphasized this feminine side, and it was probably no accident that her early audiences were constituted largely of nurses who, having had to perform the traditional female role in relationship to physicians, were eager to find an avenue to show that their role was extremely important in its own right and not simply as a "handmaiden" of the physician (based on Klass, 1981–82).

Limitations of Stage Theory

However, in some ways the book made too much sense, and Kübler-Ross' subsequent popularity as a speaker added to this. The stages were so appealing that many people accepted them as gospel, as immutable. They regarded the stages as a natural progression through which virtually everyone passed; patients who did not pass through the stages and did not arrive at "acceptance" before death were sometimes seen as failing in their tasks. This may seem strange, but it occurred. A nurse would become angry with a patient who "regressed" from depression to anger; a patient's relative would question why the patient was so long in the denial stage.

Some experts in the field claimed that Kübler-Ross' stages eventually led to a "new form of depersonalized care for terminally ill persons" (Fitchett, 1980, p. 1). One experienced chaplain pointed out that the stages gave the health care workers something to do and reduced their own feelings of helplessness; he stated that there was often more concern for getting the patient on to the next stage than for helping the dying person deal with his denial or depression. Without realizing it, many hospital staff members, and even some family members of the patients, saw dying persons who did not go through the stages at the right pace as being "management problems" (Fitchett, 1980).

Several questions have emerged:

First, do these stages actually exist; that is, do most observant people notice them?

Second, are the stages actually a natural progression?

Third, does virtually everyone pass through them?

Fourth, are these the only significant emotional responses that people have during the dying process?

Fifth, is it emotionally adaptive to pass through these stages and, particularly, to arrive at acceptance?

Sixth, should some therapeutic intervention be offered to help people pass through the stages and arrive at acceptance?

First, do the stages actually exist? They most certainly exist as familiar responses exhibited by dying persons, but they don't appear to exist as reliably recognized, nonoverlapping occurrences. One investigator distributed verbatim copies of one of the cases reported in Kübler-Ross' original book (1969) to a number of health care professionals and students and asked them what stage the person was in at the time. Just over 25% of the respondents recognized the stage as acceptance, which was Kübler-Ross' description; almost as many referred to it as denial. Interestingly enough, when the responses of experienced health professionals were separated from those of inexperienced health caretakers and students, a higher proportion among the former group thought the patient was in the denial stage than in the acceptance stage (Fitchett, 1980).

Second, are the stages a natural progression? The answer again seems to be in the negative. A review of research evidence concluded that the stages were not a natural progression and did not occur in a majority of instances (Schulz & Aderman, 1974). On the basis of his extensive clinical work, Shneidman (1973) stated that he observed frequent alternation between acceptance and denial, rather than a unidirectional movement through five stages.

Third, does virtually everyone pass through them? And fourth, are these the only significant emotional responses? The consensus is that different people die in different ways and experience a variety of feelings during the process: hope, fear, curiosity, envy, apathy, relief, even anticipation.

The answers to the last two questions are more complex. For some people and under some circumstances, acceptance of death is certainly the way to an appropriate death. For others, it is not. Perhaps anger, even fury, is the most appropriate way to die: what a mockery death is; how destructive it is; how absurd it is—there is nothing good about death, at least about *my* death, and I have no intention of being peaceful or submissive or accepting! Two quotations seem appropriate, the first from Ecclesiastes 9:3 and the second from Dylan Thomas:

> This is the root of the evil in all that happens under the sun, that one fate comes to all. Therefore, men's minds are filled with evil and there is madness in their hearts while they live, for they know that afterward—they are off to the dead!

> Do not go gentle into that good night
> Old age should burn and rave at close of day
> Rage, rage against the dying of the light

In other words, death is so horrible that the only proper response is to be angry about dying. Is this the best way to die? That depends on the individual. Of course, dying peacefully and with acceptance is easier on the hospital staff and on family members and friends. It is a unique nurse or physician who is able to remain untouched by an angry dying patient—perhaps in part because the anger is often addressed directly to the medical treatment. How much more pleasant it is (although not without pain) to encounter someone who is no longer angry or blaming.

Sometimes the reason for not accepting death is quite different. Cornelius Ryan, a writer and historian who was dying of cancer, found that the medications he was taking were not only distorting his appearance but affecting his thought processes so that he couldn't write. Rather than exchange his writing competence for pain-free time, he stated "I shall try never to feel peaceful and pain-free again. . . . These symptoms . . . may be quite closely linked to death . . . . Fast-paced mental activity and constant pain are now my criteria for being well" ("The Longest War," 1979, p. 100). The decision to accept death and to die without pain may give way to higher priorities.

Kübler-Ross and many others appear to emphasize the importance of "giving in to death," of "accepting death," of "letting go." This may reflect the feminine side of people again, the willingness to be taken care of, and to refute the masculine side, the insistence on being in control (Klass, 1981–82). The issue of whether it is an appropriate task for health caretakers, or even family members and friends, to manipulate a person into "letting go" brings up the inevitable question: For whose benefit?

The final question concerns therapeutic intervention to move people through the five stages. There seems little doubt that this would be a misuse of therapy. Two of the purposes of most therapy are to enable people to feel better about themselves and to enable them to make choices for themselves. If, in this process, they move from denial through the next three stages to acceptance, that's fine; if they don't, that is all right also. What does become dangerous, however, is to assume that progressing through the five stages is *the* best procedure for all, or even for most, people and then to apply some program, no matter how well-meaning, to manipulate them through the stages.

Another matter is also important: we do not want to depersonalize dying people by placing them in a rigid system of classification and labeling them in terms of a category. To say literally or symbolically "Oh, I understand you, because you are in the anger stage" is to remove individuality from the dying person. It is comparable to the teaching physician who takes his students to visit a patient with pancreatic cancer and says "Now, here is a pancreatic cancer." Not true. Here is a human being who has pancreatic cancer. The difference is more than theoretical, since we respond to people and things according to the labels we assign them.

The evidence is far from all in. We don't know how "most people should die." Therefore, my own belief is that we are better off following Weisman's admonition to help people die appropriate deaths—to die as much as possible the way they want to die, rather than according to a preestablished scheme.

Part of the process of dying can be described under the needs of the dying, communication with the dying, and the tasks that the dying must accomplish. These will be discussed in the next chapter.

CHAPTER EIGHT

Needs and Tasks of the Dying

"It wasn't until I learned that I was going to die that I really began to live." Have you ever had the experience of leaving a house or a community that you loved in the belief that you would never return? If so, do you recall your thinking as you parted? Perhaps you looked around in an especially loving way; maybe you carefully made note of each important item in the house or attended to all the things you had noticed before and many you hadn't as you walked or drove around the community.

When you recognize that life is finite and that your life is very likely to end within a relatively brief and relatively predictable time, you begin to notice things that you have never noticed previously. You also begin to consider the uses of your time differently from the way you had, since time takes on new meanings—or perhaps intensifies older meanings. Your situation has changed, but you are still you.

THE NEEDS OF THE DYING

What are the needs of the dying? The question is no more difficult—nor any easier—than the question "What are the needs of people?" You would probably respond to the latter query in one of two ways. You might say that individual differences are so great that no one answer is possible; or you might outline some broad areas of needs—perhaps adding that great individual differences exist. But these two answers apply as well to the dying, who, despite the labeling, are presently living individuals; the difference between them and others is that their lives are influenced by the presumed imminence of their deaths.

When we consider the needs of the dying, we often think in terms of what can be done to facilitate "death with dignity" or a "good death." Perhaps we first need to recognize that "if the dying die with a degree of nobility, it will be mostly their doing in doing their own dying" (Ramsey, 1975, p. 82). We can help create the conditions in which an individual can live with dignity until death, but we can't *give* death with dignity.

And people who live in dignity are people who are living as much as possible the way they wish to live. Therefore, "death with dignity" or a "good death" is what Avery Weisman has termed an "appropriate death," which is dying—or, more properly, living the end of life—as much as possible the way the individual wishes. If providing the conditions to permit an appropriate death is the overall goal, what are the specific needs that must be satisfied to bring this about?

There are a number of systems that classify psychological needs, but the hierarchy of needs developed by humanistic psychologist Abraham Maslow is one of the best known and will be applied here to the dying person. Maslow's system of needs assumes that the more basic need must be reasonably well satisfied before the next (higher) need can receive attention (1970a), but we need not make this assumption. Instead, we'll just address his five need categories: physiological needs, safety and security needs, love and belonging needs, esteem and self-esteem needs, and self-actualization needs.

Physiological Needs

We all require food, air, temperature regulation, sleep, the avoidance of pain, and the opportunity for elimination. The dying are no different from the rest of us in requiring these things, except that the way they express their needs and the actions that must be taken to satisfy the needs may be different. Although there is nothing about being in the living-dying interval as such that influences any of the needs, given health conditions can affect the extent of the need and the method for its satisfaction. For example, certain illnesses may make breathing difficult, so the dying person may require some help in breathing, but *not because* of dying. Similarly, diet is affected by one's health condition, so that appetite is likely to diminish with illness. Dying persons often eat less or are put on special diets, but again, not because they are dying. Knowing that someone is dying gives us only the slightest hint about what changes will occur in the nature, intensity, or satisfaction of physiological needs.

Dying is often uncomfortable and certainly can be painful—sometimes horribly painful—but as indicated above, it is not dying itself that produces the pain, but the condition causing the dying. Pain is often much more severe in health problems that don't result in death. The classic study of the painfulness of dying was reported by Dr. William Osler, a famous physician, in 1904. He stated "I have careful reports of about 500 death-beds, studied particularly with reference to the modes of death and the sensations of dying ... 90 suffered bodily pain of one sort or another" (p. 19). Although the causes of death have changed enough since Osler's time that there might be increased pain during dying, the use of analgesics and improved medical techniques should substantially diminish the proportion of individuals who suffer moderate or great pain in dying. Of course, pain is so subjective that what constitutes "moderate or great pain" is open to considerable disagreement.

Safety and Security Needs

"If a patient asks, 'What do I have?' he usually means, 'Can I count on you?'"
(Weisman, 1972, p. 19). A dying person has as much need as anyone else—
perhaps more need—to feel safe and secure. Of course, the causes of feeling
unsafe and insecure may be different.

The dying person's feelings of insecurity seem to have two major sources:
lack of trust in the health caretaking operations and fear of abandonment.
Do you trust these virtual strangers—physicians, nurses, aides, orderlies,
dietitians, X-ray technicians, hospital administrators—and the health sciences in general, to be responsible for what happens to you? Although part of
the problem is simply whether you like them, it is more a question of
trust—perhaps even of faith. You don't need to believe that they will keep
you alive forever. Rather the question is whether you trust them to give you
appropriate care as long as you live under their guidance.

The other aspect of the need for safety and security is the feeling that you
can count on your physician to care for you and on your family and friends
not to abandon you. What does the feeling of abandonment cause? First of
all, fear. I am abandoned—I am alone—I am lonely—no one will help me—no
one cares. Second, it causes me to feel vulnerable, open to attack, unpro-
tected. Third, I will feel that I no longer have any control of what is happening. Fourth, we are angry when we are abandoned. It isn't fair. Why did all of
you leave me? Frustration often leads to aggression—that is, to anger,
among other reactions. And perhaps, fifth, abandonment leads to guilt. What
have I done to be abandoned? If only I hadn't done . . . or said . . . or been . . .

When we are dying, it is very easy to feel abandoned. Other people go on
about their business; visits become fewer and fewer; the world goes on
without us. How can that be? How can everything and everyone act as
though nothing were happening *when I am dying!*

Carrying one step further the concept of the need of the dying for safety
and security, Avery Weisman proposes that a dying person needs **safe conduct** (1977): cautious and prudent behavior and guidance through peril and
the unknown. (It does *not* mean playing it safe.) Although clinical medical
treatment can contribute to the patient's safe conduct, compassion and skill
in human relationships are also required. Weisman believes that, if the
professional health caretakers cannot offer adequate safe conduct, they
should transfer responsibility for this task to others.

Love and Belonging Needs

There is no such thing as being too sick or too near death to need love. It is
possible to be so uncomfortable or so confused that you can't respond to
love, or it is possible to be embarrassed by love. And it is also possible that
knowing your death will lead to the loss of loved ones is so painful that you
avoid offers of love. But dying a lonely death—abandoned, without love,
without anyone who cares—is often seen as the worst kind of death.

Love can come from many quarters, not only from family members and
close friends. Sometimes a physician, nurse, other hospital staff member, or

other health worker can express true concern and caring; a visit from a clergyman, a telephone call from a cousin across the country, or even the expressed fondness of a dog or cat can all provide a sense of being loved. Sometimes the dying person will need to reminisce about the former love of people who have died or are not available for other reasons.

Reminiscing is enriching in a variety of ways and can be helpful for people of any age and health status, though particularly so for the dying and, most likely, for the elderly dying. It enables people to focus on the times that were deeply satisfying, to remember themselves as whole and healthy, and to see their own histories as cohesive and meaningful. Sometimes reminiscing requires guidance, since it is possible to dwell on unpleasant and guilt-producing experiences. Most of us look into the future for hope, but the dying person does not have this option. His or her present life situation may offer little in personal satisfaction, other than a visit from a friend or an exchange with the nurse or an enjoyable television show. If anticipating the future seems futile and enjoying the present seems dubious, at least recalling the past can provide considerable pleasure.

Esteem and Self-Esteem Needs

Your esteem for me and my esteem for myself are based, to some extent, on past, present, and future accomplishments, on the degree to which I believe I am a "good human being," on how much others appear to like me, and—certainly in this society—on my competence and autonomy. As the dying process develops, I may become increasingly incapacitated, helpless, and dependent and, consequently, an increasing burden and financial drain on those I love. My need for esteem is unchanged, but my opportunities to have it satisfied have diminished. I may even welcome the thought of death because only death will remove me from this unwelcome situation.

As infants, we were taught to be in control of our bodies and ourselves. As very young children, we were proud of our ability to walk, to use the toilet properly, to eat by ourselves, to catch a ball. Our self-esteem depended in large measure on how well we could do these and similar things. We esteemed our control of self and our increasing independence and autonomy.

Look what happens during the dying process: More and more decisions are turned over to other people. If you are hospitalized or bedridden, some decisions are based on institutional policy and some are made for the convenience of others. Fatigue, pain, discomfort, and weakness require that others do things or make decisions that you could previously have done or decided for yourself. Physical strength and sexual activity, both symbols of competence, diminish greatly.

Other kinds of control also become more difficult. One of the most upsetting changes that some very sick people suffer is loss of sphincter control. Not only does this produce unpleasant odors and make social contacts more difficult, but it is also understandably perceived as a regression to childish, even infantile, behavior. Its arrival at a time when other kinds of competence and control are also diminishing makes its effect particularly distressing.

Also, knowing that you will be dead in the foreseeable future means that you must anticipate not merely diminishing competence and control but irreversible loss of competence and control. For some dying persons, it is the awareness of impending losses, even more than previous losses, that is so disturbing.

Furthermore, it doesn't make much difference who you were previously. If you were once great and powerful, you will probably receive some extra attention, but you still will have little control or competence. The fact that you wrote a great novel, discovered a gold mine in Nevada, owned a factory employing thousands of people, or coached a championship team is of little importance.

How can the dying try to retain self-esteem? One way might be to reminisce about events that enhanced self-esteem. Also important are accomplishments in the present that lead to self-esteem. For the very ill, an accomplishment can be something as simple as walking across the room; for a healthier person, it might be a satisfying discussion with a friend or some work-related achievement. More fortunate persons are able to finish significant projects during their last months and weeks, so that the close of their lives resembles earlier stages and they do not confront the sorts of situations that lead to diminished self-esteem.

Self-Actualization Needs

Dying does not mean that development stops. In fact, some people seem to use the crisis of death to facilitate their personal growth. The dying person has little time to procrastinate and stall; if change is going to occur, it must occur very soon—immediately! This awareness can lead to rapid growth. Two case studies are representative of what can happen.

The first concerns a man who had a long history of psychotic behavior, including seven years in a state mental hospital, with severe delusions and hallucinations and paranoid ideation. Some years after leaving the hospital, he was able to work hard enough to maintain himself in the community, to give support to a troubled friend, and to maintain some relationship with his family. However, many of his symptoms remained. At that point, he was diagnosed as having terminal cancer, although his prognosis predicted many months of life. His psychotic symptoms and the acute tension with which he had been living virtually disappeared and did not return for the last two years of his life (Smith, 1975).

The second case study, describing the personal growth of a dying woman who was the focus of intensive research, led its authors (Zinker & Fink, 1966) to conclude that the end of life may be the impetus for resolving problems, establishing closer relationships, and even becoming more productive. Additionally, the authors noted that, over the course of time, the dying woman found her physiological needs increasingly important and her need for esteem much less so. When breathing is difficult and physical strength diminishes, more energy must be expended in satisfying physiological needs and less is left to satisfy esteem or self-actualization. Thus, as Maslow predicted, when needs lower down on the hierarchy are not satisfied, those higher are also frustrated.

THE NEED TO DENY DYING

Denial is one of the major protective psychological mechanisms that enable people to cope with the flood of feelings that occur when the reality of death or dying becomes too great. In Chapter Five we discussed the denial of death; in Chapter 7 we described Kübler-Ross' stage of denial; here we will amplify the denial of the dying process.

Numerous people are likely to deny that someone is dying. The dying person himself or herself is extremely likely to deny impending death. Close friends and family members may also deny that dying is occurring, either to themselves or in their interactions with the dying person or under both circumstances. Health caretakers may also participate in the denial; they may deny the dying to themselves, in their contacts with the patient, and/or in their contacts with the family members of the dying person. And each of these may encourage the denial of the others—perhaps to protect the dying person against knowledge of the prognosis, perhaps to gain support of his or her own denial, perhaps to avoid any need to confront the issue of death in the presence of others for whom the issue might be sensitive.

Denying Your Own Dying

Dying persons can deny the existence of information, or they can reinterpret the meaning of the information to avoid its implications. One well-known author (Weisman, 1972) has proposed three degrees of denial. The first is the denial of facts; this is exemplified by an individual who, told by his or her physician that a scheduled operation is for cancer, subsequently believes that its purpose is to excise a benign tumor. Another example would be a person, who, given a diagnosis by his or her physician of terminal stomach cancer, asks on the doctor's next visit why she is experiencing stomach pain.

The second degree of denial is denial of implications. In this case, the patient acknowledges the disease but denies that it will end in death. A woman with intense pain radiating down the left side of her body insists that it doesn't hurt much, that she will be fine; a man observing a growing lump that is becoming increasingly painful and sensitive attributes it to a bruise he received months earlier.

The third degree is the denial of extinction. This form, not applicable to persons whose deeply felt religious beliefs include some form of immortality or continuity, is limited to people who accept a diagnosis and its implications but still talk and behave as though they were going to live through the ordeal (Weisman, 1972).

Another psychiatrist (Hyland, 1978) described two kinds of denial: adaptive and brittle. **Brittle denial,** which seems to cover the first two of Weisman's degrees of denial, is accompanied by observable anxiety and agitation. Often the individual will reject any attempts to improve his or her psychological or social functioning in the situation. **Adaptive denial** occurs when an individual, aware of the diagnosis and its implications, makes the decision not to dwell on this aspect of life but to emphasize strengths and opportunities. These individuals welcome help and support. This form of healthy denial may actually prolong life, since it exhibits a formidable will to live.

Denying the Dying of Others

Often, when we are with someone who is dying, we feel a virtual compulsion to tell her how well she looks, to tell him that we know he will soon be up and around again. This occurs not as a denial that the person is dying but from awkwardness about how to respond. We rationalize our behavior and say we do not want to make the dying person feel uncomfortable, but the truth is that we are the ones who are uneasy.

If you haven't had the experience of denying that someone was dying, you might understand it better by recalling some related situation you have experienced. For example, can you remember the process you went through when an intimate relationship of yours was broken by the other person's leaving? Did you ever fail an examination that you had been positive you had passed easily? Have you ever lost a job you believed was secure? Denial is a familiar response in each of these situations.

Denial of dying—your own or someone else's—can be either adaptive and helpful or maladaptive and disjunctive; it can even be both at the same time. Denial may be used to avoid the destructive impact of shock by postponing for a time the necessity of dealing with the idea of dying. And it may function to keep a person from coping with intense feelings of anger and hurt, feelings that interfere with other kinds of behavior because they are too intense to stifle completely. It is not that denial is "good" or "bad"; an evaluation of its adaptive qualities must be done on an individual basis.

There is the temptation to support the denial of someone else because his or her pain causes us pain; our encouragement of the denial permits (or requires) that the pain not be displayed. Conversely, there is the temptation to press through denial, as we become impatient with other people's reluctance to accept reality:

> Sometimes the denial in the family is its only defense to help it get through the crisis, to give it time to integrate an unhappy truth. I didn't want to talk about Jean's impending death. I didn't want to admit he was dying. I couldn't. I preferred denial. Some of the doctors didn't understand and therefore didn't allow it [Paulay, 1977–78, p. 175].

Perhaps it was necessary for the physicians to have Ms. Paulay cease denying—perhaps not. It is impossible to make that determination without knowing a great deal more about the circumstances. What is apparent is that denial can serve an important function.

Denying the Effect of Dying

"Yeah, she/he/I/you/they is/are dying, but it isn't really having an effect on me." Another way to deny is to isolate the fact of dying from feelings that surround it. This is easy to do when you read about a disaster or war that is taking place 5000 miles away and doesn't involve anyone you know. But it is still possible when you are the health caretaker, the family member, or even the dying person. Your feelings may break through the denial, but the denial still operates.

Another way to deny the effect while accepting the process is to place so much emphasis on the growth potential and the beauty of the dying process that the "sting of death" is barely a mosquito bite. "Dying will be all right, as long as we are healthy, vibrant, and creative. Death will be all right, too, as long as it is not death" (Kastenbaum, 1982, p. 165).

It is one thing to try to turn the dying process into something that is valuable to the dying person, whether the value arises because of an increased ability to withstand pain or to provide nurture to others or to enjoy music or to contemplate the potential wonders of the hereafter. It is a totally different thing to use these themes to deny the concerns of the dying by pressuring them to "die beautifully." This is not unlike the pressure, discussed earlier, to "let go," so that the dying person dies according to the needs of those around him or her.

THE NEED TO KNOW

Does the dying person have the right to know about the prognosis? Does he or she need to know? What are the effects of knowing or not knowing? Actually, these questions are simplistic. The issues become increasingly complicated as we examine them more carefully. First, we'll look at what two medical sociologists have called "awareness contexts" (Glaser & Strauss, 1965); then we'll outline some of the issues and the related research on communicating with dying persons about their dying.

Closed-Awareness Context

Often an attempt is made to keep the patient from knowing of the terminal diagnosis. In some instances, the physician enters into a conspiracy with family members to withhold the information; occasionally he or she acts without talking to the family, or there are no family members to involve. Of course, the closer the individual is to death, the more likely he or she is to be aware that death is imminent. The communications from others, the signals from within the body, and the changing medical care procedures become much too clear to ignore or deny.

The task of keeping patients from learning they are going to die is immense. Frequently, when the patient learns that others have been shielding him or her from the truth, future relationships with those who participated in the deceit are seriously marred.

Jack Kaplan was diagnosed as having terminal intestinal cancer and was expected to live 10–12 months. The course of his illness was such that although he had to remain home and would be in increasing pain and discomfort, he would be able to do a lot of things around the house. Since he was still a relatively young man, not quite 40, and had two elementary-school-age children, his wife and his physician decided not to say anything about his prognosis until the illness became incapacitating. Nor were the children informed, except to be told that their father had a serious illness and might not get better for at least a year.

Jack accepted their story, went faithfully for his treatments, which were not fully explained to him, and remained optimistic about recovery. As time went on and his condition worsened, he became anxious and began to question his wife about his health. In order to maintain the conspiracy of silence, she avoided his questions, but this merely served to increase his anxiety and his questioning. His wife found it so difficult to be with him that she began to avoid him, which again made Jack more anxious and also angry. Some arguments began, and Jack even suggested marriage counseling, which, when his wife rejected the idea, increased his anger.

Talks with the physician were no more helpful, since although he was reassuring, he also began to avoid Jack. Jack became depressed and began to retreat from both his family and the physician. After about seven months, his condition worsened and he was taken to the hospital, where he went downhill extremely quickly and died three days later without having regained consciousness.

Jack's wife was extremely angry with the physician and blamed him for not telling Jack or having her tell Jack the truth. The physician was told about her anger and insisted that not informing Jack had been her idea. Mrs. Kaplan was depressed for many months after her husband's death and never forgave the doctor.

The core of Emily Kaplan's anger did not arise from her husband's medical treatment or even his rapid decline, since she never considered the possibility that his anxiety and depression might have hastened his death. Her own words express her feelings best: "I had only a few months left with Jack, and we could have made those good months. We could have been close and talked and had some good times with the kids. We could even have planned the children's future. Instead, I ended up cut off from my husband, and he died furious with me. My children will remember their father as an angry man instead of a loving man, and they may think of me as a distant wife instead of the loving wife I was."

Not all closed awareness situations turn out as badly as the one just described. In some instances, the dying person and others can communicate easily and warmly, while avoiding thoughts of the horse on the dining-room table. But often they can't. And after all, as a friend said to me some years ago "It's my life and my death and my suffering, and it's not up to the physician or even to my husband to decide whether or not I want to know about dying. If I don't want to know, I'll find some way to tell them that. Their task is to be competent, loving, and honest, not overprotective and deceitful."

Suspicion-Awareness Context

When the clues become too strong to overlook, patients may become suspicious that their condition is more serious than they had been told. Then a sparring match may begin. The patients may try to find out how sick they are, while simultaneously not wishing to find out that death is predicted. Sometimes patients barricade themselves against the ultimate knowledge by trying to get information first from people who are less official and whose judgments are less "final"—for example, first from an aide or chaplain, then from a nurse, and finally, if all the others imply that the patient is dying, from the physician.

When the health caretakers and the family are conspiring to keep the patient from learning the truth, the patient still has some options to gain information. The most obvious is to ask a direct question—with the expectation, not of being told the truth, but of finding clues to the truth in the voice and body language of the person queried (Glaser & Strauss, 1965). Another possibility is for a patient to tell the physician or spouse that he or she is dying and then wait to see the response. A third is to press for information about the future and also about the illness and to watch both explicit statements and what is not made explicit.

In response to the third approach, the staff may try to be as honest as possible without telling the patient the truth. They may deflect questions by saying "We're all dying" or "This treatment is taking a little longer than we had hoped, but you'll be all right" or "You're going to get worse before you get better." (This latter statement was described to me by Dr. Avery Weisman, a psychoanalyst whose contributions to working with the dying are outstanding, as a particularly clever and also particularly dishonest approach. It has the effect of predicting all possibilities and, when believed, will encourage the patient to stop asking questions.)

Mutual-Pretense Context

Not infrequently both the patient and others in the social environment know that the patient is dying, but they pretend otherwise (Glaser & Strauss, 1965). Since the patient and the hospital staff are part of one system and the patient and his or her family are part of another system, the patient often maintains mutual pretense in both systems. Sometimes the mutual pretense is only with the family; it may be part of a conspiracy between the patient and the hospital to keep the family from knowing what is taking place.

One difficulty inherent in mutual pretense is that each party only assumes what the other party knows. While, in fact, the patient may be suspicious but not certain of a diagnosis, the communication pattern established between him or her and the hospital may assume the patient's equal knowledge. Or, conversely, the patient may have come to believe that death is a certainty, while the truth is that the condition can be alleviated. Patients may misinterpret the numerous cues and form their own terminal diagnosis; then, feeling cut off from honest responses from both family and medical staff, they become anxious and depressed. Their anxieties and mistrust may even cause them to ignore the signs that signify that they are recuperating and attend only to what reinforces their belief that they are dying.

Open-Awareness Context

In the open-awareness context, the patient is aware of his or her prognosis and is able to discuss the dying process or impending death, or to plan in terms of dying and death, with both health caretakers and family members and friends. Since each of the parties is aware of the situation, each can choose to relate to the others in terms of the coming death or to ignore the death. Of course, as death comes closer, ignoring it becomes increasingly difficult and eventually almost impossible. Views regarding the desirability of open awareness have changed in recent years.

A 1953 study of physicians in Philadelphia found that 3% of the 444 respondents said that they always told the patient if he or she had cancer, while 57% said they usually did not inform the patient and 12% that they never did. By 1979, another study of physicians showed that 98% said their "usual policy" was to inform the cancer patient, and 68% said they rarely or never deviated from this policy (reported in Veatch & Tai, 1980). A study from Canada reported that 98% of physicians agreed to tell dying patients what they wish to know, 97% wanted to know about their own death and the deaths of their relatives, and 92% believed that the relatives of a dying person should be informed even if the patient is reluctant to know (Gosselin, Perez, & Gagnon, 1981).

A similar change has been exhibited among the general public, although the public has always been more favorable toward informing the critically ill or dying patient than the medical profession has. A thorough analysis of all journal articles, both research and opinion, showed that the majority favored informing the patient (Koenig, 1969). However, like physicians, members of the general public assume themselves more capable of handling such information than they believe people in general are (Kalish & Reynolds, 1981). It's obvious that the social values of people in general and, to a much greater extent, of physicians have changed in regard to this occurrence. Patients are seen as participating more in their own care, and their right to have access to relevant information is also seen as more appropriate. When patients agree to a particular health treatment program, it is now usually assumed that they are giving informed consent and, to this end, they must know what is wrong with them and what the intent of the treatment is (Veatch, 1982).

Fifteen years ago, a controversy raged over whether open awareness or closed awareness provided more advantages to the patient. The controversy now seems settled, with far more support for open awareness from both health professionals and the general public.

Given these changes toward support for the notion that the open-awareness context is normally optimum, the issue arises of the nature of the communication and with whom the dying person discusses his or her imminent death. A British study of 80 married patients who were dying of cancer (Hinton, 1980) showed that over 75% had spoken of the possibility that they were dying. Of these 62 individuals, slightly over one-third had spoken to the hospital staff and slightly over two-thirds had talked with their spouse.

Those who felt more certain that they were going to die were more likely to talk about it.

Middle Knowledge

"Somewhere between open knowledge of death and its utter repudiation is an area of uncertain certainty called 'middle knowledge'" (Weisman, 1972, p. 65). Like many powerful feelings, those feelings that say "I am dying" are not immediately integrated into our selves. We vacillate between accepting and denying, between full awareness and believing it can't possibly be. Not to me. "Patients seem to know and want to know, yet they often talk as if they did not know and did not want to be reminded of what they have been told" (Weisman, 1972, p. 66).

Weisman is making the point that awareness is not an all-or-none concept. We are aware and not aware. Recall your last exam or job interview or the last occasion in which you believed you were entering a committed intimate relationship. Did you feel, as you left the exam room, the interviewer's desk, or your "intimate's" presence, that things were settled? Probably not. If your experience was like the experiences of most of us, you had moments when you felt the job was yours, moments when you felt that you really did poorly, and moments when you told yourself it didn't really matter. You weave in and out of certainty. And this middle knowledge is what people often feel regarding their deaths.

As time goes on, living with the awareness of death may become easier, although we don't know for certain. Weisman (1972) believes that middle knowledge is especially likely to occur at certain significant transition points, like setbacks or sudden losses of capacity.

Learning I'm Dying

How do I learn I am dying? The ways are numerous.

1. Directly from a health professional. Most frequently the physician will inform the patient of the prognosis, although how the doctor communicates the news will vary. The doctor may be gentle or abrupt, lengthy or brief, encouraging of questions and expressions of feeling or not. When the physician tells me that I am dying, I may not incorporate what I'm told. Perhaps the awareness will surface later, or perhaps I will need to "learn" that I'm dying in another way—at a later time or in a less threatening setting. Occasionally the dying person learns from another health professional, perhaps a nurse or the hospital chaplain, but this is much less common.

2. Indirectly from a health professional. Standing outside the hospital room, the physician and the family members are discussing the person who is dying a few feet away from their conversation. Of course they talk only in whispers, but the sounds frequently carry amazingly well. At the end of the conversation, they enter the room in forced jovial spirits to offer encouragement to the patient. An older woman dying of cancer in a hospital told her one confidant, her son, that "whenever I close my eyes, everyone seems to assume that I'm unable to hear anything."

3. Directly or indirectly from people other than health professionals. Family members and, very occasionally, friends will directly inform a patient of the prognosis. Also common is the kind of indirect informing process described above. Once in a great while, another patient provides the information, usually inadvertently.

4. Changes in the behavior of others. The anecdote that best exemplifies this describes the ill man who, each morning, asked his nurse "How am I today, nurse?" And each morning the woman answered "You're fine—you'll be out of here in no time." Finally, one morning, the nurse read on the patient's chart that he was getting worse and was probably terminally ill. The patient again asked "How am I today, nurse?" And she answered "I'm sorry, but we're not allowed to give out that information. You will have to ask your physician."

Other changes in the behavior of friends, family members, and hospital staff also provide clues. Visits either increase or decrease noticeably; a brother from 1500 miles away "just happens" to have a business trip to the area and stops in; people who had been cheerful before suddenly seem to have been crying a great deal; conversation becomes stilted; planning for the summer vacation receives no response; the chaplain comes in to talk about religious views and immortality; body language and voices either become tense or show obviously false attempts at being casual and relaxed.

5. Changes in medical care procedures. Sometimes a significant change in medical care procedures implies that the prognosis has also changed. For example, if planned surgery is canceled, does that mean that you don't need the surgery because you'll get well without it—or that you're beyond the help of surgery? You're being sent to a room with a much sicker roommate; does that mean that you're also much sicker? The physician doesn't visit you as often; you're given sedatives more freely; a new physician has appeared and seems to be taking over from your personal physician. As you consider each of these stages, you will realize that they must be interpreted, since none of them is very clear in meaning. That's exactly the difficulty: a hospital patient is sometimes not told, and when told, not always told fully, the meaning of what's going on. Therefore, the patient is free to project the greatest hopes or wildest fears.

6. Self-diagnosis. Many patients read and talk to others a great deal about their own condition. In a melange of confusion, ignorance, and distortion there often is a fair amount of valid understanding. And even if the self-diagnosis is inaccurate, the degree to which the person accepts it and acts accordingly is extremely important. One young woman whose terminal diagnosis had been withheld from her learned it from an article describing her symptoms in *Reader's Digest.*

Part of self-diagnosis inevitably comes from the signals within the body. Pain and discomfort increase; psychomotor functioning diminishes; sedatives must become stronger in order to work properly. The fatally ill person often senses the changes within his or her own body and recognizes that the future is brief.

Given the many ways of learning that you are dying, how many people die without knowing what's happening? The answer is, as best we can tell, not very many. In our Los Angeles study of 434 adults, over 80% answered yes to the question "Do you think a person dying of cancer probably senses he's dying anyway, without being told?" Interestingly enough, 20% of the men but only 7% of the women responded negatively to this item (Kalish & Reynolds, 1981).

Studies conducted with dying patients also indicate that most are aware. One investigator, using careful personal observations, noted that nearly half the patients diagnosed as terminally ill overtly mentioned being aware of their prognosis; another sizable group avoided speaking of their future or used only vague terms. Only 5% appeared confident of recovery and 8% hoped for partial recovery (Hinton, 1972). Kübler-Ross (1969) reports that only 3 out of 200 dying persons were unaware of their true state at the end of their lives.

One large British research project interviewed the next of kin of several hundred persons who had died fairly recently. It found that numerous factors contributed to the awareness that the dying person and the next of kin had of the imminence of death. For example, a diagnosis of terminal cancer was more easily kept from a patient than other diagnoses, and the longer the individual was bedridden, the higher the probability that the patient and the next of kin knew of the prognosis (Cartwright, Hockey, & Anderson, 1973).

In a Finnish study (Achté & Vauhkonen, 1971), 100 cancer patients were interviewed about their illness; in addition, their case records were examined and their physicians and appropriate nurses were also interviewed. The investigators determined that, in 40% of the cases, the diagnosis had been spontaneously revealed to the patient by the physician. Although almost all of these admitted to fear and anxiety on hearing the diagnosis, a great majority appeared satisfied with having been told with such frankness. Another 29% were told their diagnosis in response to direct questions, and they were unanimous in approving their physician's openness. An additional 6% had not asked the physician or been told but knew that they had cancer. The remaining 24% (the status of one patient could not be determined) had not asked their physician about their illness, had not been informed by the physician, and presumably did not know its nature, although some were aware that they had some form of tumor. These figures would obviously differ in different facilities and with different kinds of illnesses, but they present at least some initial data.

The Process of Informing

How is the dying person to be informed? To some extent, the answers are obvious: with gentleness, with tact, with honesty. But there are further considerations. Avery Weisman (1972) suggests that when patients ask whether they are going to die, they may really be asking their physician (or nurse or spouse) not to abandon them. It isn't necessary to sit down as soon as the terminal diagnosis is evident and present all the information directly. This can even be a cold way of doing it, a way to say to the patient "Here, I've done everything I can for you. Now you can go off and die and don't bother me."

Instead, the physician can tell the patient enough to enable the patient to ask direct questions that would lead to a full diagnosis and prognosis. That is, the doctor may say something like "From what the tests show, your condition is extremely serious." Or "It appears that you have a malignancy." The words, of course, should not be too technical for the patient to grasp. Armed with this information, the patient may probe for elaboration and clarification, and the physician should normally respond to each question honestly and without avoiding the intent of the patient's question.

Frequently the patient will not press for complete information during the first discussion with the physician. It might be enough to know that the condition is "extremely serious" or that there is a malignancy. The patient's concern may then be to know what treatment is recommended or whether he or she will be suffering pain. It may take a week or more to digest the meaning of this intrusion into one's life. Only at the next visit with the physician will the patient ask more about what will happen. If the doctor has been honest and open, a patient will feel free to ask more when he or she is ready.

Sometimes patients are given full information before they are ready, because no one, not even a physician, can always understand the level of a patient's readiness to hear without denial. Many physicians have reported having patients who had been fully informed return two weeks later asking why they were losing weight or having pain and then become angry that the physician hadn't told them the severity of their condition the first time—even though they had been told.

In spite of these problems, the open-awareness context provides many advantages to the dying person, to family members and friends, and to the health caretakers:

- "The patient [has] an opportunity to close his life in accordance with his own ideas about proper dying" (Glaser & Strauss, 1965, p. 103).
- The dying person is often able to complete some plans and projects, to make arrangements for survivors, and to participate in decisions concerning funeral and burial.
- There is the opportunity to reminisce, to talk with people who have been important, to end life conscious of what life has been.
- Open awareness permits greater understanding of what is going on within the dying person's body and of what the medical staff members are doing.

All in all, it is easier to die when people you love and care for can talk with you freely about what is taking place, even if there is a great deal of pain and sadness in the discussions. Family members can show their grief openly, and love can be expressed openly, since it is amazing how often we neglect to tell those we love most how much we love them. Somehow, in the face of death, telling them that we love them becomes easier.

My 81-year-old aunt was extremely ill and had been for two years; the indications were that she would probably not live for many more weeks. My home was 800 miles away, but I was able to get to visit her and my uncle for a couple of days. It bothered me to see her hooked into a machine that held her life; the ugly wig she had worn during the past couple of years had been discarded, and there were only a few wisps of hair left, but at least they were hers; her teeth had been placed in the drawer by her bed since she couldn't take solid food, and at this point she was not concerned about how she looked.

My uncle and I were in her room, talking with her as she moved in and out of awareness. He was standing at the foot of the bed, and I was sitting next to her, holding her hand. He began to talk to to her about coming to visit me, as soon as she could get up and around again, probably next summer. I noticed that she tuned his comments out. Then I found a pretext to get him out of the room.

When we were alone, I stood up and kissed her. I'd like to say that it was easy, but it really wasn't. I told her that I loved her, and I realized that I had never said that to her before, hadn't even thought about it, hadn't even consciously thought that I loved her. I just—loved her.

Then I said, "Bea, I have to leave now. I may never see you again, and I want you to know how much I love you." Her eyes were closed and she was breathing strangely, but she winced at my words, and I became frightened that I'd said too much, so I hesitated. "Well, I hope that I'll see you again, but I might not." And I left.

She died before I could visit again, and I always wondered whether I should have said what I did, but it seemed important to say it. Even if it pained her to hear me, she knew it was true, and she had not shrunk from painful situations before. It had been easy for me over many years to talk and write about death and dying, but it was very difficult for me to be in the situation where someone I loved was dying. I did what I have told other people to do, and it wasn't at all natural—I had to force myself. But when I heard, three weeks later, that she had died, I considered myself fortunate to have had the chance to be with her before she died and to have been both caring and honest.

THE TASKS OF THE DYING

Like everyone else, dying persons want to accomplish certain tasks. And, like everyone else's tasks, theirs may involve deeply personal considerations. Sometimes the tasks concern ongoing relationships; sometimes they require anticipating future needs. The main tasks of the dying seem to be completing unfinished business, dealing with medical care needs, allocating time and energy resources, arranging for what happens after death, coping with losses, and encountering the mysteries of death itself. The latter two have been discussed extensively in this book. The next few pages will focus on the first four of the tasks.

Completing Unfinished Business

One of the major tasks of the dying is to deal with unfinished business—for example:

- Calling your sister in Portland; you had an argument with her 27 years ago and you haven't spoken to her since.
- Finishing the sweater you were knitting for your grandson.
- Thanking the young nurse who had been particularly nice to you when your treatments were so painful.
- Making certain that your store's books are available and that all records are up to date, so that your successor can take over without confusion.
- Telling your children that you love them.
- Making certain that your bankbooks and insurance policies are readily accessible.
- Knowing that your fourth grandchild was born healthy.

As death approaches, many unfinished tasks recede in importance, although you would need to know a person very well to predict which tasks will remain prominent and which will diminish in importance. Sometimes preparing for death means withdrawing psychologically from people and from the responsibilities that you had maintained during your life. A young mother, for example, may be deeply concerned about her children's future, and she will not feel easy until she is assured that they will be properly cared for after her death. Once she has this assurance, she can permit herself to withdraw from the responsibility and focus on herself.

A common error at this juncture is to discount the strength of feelings that dying people have tied up in unfinished business. It is often much easier to help a person complete a task than to persuade her or him that the task is no longer important. We all face each moment the possibility that we will not be alive the next moment to complete a particular task, but the probability that we will not be alive is so small that we simultaneously ignore it and deny it. For the person well advanced in the living-dying interval, the probability is much greater, and the pressure of time, therefore, is much greater. You have many things you wish to do in the next few days, months, years—in your lifetime. Although right now you are required to make some decisions and eliminate some options, you expect to have time to do most of what you wish. Those who face their own foreseeable death and probable decline before death do not have the range of options that you have, and they confront the task of deciding what can be accomplished and what must be left behind.

Dealing with Medical Care Needs

Not all people facing their deaths have changing medical care needs, and not all persons whose medical care needs are changing significantly are dying, but the connection is still obvious. Sometimes the fatally ill person prefers to leave medical decisions to others, but other times he or she wishes to take a more active role in the way medical care is obtained. This obviously requires that the individual have some understanding of the medical diagnosis and prognosis, the meaning of various kinds of treatment, and the kinds of people and facilities that can provide the care.

When the medical care decisions are made by others, the dying person is likely to become a passive participant in the care plan—following instructions (though frequently with considerable passive resistance) and doing what is required. There is considerable encouragement today to make the patient an active participant.

A dying cancer patient, for example, may decide to forgo cobalt treatment, with its secondary effects of hair loss, nausea, and extreme fatigue, in exchange for an earlier death with less discomfort. Another patient may choose to live her last few weeks at home, even though this choice probably means that death will occur sooner.

A well-known psychologist had had a severe heart attack and was informed by his physician that the only chance he had for a long life was to reduce his activity level, to stop all smoking and drinking, to eliminate sexual activity, and to change his eating habits. Rather than give up what he had enjoyed so much, he decided to live much as he had been living and to accept death when it came. He died of a second coronary about two years later, but the two years were enjoyable and fulfilling. More important, he died an appropriate death—that is, he died as he wished to die: while engaged in the excitement of a vigorous life.

Allocating Time and Energy Resources

When time and energy no longer seem infinite, people have to make choices. When people were asked how they wished to spend their last six months, their responses were highly variable (see Table 3-1). Of course, most of the people interviewed had never actually faced their own deaths, and it is difficult to know whether what they claimed would be what they would actually do under the circumstances.

Major factors in how remaining time is spent are the nature and course of the illness. A person dying from a slow-acting cancer, which brings increasing fatigue and debilitation, allocates time and energy very differently from the psychologist described above. And this brings us back to unfinished business. The pressure of certain unfinished tasks may be so great that the dying person will fight off death until a particular task is completed. Nevertheless, the illness eventually takes command, and death will occur in the face of the most powerful desire to continue.

Arranging for After Death

If you died before you finished reading this sentence, what would happen to your body? Your possessions? Your survivors? Are the things that would happen what you would like to have happen? If you haven't made any preparations for your own death, you are not alone. Table 8-1 shows that, except for having bought life insurance, most people have not made specific arrangements for their deaths; even most older people have not got around to making out a will or arranging for someone to handle their affairs.

Life insurance is the most familiar preparation made for death. In 1976 a national survey found that 90% of families with both husband and wife present had some insurance; 80% of all adult men and 65% of all adult women were insured. Even among those 65 years of age and older, 68% of the men

TABLE 8-1.
Responses of 434 Los Angeles Residents Concerning Specific Plans and Preparations They Have Made for Their Own Deaths

	Percentage Answering Yes								
	Ethnicity				Age			Sex	
Questions: Have you…	Black American	Japanese American	Mexican American	"Anglo" American	20-39	40-59	60+	Men	Women
taken out life insurance?	84	70	52	65	61	76	66	73	63
made out a will?	22	21	12	36	10	22	39	26	19
made funeral arrangements? paid for or are you now	13	11	8	14	3	11	24	13	10
paying for a cemetery plot?	22	26	12	25	7	17	44	20	22
seriously talked with anyone about your…death?	27	16	33	37	28	28	29	28	28
arranged for someone to handle your affairs?	24	17	25	42	13	44	44	26	28

From *Death and Ethnicity: A Psychocultural Study*, by R. A. Kalish and D. K. Reynolds. Copyright 1981. Reprinted by permission.

and 55% of the women carried life insurance. These figures are similar to the data reported in Table 8-1. The total amount of life insurance in force in 1982 was $4.48 trillion! Almost as many women carry life insurance as men. However, in spite of these statistics, the average coverage in 1982 was $57,300 per insured family (American Council of Life Insurance, 1983). Even allowing for the distortions of an inflationary economy, this amount of money would not keep a family going for very long.

A totally different kind of preparation for death is arranging to donate an organ—a kidney or the cornea of an eye, for example—to someone else. Only 3% of the respondents in the Los Angeles study had made such preparations (Kalish & Reynolds, 1981), and the topic did not elicit a great deal of interest. Nonetheless, many people do make out and carry with them official cards stipulating that, in the event of their death, their body may be used for transplants or donated to a medical school to be used for instruction or research.

Why bother making advance arrangements? Several answers are obvious. First, it allows what happens after your death to be as much as possible the way you want it to be; if you don't make arrangements, someone else—perhaps someone assigned by the courts—will. Second, it frees your family of the tasks so that they can deal unencumbered with their grief; they will still have ample practical matters to concern them. Third, it avoids having your estate, even if it is very small, tied up in courts for many months or longer; the better job you do in setting things up, the more quickly all matters will be settled. Fourth, if you have dependent children, you can assure them of the best living arrangement and care in the event one *or both* parents die.

One answer is less obvious. If you can arrange for what will happen when you die and if you can discuss this with persons who are important to you, you will begin to establish an open-awareness system. These individuals will know that you are capable of discussing your own death, and they will be more likely to be open with you when your death is actually imminent. Furthermore, they will feel satisfied that they are carrying out your wishes concerning your funeral, disposal of your body, and disposal of property, and this will certainly reduce the chance of tension and arguments among your survivors. Conversely, you can learn their preferences and perhaps alter some of your plans accordingly.

Why, then, do so many people never get around to making preparations? Financial costs are so low that lack of money can't explain the figures in Table 8-1; the effort required isn't greater either. Some individuals, of course, have neither dependents nor possessions, so they may not feel any pressure to make arrangements. Others assume that because they are young and healthy, they can postpone these considerations.

But there is still another reason, one that borders on superstition but is common even among individuals who aren't afraid to walk under ladders or to plan activities on Friday the 13th. If I make out a will or make funeral arrangements, I am admitting that I am going to die; therefore, I will die. If I don't make out a will and don't make funeral arrangements, I am not going to die. And the less I think about death, the less likely I am to die. Very few people will admit that their thoughts run along those lines, but my own observations are that such "logic" is more common than usually recognized.

Ironically, when a person does get around to seeing a lawyer, he or she is likely to find the word *death* avoided. Thomas Shaffer, a lawyer and law professor, reports several ways in which lawyers avoid bringing death directly into conversation, even if the entire purpose of a conversation is to prepare for death. They (1) use evasion and denial and change the subject, (2) employ raucous humor concerning death-related matters, and (3) save discussion of what happens when death occurs for the end of the allocated time, then shift the topic back to financial assets and family members as quickly as possible. They are also likely to remove the topic of children from any discussion (Shaffer, 1970). Shaffer also mentions that parents exhibit great stress when asked with whom their children should live if both parents die or are incapacitated. Disposing of money, furniture, and jewelry arouses the emotions less than dealing with the possibility that the children you love may lose you.

The tasks that face the dying person are considerable, and the psychological stresses and physical limitations that are present may render the accomplishment of these tasks even more difficult. It's useful to make some advance preparations, especially concerning some practical matters, so that your strength and resources can be applied to what is personally significant: being with those you care for, completing plans and projects, meditating or praying, reminiscing and trying to see your life in perspective, participating in activities that you particularly enjoy and that your health will permit.

CHAPTER NINE

Suicide, Euthanasia, Disasters, and Unexplainable Deaths

You often read that someone died of "natural causes." The implicit assumption is that some causes of death, such as cancer or heart attack, are natural while others, such as suicide or automobile accidents, are unnatural. The differentiation, though occasionally useful, is a dubious one. An earth-quake is certainly natural by any definition, whereas a person who dies of cancer because of having smoked three packs of cigarettes a day for 30 years or having lived where the water was polluted by adjacent factories is not necessarily dying of natural causes. Perhaps it is all an arbitrary outcome of one's personally preferred definitions.

Nonetheless, we will follow acceptable terminology for now, and in this chapter we will discuss four kinds of "unnatural death": suicide, euthanasia, disasters, and unexplainable deaths. There are other kinds of "unnatural deaths" that we won't comment on, such as homicide, accidents, death during war, and capital punishment. You may wish to pursue these issues on your own.

SUICIDE

Suicide has held a fascination for poets and psychologists, for philosophers and physicians. Some people romanticize suicide by viewing it as the one way in which a person can exercise ultimate control over his or her life; others see suicide only as an insane act. Argument rages over the moral right of a person to take his or her own life. On the one hand, if I am not in charge of my own life, I am not in charge of anything: it is my life and I should be able to take it if and when I want. On the other hand, because death by suicide affects not only the person committing suicide but many others as well, the family and even society in general deserve protection from suicides; another argument against suicide is that, though irreversible, it often arises from stresses that can be alleviated with help or simply with time.

Epidemiology of Suicide

On one matter, there is little disagreement: suicide is one of the leading causes of death in the United States and Canada, although the rates are higher in the United States. It ranks among the ten most frequent causes of death in the United States for all ages after childhood (*Statistical Abstracts*, 1982–83). Adolescent suicide, which is now dropping off slightly after a tripling of rates over a 25-year period, still accounts for a minimum of 5000 deaths yearly for persons age 24 and under. In the United States, suicide is the second leading cause of death for 15–24-year-old males and is tied for second with cancer for 15–24-year-old females (*Statistical Abstracts*, 1982–83).

Suicide attempt rates are consistently higher than suicide rates for all groups and all ages. Further, most experts in the field assume that these rates, which reflect only known suicide attempts, are substantially lower than the actual attempt rates. It has long been recognized that many attempts are never reported to the authorities, and if we extend that figure to include persons who think seriously about suicide but never make a serious attempt, the rates skyrocket.

Some people are more likely to *commit* suicide than others: those who are male, older, presently unmarried, living alone, in poor physical health, unemployed, depressed, and mentally ill (Sainsbury, 1975). Their suicides are precipitated by illness, bereavement, and loneliness. Others are more likely to *attempt* suicide: those who are female, young, married, and suffering from personality disorders. Their attempts are more likely to be precipitated by domestic crises and serious problems in personal relationships (Sainsbury, 1975).

Determining whether a particular action was a suicide attempt or whether a particular death was caused by suicide is not always easy. Sometimes it is difficult even though a note has been left, since a suicide attempt that was meant to draw care and attention but not to cause death can turn into an actual suicide by chance circumstances. For example, a middle-aged man, deeply depressed for some weeks, has talked occasionally about "getting away from it all." While driving 75 miles per hour on the way to work one morning, he hits a freeway abutment and dies immediately. Did he knowingly commit suicide? Were his stresses so great that he wasn't aware of how fast he was driving or where his car was heading?

The Meaning of Suicide

Suicide has many meanings, and sometimes a particular suicide arises for several reasons. For the person committing suicide, the act may signify the desire to end life, to be freed of feelings of helplessness and hopelessness, to gain relief from physical or emotional pain, to gain reunion with others who have died or to gain union with God, to free others from their burden of care, to cry out for attention or to punish survivors, or it may be a response to the symptoms of mental illness.

In recent years, suicide has been seen, first and foremost, as a cry for help, rather than a wish to die. The nature of the desired help varies from someone who will respond to emotional needs to providing financial aid or a job to wanting the structure of hospitalization.

Often, the person attempting suicide doesn't really want to die. He may be consciously aware that the suicide attempt is not supposed to cause death, or he may be unaware. So he swallows a bottle of sleeping pills in a motel room three miles from his family, then telephones them to say "I won't bother you any more. I'm going to die peacefully right in this room." He hangs up. Is he consciously aware that his car is parked right outside the door of the room with the license plate facing the street?

Or she engages a close friend in an ostensibly intellectual argument about the right to commit suicide—becoming increasingly emotional as the discussion progresses. The friend she selects to talk to is a clinical social worker. Has she consciously selected the one person she knows who would quickly understand the hidden message?

Sometimes the desire for the attempt to fail is even more obvious: he barely cuts his wrists enough to draw blood, or she not only makes a call from a motel room after taking pills but asks her friend for help. One familiar pattern is to use a suicide attempt to bring a separated spouse back into the household; it is not unheard of for a woman or a man to make a suicide attempt every time a frightening breakup occurs. And there are some husbands or wives who act out their part of this serious game by returning to "save" the person attempting suicide.

One procedure, called the **psychological autopsy,** has been used to try to determine whether such an act was overtly suicidal or not (Shneidman & Farberow, 1961). Persons conducting a psychological autopsy review the dead person's life very carefully, especially the events immediately preceding the death, and they put together a comprehensive chronology. Through extensive experience and research, moderately accurate predictors have been developed that appear to differentiate suicidal deaths from deaths by other causes.

If all suicides are self-destructive acts (although you might wish to debate this point), are all self-destructive acts attempted suicides? How about cigarette smoking, reckless driving, heavy drinking, or consciously living a highly stressful existence? Are these indirect ways of committing suicide? Or are they conscious decisions in which the individual establishes priorities, even though the risk is there?

Frequently the suicide attempt itself is sufficient to produce change. People become aware that death can really occur, and they realize that being dead, though solving their immediate difficulties, will also cause significant losses for them. Most persons who were kept from jumping from one of the San Francisco area bridges did *not* subsequently make another suicide attempt.

In many ways, suicide is a social act, meant to influence others. It is one type of communication, and it might be meant to say:

I am angry and I am going to punish you in the worst way possible. You will feel guilty long after I kill myself.

You never paid any attention to me—no one ever paid any attention to me—but you will pay attention to me if I attempt to kill myself.

I need help but I am not able to ask for help; I don't know how to ask for help. This is a way to ask for help.

The pain of my life is too great, and I can't stand it any longer. Either someone has to help me out of this pain or I will help myself out by dying.

I want to control you, and I can do that by attempting suicide. I will be victim and you will be rescuer.

The frequent assumption today is that people who attempt or commit suicide are either mentally ill or under great psychological stress; physical illness, financial problems, work and love losses, and other factors are rarely mentioned as causes. Nevertheless, persons who commit suicide are still sometimes viewed as cowardly, inconsiderate, or even evil (Kalish, Reynolds, & Farberow, 1974).

The meanings of suicide for the survivors are also varied, but the impact is immense. The survivors tend to feel punished, no matter what the initial intent of the suicide, and their response is often to defend themselves against the implicit blame that they weren't "doing the right things." Not only is a close family member removed, often at a time when that person was still important to others, but the survivors may feel responsible for not having intervened to stop the death from occurring. In fact, they often feel responsible for having encouraged the death through their actions.

Edwin Shneidman, a leading figure in the suicide prevention movement, has encouraged **postvention** to reduce the emotional damage done to those who are close to suicide victims. *Postvention* refers to "those activities that serve to reduce the aftereffects of a traumatic event in the lives of the survivors" (Shneidman, 1973, p. 33). There is a need for such activities because "survivor-victims of such deaths are invaded by an unhealthy complex of disturbing emotions: shame, guilt, hatred, perplexity. They are obsessed with thoughts about the death, seeking reasons, casting blame, and often punishing themselves" (p. 34).

The culture also endows suicide with various meanings: it can be viewed as sinful, as a criminal act, as a sign of weakness of character or of ego, as an indication of mental illness or "madness," as a beautiful and moving action, and as a rational response to unduly painful circumstances (Kastenbaum, 1981).

Justifiable Suicide?

A totally different kind of issue emerges in some discussions of suicide: is there such an act as a justifiable suicide? Are there times when remaining alive makes less sense than ceasing to live? Too often the responses to these questions are made too quickly, without adequate thought. Frequently lives that seem hopeless are not; the availability of one truly caring individual might cause a suicidal person to decide to live. One useful first reaction to the question of justifiable suicide is to ask about specific situations: is there any change that anyone can provide that would enable the person to wish to live? There may be. There may not be. One serious concern is that too many of us allow the idea of a justifiable suicide to absolve us of responsibility for providing another person with reasons to live.

Conversely, there are people for whom the pain of living and the total hopelessness of the future clearly outweigh any potential for life. In many instances, these individuals are already terminally ill, and their future is a matter of weeks or, at the most, months (although the differences in life expectancy between them and the rest of us are quantitative, not qualitative). In other instances, a physically ill or depressed person feels that he or she is using up too many resources or is causing too much distress for loved ones. Death is seen as liberating the ill person or liberating those the person loves.

Is there such an act as a justifiable suicide? Perhaps each of us can answer only for our own value systems.

Suicide Prevention Centers

Suicide prevention centers are now found everywhere, both in the United States and Canada and elsewhere around the world. Although programs and procedures vary as a function of the characteristics of the community, of the financial resources, of policies developed, and of the kind of organizational structure of which the center is a part, the basic purpose of these centers is the same: to develop a telephone-response system to permit people contemplating suicide to call in and receive information, personal support, and a kind of quasipsychotherapy. Suicide prevention centers also offer community education programs and may be affiliated with other community services at the local level. Some of these centers have followed the lead of the Los Angeles center, the first one established in North America, by conducting research, developing new program ideas, and trying to influence local and national policy on issues regarding suicide prevention. In addition, these centers attempt to increase national consciousness about the problems of suicide and may also provide individual counseling for persons attempting suicide or relatives of persons who have committed or attempted suicide. Most centers, however, do not have extensive facilities, and they must be content with providing telephone help, some community education, and, frequently, referrals for persons whose needs go beyond their ability to provide services.

Individual suicide prevention centers are autonomous, linked together through membership in the American Association of Suicidology and through regional associations, which are often informal. Their source of funding varies, but much of it comes through city, state, and county mental health funds, and they are likely to be city or county agencies.

Do suicide prevention centers reduce suicides and suicide attempts? That question has been debated by those within and outside the field. The answer is uncertain. Most people who call in to SPCs are not considered likely candidates for a suicide attempt (Lester & Lester, 1971). Many are lonely and depressed, seeking a friendly voice; some are chronic callers; others want information about helping a friend or relative who appears likely to make a suicide attempt or who has already done so.

That SPCs prevent some suicides is virtually certain. That they keep the suicide rate from going up is much less so. However, they provide other resources: they offer a system of aid for many isolated, depressed persons; they help people to understand the dynamics of suicide and, consequently, to become better able to help a friend or relative who has made a suicide attempt; they have helped to change attitudes toward people who attempt or commit suicide; and they have made mental health professionals aware of the need for suicide prevention.

The literature on suicide is voluminous. All I have done is touch on a very few issues. Others include causes of suicide, methods of suicide, the relationship of depression to suicide, treatment programs and psychotherapy for suicidal persons, and the role of suicide notes.

EUTHANASIA AND THE RIGHT TO DIE

Some people talk about the "right to die" and the "right to die with dignity"— both laudable concepts—without a full understanding of the implications of these issues. A person's death does not affect only the individual, and we often must consider the right of an individual to die with the rights of that person's family to have him or her live. More important, it would seem, is the right to live a life of quality.

I want to have as much power over my own life as possible, and since my death is just as much a part of my life as my work or my eating, I want to have power over my death. This means I want power over where I die, how I die, and when. Since no power is absolute, I know that I cannot have full power over these issues, but I can at least have some influence.

To an appreciable extent, I can have influence over my death by the way I live, the foods I eat, the ways I handle stress and losses, the work that I pursue, and other comparable matters. To some extent, my will to live or desire to die is also a factor. But there are many occasions when my existence is largely determined by other people, and this is particularly the case when I am very ill and perhaps near death or when, for other reasons, I no longer have control over my physical body or social environment.

The situation could certainly arise when I wanted to die but was able neither to cause myself to die nor to get anyone else to make me die. At that point, I would lose power over myself—especially the power to cause to happen the one thing that I might most wish to happen: my death. To make matters worse, this loss of power over self is likely to occur when I am ill, in pain, facing imminent death, and running up immense medical costs—all of which combine to bring great distress to my family. All these factors would conspire to make certain that I am not dying with dignity.

Before proceeding, I would like to present a few issues for consideration:

- Does my "right to die" or "right to die with dignity" depend on what I decide or on what someone else decides?
- Does it depend on my decision—no matter how I arrived at it—or must I present a persuasive case for it?
- Must I cause my death directly, or will someone do it at my request?
- Can I cause my death, or have someone cause it, by some active agent (for example, poison, sleeping pills), or am I limited to refusing further treatment, which is always a legal prerogative unless I am stopped by some court action?
- Does it matter whether someone—spouse, child, employer, clergy—opposes my death?
- Am I permitted only to hasten my inevitable and predictable death, or am I permitted to determine myself the conditions under which I may choose to cause my life to stop?

The Issues

Who is entitled to define the end of life? Physicians? Lawyers? Philosophers and theologians? Judges and politicians? Everyone equally? Who is entitled to say whether death should be defined as the irreversible end of consciousness or the end of heart or brain activity?

My own feelings here may well be in conflict with yours. I think the issue is a philosophical or theological one that must be settled in the social-political arena, not in a medical center. Physicians, of course, must make the determination of what is physically possible to do; they have the technology and the experience to understand whether instruments are available that can accurately evaluate the irreversible end of consciousness or the termination of heart activity. But whether the end of consciousness should be used to define the end of life is a moral, not a medical, question (see also Veatch, 1976). The definitions, it seems, need to be developed (or left undeveloped, which is a possible decision) by legislative bodies, with advice from medical, religious, psychological, and other experts, as well as from others who are concerned with the issue.

For any given person, of course, a physician is likely to determine whether life is continuing or not. Thus, although I would like to decide for myself whether I want to have my life declared over when my consciousness stops forever, I must permit a physician to decide whether my condition is indeed irreversible.

Another controversy that often emerges is whether there is a difference between **active euthanasia** and **passive euthanasia.** The former occurs when something is done to a patient to cause death; the latter refers to situations in which no action is taken to prolong life under circumstances in which action might have permitted a patient to live longer. Removing a patient from a respirator that was maintaining life would be an example of active euthanasia; an example of passive euthanasia might be withholding treatment for a heart-attack victim that might have kept that person alive but probably without adequate brain function. Some people argue that active euthanasia is morally wrong but that passive euthanasia is acceptable; others contend that they are merely two sides of the same coin and that either—or neither—is acceptable.

Many states have enacted legislation permitting an individual to describe the conditions under which he or she would want life-sustaining procedures withheld or withdrawn. One necessary condition is that the individual already have a terminal, incurable disease. The legislation requires that a document, frequently termed a **living will,** be made out when a person is capable of understanding its implications and that its signing be appropriately witnessed.

The right to commit suicide has also undergone change. Once forbidden, suicide is still disapproved by custom and by most religions, but legal sanctions against persons who have attempted or committed suicide are no longer in practice. One exception is the limitations some life insurance companies have on paying beneficiaries of a completed suicide—especially if the suicide occurred shortly after the policy was initiated.

The Attitudes

Feelings about euthanasia and the right to die can become intense, though often less intense than those regarding abortion. However, the "right to die" does not exist in a vacuum. The next question that must be asked is "The right to die under what circumstances?" Should a person be able to die any time he feels like it? Or should a person be able to die if she is in great pain, with an incurable disease that will in all likelihood cause death in the near future anyway?

Research goes back many years. In 1939 an opinion poll reported that nearly half the people interviewed answered yes to the question "Do you favor mercy deaths under government supervision for hopeless invalids?" Some years later, Professor Thomas Eliot, perhaps the first sociologist to call attention to the paucity of research on death and bereavement, asked 118 men and 12 women, all military veterans, for their reactions. About as many expressed willingness for the physician to hasten death as opposed such action (Eliot, 1947).

In numerous recent studies, from at least half to nearly 90% of the respondents favor euthanasia (for example, Haug, 1978; Kalish & Reynolds, 1981; Ostheimer, 1980), and a well-conducted national survey indicated that nearly 2 of 3 adults approved of ending a person's life if agreed to by the individual and his or her family and if the patient was confirmed as incurable by a board of physicians (Jorgenson & Neubecker, 1980–81).

As would be expected, willingness to accept euthanasia varies widely among groups of people. Those most accepting are men, those who don't declare themselves to belong to any of the major religious groupings, Whites /Anglos (as opposed to Blacks, Hispanics, and other non-Whites), persons with higher education, political liberals, and younger persons (Jorgenson & Neubecker, 1980–81; Ward, 1980).

And people also differ as a function of the conditions under which such deaths are to be permitted. In the multiethnic Los Angeles study, when we asked about approval of the right to die, approximately half of the Japanese-American and Black respondents and over 60% of the White respondents said yes; only the Mexican Americans were largely opposed. However, there was considerable sentiment to permit the hastening of death only if the person was dying anyway or in great pain; only 1 person in about 15 believed that wanting to die is sufficient reason for permitting someone to die without other justifications. The major reasons for opposition to permitting a person to choose his or her death were the views that only God has the right to take a life and that, no matter how bleak matters seem, there is always hope (Kalish & Reynolds, 1981).

A comparable study in the Midwest, conducted several years later, found that 75% of the research participants believed that people in the last stages of terminal illness should be permitted to have their deaths hastened (Haug, 1978). If allowances are made for the differences in the phrasing of the question in the two studies, the two sets of results are amazingly consistent: the right to a more rapid death is generally acceptable under specified conditions.

But when we permit people to hasten their deaths because they are dying anyway, the hazard is that since we are all going to die someday, any one of us could be a candidate for a hastened death. I know the response to the previous sentence: But these people are in pain and their lives don't have meaning anymore, so why not let them die in dignity instead of living in torment?

The answer is simple, but implementation is exceedingly complex. Letting people die can be the most humane approach; it can also be an excuse for not providing optimum medical and human care. Obviously many dying people don't want to hasten their deaths—some because they are afraid of dying but many because life still has some meaning for them. It thus seems important to extend every effort to every patient, whatever the condition of the person's health, to control pain and to make life meaningful—no matter how brief the potential life is. Otherwise we run the risk of using the concept of death with dignity as a rationalization for our own failure to provide life with dignity.

DISASTERS

We can all be struck by disaster: earthquake, tornado, radioactivity from a nuclear plant or carrier vehicle, explosion, fire, crippling snowstorm, volcano. But an individual tends to ignore warnings, perhaps because he or she feels "I am immune—it can't happen here, but if it does, I will survive." After the disaster has occurred, we may blame the carelessness of others, the cynicism of bureaucrats, the lack of good warning systems, the cost-cutting of industrial executives, payoffs to inspectors. But this is all after the fact. "The failure of the warning-predicting-preventing system often is associated with the most common and ordinary attitudes and practices of our society" (Kastenbaum, 1981, p. 93).

During a disaster, some people emerge as true heroes: they devote their time and energy and risk their lives to help others. Other people are consumed by fear for their own lives or property or by anxiety for the well-being of those they love. Some disasters cause so much death and destruction that immense stress and anxiety are generated.

One author, who is a professional sociologist and has been a professional funeral director, describes eight practical matters that must be attended to in disasters (Pine, 1974):

1. The victims who survived the disaster need to be cared for, fed, given medical attention, housed, and so forth.
2. Persons who are not directly involved usually need to be kept away from the area. (The problems of helping disaster victims when surrounded by sightseers or scavengers are familiar ones.)
3. The disaster area should be left as undisturbed as possible, in order to facilitate subsequent investigations.
4. When people have died, the locations of their deaths are usually marked and recorded before removing the bodies.
5. When possible, the bodies of the dead are identified, and their deaths are legally certified.
6. The next of kin need to be notified.
7. The final disposition of the dead is accomplished.
8. The psychological and social needs of the family members of the dead should be considered and given attention.

The final item, caring for the needs of family members, is often overlooked because of the stresses of the disaster, the numbers of persons who must be notified, and the usual lack of an effective system for handling such matters. We cannot anticipate and plan for all disasters, and frequently the cost and the time required to take even modest precautions are considered too high.

Perhaps the greatest disaster of modern times—certainly the disaster that has had the greatest impact on the modern world—was the dropping of atomic bombs on Hiroshima and Nagasaki. Although you may not wish to consider this a disaster since it was the consequence of a human act and not a natural disaster, its impact was like a disaster's all the same. Probably the best psychological book about Hiroshima was written by psychiatrist Robert Lifton (1967). Based on hundreds of interviews and many months of observations and discussions, the book describes the first experiences of the bombing as involving an initial *immersion in death* and subsequent psychic closing off, during which people "simply ceased to feel. They had a clear sense of what was happening around them, but their emotional reactions were unconsciously turned off" (1967, p. 31). The next reaction, which Lifton termed *survival priority*, was the guilt that the *hibakusha**felt about having survived while so many others died. The dead, the dying, the disabled were

*Survivors of the atomic bombing of Hiroshima and Nagasaki in 1945.

so numerous as to be overwhelming; so many people cried out for help that no survivors were immune to the feeling that they had failed to help at least one person who needed it. In most, perhaps all, instances, guilt and shame grew over the years, as more deaths resulted from the radiation. And, of course, the survivors experienced anger and fear as it became apparent that all those who were affected by the radiation had to deal with illnesses and disabilities, which they hadn't originally anticipated.

Another kind of disaster, though not always classified as such, is the Holocaust, the years of terror brought about by the Nazis in Germany and elsewhere in Europe over 40 years ago. The horror of what happened in the camps was so great that wholesale denial occurred, both among persons living thousands of miles away and among those who could actually see the smoke rising from the chambers where tens of thousands of Jews and others were being gassed and cremated.

The effects of the Holocaust are still being felt, not only by the survivors but by their children and grandchildren as well. The child of a couple, both of whom had survived the camps, was frightened of anything bearing the Nazi insignia until she went into psychotherapy; another child of survivors would wake up during the night with nightmares of the Nazis entering his home to take him away to the camps. On the surface, most of the survivors have been able to function well in society; however, one experienced psychotherapist told me years ago that "there isn't one survivor of Hitler's camps who isn't psychologically scarred in some significant way."

The victims of the Holocaust might be expected to show the scars of their experience of fear and terror and of physical and emotional pain and deprivation. That their children and grandchildren identify as they do and take on some of the fear and pain of their parents and grandparents might not have been expected. It seems imperative, therefore, to investigate the possibility that children whose parents have suffered in other ways will also be deeply affected, even if the child was born after the event occurred. This could be true of earthquakes and fires, as well as occurrences not usually considered disasters, such as imprisonment or criminal victimization, particularly when a physical assault or rape is involved.

There is little doubt that surviving any major disaster leaves an indelible mark on the survivor and often on future generations as well. "Personal disaster is not forgotten but stays with the individual as a reference point in his existence. He may change his life following it, he may attempt to repress it, but in anniversary phenomena, in his memory and attempts to interpret it, the disaster remains an ongoing part of his experience" (Raphael, 1983, p. 351).

UNEXPLAINABLE DEATHS

Can you wish yourself to death? If so, does your wishing or your willing make itself felt through reduced appetite, poor digestion, reduced circulation, and other direct influences on your physical organism, or does it operate in some other fashion? Is there such an event as a voodoo death? If so, what is it that causes the death? Conversely, can you wish or will yourself to remain alive, long past the time at which any knowledgeable physician would have predicted your death? If so, what are you doing to make it happen?

No question exists that competent medical, nutritional, and other health-related care can extend life expectancy. Similarly, poor medical and nutritional practices and care will reduce the life span unnecessarily. More speculative, however, is the possibility that social and psychological means can successfully influence the physical health and, therefore, the life expectancy of an individual.

Predilections for Death

We know that some people wish to die. The more formidable question is whether some people hasten their own deaths through means that are not normally termed suicides. Most people seem to accept this possibility. In our Los Angeles attitude study, we found that well over three-fourths of the 434 adult respondents agreed that "people can hasten or slow their own death through a will-to-live or a will-to-die" (Kalish & Reynolds, 1981), suggesting that each of us can control, to some extent, the timing of our own death.

Many physicians have described incidents in which patients appeared predisposed to die. One article described six persons who died during or shortly after being operated on, although each had had a good prognosis and none was considered suicidal, depressed, or anxious. Yet prior to their deaths, they were all convinced that they would die and fully accepted their impending deaths. In each instance, the death was viewed by the authors as being appropriate; that is, death appeared understandable as a solution to medical and personal problems. Such persons are said to have predilections for death (Weisman & Hackett, 1961).

Some years ago, a professor of education told me of an extremely dramatic "unexplainable" death that he felt he had inadvertently caused:

> In the early 1920s, he was a young high school English teacher in a small rural community whose population represented a variety of ethnic backgrounds. As a class assignment, he asked his students to write a story based on a folk legend of their particular ethnic group. One student, a girl of Portuguese background, mentioned that she knew a folk story she thought would interest him but that she had been told a great calamity would occur to anyone who divulged the legend outside her ethnic community. The teacher finally persuaded the girl to write that story as her assignment.
>
> Within a very few days, the girl's fiancé was brutally killed in an industrial accident. Within two months, following a lengthy period during which she steadily weakened, although she did eat fairly regularly, the girl died of no medically recognized cause.

Shneidman (1973) labels persons like this girl **Psyde-facilitators**—one of his numerous classifications of orientations to death. The Psyde-facilitator is a person who is " more-than-passively unresisting" to death when illness occurs and both psychic and physical energy is low. This definition accords with the following description, quoted from the coroner of a large city: "Every year men die after suicidal attempts when the skin has scarcely been scratched or only a few aspirin tablets have been ingested" (Richter, 1959, p. 311).

The desire to die is not always as obvious as in the above cases, and other kinds of unexplainable deaths have also been described. Reports from North Korean prisoner-of-war camps in the early 1950s told of American prisoners who died much more rapidly than the physical conditions alone warranted (Strassman, Thaler, & Schein, 1956). Viktor Frankl (1963), the existentialist writer, has pointed out that apathy, signifying perhaps a lack of meaning in life, was often predictive of death among inmates of Nazi concentration camps. Equally dramatic are the well-known descriptions of infants who died from marasmus (Ribble, 1943), a wasting illness associated with young children and not attributable to any particular known disease. The children who died had been institutionalized and not given proper loving care, although their physical needs were often met. Both the POW deaths and the marasmus deaths can be understood in the context of hopelessness and helplessness (the two frequent criteria for explicit suicides); the will to live is lost.

A psychiatrist, interested in the possible connection between intense emotional upset and sudden, unexpected death, collected 275 newspaper clippings describing such occurrences. He developed four major categories: first, the extremely traumatic disruption of an intimate relationship or the anniversary of such a loss (135 deaths); second, situations involving danger, struggle, or attack (103 deaths); third, loss of something very important, such as status, self-esteem, or highly valued property, or defeat, disappointment, or failure (21 deaths); and fourth, a moment of triumph, public recognition, or reunion—what the author terms "happy endings" (Engel, 1977). Presumably, these persons encountered highly stressful experiences, some continuous and others sudden and unexpected, that produced physiological changes too great for the person's system to handle. Dr. Engel's own determination from the data he collected is that the sudden, unexpected deaths were due primarily to cardiac problems.

Perhaps the elderly are even more susceptible to death from despair and helplessness than persons in other age groups. It isn't unusual to hear an aide at a nursing home say something like "When his children didn't visit him that Christmas, he turned his face to the wall; two days later he died." Living in an institution with few pleasures makes visits and maintaining old relationships even more important than they otherwise would be; when other people no longer seem to care, the institutionalized older person just gives up on life. One group of authors (Maizler, Solomon, & Almquist, 1983) define this as the **psychogenic mortality syndrome**, which they then operationalize as "giving up." It obviously involves depression and may be parallel to John Bowlby's (1961) description of infants who, when removed from their parents, went through stages of anger or arousal, despair, and then apathy and withdrawal.

Voodoo Deaths

Voodoo deaths, hexing, and bone-pointing offer a journey into the exotic for the individual who wearies of the more mundane world in which she or he lives. In voodoo death, the person who desires the death is not the person who is to die, but someone else, perhaps an individual paid to place the hex or perhaps an individual who has cause to wish the death to occur.

Authorities are not in agreement about the effectiveness of voodoo death. One study by two psychiatrists indicated that medical authorities in communities where voodoo was freely practiced were in essential agreement that voodoo deaths did occur (Hackett & Weisman, 1961). Another physician made the case that voodoo deaths are not psychological but, rather, occur because the hexer actually murders the victim, often by poison, in order to collect his fee; however, he makes it appear that a spirit power caused the death (Barber, 1961).

Not all voodoo stories have unhappy endings. A professor of psychiatry observed a fascinating series of events while he was a visiting professor in a foreign country:

> A man was brought to the hospital, obviously near death and also extremely frightened. Once we ascertained that his fear was not because he was dying, but because of a curse placed on him, the head physician decided to try an experiment. He went to the medicine man and threatened him with homicide charges in the event that the patient died. Of course, this was against local law and also had no chance of succeeding in court, but the medicine man didn't know that. Although he denied any responsibility for the hex, he did agree to visit the patient in the hospital where we observed him give some message to the dying man. Within one day, the patient's condition began to improve, and within a week he was completely recovered and returned home [M. E. Wright, personal communication].

Explaining the Inexplicable

What causes unexplainable deaths? One possible answer depends on mystical, extrasensory, or supernatural interventions. People who desire to die just "go ahead and die"; the curse from a voodoo hex is sufficient by itself to cause death.

Another possibility, which is certainly more in keeping with most modern thinking, is that changes in living patterns lead to death. People under a curse learn about the curse and, believing in its efficacy, they become frightened; their fear then changes their eating patterns, so that their nutritional intake is reduced or they can no longer adequately digest what they do eat. At the same time, their sleep patterns are disturbed, and they become fatigued. Between the lack of adequate nutrition and the increasing fatigue, their resistance to a variety of illnesses is reduced; they easily become ill and die. The same explanation could be applied to the prison-camp deaths and even the postoperative deaths. Furthermore, many of these people have already suffered social deaths: they are isolated from persons who matter to them, and they receive little cognitive stimulation, since they do not attend to the stimulation that is available. This social pattern exacerbates their increasingly precarious health condition, and the result is organic breakdown (Kalish, 1970). Hackett and Weisman (1961) suggest that truth and mutual trust might provide a counterhex.

Another tack is to look at the studies of stress and psychosomatic illness. One author concluded that "death may be instigated by radical alteration in physiological functioning in response to a psychologically stressful situation" (Lachman, 1982–83, p. 348). This requires that the victim believe in the effectiveness of the cause (that is, bone-pointing, sorcery, incantations, hexes, and comparable events) and that he or she know that the voodoo process has been set in motion; the more suggestible the individual and the more volatile the person's body physiology, the more likely the "curse" is to work. It also requires that the changes that occur within the body be sufficiently intense and of sufficient duration to lead to the illness and/or death (Lachman, 1982–83).

Another possibility, which does not really contradict the previous ones, is that voodoo and hex deaths are produced by strong fears that cause intense action of the sympathetic-adrenal system and a rapid fall of blood pressure (Cannon, 1942). One well-known study described rats that had their whiskers clipped and were then put into jars filled with water. The rats died, but their lungs contained virtually no water; rather, they apparently died of slowing of the heart (Richter, 1959). This suggests they died of despair rather than of fear. The general consensus among those who have written on this topic is that the unexplainable deaths are caused by depression, which arises from despair and helplessness.

Magical Numbers

- I am a 42-year-old woman with two children. My parents and their parents all died before the age of 45; my older brother died at the age of 45; my father's two brothers were killed in the war, and my mother's brother died as a child; the only cousin I have who was born before I was born died at 44. The deaths in my family resulted from a variety of illnesses and accidents, so there is no particular pattern in that regard. Will I be alive for my 46th birthday?
- I am the father of three sons, the oldest of whom has just had his twelfth birthday. My father died when I was 13. Will I die when my oldest son is 13?
- Both my parents were physicians, and all my life I heard them called Dr. Albans. I always felt that if I could be Dr. Albans also, I could die happy. Finally, when my youngest child went into third grade, I was able to get into medical school. Next month, I will also be Dr. Albans. Will I then die?

Perhaps you will understand these magical numbers, or perhaps you will have little feeling for why they are important. It is not unusual to feel that one's life script calls for death at a particular age, based on family history or some fantasy. Do people die according to these scripts? From time to time, I have been told of someone who has, yet I also know that most people live past the age or situation that they imagine calls for their death. No research has been done on this topic, and research would be extremely difficult to conduct—although investigations of the effects of anniversary reactions on other events, such as mental illness and suicide, do suggest significant influences.

Magical numbers can also work in the opposite direction.

- I was born in 1925, and I always wanted to see the new century in. I used to think that was the year 2000, but I learned some years ago that next century doesn't begin until 2001. I *must* live to see that year.
- My youngest child has always been troublesome, but I know he will settle down when he is older. I *must* live to see him settled down.
- All my life I have been fascinated by China; I have read everything possible on China, and I probably know more about it than most State Department experts. I *must* live to see China.

None of us knows how these magical numbers and events work or even whether they have any effect at all. Nevertheless, they are part of our feelings and beliefs about ourselves, and if you believe that we do have some control over how we live and when we die, then you can at least consider them as possible influences in our future. One psychotherapist frequently asks clients in family therapy to tell her about how they see their deaths, and she states that very few adults are unable to respond. Their magical numbers influence not only the possibility of their dying but also how they plan their lives. Those whose magical numbers call for an early death may press for early success or may decide to spend a lot of time with their families. Those who anticipate a late death or have never considered the possibility of dying (however unrealistic the latter is, many people fit the description) may plan a very different kind of life for themselves.

"Death Dips"

Another kind of magical number is exhibited in what are sometimes called **"death dips."** For some people, certain dates have developed a death-related significance. I will discuss this in Chapter 11 when I discuss bereavement in general. Other dates are unrelated to grieving for loved ones. For example, Christmas, which is presumed to be a time of happiness, intensifies unhappiness and depression in some individuals and is a season of suicide as well as of pleasure.

Some fascinating research has shown that people are more likely to die after such occasions as Christmas or Yom Kippur and their own birthdays than before (Phillips & Feldman, 1973). One study showed that many more people die in the three months following their birthday than in the three months preceding that occasion (Kunz & Summers, 1979–80). As you might assume, not all research investigators obtained consistent results (for example, Harrison & Moore, 1982–83), so there is still doubt whether the death dip actually operates. Nonetheless, it is an intriguing idea with enough research support to take seriously.

Now that you have finished the chapter, you will recognize my biases: that "unnatural deaths" are as natural as any other kinds of death, that unexplainable deaths are not truly beyond the possibility of explanation. Our nomenclature isn't always perfect, but sometimes it is all we have.

This chapter has discussed four causes of death. Suicide and euthanasia are often grouped together, since each involves someone's making the decision that a particular person (oneself or someone else) would be better off dead than alive. The third cause, disasters, is seldom grouped with the other two, and the fourth, unexplainable death, is really a collection of various causes. Consider how the responses of the bereaved might vary as a result of a death from each of the four.

GRIEF
AND
BEREAVEMENT

"IF YOU REALLY HAVE
NOTHING TO LOSE,
YOU HAVE NOTHING."

Seven Days

It was really a lot more like seven months. But I will try to tell the story coherently, or at least chronologically. I will try.

My father died the summer I was eighteen, and I was on holiday, staying with my aunt and uncle in Ecuador. We had come to the United States from Ecuador five years before, and this was my first return visit.

Just as the summer was reaching its end, I felt an overwhelming and inexplicable need to talk to my father, and I called him. I couldn't reach him by phone or amateur radio, and my unhappiness was taken for adolescent moodiness, so no one took me very seriously. And then my mother called. She asked me to return home immediately, because she needed an operation and wanted me by her side. I asked to talk to my father. She said that he was not there. I told her that he was dead. She denied it. I asked why he wasn't the one to call if she was ill. She said that he was very busy. I said that he was dead. She denied it again and tried to comfort me. And the phone was taken from me. Tío Leon had a long conversation with my mother and then with relatives who suddenly appeared from nowhere. The place became crowded and smoky, and the hushed whispers made my ears hurt, and I must have been hysterical, because someone gave me a pill of some kind and a cigarette and told me to hush.

I kept insisting that my father was dead, and everyone looked at me a lot but said nothing, except in low tones to each other. Of course, now I understand why. They were in shock and under orders not to tell me that my father had died, because, according to my mother, "it would be too traumatic." So they legitimately had nothing to say.

Tío Leon's wife, Lili, packed my suitcases. I remember thinking that she probably had never seen a hanging suitcase before, because she packed mine as if it were an ordinary case. I tried to tell her, but no matter what I thought, or what I wanted to say, the only words that would come out of my mouth were "My father is dead."

The next three days were crazy. There were no seats on any planes leaving Quito, and finally we went to Guayaquil in order to catch a plane there. This involved a trip from the Andes to the coast, and although we obviously made it, to this day I do not remember how. Anyway. We got there, made reservations for the next morning on a direct flight to New York, and checked into a hotel. I was despondent, and Tío Leon, along with some of his friends who appeared without explanation, took me driving to raise my spirits. We passed a club I remembered from my childhood, and when I heard the music, I suggested that we go in and have a drink. Tío Leon became very upset. He would not allow it, and he would not explain why. I knew then, as well as I know today, what the reason was. My father had died, and in Jewish law, music is forbidden for a year after the death of a parent. But still, no one would admit that he was dead. Somehow, the day passed, and we went to our rooms.

Sometime in the middle of the night, I received a phone call from Tío Leon, who was in a room down the hall. When I answered it, he said "Tampoco puedes dormir?" (Can't you sleep, either?) I was quiet for a while and finally whispered "no." Tío Leon came to my room, and we sort of talked for a while. Then, unrelated to anything, he told me. "Your father has died, and you have no father anymore, and so I will be your father." And he started to cry. Hard. So hard that his false teeth fell out, and it took me a little while to find them in the dark. And then I comforted him and became very calm. Or at least I think I did. I may have been numb. Mostly, I felt painfully victorious, for I had known all the while. Yet, now that Tío Leon had actually confirmed that my father had died, I could not believe it.

When he quieted, he remembered me and asked me what I wanted to do. I wanted to go for a walk in the park to look for a friend, who, I told Tío Leon, would probably be there. Naturally, my friend was not in the park. Who walks around parks in the middle of the night anyway? But it seemed to make a lot of sense then. The morning eventually came, and I thought that I had slept most of the night, yet at the airport I overheard Tío Leon telling someone that my eyes had been open all night and that I didn't even blink. I remember smiling and thinking that maybe I had slept with my eyes open. While I was waiting, I felt very isolated. They talked to each other but not to me. In fact, it seemed as if they did not want to come close. I wanted to tell them that death is not contagious and that I couldn't give it to them as if it were a cold. I felt like a pariah. I liked the sound of the word, and in my mind, I set it to music. Soon I was inaudibly singing "Pariah, pariah, pa-pariah...." Somehow, I kept changing the sound of the word until it became "princess," and I decided that the attractive young woman under the big floppy hat and the dark glasses was a princess on a secret mission, traveling incognito. And that is who I was all the way to New York. It was sort of fun, in a strange, guilty kind of way. And then the plane landed, and I had to deal with the reality that I was an eighteen-year-old girl whose father was dead.

My mother was so sedated when I got home that she hardly knew me. The funeral arrangements had been made while they were waiting for my return, and if Sears & Roebuck had made them, they could not have been more impersonal. My father was to be buried in New Jersey. (New Jersey? He would not even have been able to find the cemetery in life. None of us had ever been to that part of the state.) The funeral service was to be held by someone who had never met my father, in a synagogue which none of us had ever entered. (When the time came, he said the usual, applicable-to-anyone things.)

Someone went out to buy me a black dress, and the funeral people tore it in several places. I put on my rent garment, and the dance began. And it lasted seven days. Seven days of shovelfuls of dirt in my dreams, roses falling into graves. Red for mothers. White for daughters. Seven days of covered mirrors and windows, sitting on little backless stools, eating food brought by others, praying—because we did pray. And although my father had no sons, the prayer for the dead was said for him twice a day for seven days. And to the astonishment and perhaps disapproval of friends and family, I was the one who prayed for him. A female child.

It is twenty years later now, and I still remember many things. The casket, for instance. I knew that my father would not have liked it, and besides, I was not entirely sure that he was in it. A big part of me thought that he had run away from all these people—people who appear only at funerals and feed on grief. Perhaps that is unfair, but it certainly seemed real then. My father's hands. I could not forget my father's hands, any more than I could remember his face without looking at a photograph. The emptiness I felt. If emptiness can be felt. Because I did not feel anything, except maybe anger. The whisky that I drank as if it were water, and with little more effect than water would have had. My guitar. I couldn't play it, but I held it. My mother swaying and chanting on her little stool. Let me explain the little stools. In the seven days following the burial of a Jewish person, the immediate family sits on stools that are lower than the rest of the chairs in the house to symbolize grief. These stools have no backs, to symbolize discomfort, but I quickly found that there is no symbolism there. More than anything else, those little stools made me want to stop grieving. When Shivah, the seven days, was over, I burned mine.

More memories: Washing our hands after returning from the cemetery and before entering the house. Because you may not bring death into the house. And in a strange way, we didn't. The insurance salesman, whom I finally called a vulture and threw out of the house. The ten faceless men who gathered morning and evening. Because it takes ten men for a minyan: a prayer quorum. I remember asking myself: "If I pray by myself, will God hear? Would he hear nine people? How about eight who really meant it?"

The seven days finally ended. After a long time. We washed and changed our rent garments for clean ones, without death and suffering torn into them. And we went on. It was difficult at first, and it got more difficult later. But we survived. Through it all I wanted to die many times. In fact, I became fond of saying, only half in jest, that the thought of suicide saw me through many a bad night. It was all over one day, inasmuch as grieving is ever finished. And I had learned something. Life is as irrevocable as death.

Toni C. Mehler

CHAPTER TEN

The Grieving Process

Anything that you have, you can lose; anything you are attached to, you can be separated from; anything you love can be taken away from you. Yet, if you really have nothing to lose, you have nothing.

There are numerous kinds of losses that each of us suffers, and there is no way we can avoid loss in our lives. Consider your own life and ask yourself how often you have lost each of the following:

- A parent, brother or sister, spouse, or child through death.
- A familiar relationship with a spouse, parent, or child through divorce.
- A job that you either liked or had become attached to.
- A familiar neighborhood.
- A home you either liked or had become attached to.
- Some physical capacity, such as the ability to walk or to hear.
- A pet, through death or other cause.
- Faith in or respect for an important system of religious, moral, or political beliefs.
- Something you owned that was important to you, such as a wedding ring, a car you loved, or a family heirloom.
- Membership in a group that was important to you, such as a social club or a group of close friends.
- Anything else that really mattered to you.

There are other kinds of losses: the loss of a wonderful dream for the future, carried by so many young and some not-so-young; the loss of innocence, when, for example, a child first learns that the world can be cruel or adults malevolent; the loss of sexual virginity; the loss of respect for someone previously idolized. Each of these losses can lead to bereavement, grief, and mourning.

Bereavement is a state involving loss. In fact, to *bereave* means "to take away from, to rob, to dispossess." Although the term usually implies that the loss produces unhappiness, this is not essential to its meaning: my father, to whom I am very close, dies, and I am bereaved; my mother, who has been both physically and psychologically absent from my life for 15 years, dies, and I am also bereaved—perhaps equally so in the strict definition. In both instances, I have had something taken away from me, although the value of that something differs greatly.

Grief refers to the feelings of sorrow, anger, guilt, and confusion that can arise when you have suffered a loss or are bereaved. It seems fair to say that you can't grieve without being bereaved, but you can be bereaved and not grieve. Although the process of grieving seems necessary to full recovery from a significant loss, grieving itself means pain and suffering.

Mourning is the overt expression of grief and bereavement. The ways in which we mourn are heavily influenced by our culture; we may dress in black or in white, attend funerals or say prayers at home, drink and laugh at the wake, or take tranquilizers and cry at the funeral.

THE NATURE OF GRIEF AND ITS PAIN

"The pain of grief is just as much a part of life as the joy of love; it is, perhaps, the price we pay for love, the cost of commitment" (Parkes, 1972, pp. 5–6).

> I always emphasize to my clients that they only do what they choose to do. When they say they don't have any choice, I point out that they have a choice, but that the alternative is too unappealing to be considered. One young man was telling me of the pain he was suffering because of the death of his father, and he challenged me by saying that he hadn't wanted his father to die and he hadn't wanted the pain of his grief. I asked him why his father's death pained him so much, and he responded by saying that he had loved his father. I then suggested that he could have avoided the pain by not loving his father. He was quickly aware that the love he had for his father was well worth the suffering he was experiencing. Realizing that he had made a choice and that his choice was a good one, he felt less unhappy and much more willing to accept the pain and survive it [Personal communication, printed by permission of John Enright].

Human beings are not the only form of animal life to suffer grief. Other animals, especially primates, also grieve when loss occurs, especially when an infant dies or when captivity separates them from companions or mates (Averill, 1968). Although the evidence for grief in animals other than primates is limited, some individuals report observing similar behavior in dogs and even birds. "The loss of a mate by one of these birds [jackdaws and geese] typically occasions frantic searching and calling. If this is unsuccessful in reuniting the pair, a period of depressed activity may ensue, including a loss of sexual interest in potential new partners" (Averill, 1968, p. 732).

The extent and duration of grief vary from person to person, probably on the basis of both the centrality of the relationship and the preventability of the death (Bugen, 1977). This means that the grief will be more intense and last longer for survivors (1) for whom the death led to the loss of important roles and relationships and (2) who believed the death might have been prevented; the latter is especially true if they see themselves as having been potentially able to prevent the death.

The Purpose of Grieving

Grieving seems necessary to effective functioning. Assuming that the nature of the loss appropriately leads to grief, the grief requires some form of expression. Whether this happens early in the bereavement or later, with great initial intensity or spread out over time, through public display of tears or through private sorrowing, by means of overt behavioral expressions of grief or by means of physiological changes, grief will virtually always be expressed in some fashion.

Worden (1982) outlines four tasks that need to be accomplished in order to move beyond grief. First, the grieving person must accept the reality of the loss—that the death has in fact occurred. Denying the death or even denying the meaning of the death or the irreversibility of the death can often lead to prolonged and unhealthy or, occasionally, pathological grief.

Second, the grieving person must accept that grief is painful. Use of alcohol or drugs of any sort, including tranquilizers; avoidance of the feelings of anger or remorse or sadness; unnecessarily deep involvement with work or sex—these are some of the devices that people use to avoid the pain of grieving.

Third, the grieving person needs to adjust to an environment that no longer includes the person who has died. This means taking on new tasks ("My husband always took care of all checks and financial arrangements, but now I do that"), doing things alone, and remaining a functioning individual in situations that once depended on the now-deceased person.

And fourth, the grieving person needs, over time, to be able to withdraw much of the emotional energy once invested in the dead person and begin to reinvest it in other relationships. This is not a betrayal of the dead person's memory but is more often a tribute to that person's meaning.

A mother in her midthirties was left widowed with three small children. Before his death, she and her husband had many long discussions about their love for each other and about her ability to go on living effectively after his death. The last few weeks of their life together were upsetting, because of his growing cancer, but were also very rich in terms of their feelings for each other. A child psychiatrist, he maintained his practice until a week before his death. Having had a satisfactory relationship with her husband, the widow was freed from guilt and anger after his death. Within a year she had met a somewhat older widower, and they were married several months later.

To withdraw emotional energy does not mean to forget the dead person but to become able to develop healthy new relationships.

Stages of Normal Grief

Stages of grief, like stages of dying, have frequently been described in the literature about death. Many people have applied Elisabeth Kübler-Ross' five stages of dying to the process of grieving as well, and this application can serve as a useful framework. Other stage theories of grieving may do the job better. Averill, for example, proposes three stages of grieving: shock, despair, and recovery. British psychiatrist Colin Parkes suggests four: numbness, pining, depression, and recovery.

In comparing these theories, one sees that the last two are almost identical, except that Averill encompasses Parkes' two stages of pining and depression in the one stage of despair. Kübler-Ross' denial stage is comparable to the first stages described by Averill and Parkes; she has no stage similar to Parkes' pining, but her stages of anger and depression are counterparts of despair and depression; her final stage of acceptance is the equivalent of recovery. So the three theories parallel one another.

In reviewing these theories one should keep in mind that the stages of grieving are not invariable or even, necessarily, adaptive. Perhaps it is most useful to heed Parkes' (1972) reminder that grief is a process and that what is observed early in the process of grieving differs from what is seen later. There is also a strong tendency to underestimate the time it takes to move from the initial shock of death to moderate recovery. People, of course, return to what appears to a casual observer to be normal functioning in a few days, but the pangs of grief continue for weeks and months, though with diminishing frequency and intensity. A reminder of the dead person or simply a period when the level of general stress is high may produce a wave of grief one, two, or several years later. Certainly it takes at least one year for a reasonable recovery in most instances, and a two-year period is not unusual (a time period also proposed by Weiss, 1975, for recovery from divorce). In some ways an important loss always remains with us.

Normal Expressions of Grief

Grief can be expressed overtly through traditional mourning behavior or in ways that do not coincide with cultural expectations but nonetheless represent the feelings of the individual. Expressions of grief can be encouraged by the situation, such as a funeral where many people are sobbing, so that your own sadness becomes expressed through sobbing. Or such expressions can be restrained by the situation, as when you and your sisters are negotiating to divide your mother's jewelry, and you don't wish to permit your emotions to dominate you. Grief can also be expressed unconsciously: your tears at the third-rate movie are far greater than the film deserved, and you realize some hours later that the scene where you cried the most was very similar to your own experiences with the recent death of your grandmother.

There is no "correct" way to express grief, but some ways appear to lead to more effective recovery from the distressing aspects of grief. Rather than talk about "abnormal" grief, I prefer to think in terms of healthy grief and unhealthy grief, with the knowledge that unhealthy grief occasionally becomes extreme enough to be considered pathological grief. We can judge the extent to which grief is healthy or unhealthy by determining whether it leads to long-term personal well-being and effective functioning or to distress and disrupted functioning. Another way of looking at healthy and unhealthy grief is to determine the extent to which it enables the grieving individual to accomplish the four tasks described above.

For grief to be pathological, not only must it fail to accomplish the four tasks but it must be either of such lengthy duration or so disruptive of other aspects of life that the meaning of the death or other loss cannot come near to providing an explanation.

Grief may be manifested in many ways. William Worden, a long-term researcher in the areas of dying and grieving, has proposed that these be viewed as falling into four global categories, while recognizing that the categories cannot be seen as having rigid boundaries. These categories are physical, cognitive, affective, and behavioral.

PHYSICAL EXPRESSIONS OF GRIEF

Physical expressions of grief range from lack of energy to the possibility of fatal illness. These can be divided into two categories: bodily feelings, such as a dry mouth, and physical health concerns. In keeping with Worden's (1982) categorization, we have placed some physical issues, such as sighing or crying, in the section on behavioral responses.

Bodily Sensations

Undoubtedly Erich Lindemann's 1944 article on the symptomatology of grief is the most influential single piece of writing on the topic. Basing his comments on interviews and psychotherapy with over 100 bereaved persons who had lost family members in a catastrophic night-club fire, the psychiatrist developed careful descriptions of normal and pathological grieving reactions.

One set of symptoms common to all the people whom Lindemann interviewed included "sensations of somatic distress occurring in waves lasting from twenty minutes to an hour at a time, a feeling of tightness in the throat, choking with shortness of breath, need for sighing, and an empty feeling in the abdomen, lack of muscular power and an intense subjective distress described as tension or mental pain" (1944/1965, p. 187). Parkes (1972) refers to this constellation of reactions as "pangs" and indicates that they are the most characteristic single response to grief. Adding sobbing and crying to Lindemann's description, Parkes says these pangs begin shortly after the death—a few hours or a few days later—and last from a few days to about two weeks. Over time, the pangs occur less frequently, until eventually they are expressed only when there is an anniversary or other reminder of the death.

In instances in which grief pangs do not occur right away, the bereaved frequently feel numb; that is, they perceive themselves as being without appropriate feelings and sometimes without any feelings at all (Parkes, 1972). The numbness is not continuous; strong feelings will sometimes interrupt, and it tends to pass within a few days. In effect, it appears to be the counterpart of a state of shock after an accident. Persons falling from

mountains describe a similar state (Noyes & Kletti, 1972), which is characterized by a sense of unreality and lack of feelings.

One grief counselor noted the most common physical responses to grief he
had observed among those coming to his center for help (Worden, 1982):

- Hollow feeling in stomach
- Tight feeling in chest
- Tight feeling in throat
- Oversensitive reaction to noise
- Sense of depersonalization (nothing seems real)
- Breathlessness, feeling short of breath
- Muscular weakness
- Lack of energy
- Dry mouth

It's obvious that many of the symptoms that Worden frequently notes are
virtually identical to the reactions described by Lindemann (1944/1965) and
Parkes (1972) in different contexts.

Physical Health Concerns

The metaphor of the broken heart is an old one, but it appears that the
metaphor may have a strong basis in reality. A British study of 4500 widowers over the age of 54 found a major increase in their death rate during the
six months following bereavement, after which it dropped back to expected
levels (Young, Benjamin, & Wallis, 1963). When a further analysis was made
of the causes of death, a very high proportion was due to heart disease
(Parkes, Benjamin, & Fitzgerald, 1969).

Many other studies have documented significant increases in illness and in
death following bereavement (Jacobs & Ostfeld, 1977). One comprehensive
review of numerous such investigations supports the existence of the relationship, largely for the six months or so after the death (Rowland, 1977).
This appears to be true not only for widows but for parents, brothers and
sisters, and children as well (Parkes, in press). The responses of infants and
very young children to separation may offer some explanation of this phenomenon. Many years ago, it was observed that children who had been
placed in institutions both had a high rate of illness and underwent a pattern
of protest followed by despair and then by apathy (Bowlby, 1961; Ribble,
1943). As the children became apathetic, they appeared to give up, and many
became sick. The symptoms were termed **marasmus,** but the condition was
somewhat different from that normally defined by the medical term. This
syndrome was believed to be a response to separation, and concern about
separation was termed **separation anxiety.** Despair and apathy might be
seen as paralleling Parkes' stages of pining and depression.

Parkes, who is often cited in these pages, had worked closely with Bowlby,
whose work on separation has made a tremendous impact on the field of
infant and child development. In pursuing the work with adults, Parkes
(1964, 1972) found, as have subsequent researchers, the previously men-

tioned increase in physical problems, including health problems leading to death.

Other studies comparing nonelderly widows with comparable married women showed that the widows had many more symptoms, including nervousness, depression, fear of "going crazy," persisting fears, nightmares, insomnia, reduced work capacity, and fatigue. All these had been considered typical symptoms of grieving, but these widows also complained of headaches, dizziness, fainting spells, skin rashes, indigestion, vomiting, palpitations, chest pains, and other physical symptoms (Maddison & Viola, 1968).

What produces these physical symptoms? One obvious explanation is that the fatigue, poor diet, irregular habits, and social restrictions often experienced by persons caring for the dying and by others who are deeply concerned may reduce the body's ability to protect itself from disease and to recover from disease once it occurs. There is also the possibility that the depression and hopelessness that often accompany bereavement have a direct effect on body chemistry that alters its resistance to disease. Schulz (1978) has combined these two ideas and called them the "desolation effect."

COGNITIVE EXPRESSIONS OF GRIEF

Worden (1982) lists a number of ways in which the bereaved express their grief cognitively: disbelief, confusion, preoccupation with thoughts of the dead person and perhaps of the dying process, and encounters with the dead person in ways that make that person seem still alive. These are all well-known reactions to a significant loss.

Less well known, but probably equally common, is the tendency to go over, again and again, all the events that led up to the death. This can become a virtual preoccupation for some individuals, but almost all of us partake of it to some extent. In the days and weeks after the death, the closest family members will share experiences with one another—sometimes providing new information and insights into the person who died, sometimes reminiscing over familiar experiences. Each person offers his or her own piece of the puzzle of death. "When I saw him last Saturday, he looked as though he were rallying." "Yes, but the next morning, the nurse told me he had had a bad night." "Do you think it might have had something to do with his sister's illness?" "I doubt it, but I heard from an aide that he fell going to the bathroom that morning." "That explains that bruise on his elbow." "No wonder he told me that he was angry because he couldn't seem to do anything right." And so it goes, the attempt to understand why someone who was rallying on Saturday was dead on Wednesday.

When a death is caused by an accident or a disaster, the effort to make sense of it is pursued more vigorously. As added pieces of news come trickling in, they are integrated into the puzzle. The bereaved want to put the death into a perspective that they can understand—divine intervention, a curse from a neighboring tribe, a logical sequence of cause and effect, or whatever it may be.

Eventually each of us finds an adequate "story of the dying and death"—of John Kennedy or of our father or of a friend. Versions of the death may differ—whether the physician really did all she could to save the patient, whether Aunt Bella showed up frequently at the hospital or not, whether the operation succeeded or didn't quite succeed, whether father was ready to die or would have lived longer if possible—but each person's version satisfies him or her, and that version, with slight modifications, becomes the official version for the teller.

The stages of dying eventually end, but the stages of grieving do not. Even full recovery does not mean that all sense of loss, all sense of sadness and deprivation, all sense of anger and guilt have ended. Nor, as Victor Marshall has pointed out, should we wish this to be the case (personal communication, 1979).

AFFECTIVE EXPRESSIONS OF GRIEF

There are numerous ways in which we express grief emotionally. Those to be discussed here include (1) depression, sadness, and sorrow, (2) relief, (3) guilt and anger, and (4) denial. A final section will describe some of the psychiatric issues that have emerged as possible results of grief.

Depression, Sadness, Sorrow

Everything we know about grief indicates that sadness and sorrow that may be intense enough to be considered depression are among the most familiar characteristics of grieving. The death of a loved person is an objective loss, and we are sad when we lose what we love. The grandfather of bereavement research, sociologist Thomas Eliot (1955), described this sorrow as "inevitable but not insurmountable."

We expect that people who are grieving will behave in ways that we might consider pathological under other circumstances (Averill, 1968). Numerous investigators have found that widows and widowers describe many more depressive symptoms than do people in carefully selected nonbereaved comparison groups (for example, Maddison & Viola, 1968; Parkes & Brown, 1972). One study found that 35% of a group of 109 widows and widowers who were evaluated one month after bereavement displayed symptoms similar to those of depressed psychiatric patients. The only real difference between those who were very depressed and those who were not was that fewer of the former had children to whom they felt close living nearby. The investigators proposed that this group's lack of access to emotional support from their children had contributed to their depression (Clayton, Halikas, & Maurice, 1972). Not having children available and no longer having the companionship of a spouse, these individuals may have become lonely and isolated.

A follow-up study with the same persons a year later produced additional interesting results. At that time only 16 of the 92 participants located were considered depressed; 12 of the depressed widows and widowers had been depressed a year earlier, and 4 who previously had seemed healthy had become depressed. However, 24 of the 36 persons who had been depressed after the first month of bereavement and 52 of the 56 persons who had not been depressed were not depressed a year later. The depressed group also reported a high incidence of dizziness, blurred vision, chest pains, and poor general health (Bornstein, Clayton, Halikas, Maurice, & Robins, 1973).

At the end of the study, the authors make an extremely important point: "Grief is not a model for psychotic depression. Although some of our patients had depressive symptoms, none could be called psychotic at 13 months. . . . The normal depression of widowhood . . . is . . . different from clinical affective emotional disorder" (Bornstein et al., 1973, p. 566).

Results from another longitudinal study (Parkes & Weiss, 1983) confirmed these findings. These investigators were working with both widows and widowers, albeit more of the former, under the age of 45. In their follow-up 13 months after the death, the bereaved were compared with a group of nonbereaved persons. Those who had suffered the death of a spouse were more depressed than the control group; they were also more worried about loneliness, more restless, more likely to view life as not worthwhile, and more likely to experience physical illness having an autonomic-nervous-system basis, which implies health problems with emotional origins (Glick, Weiss, & Parkes, 1974).

Most of the research participants were interviewed again, between two years and four years after the death. At this time, those who were seen as having made a good recovery from their grief were compared with those whose recovery might be deemed unhealthy. The latter were much more likely to have talked about wishing for their own death early in the research, which indicated depression (Parkes & Weiss, 1983).

Relief

Mingled with other emotions after a death are often feelings of relief. Now it's over. Now I don't have to wonder when he will die or whether she will be in pain. Now I don't have to look at him, lying in the hospital and suffering— and suffer myself as I do. Now I don't have to spend hours every day, changing the bedding and cleaning up. Now I don't have to wake up two or three times every night to respond to her call bell.

Some of the relief comes from being relieved of the caretaking responsibilities and from no longer having to watch someone who is dearly loved suffer and die. Some of the relief comes from the return to familiar routines. The dying process often requires that old and preferred routines be discarded for new ones. Death offers the possibility of returning to the earlier ways of living: a dutiful daughter who left her job to care for her mother can now return to work; a grandson who came home every day after school to attend to his grandfather can now play instead; a husband and three children can now have dinners with their wife/mother, who no longer needs to visit her mother in the hospital after work every day.

Relief comes also from a new sense of freedom—although it may have a considerable admixture of guilt. Since any relationship presents some restrictions, becoming freed of that relationship offers new options in life. I very much love my mother, father, sister, brother, spouse, son, daughter, but if that person were not around, how much freedom I could have! Sometimes a person's death gives one freer access to money, to work, to better social position, or even to people. The death of a monarch, for example, permits the next in line to assume the throne; the death of a father permits a son to take over the family business; the death of a woman permits her husband, whom she was divorcing, to regain the opportunity of parenting his young children.

Relief, of course, like other emotions evoked by a death, occurs in conjunction with a variety of feelings, such as guilt, anger, and "emptiness." Consider the implications for guilt, for example, in the situations described in the previous paragraph.

Guilt and Anger

When Parkes and Weiss (1983) looked for differences between widows and widowers who had shown a good recovery from the death of a spouse two to four years earlier and those whose recovery was poor, two of the most significant early predictors were anger and self-reproach. In other words, those bereaved who expressed anger and self-reproach or guilt a few weeks after the death were found to have made a much poorer recovery from grief two or more years later.

The authors believed that the poor recoveries represented marriages in which ambivalent feelings, rather than loving or completely nonloving feelings, were prevalent. They also learned that bereaved spouses who indicated shortly after the death that their marriages had had many conflicts not only showed less emotion just after the death but displayed many more problems when interviewed both 13 months and 24–48 months after their bereavement (Parkes & Weiss, 1983).

Parkes (1972) further reports that most of the British widows he interviewed admitted strong feelings of anger at some time during the first years after the deaths of their husbands. This anger, related to restlessness, tension, and a rigidly controlled impulsiveness, was expressed in comments like "My nerves are on edge" or "I feel all in a turmoil inside."

Why did the widows feel anger, when they were still alive? Part of their anger probably came from guilt, as explained earlier. However, another major source probably was the sense of having been abandoned. The bereaved may implicitly feel that persons who have died did so on purpose—to make them feel bad or to cause them to fend for themselves. A grieving person recognizes consciously that this isn't true; nevertheless, it is a way of expressing anger over having been abandoned.

Bowlby (1961), in describing the process that infants go through when separated from their mothers, cites the stages as (1) protest, (2) despair, and (3) apathy. The anger that a grieving person feels is comparable to the protest expressed by the infant. After all, both feel abandoned; both are suffering from separation. As an example, when an elderly woman was told by her daughter that her son-in-law was going to die of cancer soon, she sat down abruptly, shook her head mournfully, and cried out "Oh, that this should happen to me!" In a way, of course, she was being self-centered, since her son-in-law was about to die, her daughter was about to be widowed, and her grandchildren were about to become fatherless. On the other hand, her cry was very human and understandable: she was expressing her own protest and anger.

Anger is frequently displaced. The older woman mentioned above was not so much expressing anger with her son-in-law as expressing a generalized, undirected anger, comparable to Bowlby's protest. But victims of displaced anger are common, and they often are not aware of what is happening. (Similar reactions occur during the period following a divorce.) The grieving person may direct his or her anger at others who are around and who are often trying to be helpful. Also, anger may be directed at God, at the medical profession in general, at a particular hospital or physician, or at others who might possibly have had some responsibility. And, of course, the dead people themselves can become lightning rods for the anger and can be accused of not having taken adequate precautions or not having "tried hard enough." "Widows often seem to regard the pain of grieving as an unjust punishment and to feel angry with the presumed author. The death is personalized as something that has been done to them and they seek for someone to blame. . . . God and the doctors came in for a lot of angry criticism since both were seen as having power over life and death" (Parkes, 1972, p. 81). Others also become scapegoats: family members, employers, funeral directors.

That the loss of a spouse or other loved person also evokes guilt is well-known. Because this feeling is painful, it, in turn, elicits anger directed toward the dead person who is the source of the guilt. But being angry with someone who is dead is obviously unfair and inappropriate, so the anger engenders still more guilt.

The guilt arises from a number of sources. Most familiar is the "If only I had . . ." syndrome: If only I had kept him from driving that car; if only I had not permitted them to operate on her; if only I had been a better parent; if only I had been more attentive while she was alive; if only I had. . . . That is, guilt can arise from feeling both that you could have done something to prevent the death and that you did not treat the person right while he or she was alive.

People trying to comfort bereaved persons can respond by saying, for example, "There is nothing you could have done" or "She/he would understand." Often, of course, this kind of affirmation is less important than simply listening and indicating that you like and understand the bereaved person.

An excellent example of guilt arising from the feeling that one could have prevented a death—and of a double-bind situation—may be the case of a person recovering from a serious heart attack. Let's say the heart patient, a man, has returned to near-normal functioning but has been put on a fairly strict regimen in which he has to watch his diet, eliminate smoking, keep sexual activity moderate (no one has ever figured out exactly how to interpret that admonition), exercise moderately, and avoid stress. If the heart patient does not stick to his regimen, what is his wife to do? If she tries to control his diet and presses him to work less and exercise more, she may be inducing him to circumvent her or she may be causing an increase in stress. Conversely, if she permits him to continue as he is doing, she is permitting life-threatening practices. If her husband then has a second major coronary and dies, the wife can find justification for her guilt in whatever she had attempted to do. (This example is drawn from Schoenberg & Stichman, 1974.)

Sometimes the guilt arises from having had unconscious (or even conscious) death wishes directed toward the dead person. Now that she or he is really dead, there is some implicit sense that you caused the death or, at the very least, that your wishes were evil.

> An attractive young woman married a very close and extremely wealthy friend of her father's when she was 22 and he was 42. Within a few years, she became restless in the marriage and left her husband, whom she angrily accused of being insensitive to her feelings and of maintaining other sexual relationships, and he eventually sued for divorce. By the time the suit had begun, she was seeing a man her own age, a graduate student in history. Her husband was debating whether or not to settle the divorce suit out of court when his sports car rear-ended a medium-sized truck and he died before reaching the hospital. His wife, now an extremely wealthy widow, remarried shortly after.

In this story, a perverse Cinderella story, one matter is omitted: given her anger with her husband before his death, the wife felt tremendous guilt for her death wishes and was never happy in her new marriage.

The above events are all true, other than some minor changes caused by my own uncertain memory, except for one: I don't have the vaguest idea whether the wife felt guilty or not. The one time I visited her and her new husband, she seemed gloriously happy, but she and I were not close friends and she would certainly never have confided any guilt feelings to me. Since I don't know the real ending, I made up my own. You can do the same.

The above example suggests a further source of guilt: benefiting from someone's death in some fashion. For example, your uncle, whom you cared for deeply, died and left you a large inheritance. You are simultaneously pleased and sad over his death. Or you received a promotion at work when your supervisor died; you feel guilty because you are glad that he is no longer preventing your moving up in the company.

Death wishes need not be as potentially obvious as in the case of the young woman described above. No important relationship is entirely positive, and few or none are entirely negative. Therefore, every death produces both gain and loss. Think for a while of the person you love most in the world. You may imagine that if that person died, you would never stop grieving. Yet, think of some of the freedoms that the death of that person would offer: freedom to leave where you are and go elsewhere, freedom from having to adjust to someone else's eating and sleeping patterns, freedom to have social or sexual relationships with people who are now forbidden to you, freedom to dress or drive or speak in ways you now feel uncomfortable in doing. These kinds of feelings and tensions do not mean that the relationship is not good, only that no relationship is entirely satisfactory. When someone important to us dies, our grief is a strange, often unexpected mixture of many feelings, among which are frequently guilt and anger.

The final source of guilt to be examined here is survival itself. In some instances, survivors feel guilty for having survived. Survival guilt has been noted in people who have lived through active combat or the Nazi Holocaust or the Hiroshima and Nagasaki atomic bombings. Survival guilt caused them to ask "Why did I deserve to survive?" Those who lived felt fortunate, but at the same time they felt that, in some fashion, their lives were paid for by other people's deaths. A middle-aged woman recalls her childhood in a Nazi concentration camp. Prisoners were lined up and counted off by fives; on any day all the number threes, or perhaps the fours, were marched off to extermination in the gas chambers. Had this woman been a "three" on the wrong day, someone else would have lived, and she would have died. A soldier who fought in Korea still wonders why he survived hand-to-hand combat when so many men with young children were killed.

Denial

When death occurs suddenly and unexpectedly—and even in some other circumstances—the response of close family members may be denial. Sometimes this denial is so radical that the survivors do not believe that the person is actually dead. More often, however, their feelings are split, knowing the person is dead yet not able to believe it. You continue to make plans that implicitly assume the person is still alive; you think, for example, as you drive home from work, how nice it will be to discuss your exciting new development program with—and then reality intrudes (see pages 85–86).

Denial may take other forms. Someone will maintain a child's room just as it was when he or she died. A widower, for example, will continue to say "we" even though only one person is now involved. It's difficult to know exactly how much each of these actions depends on denial and how much on other factors, but denial is normally at least partly involved.

Later Psychiatric Problems

Increased illness rates are noted shortly after bereavement, and the studies of death following loss have been restricted to a fairly brief period. However, other possible consequences of bereavement take longer to emerge. For example, numerous studies have investigated the possible relationships between bereavement and mental hospitalization, suicide, and illegal behavior. Despite some conflicting results, the weight of the evidence would seem to support correlations between bereavement and these events.

It isn't, however, sufficient to establish the relationships. One must ask whether early childhood bereavement influences later psychiatric problems and whether recent bereavement influences psychiatric problems in general. One review article cites six studies that found schizophrenic patients had a higher-than-expected rate of childhood bereavement and five studies that showed no such relationship (Bendiksen & Fulton, 1975). More recently, other investigators have shown that early childhood bereavement is related to later schizophrenia (Watt & Nicholi, 1979) and to depression in the adult years (Brown, 1982).

Even the evidence from these studies, however, does not establish that it is the death itself that causes the psychiatric problem. When a significant person, such as a parent or child, dies, many aspects of life are disrupted; for example, there are major changes in financial status, in opportunities for love and care, and in family relationships. Thus, it might be these subsequent changes acting alone or acting in interaction with the impact of death that produce the difficulties, rather than just the death alone.

Sometimes the immediate response to a death and subsequent behavior appear to be pathological. As Freud has said, "Melancholia instead of a state of grief develops in some people, whom we consequently suspect of a morbid pathological disposition" (1917/1959b, p. 153). The features that Freud observed in these individuals included dejection, loss of interest in the outside world, loss of capacity to love, lowered activity level, poor self-concept, and a "delusional expectation of punishment" (p. 153). According to Freud, most of these are the same symptoms found in normal grief; it is poor self-concept, which includes self-recriminations and a feeling of worthlessness, that accounts for the pathology. This suggests that the sense of loss, rather than involving the dead person, is actually involving the individual himself or herself. "In grief the world becomes poor and empty; in melancholia it is the ego itself" (Freud, 1917/1959b, p. 155).

Some 50 years later, when Parkes (1972) compared the experiences, feelings, and behavior of bereaved psychiatric patients with those of widows displaying normal grief, he found that the former group expressed their grief over a longer period of time and took longer to begin to express grief. In addition, there was only one symptom that was not shared by psychiatric patients and widows with normal expression of grief: the patients had markedly more ideas of guilt and self-reproach. This would appear to be a direct confirmation of Freud's earlier formulation.

Studies investigating the relationship between early bereavement and illegal behavior show comparable findings. An early study described a series of cases of juvenile delinquents whose behavior appeared to have been a direct outcome of their bereavement (Shoor & Speed, 1963). Later, other investigators analyzed data from a large sample and concluded that childhood bereavement was predictive of individuals who would be convicted of illegal offenses by their early 20s (Markusen & Fulton, 1971).

BEHAVIORAL EXPRESSIONS OF GRIEF

If Worden's (1982) list of cognitive expressions of grief was brief, his list of behavioral reactions is not. They include—

• Sleep disturbances, such as insomnia or sudden awakening.

- Appetite disturbances, usually undereating.
- Absent-minded behavior, such as getting lost while driving because of taking a wrong turn, or missing appointments.
- Social withdrawal from other people, especially early in the mourning process.
- Dreams of the dead person, both normal dreams and nightmares.
- Sighing a great deal.
- Restless overactivity, such as having to get out of the house or not being able to concentrate on reading the newspaper.
- Crying.
- Avoiding reminders of the deceased.
- Visiting places or carrying objects that are reminders of the dead person (the opposite of avoiding these reminders).
- Treasuring objects that belonged to the deceased, such as keeping his or her room exactly as it had been, including clothing in the closet.

Systematic research supports many of Worden's observations. For example, the bereaved exhibited an increase in insomnia and weight loss, probably a reflection of poor appetite, considerably more frequently than the nonbereaved; and they showed a 28% increase in tobacco use, a 28% increase in alcohol consumption, and a 26% increase in use of tranquilizers one year following the death (Glick, Weiss, & Parkes, 1974).

Each of these forms of expression can have significance for the day-to-day functioning of a grieving individual in that the person's behavior can become less effective, which, in turn, may serve to prolong the grieving process. However, for the most part, it is only if these behaviors continue for a long time or remain intense longer than appropriate that they interfere in a meaningful fashion.

Another extremely important behavioral expression of grief is sometimes called **searching.** This is a restless activity, accompanied by preoccupation with thoughts of the dead person. It often includes a perceptual sensitization, so that others look like the dead person and varied events constantly recall general or specific memories of him or her. Sometimes grieving persons turn over specific past events in their minds, perhaps in an attempt to hold onto the person who died. When one recent widow told her two young children that their father had died, they took his clothes out of the closet and curled up under them. And my own experience is relevant here.

> When I was a junior in college, I wrote a short story about a young man who had gone to the cemetery to visit his father's grave. He had never been there before, but he felt certain that he could find the grave without directions. In effect, he believed he would have some form of mystic guidance. However, he never found the grave, and it was a deeply upsetting experience for him.

The odd thing is that I don't really know today whether I was writing about my own personal experience or not. I don't think I ever tried to visit my father's grave (I had not been at the burial itself, which was some 500 miles from where we lived at the time), but I'm not completely certain that I didn't make the attempt. This is a dramatic example of the search for the dead person and the confusion it can create.

RECOVERING FROM BEREAVEMENT

Some people recover from the death of another in an appropriate time period and with minimal vestiges of disrupted behavior; for others, time seems of little use as a remedy and personal behavior remains disrupted. What differentiates these groups?

One expert has offered five propositions:

1. The better the previous relationship with the deceased person was, the better recovery will take place; ambivalent feelings and dependent relationships lead to poor prognoses.
2. Deaths that neither the dead person nor the survivors had much opportunity to anticipate lead to slower recovery.
3. The bereaved person will fare better if the family and the social network in general are supportive.
4. If the stress caused by the death is compounded by other major sources of stress or other major crises, recovery is slower.
5. When previous deaths, especially in early years, were not well resolved, then it becomes more difficult to resolve this loss (Raphael, 1983).

To these, others may be added:

6. Deaths caused by suicide, homicide, or self-neglect are more difficult to resolve.
7. When the bereaved person believes himself or herself responsible in part or totally for the death, the grieving process will take longer and will be less effective.
8. Deaths that are so painful, prolonged, and drawn out that the survivors remain in a state of upset or even become impatient for the death will require a more demanding grief process.
9. When caring for the dying person is especially distressing to the eventual survivor, the death will elicit a more unhealthy grieving.
10. When no body is available, for whatever reasons, recuperation from the death will be more difficult (Simpson, 1979).
11. When grief is not appropriately expressed within a reasonable time after the death, the grieving will be less healthy (Parkes, 1972).

Research, as well as clinical experience, is essentially supportive of these propositions. For example, Parkes (1972) described three patterns of grieving among widows. One group became severely disturbed right after bereavement and remained disturbed for about two months; by the third month they were only mildly upset. The second group showed only moderate disturbance initially, then a week later became intensely upset, and subsequently recovered more rapidly than the others. The third group showed little or no emotion until toward the end of the first month after the death and did not show intense emotion until around two months later. Parkes concluded that grieving can be postponed but not altogether avoided. However, the postponement takes its toll; members of the group that postponed grief longest had more physical and emotional problems one year later than did people in the other groups.

Lindemann (1944/1965) describes a teenage girl whose parents and boy-friend all died in the Cocoanut Grove fire; while recuperating from her own burns for ten weeks following the deaths, she was cheerful and displayed no signs of distress. Only then did she begin to express her normal grief. In this instance, the delay may have been adaptive—allowing the girl to survive a highly stressful period. In other instances, in which delays are considerably longer or the grief is never expressed, the individuals may pay a high price in later emotional and health difficulties.

In a study we have referred to before, 68 widows and widowers were interviewed shortly after bereavement and again 13 months later. The persons who were having the most difficulty coping with their loss a year later were those from lower socioeconomic backgrounds, those whose spouses had died after a very short illness with little warning of death, and those who had another life crisis during the first 13 months (Glick et al., 1974). When more than two years had passed since the death, the factors differentiating those making a good adjustment from those not doing so seemed to be (1) the ability to anticipate the death and make some adjustments to it, (2) having had a good marriage before the illness and death, and (3) not expressing significant guilt or anger just after the death (Parkes & Weiss, 1983).

One of the reasons that different studies come to different conclusions is that they ask different questions. This is simultaneously one of the exciting and one of the frustrating elements in trying to integrate various research findings into a meaningful pattern. Therefore, when a group of Canadian researchers approached the issue of what leads to recovery from bereavement, they investigated social supports, situational variables, and personality. As might be expected, they found that widows (mean age of 54, with a range from 27 to 69) who were most distressed two years after the death had (1) fewer social supports, (2) greater health problems, (3) greater financial stress, and (4) lower emotional stability and higher anxiety (Vachon et al., 1982).

Anticipatory Bereavement

Bereavement, grief, and mourning before a person's death have been called **anticipatory bereavement** or **anticipatory grief** (Lindemann, 1944/1965). Although some controversy still exists, the evidence seems strong that (1) it occurs, (2) it leads to greater calm and acceptance of the ensuing death (Fulton & Fulton, 1971), and (3) it permits the bereaved person to regain full capacity for effective functioning and subsequent happiness more rapidly.

The longitudinal study of 68 widows and widowers under age 45 found that the opportunity for anticipatory grieving diminished the likelihood of psychological difficulties 13 months later (Glick et al., 1974). And in the follow-up two to four years after the death, those research participants who had had less than two weeks to anticipate the death were still having many more problems than those who had had from two weeks to many months to prepare. Sudden death was extremely likely to lead to later difficulties (Parkes & Weiss, 1983).

Another study (Ball, 1976–77) examined the experiences of 80 widows, also approximately one year after their husbands' deaths. Those under 45 years of age who reported that they had been given at least six days to prepare for the death also indicated that they had less stress; for middle-aged and elderly widows, the preparation time seemed to make no difference. Perhaps as people become older, their spouses begin to anticipate their deaths on a more regular basis even during times of health. And finally, a third study found that parents of dying children were more accepting of their loss when there had been time for anticipatory grieving—again the issue of a sudden and unexpected, or at the very least untimely, death (Binger, Ablin, Feuerstein, Kushner, Zoger, & Mikkelson, 1969).

> A 35-year-old nurse was told that her father was going to die of cancer in about six months; she subsequently said that she felt stronger grief at that moment than she ever felt later. She brought her father to her home and cared for him there, with the warm support of her husband. She and her father enjoyed their time together, and they even valued the occasions when they just sat in the same room, watching television. After seven months, he slipped into a coma and died three days later. When I interviewed her, about a year after his death, she told me "I never cried when he died—I think I'd finished with crying by that time."

Anticipatory grief has its dangers. For example, if the mourning period prior to the actual death is extremely successful—that is, if the person finishes grieving—what is the basis for continuing the relationship? After all, the dying person is still alive, yet mourning has been completed. It has been suggested that the bereaved persons may abandon the dying person if they complete mourning before death occurs (Fulton & Fulton, 1971). Moreover, the significance of the funeral is diminished, since its function as a way to permit the expression of grief and family solidarity has already been superseded by the previous grieving. This may be a particular problem with the death of the elderly, especially the very old and the institutionalized, for whom there have been years of anticipatory grieving in some instances and whose death therefore has relatively little impact (Fulton & Fulton, 1971).

And another prominent investigator warns that we may be oversimplifying the issues. What is important isn't just "sudden" versus "nonsudden" death but the nature of other conditions that accompany these deaths. For example, in many sudden and unexpected deaths, not only do the bereaved receive little warning, but their support systems are often not as effective (Sanders, 1982–83). This is confirmed by data from another longitudinal study of widows, in which the percentage of those without adequate outside social supports who were still distressed two years later was slightly over twice that for those who did have adequate social supports (Vachon et al., 1982). So it seems that we can decide that *on the whole*, sudden death leads to greater problems for the survivors, both early and later on, than nonsudden death, but that we need to move into investigations of the factors that lead to this difference. And, of course, this may lead us toward improving our understanding of how to help the grieving recover more quickly and more effectively.

Traditionally, guidelines have indicated how to behave following a death. Wakes, funerals, and a variety of other rituals and ceremonies all took place without much decision. Today, more choice is offered, including the possibility of not performing any rituals, participating in any ceremonies, or changing one's everyday behavior at all. Although the vastly increased number of options certainly increases personal freedom, it also may make grieving more stressful. And this stress may be exacerbated by the lack of a system of meaningful, cohesive religious beliefs (Gorer, 1967; Parkes, 1972).

Anniversary Reactions

The term **anniversary reaction** refers to a significant change in behavior or feelings on the anniversary of a death.

> I was 46 years old when this happened, over 30 years after the death of my father. That evening I was driving some 40 minutes to meet with a friend when I became aware that I was extremely restless, agitated, and tense, for no reason that I could ascertain. I kept turning the radio from station to station, both AM and FM, without any satisfaction. If I hadn't been driving, I would not have been able to remain seated. Since I was going to be slightly late, I continued to drive but decided to try to reduce my agitation by figuring out what was causing it. My mind flipped from idea to idea without consequence until, less than five minutes from my friend's home, I asked myself what the date was; and then I realized it was the anniversary of my father's death. At the moment I understood that, I was able to relax. In later reviewing the events of that drive, what surprised me most was that over the years I had paid little attention to that anniversary, often not even being aware of it until days later. And I knew that I had had no reminders of the death earlier that day—my response was unconsciously motivated. The only circumstance that might have explained my anniversary reaction was that my son had turned 15 some months earlier, which was my age when my father died. I had been writing about these occurrences for two decades, but when I actually experienced them, I was still surprised.

One study, for example, showed that 100% of 16 bereaved persons who had been classified previously as depressed and over 60% of 76 people who were not so classified described either a mild or a severe reaction on the anniversary of their spouse's death (Bornstein & Clayton, 1972). Another project found evidence that suicides are more likely to take place within 30 days of the anniversary of a parent's death than would be expected by chance (Bunch & Barraclough, 1971).

The term *anniversary reaction* has another use, which is close enough to the first definition to be confusing. When an individual attains the age at which one of his or her parents died, there is a higher-than-chance occurrence of various signs of distress. Thus, mental hospital admissions occur more frequently to persons at or near the age when a parent died than would normally be assumed (Hilgard & Newman, 1959). Similarly, there is evidence that admissions increase when a person's oldest child becomes the same age that the person was when his or her parent died. That is, if your mother died when you were 12, it will be somewhat more likely than would happen by chance that you will be admitted to a psychiatric hospital when your oldest child reaches 12 (Hilgard & Newman, 1961). In effect, the disturbance apparently results from a reestablishment of conditions similar to those at the time of the original death: now I am the parent, and my child is me, and a parent dies when the child turns 12.

However, research does not always support the idea that psychiatric hospitalization is related to anniversary reactions. Furthermore, the chances of any one individual's being hospitalized or committing suicide on a significant date are extremely small; they are only slightly higher than the likelihood that either would occur on any other date. However, the increase in depression on anniversaries and on other significant dates appears beyond dispute.

We are all affected by loss at one time or another, and therefore we have all experienced some kind of grief. Frequently we do not respond as we would have expected; sometimes we are not even aware that what we are doing or how we are feeling has been affected by grief. And although when and how we mourn are greatly influenced by our culture, there is probably no culture that does not recognize and make allowance for grief in some form.

CHAPTER ELEVEN

The Social Context of Bereavement: Roles, Relationships, Rituals

Each death occurs in a social context, and each grieving person lives in a social context. Like the pebble tossed into a quiet pond, a death has effects that ripple outward and downward, affecting all around it. The death produces varied feelings in the survivors, discussed in the previous chapter. The death also alters the lives of the survivors by influencing their roles and relationships and by leading to rituals and ceremonies that are, in turn, presumed to make the role transitions and relationship transitions easier.

LOSSES OF ROLES AND RELATIONSHIPS

Roles are sets of expectations that a society has of persons who fill certain positions, such as parent or leader or worker; these expectations are basically shared by members of the group and are seen as appropriate. When a person dies, he or she is no longer able to perform that role, and others must work out ways to cope with this loss.

The meaning of a person's death for the survivors includes both the loss of someone to whom they were deeply attached and closely related and the loss of someone who performed significant roles in their lives. Therefore, the loss is actually twofold: this person is no longer available to feel close to *and* this person is no longer available to function as a parent to your children, for example. The death also affects the broader community, including persons not appropriately recognized as "survivors." This occurs directly through the individual's removal through death and indirectly through the effect of the death on family members.

Effects on the Community

In our culture, the death of an individual and the grieving of the survivors affect the community in a variety of ways. First, various of the community's institutions go into action, either to help the survivors or to protect the community. Thus, the death is recorded and entered as a statistic; the survivors may become eligible for life insurance or some kind of financial aid, such as death or survivor's benefits under Social Security; the body is removed from the hospital or home and "disposed of" for public health, as well as religious, reasons; the funeral and burial bring the social support network together, at least briefly; the church may contribute to this support; the work setting permits a brief absence to the survivor while also arranging a replacement for the dead person.

If the death means that some survivor now requires additional help, the community may provide this also, unless the family is willing and able to do so. An elderly mother who had depended on her daughter for care now has to depend on the community for care; two young children are orphaned by an automobile accident; a middle-aged mentally retarded woman no longer has her elderly mother to care for her.

With few exceptions, however, the social system will continue to function well in spite of a death, no matter how significant the roles of the person who died. (When many deaths are caused by war or disaster, this may not be the case.) Small businesses, creative enterprises, and other endeavors with one or two key persons would perhaps be exceptions. However, the nation has weathered the sudden, unexpected deaths of several presidents; Walt Disney Enterprises continued to operate successfully after the death of Walt Disney; movie and television studios seldom stop production after the death of a star.

In many instances, plans are made in advance for handling the death of an individual, whether important or not. The vice-president becomes president; the assistant manager becomes acting manager; the second-string shortstop becomes the first-string shortstop. Frequently numerous people move to fill in for the dead person until other arrangements can be made: when the professor becomes ill and dies, other faculty members take over her courses for the remainder of the term; when the school crossing guard suddenly dies, two or three retired crossing guards are pressed into service until a regular replacement is made.

From time to time we will observe an organization that is tightly controlled by a single individual who has not made arrangements for his own replacement. If that person dies suddenly, either there is confusion, since no one else may be capable of running the organization, or there is tremendous struggle by subordinates or even outsiders to fill the vacuum left by the death. This can be just as true of an entire nation as of a small business.

Effects on the Family Structure

When a family member dies, the person leaves empty roles and severed relationships. The nature of the grief experienced by the survivors reflects the type of relationship ended by death; for example, bereaved adult children of very old parents express their grief differently from middle-aged widows and widowers (Owen, Fulton, & Markusen, 1982–83). Further, if the person is very old or very young, the empty roles may not affect others very much: the elderly woman dying quietly in the nursing home may leave behind family members in deep grief, but it is unlikely that her present roles will be missed (the chances are that she has already given up most of her significant roles); a 6-month-old infant who dies suddenly will cause immense grief and loss of relationships, and the death may have a devastating effect on the family, but—other than being the recipient of affection and hopes—he leaves no significant roles empty, although the death may leave future or anticipated roles empty.

The first response to the death of a family member is to make certain that the important roles are taken care of. An informal network emerges: grandmother takes over some of the cooking; an uncle serves as an occasional surrogate father; an older cousin provides some household help and instruction. The particular tasks, of course, depend on what the dead person left and what the others are capable of providing. If the death is that of a parent of dependent children, the remaining parent will take over many of the tasks and responsibilities of the dead spouse, perhaps delegating others to those children old enough to perform them.

However, the new family structure is likely to be unstable initially. Grandmother may continue to help with the cooking, but uncle tires of surrogate fathering. Other roles may also change. Mother had previously been housewife, mother, and part-time employee; now she becomes full-time employee. Older daughter is now designated as part-time housekeeper and caretaker of the younger children; this role may be given to her formally or informally, or she may take it on herself. Middle child/son has performed the role of rebel and troublemaker; he may take on the role of home-repair expert and errand runner, and in so doing, he may leave behind the roles of rebel and troublemaker—or he may not.

Obviously this family structure or system will continue to change over time, but it will never be the same as it would have been had father remained alive. Eventually a new man may enter the picture and may take over a portion of father's roles. However, by this time older daughter and son have already been providing those roles, and they may resent losing the status that they achieved with the roles, even though they might not have liked the particular tasks demanded of them.

When Roland's wife died, his daughter was a high school junior, and the two sons were several years younger. Tish quickly took over and ran the household, while her father's income fortunately permitted a once-a-week cleaning woman. Tish was efficient and the household ran smoothly; the two boys did their chores (reasonably well) and maintained their schoolwork; and Roland's life was amazingly smooth.

A few months later Roland began to see other women, initially on a casual basis and eventually with greater emotional involvement. By this time, Tish had become so valuable to him that he would discuss these women with her, and Tish carefully promoted or deflated each relationship in accordance with whether it threatened her status in the household or not. By the time Roland met Andrea, Tish was ready to graduate from high school and wanted to attend a college several hundred miles from home. Tish and Andrea looked each other over and, without ever doing so explicitly, decided to make common cause. Tish approved Andrea, and Andrea made no attempt either to compete with Tish or to become a parent to her. The two boys were not overjoyed that Andrea had come into the family system or that Tish had left for college, but Tish quickly made it clear that Andrea was "entitled" to replace her. The family unit, with the addition of Andrea, once again stabilized.

Had Andrea had children of her own or had she not been willing to let Tish retain her previous power, the results might have been far different.

The "presence" of the dead person does not cease at the time of death. Chapter Four described some of the ways in which the physical presence continues to be felt after the death. This chapter is concerned with the psychological and social impact. The widow or widower may view prospective mates in terms of their capacity to replace the roles and reestablish the relationships left vacant by the dead person; the children may think of succeeding in school or in their careers in terms of how they believe they would have gained the approval of the deceased parent. Clinical research suggests that the connection with the dead spouse is much stronger and more durable than has been assumed. Themes representing this connection include caring, intimacy, commitment, family feeling, and reciprocal identity support (Moss & Moss, 1980). In fact, it is not unknown for adults to realize they had been guided throughout their lives by the presumed expectations and personal qualities of a parent who died before they were out of infancy.

Effects on Individual Survivors

Replacing the lost relationship of the dead spouse and parent is probably more difficult than replacing the lost roles. If one parent has died, the other can usually find some way to have money or find someone to take care of the house and the children. Often today, since traditional roles are viewed more flexibly, the mother is totally capable of earning sufficient income, while the father has the ability to care for the house and children.

When one parent dies, the other parent has multiple new responsibilities, which can interfere with his or her grieving. Children need to be cared for; arrangements must be made for future income; legal arrangements may be necessary (for example, transferring title to a house to a widow, changing names on bank accounts); and decisions concerning moving, schooling, and related matters must be made. Given all these demands, the grieving person may find no time to express his or her own grief, especially after the first burst of community and family help has been spent.

One woman phrased this with poignance: "You hold the kids when they cry, but there was no one to hold me when I cried." Sometimes there isn't even opportunity to cry. The needs of a grieving spouse for a loan or for a friend to make a meal are easily understood; the need for someone to stay with the person's children while he or she takes off alone or with a close friend for the weekend is often not recognized.

Because in our society adults function as couples, in many communities a single person may have difficulty developing social relationships. Since most singles' and single parents' groups are concerned with the divorced and the never-married, widows and widowers frequently have trouble finding responsive friends. Thus, the companion role provided by the spouse is also difficult to replace.

However, it is probably the loss of the caring relationship that takes its greatest toll on the survivor. Someone to talk to, to sleep with, to hold and to be held by, to be familiar with your habits and likes and dislikes, to share experiences with, to share tasks with—these are the components that are missing after a spouse dies.

In many marriages, of course, the wife and husband did not talk to each other, often didn't sleep with each other and very seldom made love, and did not hold each other or share very much with each other. Yet there is still a bonding or attachment that occurs. Consider the metaphor of a large spider web, with many strands of differing strengths. Death cuts the web down the middle, severing almost all the strands (the sense that the dead person is still in some kind of contact or communication or is waiting in a subsequent existence suggests that two or three strands still exist). The cutting of each strand is painful, and cutting all the strands is immensely painful. As time goes on, the surviving spouse will often see the severed strands, with the ends just hanging there limply and unconnected, and this association will serve to revive the pain.

Frequently the dead person and the severed relationship are idealized. "Don't speak ill of the dead" is a familiar expression, one to which many adhere. Troubles and tensions are forgotten, repressed, or ignored, and the dead person is recalled as a paragon of virtues. This position is encouraged not only by close friends and relatives but by the eulogy at the funeral and by society in general.

It's not unusual for the pain to be so great that the survivor expresses a desire to avoid any such strong attachment in the future. The fear that a new intimacy will also end in death is too great to permit. Nonetheless, replacement relationships do occur, although, as a very wise friend of mine said, "No relationship is ever really replaced; every relationship is unique." So it isn't, strictly speaking, a replacement, but rather a relationship that offers some of the same qualities and responds to some of the same needs and role requirements.

At the turn of the century, it was common for a young wife to die in childbirth or succumb to illness or epidemic and leave her husband with young children. He would eventually remarry, and his second wife was, not infrequently, a considerably younger woman. Today the situation has changed. It is more likely that the father will die and his role will need replacing. Since the average widow loses her husband when she is 56 years old, their children are probably at least in their teens and, more frequently, in their twenties. Nonetheless, even today about 20% of children in the United States will lose one parent before age 16 (Simpson, 1979). Because of the high divorce rate, new attention is being paid to women who return to singlehood during their middle years, and this concern will benefit middle-aged and elderly widows.

Bereavement Overload

The death of one close person produces extensive loss in relationship and a major restructuring of the family system. Sometimes the usual process of grieving and coping with the disrupted family system is made much more difficult by what Kastenbaum (1969) has termed **bereavement overload**. This concept can be understood in two ways. First, the death of one person leads to many losses; for example, the death of a young father means that his children have lost someone to whom they were deeply attached; it is also possible that they will now see less of their mother, who will need to work; changes in the financial situation may require that they leave their home, move to another neighborhood, enter another school, and reside too far from their old friends to play with them. Thus, a father's death sets into motion a series of related losses.

The second, and original, use of the term refers to the frequency with which someone, most often an older person, will suffer several significant deaths within a brief period of time. A 60-year-old woman may lose her husband, her brother, and her mother within a period of 18 months. Before she has time to recover from one major loss, she is caught up in another, and if one bereavement is not adequately mourned, a subsequent death is probably much more difficult to work through.

Widows and Widowers

There are presently over 11 million widows in the United States who are not remarried—roughly 1 of every 8 women 14 years of age or older; of women over age 65, slightly over half are widows. There are some 2 million widowers in the United States, about 1 in every 40 males over age 14, and under 15% of men over age 65 are widowers (Metropolitan Life Insurance Statistical Bulletin, September, 1977; Brotman, 1982). Three explanations probably account for the discrepancy: women live longer than men; women marry men older than themselves; and widowers are much more likely to remarry than widows (Bequaert, 1976).

In viewing widows and widowers as two groups rather than as individuals (admittedly a hazardous practice), certain important differences emerge. Compared with widows, widowers will

- be older and, therefore, less healthy
- be less numerous, leading to greater difficulty in establishing friendships with other men their age but less difficulty in finding women available for friendship and marriage
- have more money
- be less able to do housework and child care but more capable of earning money and performing home maintenance

- have developed fewer social and verbal skills
- be less willing to seek either professional or personal help
- be more willing to drive at night and to go places alone at night
- be more experienced in financial matters (Kalish, 1982)

The fact that women outlive men is often presented as one of the advantages of being a woman, but even that is questionable. Wives tend to nurse their husbands through the final illness, arrange for a funeral and burial, and then work out a way to live a number of years without the valuable support of a spouse. Their income is often severely diminished at that point, and their age frequently makes it difficult to enter the job market, unless they already have a work history. The number of men available for dating or remarriage is also limited, in particular for older women in our society.

So widows tend to socialize with other women; some of them are previous friends who are still married, but many of them are also widows. Obviously some widows maintain friendships with both members of a couple, but there is a strong tendency for couples to participate socially with other couples. In one study, 38% of the widows stated that they had a less active social life than before the death of their husbands, but 43% claimed to have perceived no change, and 12% even had a more extensive social life (Lopata, 1973).

Widows were observed to speak of their deceased husbands in such glowing terms that one sociologist became suspicious. Her research found that some widows idealized both their dead husbands and the past marital relationships. Referring to this as "sanctification" of the husband, the author (Lopata, 1979) pointed out that such distorted memories appear to give meaning to the previous life of the widow while also justifying any desires she might have to avoid the risk of new relationships.

Widows themselves give three reasons for strains in their relationships with married women. First, they feel that being a widow is like being a fifth wheel; second, they believe that other women are jealous when their husbands are around widows; and third, they have had the experience of being propositioned by the husbands of their friends. Although these views are not held by a majority of widows, they represent the experiences of some (Lopata, 1973).

Those women who do develop satisfactory friendships tend to have more formal education, a reasonable income, and "the physical and psychic energy needed to initiate change" (Lopata, 1973, p. 216). Since these are likely to be characteristics related to many kinds of success for both women and men, it would seem that people who do things better and have more resources continue to do things better and get more resources.

In addition to the difficulties of coping with their grief and maintaining friendships, widows suffer the additional problems of stigmatization (Parkes, 1972). The taboo of death appears to rub off on the widow, and she may be treated much as funeral directors are treated. In some societies, widows are approached as unclean, and among the Agutainos of Polawan, they must announce themselves as they approach others, since to see them is to court one's own death (Cochrane, 1936). We don't ostracize widows in our society, but we often don't know what to say to someone who has recently lost a spouse, and we are more comfortable when we can avoid people to whom we have trouble talking.

That widows and widowers are deprived is evident. Each has lost someone important, even if the previous relationship was far from ideal. During the relationship, a network of close associations and shared experiences developed over a period—often a lengthy period—of time. Prior to the marriage was a courtship period when this association began and received its initial testing; mourning is like the courtship period in reverse, as the widow or widower begins the process of reducing emotional involvement or attachment in the relationship with the dead spouse (Marris, 1975). Often, perhaps usually, some sense of attachment, of connectedness, continues indefinitely.

Both widows and widowers cite loneliness as one of their major problems after their spouse's death, and it is often the most important single concern. Over half of one group of widows and over one-fourth of a group of widowers listed loneliness as the most important problem at that point. Widows went on to say that they also had problems making decisions and doing things by themselves; widowers were more concerned about the practical problems of running a household (Carey, 1979–80).

Nor do the problems of widows and widowers diminish much over the years. In studying changes in morale, participation in activities, health, and optimism about the future, two investigators observed little change as a function of the number of years since the death. They concluded that "we give time too much credit as a healer" (Barrett & Schneweis, 1980–81, p. 102). Their findings are in conflict with what others have found, and it may be that some kinds of well-being do improve over the years, while other kinds show little change.

In focusing on the problems of bereavement, one can easily overlook the practical problems of widows and widowers. A 35-year-old widow with three school-age children and a 55-year-old widow with grown, self-sufficient children obviously have very different practical problems. The same is true of men, except that widowers with children are considered to need a woman's help, and they are more likely to be aided by women (mothers-in-law and sisters-in-law are especially supportive); widows may require financial aid, and much of their help comes from brothers-in-law. And whereas widowers receive relatively more help from family and friends, widows are more likely to seek help from social workers, physicians, or others (Glick et al., 1974). Clergy, however, probably provide more support to both widows and widowers than any of the other categories of professionals do.

Many people in the helping professions underestimate the importance of financial problems and overestimate the importance of emotional stresses. In one study a group of widows overwhelmingly agreed that financial knowledge was the most important way to help women prepare for widowhood (Barrett, 1978a). Another study found that 71% of the husbands of over

1700 women widowed before they were elderly had not made out wills; in these cases the average family income dropped to only slightly more than half of what it had been before the husband died (Nuckols, 1973). Having to cope simultaneously with the emotional pain of the death and the practical changes in financial status can be an inordinately great task.

Discussing financial matters when death is not pressing anticipates this difficulty. Yet, because denial often operates, people frequently feel that talking about money and death is in poor taste or that, in some magical fashion, it will cause a death to occur. One young woman whose husband was dying of cancer said that she rejected his attempts to discuss money as a part of her own denial that he was dying.

When (and if) remarriage does occur, it is more likely to be with someone else whose spouse has died than with a divorced or never-married person. To some extent, this undoubtedly reflects age differences—widows and widowers are generally older than most people in either of the other groups—but it probably also reflects the understanding that these people have of each other. A wife who cherishes the memory of her dead husband can accept her new husband's continued attachment to his deceased wife; a divorced woman will not have shared the same experience and may be less patient with his fond reminiscences.

THE CULTURAL MILIEU

Bereavement and mourning are directly affected by one's culture; grief is indirectly affected by it. Thus, the situations in which a person will be bereaved are culturally defined. If I live in a society with strong extended family networks, I might be bereaved by the death of a second cousin or my mother's brother's father-in-law. If I live in a society based on strong nuclear family attachments, such deaths would not necessarily be the basis for bereavement, although I might still view myself as bereaved if I cared particularly for the person. For example, among the Trobriand Islanders in the South Pacific, only the losses of maternal kin are sources of bereavement; the loss of paternal kin or even one's spouse is not considered as profound (Volkart & Michael, 1957). A spouse, however, is allowed to grieve because of her or his sadness.

Similarly, if I lived in a society with a very high fetal and infant mortality rate, I might not be considered bereaved if my fourth child were stillborn; in nations with very low infant mortality, I would be bereaved.

Defining the Time of Bereavement

Bereavement is not always culturally defined as occurring at the time of a death. Among the Kotas of South India, an initial funeral is held shortly after a man dies, but his spirit does not leave for the afterworld until a second funeral is conducted; this latter funeral is held once a year for all persons who have died since the previous community funeral. If a widow becomes pregnant before the second funeral—and she is likely to try to do so—the child takes the name, clan, and property of the dead husband (Mandelbaum, 1959). Thus, to some extent, the widow does not become bereaved at the time of the death. Although this implies that the way she mourns will be affected by the community's definition of bereavement, she may, in fact, still suffer grief as intense at her husband's death as a widow in Minneapolis, Osaka, or Kiev would.

The duration of mourning is also culturally influenced, although the individual's grief is a determining factor. Table 11–1 shows some cultural norms for bereavement. Each person was asked how long a person of his or her sex, ethnic group, and approximate age should wait before doing each of the things listed in the table. Note that appropriate mourning is not an all-or-none matter; people believe that certain aspects of mourning should last longer than others.

TABLE 11-1.
Responses of 434 Persons in the Greater Los Angeles Area Regarding the Length of Time Following a Death of a Spouse before Each of the Indicated Actions Would Be Appropriate for a Person of Respondent's Age, Sex, and Ethnicity

	Percentage of Black Americans	*Percentage of Japanese Americans*	*Percentage of Mexican Americans*	*Percentage of "Anglo" Americans*
To remarry				
Unimportant to wait	34	14	22	26
1 week–6 months	15	3	1	23
1 year	25	30	38	34
2 years +	11	26	20	11
Other (including never/depends)	16	28	19	7
To stop wearing black				
Unimportant to wait	62	42	52	53
1 day–4 months	24	26	11	31
6 months +	11	21	35	6
Other/depends	4	11	3	11
To return to his/her place of employment				
Unimportant to wait	39	22	27	47
1 day–1 week	39	28	37	35
1 month +	17	35	27	9
Other/depends	6	16	9	10
To start going out with other men/women				
Unimportant to wait	30	17	17	25
1 week–1 month	14	8	4	9
6 months	24	22	22	29
1 year +	11	34	40	21
Other/depends	21	19	18	17

From *Death and Ethnicity: A Psychocultural Study,* by R. A. Kalish and D. K. Reynolds. Copyright 1981. Reprinted by permission.

Nor need mourning ever cease completely. On the anniversary of a death, Jews light candles and say special prayers for the Jahrzeit (year-time). The survivors may continue this practice for the rest of their lives. Many other societies have designated a lengthy mourning period.

Culture affects grief, the feelings that we have, less directly. "Many European cultures, such as those of the Greeks and Italians, have quite clear expectations of open and strong emotional release; whereas Anglo-Saxon society may view public display of feelings as unseemly, praising the person who shows strong emotional control" (Raphael, 1983, p. 38). We don't know for certain that Greeks and Italians *feel* greater grief, however; all we know is that they *express* the grief that they feel.

Or, if you wished to press the issue, I would need to admit that we don't even know for certain that they are expressing grief that they feel. They may be expressing grief that they believe they *should* be feeling. One funeral director told me that people often wailed and sobbed so loudly as they passed the open casket that it interfered with the ability of others to participate in the funeral. He finally decided to place the open casket behind a curtain, so that people were hidden from the view of most others as they passed it. This device, he explained, reduced the wailing by about 75% and also permitted each person a "moment alone" with the deceased.

Cultures also influence the kinds of attachments that we develop, and grief occurs when we lose a relationship in which the attachments are strong. When many people are equally important in someone's life, the death of one of those persons is not likely to cause immense grief; however, when only a few people are very important in one's life, the death of one of them will probably lead to grief and suffering. We can at least speculate, then, that our system of nuclear families makes each individual in our system more important, so that the death of one will bring greater grief, but to fewer people.

Forms of Mourning

The cultural differences in mourning are considerable. They range from *suttee*, the Hindu practice of burning a dead man's widow to enhance his memory and his family's prestige (which, incidentally, was optional) (Kroeber, 1948), to wearing a black armband for a year following the death to having a ceremonial meal.

These variations occur for all aspects of mourning. They "may last for days, weeks, or years; they may require abstentions from communication concerning the deceased, or they may enjoin public proclamation. The emotions of the bereaved may be publicly displayed in weeping and wailing, suppressed with stoic resolve, or camouflaged behind the mask of some other affect, for example, with smiling and laughter" (Averill, 1968, p. 722).

Washing and cleanliness are rituals frequently associated with mourning; sometimes anyone who has touched a dead body is expected to be cleansed with water (Frazer & Gaster, 1959). Celibacy for the survivors, especially the surviving spouse, may also be required. In our society, we seem to have a strange mixture of feelings about sexual behavior following the death of a spouse. On the one hand, "proper" respect is defined in part as abstention from sexual behavior for a time; on the other hand, widows often report being propositioned by men who claim to assume that, having been cut off from a sexual relationship with their husbands, these women are in need of sex and must be provided for.

The anthropological literature is filled with descriptions of mourning behavior, and there are reviews of these studies in reference sources as well (for example, Frazer & Gaster, 1959). When you read these, it is important to avoid finding the customs of other societies "cute" or "strange"; they need to be understood in terms of the entire societal milieu, not taken out of context as we tend to do. After all, think how strange our relative lack of ritualized mourning behavior would seem to persons from other cultures. It probably appears that we do not respect our dead relatives, since once the funeral is over, little or nothing is expected from the survivors. The differences among ethnic communities in the United States are good evidence of this. Japanese Americans and Mexican Americans were far more likely to believe that visiting the spouse's grave is a necessary and appropriate action, both one year and five years after the death, than Black and "Anglo" Americans (Kalish & Reynolds, 1981).

FUNERALS

Because anthropologists and historians have paid so much attention to funerals and burial rites, we have a rich literature of these death-associated rituals throughout the world. Once again there is the tendency to find the customs of other people either strange and funny or strange and admirable. Within the proper context, the customs of most other people make excellent sense, but this volume does not permit the opportunity to describe these contexts.

One major cultural difference involves what happens to the body. In our society most people are interred in caskets under the earth or in mausoleums. Some people are cremated; among these, most are content to have their ashes scattered in the garden of the crematorium, but again there are those with other plans, such as having their ashes taken to places of special significance: "I arranged for an airplane to drop Mom's ashes in Hawaii over Haleakala, where Dad's ashes are also. That has been their plan since I can remember—it was the place that they both loved best."

In some countries, such as Nepal, bodies are not cremated in private but are burned in public. When we visited Katmandu in 1963, we observed a funeral pyre on a small barge adjacent to the shore of a river. When the body on the pyre was burning, we seemed to be the only ones to notice. The Nepalese either considered it not worth their attention or were too polite to pay attention.

Water burial is also common, though limited in our culture to persons who have died at sea. Tibetans can choose among earth burial, cremation, water burial, and "air burial." In the last-named, the body is left exposed to be eaten by vultures or dogs or to decompose. These four methods of disposal derive from the Tibetan view that because the universe is composed of these four elements (certainly similar to early Western thought), the body should return to one of them (Habenstein & Lamers, 1974). Each of these modes of disposing of the body is accompanied by its own unique rituals; for example, before air burial the body is ceremonially cut apart. In addition, each kind of burial is used relatively more often for certain kinds of persons than for other kinds; water burial is used for beggars, lepers, babies, and the poor, while cremation is usually reserved for high lamas (Habenstein & Lamers, 1974).

Lavish funerals and prestigious burial sites have long been used to indicate wealth and status (consider where Washington, Jefferson, Lincoln, Grant, Roosevelt, and Kennedy are buried). Conversely, people who have had relatively little during their lives may be given lavish funerals to provide them at their deaths with what they were not able to have during ther lives.

In the United States, cremation is used between 7% of the time (*Statistical Abstract of Funeral Service Facts and Figures*, 1983) and 12% of the time (Cremation Association of North America). The former figure is provided by the funeral industry, many of whose members disapprove of cremation, and the latter figure by the Cremation Association, whose members obviously wish to encourage cremation. Perhaps the 9% that was proposed by Howard Raether of the National Funeral Directors Association in 1979 (personal communication) is the most accurate. In most instances when the body is cremated, there is first a funeral with the body present. Public services that include a viewing of the body preceding the service and a committal at the burial site still represent over 75% of all deaths (Raether & Slater, 1974), although different communities and different parts of the country vary in this practice.

At one time, funeral attendance, ritual mourning, and cemetery visits were routine. Not so anymore. A seminary professor noted that fewer than half the students in his class, most of whom planned to join the clergy, had ever attended a funeral (Raether & Slater, 1974). Among Los Angeles residents, 42% of those between 20 and 39 had not attended a funeral in the previous two years, and an additional 51% had attended fewer than three. More surprising, more than one-fourth of those 60 and over had not been to a funeral in two years, and another 36% had not been to more than three (Kalish & Reynolds, 1981).

The Meanings of Funerals

Funerals have many purposes, and these change over time within any given culture. One author has outlined six such purposes:

- To provide a rite of passage for the soul of the deceased
- To offer a way to dispose of the body, based on ritual
- To declare the dead person's status in society
- To help the survivors acknowledge their loss
- To help the survivors grieve

- To reaffirm the ability of the social system to exist after the loss of one of its members (Rodabough, 1981–82)

An additional purpose, which may be at least as important as any of the above but which is an indirect outcome of the funeral, is to provide a vehicle for bringing together members of the family and friendship support system, to aid the survivors in getting through the first days following the death. This purpose has become important only as family members move physically away from one another, so that they are no longer close enough to "drop in" for a casual visit, yet also have access to rapid transportation to permit them to cover great distances quickly enough to attend the funeral. In short, this purpose is symbolic of contemporary Western culture. "The funeral provides a setting in which private sorrow as well as public loss can both be expressed and shared" (Fulton, 1979, p. 251).

The tendency to deny death, to feel that the death did not really occur, has been mentioned frequently in this book. I earlier provided a lengthy description of one of my own experiences in denying a friend's death. Attending a funeral seems to make it much more difficult to deny the death. There is something about sitting with others, sharing their feelings, and focusing attention on the person who has died that encourages the realization that "this person is really dead." This may be particularly true if the body is openly displayed, even though it may have been subjected to cosmetics and other artificial appearance changes (Fulton, 1979).

Funerals obviously have different meanings to different people, and one sociologist (Rodabough, 1981–82) decided to look more carefully at how these differences are manifested at the funeral itself. He attended 100 Southern Baptist funerals in a Southern state and came up with a substantial number of what he called "funeral roles." I have selected a few and will present his titles without comment.

Roles of ministers:	• The young seminarian
	• The political gladhander
	• The eternal evangelist
	• The Scripture quoter
	• The ebullient eulogist
	• The comforting shepherd
Roles of family members:	• The coping griever
	• The bewildered novice
	• The hysterical performer
	• The stoic spartan
	• The party queen
Roles of friends:	• The respect payer
	• The party goer
	• The status accountant
	• The family supporter
	• The professional griever

In spite of the humorous descriptive titles, each of these describes an observed funeral-participant role, and none is meant to be pejorative.

In summing up the meaning of a funeral, one article proposes that "a funeral becomes that experience in which a person can face the reality of what has happened, let memory become a part of the process of grieving, and, in the experience, express honest feelings, accept the community support that is freely proffered, and attempt to place the death in a context of meaning acceptable to the individual experiencing the trauma of separation" (Raether & Slater, 1977, p. 237).

The Controversy over Funerals

Funeral directors and their supporters contend that the funeral itself provides a kind of closure to the relationship with the dead person and that this is especially true when there is an open casket. The "antifuneralists" disagree heartily, arguing that the funeral directors are only trying to make more money and that the embalmer's art is grotesque. The verdict of the bereaved is also split. Parkes (1972) found that about half the widows he interviewed were upset by seeing their husbands' bodies at the funeral, while the other half felt their last view was helpful. One limitation, of course, is that the embalmed body is only *relatively* lifelike: the pallor still indicates that it is a corpse, not a person. (Of course, if it looked completely lifelike, other stresses might ensue.) Embalming does not preserve the body indefinitely, as is often assumed, but it does preserve the body through the funeral and for a period thereafter (Simpson, 1979).

Objections to funerals are similar to objections to other rituals, such as weddings. One frequent complaint is that funeral directors use dubious selling practices; a second is that today's elaborate funerals are too expensive and that people who can't really afford them are manipulated into having them; third, some people say that funerals should be simple, plain, and concerned with religious beliefs and support for the bereaved but that today's funerals concentrate on lavish caskets and motorcades. The same complaints are leveled against car salespersons and people who have expensive weddings or bar mitzvahs, but the anger directed at morticians is more intense. This anger arises in part because the bereaved are such highly vulnerable consumers that exploitation is easily accomplished and partly because many death-related angers and anxieties are readily displaced onto funeral directors.

Obviously, one way to avoid the exploitation that can occur when bereavement makes one vulnerable is to make funeral arrangements in advance. Among the adults interviewed in Los Angeles, only 3% of those 39 years of age and under had made such arrangements, and only 24% of those 60 and over had done so (Kalish & Reynolds, 1981). There are two ways to make such arrangements. One is directly with a funeral home, which can record the kind of funeral you wish, with the assurance that you can get it at an acceptable price when the time comes. The alternative is through a memorial society, a loosely associated group of local organizations that contract with one or more local mortuaries to get funerals at the lowest possible price. Members, who join for life by paying a very small amount for themselves and their families, select the funeral home they wish and the funeral they wish (that is, the point on the plain-to-lavish continuum), and they fill out a form so indicating, which is their arrangement with the mortuary. In effect, membership signifies that the person wishes a modest and inexpensive funeral and burial; the extent to which clergy and others are involved must be settled separately.

Does viewing the embalmed body at the funeral help heal the survivors' grief, or is it destructive to that process? Does the funeral help provide a sense of closure, a feeling that the death has actually occurred, or is it of little use in this regard? Is it appropriate or inappropriate to spend money on a funeral, money the survivors could have used for more immediate needs in life? Answers to these questions depend so much on individual circum-stances, and good evidence is so scanty, that we need to consider our own value systems rather than pretend to any objective information.

Perhaps my own personal experiences will illustrate the complexity of just one of these issues. The first time I attended a funeral of someone I loved, I was disturbed by the cosmetic job that presumed to make him look "just like he did when he was alive." Not only could the embalmer not overcome the ravages of cancer, but I resented the waxy appearance. Some 30 years later, I attended a funeral with a closed casket that was positioned between mourners and the pulpit, and I found myself resenting the absence of the person within the casket. I was angry because I felt that the empty box did not represent the person I loved. Of course, the box was not empty, but it felt empty to me. I wanted the dead person to be there, and if he couldn't be there, I wanted something that appeared more like him than a covered container. Thus, in one instance I was upset because the body was on view, and in the other I was upset because it wasn't.

The process of dying and the process of grieving are both extremely complex matters, and policy decisions need to be made on the basis of the best available information. But we need to know when we make a decision based on sound information and when our decision reflects feelings, beliefs, or implicit values. Grieving has only begun at the time of the funeral, and it continues for many months. The grief expressed at a funeral represents only a small portion of the grief a person will express. Therefore, we need to take care that we neither overestimate nor underestimate the significance of this ceremony.

A LIFE-SPAN
PERSPECTIVE

"THAT'S WHERE THE
DEAD PEOPLE LIVE."

I. Warsaw—1939

The funeral house was not far away, although the walk to it was long enough. Long enough to think, and to remember. Long enough to become angry and confused. And yet, when I saw him, I wished that the walk would have never ended.

He stood, rocking and whimpering, in a corner of the large room. As I drew near, the body of his dead child appeared bigger and bigger. The gash in her neck seemed to pulsate. She can't be dead, I thought. She's moving. She's too young to be dead. I just saw her jumping rope yesterday. Children don't die. Old people die. She's not dead. Where is my son? Is he all right? He forgot his lunch this morning, and I was angry with him before he left. If he dies today, he will take that anger with him. Stop it. Stop it!

I corraled my thoughts just in time to reach for him as he fell to his knees. His taut face and diminutive frame, which had bent over me so long ago, and for so many different reasons: to teach, to discipline, to whisper something funny—now seemed divested of all their dignity and power. His daughter was dead. Murdered.

His wife cried in another room, and other women cried with her, but he was among his sons: his clothes torn, his face and beard smeared with ashes. And he rocked and sobbed. Rocked and sobbed.

> —I'm sorry, I said.
> —God has abandoned me and all his people.
> —The prayers will be held here, late this afternoon.
> —Will the prayers bring my daughter back to life? Will they give her breath? Will they?
> —When the sun sets, I said. What else could I say?
> —My God has abandoned me. . . .

I left. As I walked home, I went over it again—as I still do today. The voices in my head were loud. So loud.

> —But you stopped me! my brother screamed, standing so close to me that I could feel the heat of his words. When that dog slapped my father, you stopped me! And when the girl. . . .
> —They would have killed you.
> —At least I would have died fighting!

Not long after, he did.

II. Anywhere. Any time.

Work had been unusually difficult and unpleasant these last few days, and all the old people were beginning to look alike to her. They smelled alike too. Sort of stale: leftovers of something that had not been too terrific even when it was new. If it had ever been new.

And now this one had to die, just half an hour before quitting time. Well, she knew the routine. Clean the body. Same as when they were alive: lift, turn, wipe, change. At least this one would not whine or try to bite her. Now wrap the body. Her supervisor had already gone, so she used a sheet that was in her laundry bin from the recent round of bedmaking. It never made sense to her that her supervisor insisted on clean sheets. No one would see. Hell, no one ever saw their sheets when they were alive. No one cared anyway. Except for that one lady who had come to visit some old crock, and before she left gave the aides some money. She never came back, though. Now strip the bed. Empty the nightstand. Wait for the people to pick up the body.

She sat down to wait and looked around. He's better off dead. Couldn't feed himself. Never had been able to, her supervisor said, not since he got here. Couldn't talk. Didn't know anybody or anything. And always needing some kind of cleaning. Nose. Mouth. Those awful sores. And the other. Poor thing, she thought. I might have been his sister. I might be him some day. Life is unfair. But, hell, so is death. Well, anyway, this time, it's a good thing.

They came to pick up the body. She cleaned the room, and as she passed the window she saw the truck. Potter's Field. That's where most of them went. If she didn't find another job, that's where she would end up, she thought. Well, at least I'll be dead.

As she left that day, passing by the other beds, it seemed to her that the old people were looking at her—into her. She was being silly, she told herself. These were old crocks, vegetables, seniles. And some of them were plain crazy. And she must be crazy too, she thought. There was no way that these others could know that she had wrapped him in a dirty sheet.

Toni C. Mehler

"I. Warsaw—1939" and "II. Anywhere. Any time," by Toni C. Mehler. Copyright © 1984 by Toni C. Mehler. Reprinted by permission.

CHAPTER TWELVE

For Children
and Adolescents

According to legend, Gautama Buddha's father tried to protect his son from learning of the pain that exists in the world by discouraging him from leaving the grounds of his several palaces and by keeping the roadways clear of any signs of worldly suffering. Eventually the gods, determining that Buddha should have such exposure, arranged that he view old age, disease, and death. Gautama found these experiences so upsetting and his subsequent encounter with a calm ascetic so inspiring that he left his household to venture into the world (Noss, 1969).

For our present purposes, this legend says two things: first, we cannot protect people from knowledge of pain in the world, and, second, when we do try to protect people from knowledge of such suffering, their distress when they eventually—and inevitably—encounter this pain is even greater. However, the encounter with suffering can produce a richer understanding of the world. Early Buddhist writings quote Gautama Buddha as saying "I also am subject to decay and am not free from the power of old age, sickness, and death. Is it right that I should feel horror, repulsion, and disgust when I see another in such plight?" (Noss, 1969, p. 126).

We seem to work very diligently in our culture to maintain the innocence of children. Much of society's early rejection of Freud came from his emphasis on the sexuality and sexual awareness of young children, which contradicted the assumed contemporary knowledge of their innocence. Although today we have largely come to accept the validity of Freud's interpretation of childhood sexuality, we now maintain that children are innocent of death. We more than maintain this notion—we often insist on it and then do whatever we can to make our prophecy self-fulfilling.

HOW CHILDREN VIEW DEATH

No matter how much we protest that children are ignorant of death or that children should be kept ignorant of death, children are no more ignorant of death than they are of sexuality. They may lack an adult understanding of the phenomenon, but they know it exists. My daughter at age 2½ came in from the backyard, where she had been playing by herself, with a dried leaf that had fallen from a tree. She solemnly deposited it on the kitchen table, announced "Leaf dead," and went about with her play. Of course, she might have heard neighborhood children talk about dead leaves, but I believe she had already picked up the concept of "dead" and applied it to the leaf.

Children in our society often do not encounter a personally significant death until they are at least well into their teens. They may read about thousands of people being killed in an earthquake or hear about a suicide of someone in their community, but these events normally have no emotional impact on their lives: they are impersonal deaths. A hundred years ago, the deaths of children and young adults occurred frequently, but today very few children experience the death of brothers, sisters, parents, aunts, uncles, or cousins. Grandparents, of course, do die, but even most grandparents are not in their sixties until their grandchildren are in their teens; moreover, with geographical mobility, some children are isolated from close relationships with grandparents.

In other times and other places, very young children were exposed to death in a very personal and meaningful way. A family member would die at home, and the child would be involved with this person throughout the dying process; children in rural communities would experience both the births and deaths of animals, including the slaughter of animals for food; in wartime and during natural disasters, children often saw the dying and the dead all around them. There was no way to hide death from these children, and the deaths had to be explained to the children, who needed to incorporate them into their own cognitive framework. Today, when death is the province of the elderly and takes place in hospitals, these experiences are no longer familiar. At most, the child will be told that a grandparent is dying; later, he or she may attend the funeral and, perhaps, view the body in an open casket.

Early Exposures

Ask some of your friends about their first personal and meaningful exposure to death, and frequently the responses will describe the death of a pet during early or middle childhood. Although such animals as dogs, cats, and horses are most likely to affect children, even the deaths of goldfish and turtles can be significant. Children up to 6 or 7 years of age seem most concerned with why their pet no longer responds to them or moves, and they can also be deeply upset if the parents dispose of the pet's body in a way that seems inappropriate. Flushing a 3-year-old's goldfish down the toilet, one parent reports, served only to stir up numerous lengthy conversations (Gordon &

Klass, 1979); another young child buried and dug up his lizard on several occasions (Zeligs, 1974). Placing the dead pet in a box and burying it, perhaps with some brief and age-appropriate ritual, may well serve both to introduce the child to death in a useful fashion and to permit the necessary grieving and eventual closure.

By the time a child is 8 or so years old, the death of a pet can open up the topic of death for discussion with parents or other adults. By this age, children recognize that animals are very different from people, but their attachment to their pets may be so intense that they will need time and opportunity for grief and coming to terms with the loss (Gordon & Klass, 1979). The death of a beloved pet is a real tragedy for the child, and well-meaning adults who try to assuage the child's feelings by promising to buy an immediate replacement or by insisting that "it was only a dog" are denying the reality of the child's feelings. If a boy's younger sister had died, would his parents have said "Don't cry—we'll get you another sister"?

> When Anthony's mother returned from dropping him off at nursery school, she saw their golden retriever puppy lying in a pool of blood in front of the driveway, obviously a victim of an automobile. She called Anthony's father, who decided to replace the dog immediately, and by the time Anthony returned from school for lunch, a new and virtually identical dog was playing in the yard. But the new dog did not seem the same to Anthony. She didn't come up to Anthony the way the other puppy had; she didn't like the same food; she didn't sleep at the foot of his bed in the same way. Not understanding what had happened and never guessing that this wasn't his old pet, Anthony assumed that the dog had changed to such a drastic extent that he no longer wished to play with her. Anthony became deeply distressed by these events, and his parents eventually gave the dog away.

By trying to protect Anthony, his parents actually intensified the pain of loss, and Anthony ended up totally confused about how animals behave. He could have learned something important about life and death had his parents permitted him to grieve, and at a later time, he would have accepted another animal as a pet. As it was, his parents found a way to avoid their own anxiety, but at a substantial cost to Anthony.

Given the tendency of adults to protect their children against the realities of the deaths of animals, it isn't difficult to imagine how much more effort is put into hiding the deaths of people. It is likely, for example, that the hospital where grandmother is dying has rules against bringing children onto the units. Although informal arrangements are possible—for example, in one Veterans Administration hospital, the nurses would help parents bring their children up a back stairway to visit a dying grandparent—they are seldom convenient, and the message that these rules communicate to the children is that death must be hidden from them. (The basis for these rules, as explained to me by one hospital administrator, is that young children often carry communicable diseases that might infect an entire unit of seriously ill persons. I was not convinced by the explanation.)

In discussing this issue, Gordon and Klass (1979) have several suggestions.

First, since dying people—like everyone else—have good days and bad days, try to bring the children to visit on days when they're feeling better. Second, keep in mind that young children have short attention spans, and don't expect a young child to conform easily to your personal schedule. Third, encourage the child to bring a small gift, perhaps a drawing from school or a cookie he or she has helped to bake. Fourth, "It helps if there are no secrets about the impending death, so the dying person and the child can say what is in their hearts at this time, knowing it may be the last" (p. 51).

A death in the family, like the death of a pet, offers an excellent opportunity to talk with the child about death, making certain that the discussion is carried on at the child's level and with the child's determination of how long it lasts. A recent study found that the personal life experiences of 5- to 10-year-olds with death were one of two important predictors of their understanding of the meaning of personal mortality; the other was their level of intellectual development (Reilly, Hasazi, & Bond, 1983). It is likely that children will find it easier to handle the truth, and to suffer its pain, than to be kept in the dark and confused and wonder why everyone else is behaving so strangely.

One study of how mothers communicate with their young children about death (McNeil, 1983) sheds some additional light on this issue. Interviews with 100 mothers confirmed the belief that parents do find it difficult to talk with their young children about death and that they tend to feel inadequate in knowing what to say or how to say it. Nonetheless, most of them feel obligated to respond to their children's questions in an appropriate fashion, and they welcome the chance to improve their ability to do this. These mothers did not find it troublesome to answer questions that their children might have posed out of normal curiosity, but dealing with particular deaths that were emotionally involving was very difficult. The best time to talk with children about death, of course, is when the children bring it up themselves or when events in their lives cause death to be significant (Gordon & Klass, 1979).

Developmental Stages

Very young children, 2 or 3 years old, probably have little understanding of death. They live in the present and do not comprehend the nature of passing time (Jackson, 1965). I once asked my son, when he was about 3, where he was before he was born. He had learned his lesson well, and he told me that he was in his mother's "tummy." When I asked him where he was before his older sister was born, he appeared to recognize the unlikelihood that both of them had occupied the same stomach at the same time. Then he began to talk of other matters: either the notion of his own nonexistence seemed irrelevant or he found the idea too confusing.

The idea of nonexistence—either not yet having been conceived or no longer being after death—is incomprehensible to very young children. However, it is possible that, even at an earlier age, they do have an awareness of not-being. Several authors have proposed that the game of peek-a-boo is an initial attempt to test the possibility of going into a void and returning to the familiar environment. What is not accessible to the infant through his or her senses often does not exist for that child. The fact that peek-a-boo can engage even an infant for several minutes at a time, a long period to maintain attention, attests to the compelling nature of the activity. The shrieks of pleasure on the infant's return to the known world offer supporting evidence (Maurer, 1961).

That children develop conceptual awareness in stages is at the core of the theories of the famous psychologist Jean Piaget. The best-known stage approach of concepts of death was developed by a follower of his, from written compositions and drawings by and discussions with 378 children living in Hungary (Nagy, 1948). The author constructed three age-related stages from the children's responses.

Stage one.   Before age 5, children do not perceive death as irreversible. Rather, they view it as a departure or a sleep—in effect denying the permanence and irreversibility of death. Life continues in spite of death. The dead person continues to think, to grow bigger (if the dead person is a child), to remain aware of what goes on in the world. One young child commented as the family car drove past the cemetery "That's where the dead people live."

At the same time, the child recognizes that the dead person is gone. The pain of loss through death for these children is the result of separation. They may ask where the dead person is now, how she feels, whether she is ever going to return. Since death is departure or sleep, the child may become fearful of sleep—a condition that may be exacerbated if she recites the familiar prayer "Now I lay me down to sleep . . ." and contemplates its meaning—or become anxious when a parent leaves for a business trip.

Children at this age take much of what they are told very literally, and this includes the platitudes they are offered as explanations for death or the present whereabouts of a dead person. One young child, told "God has taken your baby sister to be with Him," was subsequently overheard talking with God—asking for his sister to be returned and begging God not to take him also. The boy's tone was one of extreme anger mixed with fear.

Stage two.   From the age of 5 or 6 to about 9, children tend to personify death. Death is a skeleton, a bogeyman (often an unconscious euphemism for death), a wicked person, a killer. Death "has big eyes and white clothes. It has long legs, long arms" (Nagy, 1948/1959, p. 91); "it takes [people] up in some kind of carriage" (p. 91); "death angels are great enemies of people" (p. 92). Death has a personality, may be invisible, and literally carries people away. Now, instead of denying the permanence of death, the child places death as an entity outside of her or his own self.

Stage three.   After age 9, children recognize that death marks the cessation of life and that it operates from within the body. It is now inevitable and irreversible, and it results in the end of bodily life.

A later study (Portz, 1972) confirmed the general sequences suggested by Nagy. Children at each of three age levels (3–4, 5–6, 8–9) were interviewed, and their responses were coded and scored. The two younger groups were significantly more likely to view death as reversible; they also tended to personify death and to believe that their personification could think and have feelings. The youngest group perceived death as primarily a "going away"; slightly older children viewed death as a drastic personal change; and the oldest group saw death as a loss of life.

It also seems that a strongly expressed affective response to death is unlikely to occur until age 9 or so. In one study (Menig-Peterson & McCabe, 1977–78), children were encouraged to discuss experiences in narrative fashion; the project was set up so that they would talk about their experiences with death during the process. Children younger than 9 described deaths of strangers, pets, and even family members in objective, unemotional terms. Only the older group discussed feelings and emotional attachments. This did not mean that the younger children were unfeeling—only that their expressions of emotion were limited.

> When 8-year-old Jimmy's mother returned from the hospital, Jimmy was ready to go out to play baseball; his cap was on his head, and he was carrying a baseball mitt. Jimmy's mother told him that his father had died, and then she went through some statements that she hoped would be helpful: "It's just the two of us now." "We still have each other." "Always remember that your daddy loved you." And so forth. Jimmy waited patiently until his mother seemed to have run out of loving statements. Then he pushed the visor of his baseball cap to one side and said "Now can I go out and play baseball?"

Other investigators have reached conclusions at variance with Nagy's. There has been considerable criticism of her stages for ignoring differences in the children's social, economic, and cultural backgrounds (Bluebond-Langner, 1977). The most challenging attack on Nagy's stage theory has been based on research with terminally ill children that showed them to be aware of the meaning of death at much earlier ages than Nagy had found (Bluebond-Langner, 1977), as discussed later in this chapter. It may be that younger children have an immature understanding of death because they lack experience with the phenomenon, not because they are unable to comprehend its meaning (Bluebond-Langner, 1977). Any final decision must be held in reserve, but a review of the literature suggests that two modifications are made with fair consistency in Nagy's findings: first, children's awareness appears to occur somewhat earlier than her findings indicated, and second, there is relatively little support for personification as the keystone for the second stage (Kastenbaum, 1981; Stillion & Wass, 1979).

Separation and Abandonment

Children's feelings and attitudes about death reflect numerous factors: the children's level of development and cognitive understanding, their personal experiences with death and with separation, the knowledge they have acquired from their parents, peers, and others in their environment.

The theme of separation occurs again and again. Even very young children have experienced a variety of kinds of separation, ranging from being apart from their parents to having a favorite toy fall apart and disappear into the rubbish. They learn that some kinds of separation are not permanent (parents return) and some kinds are permanent (the toy does not return). If their basic life is stable and they feel loved and cared for, separations may be mildly disturbing but probably are not seriously disruptive. Conversely, if the fabric of the child's life is not stable and if the child is anxious and uncertain about what is going to happen next, separation may add to feelings of anxiety and concern.

As children come to understand that death means permanent separation, they are likely to become afraid of death. As they learn that death is inevitable and that they are powerless to prevent it, they will feel helpless, which is a very unpleasant kind of feeling to have. Very young children believe themselves to be all-powerful, and learning of their impotence in the face of death is a direct challenge to their assumptions of omnipotence. Becker (1973) contends that these feelings are inevitable and occur to all of us, that they are part of our recognition that we are human and temporary and vulnerable, and that the dread of death is therefore universal. This dread obviously begins in childhood and would be especially strong in children who do not feel cared for and protected by their parents or other adults.

Since death is often described by adults as a kind of sleep and since children may make a similar interpretation, some children come to fear going to sleep. Their powerlessness and vulnerability while asleep may contribute to their fear. Death-related nightmares are not unusual, although it is difficult to determine the extent to which these represent separation fears more than specific death fears. Another "contaminant" in the same sense as fear of separation, is fear of not growing up, which Erikson (1963) says is common among children. Death may be felt as a threat mainly because it would mean an arrest of development: "If I died now, I'd always be 5 years old."

When children become intensely afraid of separation, they may be fantasizing that their parents will abandon them. One group of children received word-association tests to evaluate their associations with death. Nearly half of the 91 7-year-olds mentioned "death" in response to "very sad," and the death of mother was especially prominent (Mitchell, 1967). Mother's death is certainly a legitimate cause for both sadness and fear of abandonment.

Guilt and Responsibility

Children often become angry enough with their parents, their siblings, or their friends to wish them spirited away. "To think of a thing is the same as doing that thing" (Zeligs, 1974, p. 34) for many children, and if that "thing" occurs, they may see themselves as responsible. One mother who often said to her children "Oh, you'll be the death of me yet" died when they were still young, and one son couldn't help feeling that he had caused her death. Another child was living with an elderly grandmother who was extremely ill;

her mother told her not to let the screen door slam, because it would disturb her grandmother. One day, when she let the door slam, her mother shouted out the usual irritated complaint; that evening her grandmother died, and for years the girl felt she had caused her grandmother's death.

Not only do children feel that their thoughts and words can have lethal effects but they may also fear reprisal. Since, for young children, death is reversible and dead people still exist in some altered form, it stands to reason that if the child has the power to wish someone to death, that person is going to wish the child to death (Zeligs, 1974). If slamming the screen door can cause grandmother's death, the grandmother, in whatever earthly or ghostly form she wishes to assume, can slam the screen door right back. To undo this possibility, the child may perform a ritual—for example, a prayer that blesses all people he or she loves (Zeligs, 1974).

Much of this behavior fits with the concept of the Oedipus complex, the personality dynamic discussed by Freud that describes the desire of children to rid themselves of competition with the same-sex parent in order to possess the opposite-sex parent. Eventually children resolve the Oedipus complex by identifying with the more powerful same-sex parent and possessing the opposite-sex parent indirectly through this identification process. However, if the competing parent dies before the identification process is completed, the death wishes against that parent may lead to guilt and fear of retribution.

Expressions of Death Awareness

Children, like everyone else, can discuss death directly and indicate their feelings about death indirectly through play, metaphors, and puns. Since children's use of language and their ability to apply abstract symbols are still limited, indirect communication may be more important for them than for adolescents or adults.

Chapter 1 pointed out that the centuries-old game, ring-around-the-rosy, was originally a device that children used to express their feelings about death. It isn't the only one. When children play cops-and-robbers or cowboys-and-Indians, they act out a death that is always reversible. However, the richest play media for expressive feelings about death are dolls, puppets, and other kinds of unstructured imaginative play. Wishes, fears, and experiences all emerge projected onto the dolls or through characters in creative play. The doll representing baby sister dies a horrible death, then is returned to life by a kindly and all-powerful big brother doll; a fantasized bogeyman comes to take two children, who successfully fend off the specter; a father doll dies, is buried, becomes a baby, and returns. The representation of perceived reality occurs in play.

Children's misunderstanding of adult language can lead them to express their feelings about death in ways that the adults cannot understand. One boy, aged 2½, who had been weaned from his bottle for many months, began to demand the bottle again, with a real urgency in his voice. "It was . . . the fear of death that I heard in his voice" (Brent, 1977–78, p. 286). The basis for the child's fear, it turned out, was that when the family car had run out of gas three times, he had picked up the comment that the motor had died because of lack of fuel. In addition, the boy had heard that his baby sister had been having gas because of her bottle. You can put the rest together easily enough.

Sometimes it isn't that the child doesn't understand adult language but that adults don't listen hard enough to what the child is saying. A young girl whose sister was dying told a psychiatrist that she wanted a "crying doll" for Christmas. When the psychiatrist pursued the issue, the girl said that she was unable to cry because her mother wouldn't cry with her, and they couldn't cry together; therefore, the girl felt she had to restrain her own tears. The crying doll, of course, could give the girl the tears that she was not being permitted to display. The psychiatrist enabled the mother and daughter to share their sorrow, and as she left the room, the child told her that she didn't need a crying doll anymore (Kübler-Ross, 1974b). All of us speak of our deepest concerns in indirect ways—children perhaps more than adults—and death-related issues are so powerful that direct language is often difficult. Nevertheless, most people working with the dying would agree with Kastenbaum that "in speaking with children about death, simple and direct language is much to be preferred over fanciful, sentimental, and symbolic meanderings.... Try to provide them with accurate information.... See if they understand what you have said... and if that is really what they wanted to know in the first place" (1981, p. 120).

THE DYING CHILD

So few children die in the wealthier nations of the world that it is easy to forget that personal, imminent death remains a major issue for thousands of children and their family members. A large proportion of infants and children who die do so shortly after birth. In fact, slightly over 1% of infants died in 1980 during the first year of life, but the death rate dropped to 1/10 of 1% for ages 1 to 4; the comparable figures for 1900 were 16% and 2% (Mortimer, 1983).

Deaths at or just after birth are usually due to genetic abnormalities, prenatal infarctions, damage to the fetus as a result of toxins, drugs, and oxygen deprivation, and a variety of still-unknown causes (Carlin, 1977). Sudden infant death syndrome accounts for 15–20% of all infant deaths (Mortimer, 1983). Several decades ago, deaths during childhood were caused by what were termed "childhood diseases," such as measles, whooping cough, scarlet fever, and diphtheria, but these have virtually vanished in countries like the United States and Canada. Although cancer and other illnesses do cause some deaths in children, accidents and homicides are the major killers during childhood, accounting for two-thirds of deaths between ages 1 and 9 (Mortimer, 1983).

Awareness and Communication

When children are still very young—2, 3, or 4 years old—their perceptions of what is happening to them are a direct reflection of their parents' behavior. If they are confident that they are not being abandoned by their parents, children can cope amazingly well with pain and unpleasant treatments. Before children can grasp the concept of their own deaths, even at a simple level, they must have (1) a concept of their own unique separateness, of not being a part of the parents, (2) a sense of continuity of time—past, present, and future—and (3) an ability to fantasize change in their physical selves (Easson, 1974). This means not that they are unafraid when they are dying but that their fears are in response to the reactions of others, rather than to their own dying.

Eventually, perhaps around the age of 8, children do understand that their "physical being" may cease to exist. They also have begun to comprehend the medical jargon that they hear from parents and health caretakers. Now they can become afraid of death itself (Easson, 1974).

However, some children have enough comprehension of what dying means and what is happening to them to develop this fear before 8. A group of medical investigators working with terminally ill children contended that those as young as 4 or 5 were aware of the consequences of their diseases and their imminent deaths, although the parents of many tried to shield them from the knowledge. Even younger children displayed concern about separation, disfigurement, and pain (Binger et al., 1969).

A number of observers have commented that young children do not ask questions about their own dying (for example, Richmond & Waisman, 1955). Although such statements are correct, there are several possible interpretations of this behavior. One is simply that the child does not comprehend what is happening. However, it is also possible that the child is aware that something extremely serious is going on, which might lead to death, but doesn't ask because he either doesn't wish to know more or assumes that the all-powerful adults will bring back his health. A third possibility is that the significant adults in the child's social milieu have communicated to the child that questions would be troublesome, so that the child is protecting the adults. When parents, physicians, or nurses continue to tell a child that "everything will be all right," the child may feel that questioning would be challenging the authority of adults. Since the support of these adults is so important, the child is reluctant to risk alienating them by probing with unwanted questions.

One investigator worked with 64 children between ages 6 and 10. Some had been diagnosed as having chronic illness that would lead to death; some had chronic diseases with good prognoses; and others either had brief illnesses or were not ill at all. The fatally ill children showed much greater general anxiety and much greater anxiety related to death, mutilation, and loneliness than the other children, including the other chronically ill children (Waechter, 1971). A later study found essentially the same relationship (Spinetta, Rigler, & Karon, 1973). This suggests that these children were somewhat aware of their condition; they may even have had a realistic knowledge that they were going to die. An alternative explanation, though one that does not necessarily rule out the previous interpretation, is that their anxiety reflected the greater anxiety that their parents and the hospital staff exhibited in their presence. As adults, in general, become better able to be honest with children, the anxiety of both children and adults may diminish.

Another author makes an even stronger case that children have knowledge of their prognoses. Bluebond-Langner (1977) worked with a group of children, mostly between the ages of 3 and 9, all of whom, she believed, came to comprehend the state of their health. Some of the signs she noted were preoccupation with death and disease, marked fear of wasting time, avoidance of any discussion of the future, death imagery in their play and art work, and preoccupation with having things done immediately. The author concluded that all children eventually came to understand death as "mutilating experiences, bringing in their wake separation and loss of identity. Death . . . is a final and irreversible fact of life" (1977, p. 60), although children obviously expressed their feelings in less sophisticated terms. Apparently children who are terminally ill do not understand death, at least their own death, in the way indicated by the stages Nagy proposed in 1948 (see p. 226); rather, they attain a much more sophisticated awareness than has usually been assumed.

Bluebond-Langner (1977) has suggested five stages of understanding that dying children go through, almost regardless of age:

1. becomes aware that the illness is "serious"
2. learns the names of drugs and side effects
3. learns purposes of treatments and procedures
4. experiences the disease as a series of relapses and remissions
5. experiences the disease as a series of relapses and remissions that will eventually cease with the advent of death

As the children go through these fives stages of acquisition of knowledge, they also go through five coordinated stages of self-perception (Bluebond-Langner, 1977):

1. seriously ill
2. seriously ill but will get better
3. always ill but will get better
4. always ill and will never get better
5. dying

For each stage to occur, certain conditions must be met. For example, the child does not move to stage five until he or she learns that another child has died. Neither age nor intellectual ability has much to do with the progression from stage one to stage five. Rather, the child must have gone through appropriate experiences: had the condition for a while, visited the hospital, and lost friends of the same approximate age and with the same illness (Bluebond-Langner, 1977). This author's conclusions, based on her research with leukemic children, are still controversial, since they contradict other opinion and research. I personally believe that most of her work will be confirmed by others who study the self-awareness of dying children.

There is more reluctance to discuss a child's death with that child than to discuss an adult's death with the adult. Many hospitals still retain rules against such discussions (Doka, 1981–82). However, children, like adults, eventually learn that they are dying, and they tend to find out in much the same ways: from overheard conversations, from changes in the ways others respond to them, from changes within their own bodies, from being taken off one medical regimen and being placed on another. It was noted from careful observations on hospital wards for dying children that staff members spent considerably less time with those children who had been diagnosed as terminal and beyond help; they devoted their efforts to those children who were critically, but not fatally, ill (Doka, 1981–82). There is little doubt that many of the children learned they were dying from noticing the changes in staff attention.

Children who are 7 and older can usually understand what their sickness is likely to lead to, and they can discuss it with their parents and medical staff members. As with adults, it is usually easier to develop close and intimate relationships with children who understand what is happening to them than with those for whom the prognosis is carefully shrouded in attempts at secrecy (Gordon & Klass, 1979).

Encouraging dying children to stay in school (or receive home tutoring) as long as possible is also valuable. Adults who are dying and who sit around and do nothing are often depressed; the same is true for children. And continuing with schoolwork and personal relationships for these children is an indication of being normal. In this regard one author writes about using art and poetry with dying children and states "Children who are dying . . . need to master their external environments since they often feel they have lost control of their own bodies through their illnesses" (Hodges, 1981, p. 56). The issue is an important one: helping a person, regardless of age, to remain autonomous and in control as long as possible and to the extent possible.

When all is said and done, we still know that some children want to know more about their conditions, some want not to know any more than they do, and all want to learn at a pace that they can control. In serving the needs of the child, we must be sensitive to what each individual child is communicating to us. This requires that we not impose our desires on the child—that is, that we not inadvertently communicate to a child that *we* want to protect *ourselves* from having to cope with her or his emotional and physical pain. At the same time, we should not lose sight of the importance for the child of an emotionally supportive social environment.

Reactions of Dying Children

Generally, the feelings children express about their own dying and death are the same as those expressed by people of other ages: guilt, fear, anxiety, anger, denial. Some children regress to behavior that they had previously outgrown. So do some adults. Because their cognitive development is not yet complete, however, children may interpret their impending deaths in somewhat different fashions.

One interpretation children make is that their death is a punishment for having been "bad." Although adults may feel this way also (see Chapter 3), their intellectual understanding casts a different light on the feeling. Eight-year-olds, for example, are at a stage in their lives when they believe "there is a logical, inevitable planned sequence to events" (Easson, 1974, p. 26). Therefore, having a fatal illness can only be understood as a dreadful punishment for a dreadful transgression. Since all children misbehave in some fashion, the opportunity for projection is always available (Easson, 1974).

The course of the illness is also an obvious factor in determining a child's feelings. Being unable to play with friends, undergoing unpleasant treatments, observing the strain on the family, encountering the ambivalence of brothers and sisters—all can occur during the course of a fatal illness. Children become cognizant of being different but don't know how to cope with this. Resentment builds as treatments become more complex and the opportunities for normal living become more limited (Toch, 1977).

Separation fears, death fears and anxieties, and mutilation fears are reported with considerable consistency in studies of dying children (Morrissey, 1963; Natterson & Knudson, 1960). These feelings, of course, occur at all ages, and it is difficult to know how much they are reactions to treatment, hospitalization, pain, and the fears and anxieties displayed by others and how much they are generated directly by the knowledge of impending death.

The importance of understanding the sources of these fears extends beyond intellectual curiosity. If children are fearful of their actual death, it might be appropriate to respond by permitting them greater freedom to discuss their fears in an open-awareness context. However, if the fears are based on a lack of understanding of the treatment procedures or on perceptions of the anxieties of others, we can attempt to deal with these matters directly. In either instance, the fear of abandonment and separation is likely to occur, and the child's anxieties can be partly assuaged both by verbal reassurance and by tangible proof that caring adults will continue to be available.

THE BEREAVED CHILD

Children are most certainly affected—and deeply affected at that—by the deaths of those who are close to them. Even infants are deeply distressed by the death of a familiar person, usually a parent, although their reactions are not recognized as or expressed as grieving in the way that older children or adults would grieve. At this early age, infants respond to the absence of someone on whom they have depended by following the process described by Bowlby (1961) as protest, despair, and apathy.

Throughout this book, it has been emphasized that age is a significant factor in understanding how individuals respond to events. Age is probably the most obvious factor that influences how infants and children respond to the death of a parent or some other significant person. Since infants don't recognize that objects exist separately from themselves, they cannot grieve for another person; rather, they will grieve as though a part of themselves were missing (see p. 96). Children at age 3 years or 7 years or 11 years all have much different understandings of the world, of causality, of the irreversibility of death, of separation, and they will view parental deaths in terms of their cognitive awareness of the world.

Many other factors influence the ways in which children perceive the death of someone they love and how they respond to it: the nature of the relationship, the ability of others to fill in for the missing person, the child's personality, the ways the death is communicated to the child, the use of euphemisms or the pretense that the dead person will return to the child's life, how the child's friends and teachers respond, and so forth. Each of these factors can also be applied to adults, but the specific nature of the situation is often very different for children from what it is for adults and very different for children of different ages.

> When Robbie's father died on a business trip, 5-year-old Robbie was initially told that his father had simply decided to extend the trip. It was two weeks before Robbie was told his father was dead. In the meantime, the obvious chaos in the household, the suffering of his mother, and the repeated assertions that his father would soon return all left Robbie in a state of high anxiety and complete confusion.

> A few weeks after her father's death, 3-year-old Cheryl was noticed talking to some robins in the backyard. This occurred several times, and eventually her mother realized that Cheryl had been told "Your father is in heaven with the angels." Cheryl, not having access to any angels, was trying to get information from the birds about her father, since these creatures obviously were familiar with heaven as she understood it.

Several studies have compared the responses and later behavior of children whose parents had divorced and children whose parent or parents had died. One study found that the latter seemed to have more serious problems involving shyness and anxiety, while the former acted out more and expressed more aggressive behavior (Felner, Ginter, Boike, & Cowan, 1981). Although divorce often elicits grief and mourning, so many of the circumstances differ that the overall effects are quite different: the child normally has ongoing contact with both parents; the custodial parent's relationship with a divorced spouse is much different from the widowed parent's relationship with a deceased spouse; the support of others in the community is both qualitatively and quantitatively different.

Responding to Death

Children between 2 and 5 don't fully comprehend the meaning of death, and they may continue to ask where their dead parent is and why he or she doesn't return. They are likely to express confusion and bewilderment and often a form of clinging behavior. Sometimes they will return to wetting or soiling and to babyish ways of talking or eating and they may want to return to the bottle or even the breast (Raphael, 1983). Since other members of the family, including those on whom the child most depends, are also grieving and suffering their own pain, they sometimes lack patience in responding to the child, so that the preschooler does not receive either sufficient nurture or appropriate answers to questions.

It's difficult to determine the extent to which children grieve in response to their own sense of loss and the extent to which they are reacting to the obvious grief and loss of others, as well as to the changes in household routine and similar matters. And it's also difficult to know how much of the child's grief actually represents an intensified sense of personal vulnerability: with the death of one parent, the possibility that the other will also die becomes even more frightening, and its consequences for the child become still greater (Raphael, 1983).

As children become older, they develop a better understanding of the meaning of death, and their grieving becomes more similar to that of adults. They may not only request love and caring but, often, offer love and caring to others who are also grieving. However, since the nature of death is still imperfectly grasped, there may still be magical attempts to bring the dead parent back (Raphael, 1983).

In older school-aged children, denial, often accompanied by a high level of distress and anxiety, is a familiar initial response to parental death. These children may view the death as incomprehensible, even though they have the intellectual resources to know what death means. Other patterns may also emerge: involvement, symbolic or otherwise, that links the child with the dead parent, such as reading the dead parent's books or using a phrase the parent used; emulating adult roles and behavior in an attempt to appear adult and, therefore, less vulnerable; developing certain neurotic behaviors, especially phobias and hypochondriasis (Raphael, 1983).

It was mentioned in Chapter 11 that the death of a family member requires that the family system become restructured. This is obviously just as true for a child as for an adult. The child's role in the family may change; expectations of the child change; daily routines, the family's standard of living, even the ability of the family to continue residing in the same house are all threatened with significant change. And what constitutes "my family" is inevitably altered over time.

Not all important deaths experienced by children are those of a parent. Certainly the most common initial bereavement occurs when a grandparent dies. Other family members and close friends may also die. And among the most painful and significant deaths are those of brothers and sisters.

The Death of a Sister or Brother

Since children are still often assumed to be innocent of knowledge of death, family deaths are often kept from them. Yet there is good evidence to believe that these deaths affect them in many ways. Exploratory observations of the reactions of children to their mother's miscarriage (Cain, Erickson, Fast, & Vaughan, 1964), the death of a sibling (Cain, Fast, & Erickson, 1964), or the death of an identical twin indicate that these deaths do affect the children, almost regardless of their age. If, indeed, the child is too young to know that a death has occurred, he or she is still likely to be aware of some stress and disruption. Later it might become evident to the child that the stress was an earlier death.

The effect of sibling death is probably greatly underestimated, even if the brother or sister died before the birth of the present child. In fact, there have been some studies of "substitute" or "replacement" children (Cain & Cain, 1964). One young woman I knew slightly had been conceived about two months after the death of another child in the family, and she was even given the name of the dead child. When she told me about this, as an adult, she admitted that she was never sure of who she was. Am I myself? Or am I the girl who died? Who is Janet Farr? And she also wondered whether the love she received from her parents was for her or for her dead sister. Although you might think she was just being foolish, hers is not a unique response.

After the death of a child, parents are likely to be anxious about their next child, and this may take the form of being overprotective. "It is not unusual for parents to find themselves watching their sleeping child and envisioning how they are going to react if they should find this child dead, too" (Szybist, n.d., p. 18). Getting pregnant again as quickly as possible is not a way to heal grief (nor is getting a new dog for a child right after the death of his or her beloved pet a good way to heal that grief); decisions need to be made on the basis of wanting or not wanting another child for its own sake.

THE ADOLESCENT EXPERIENCE

As children move into adolescence, their cognitive capacities increase, their emotional responses become more mature, and they accumulate experiences that add to their general understanding. All in all, they become more like adults. They also become more aware of themselves and more concerned with their identities than they had been as children—perhaps more concerned than they will be as adults. They are much more likely to think about and plan their future, and since death is part of their future, their awareness of death in general and of their own death in particular also increases.

The Adolescent and Death

You often hear that adolescents don't think about death because it is so unreal and so far in the future. Not true. Adolescents apparently think of death a great deal. Sometimes they fear it greatly; sometimes they romanticize it, like the 19th-century poets, so that it seems beautiful and often even desirable; sometimes they view death as their inevitable fate in a world that is racing toward an absurd and total destruction; sometimes they think of death as a release from the stresses of adult life that they are beginning to face, not always with equanimity. But they do think about it.

In early adolescence, death seems very remote; intellectually it's recognized that it will occur someday, but that day is placed in a far-off and vague future. Younger teenagers probably do not integrate into themselves the idea that death will someday cut them off from a meaningful life. By age 14 or 15, adolescents have become somewhat more independent in their thinking and are more able to contemplate their own deaths. Now is the time for philosophizing and daydreaming about the future. The idea that death will someday put an end to that future can be very upsetting. Adolescents probably think more about death at 14 or 15 than they have at any previous time (Kastenbaum, 1967b; Zeligs, 1974).

A great many studies of college students' attitudes toward death have been conducted, but very little published research is available on people between the ages of 12 and 18. Nevertheless, we do know some things: we know that their death rate is the lowest of any age group and that accidents and suicides account for a large proportion of the deaths that do occur; we also know that many high school students have attended courses, written term papers, and worked in values clarification programs involving death and dying.

Furthermore, we know that in many ways adolescents' perceptions of death resemble those of adults. I was very much impressed when I was asked to discuss death with a seventh-grade English class that had just finished studying *Romeo and Juliet*. The pupils asked many of the same questions and brought up the same issues normally discussed by college students and adults. They had obviously done a great deal of thinking about death, and their reflections apparently preceded their reading of the Shakespeare play. But these were particularly intelligent students, who were in an accelerated class. One author has suggested that it is generally the brighter teenagers who think a great deal about death (Kastenbaum, 1967b); another found in her research—not surprisingly—that higher-achieving high school seniors had more mature concepts of death (Maurer, 1966). And although I have no specific data to prove my contention, I assume that the individual differences among adolescents in viewing death are greater than the individual differences among children.

When a friend or acquaintance does die, the prematurity of the death and its suddenness and unexpectedness make it especially difficult and upsetting. People are caught totally unprepared, in part because the death has occurred out of time sequence. The death of a high school student often disrupts the entire school: students, teachers, and staff. Sometimes the death is handled openly, even if caused by suicide, which has been increasing as a cause of adolescent death, and everyone can mourn together. On other occasions, the school does not officially acknowledge the death, and the administration and staff insist that everything must proceed as though nothing had happened. It is likely that the denial required by the latter circumstance is normally much more difficult for teenagers to handle.

Obviously this area is largely unexplored. It would be particularly useful to know (1) the developmental changes in concepts of and feelings about death from ages 12 through 18, (2) the extent to which adolescents are vulnerable to death fear and anxiety (Zeligs, 1974, has hypothesized that they are especially vulnerable), (3) the differences, if any, in death fear between adolescents whose parents have divorced and those who reside with both parents, and (4) the changes in adolescent views of death that the high adolescent suicide rate may signal.

The Dying Adolescent

The period of adolescence is the healthiest period of the entire life span. The vulnerability of infancy and childhood has been replaced by a much more robust quality, and the accrued health problems and stresses of the adult years have not yet begun. When those from age 15 to 24 to die, it tends to be from accidents, suicides, and homicides. Cancer is the fourth most common cause of death, followed by heart disease, stroke, and pneumonia and influenza (*Statistical Abstracts*, 1982–83).

To understand what dying adolescents confront, consider what their life circumstances are likely to be. For example, they are assumed, probably with justification, to be extremely self-conscious about their physical appearance and deeply concerned about what others think of them. They are just beginning to establish their autonomy from their parents and their own identity. They have begun to look forward to the end of their schooling and the beginning of what some of them see as their "real life." Death changes all this. So although teenagers display most of the kinds of responses to death that adults express, they do so within the context of their own life circumstances.

And teenagers have only begun to live their lives. Thus, to die is to be cheated out of what they had taken for granted. It would seem logical that adolescents would be very angry on learning they were going to die, since they had not yet had an adequate opportunity to live.

Because accidents, suicides, and homicides account for such a large proportion of adolescent deaths, many adolescents die suddenly and unexpectedly or after a fairly brief period of intensive care. For those who die from cancer, heart problems, and other chronic illnesses, the dying trajectory is much like that of adults suffering from the same conditions.

When 1500 Australian high school students were asked what distressed them most about their own death, 43% indicated concern about physical pain and 41% expressed unhappiness because their friends and relatives would suffer grief; an additional 29% mentioned uncertainty about what would happen to them after death. Just over one-fourth described upset at being cheated out of experiences that they had not yet had time to enjoy (Tobin & Treloar, 1979, reported in Raphael, 1983). Except for the last-described, these figures do not differ greatly from those obtained with adults.

Adolescent Bereavement

In the same study of Australian high school students, somewhat over one-third stated that their first encounter with a personally significant death had been that of a grandparent (Tobin & Treloar, 1979, reported in Raphael, 1983). Relatively few teenagers lose a parent through death, although even this number is more than usually assumed.

Adolescent reactions to the death of someone close resemble the reactions of adults in many ways. Adolescents also express anger at the loss or guilt over some real or imagined contribution to the death or slighting of the dead person. They suffer depression; they are concerned about their own future and wonder whether their lives will need to change drastically. In other words, they respond just like other people, in terms of the nature of the loss, their social and emotional maturity, their supports, and their own unique circumstances.

It is obvious, on summary, that children and adolescents of all ages respond to the deaths of those whom they love and that they do so in terms of the meaning of the loss, the nature of the relationship, the availability of support and caring from others, their present situation, and their personalities. Above all, they do so in terms of their cognitive development and their ability to understand what is happening and how they interpret these happenings. These children are in considerable need of ongoing caring relationships from the important people in their lives, and the people who care for them need to know that the children are capable of surviving loss and emotional pain but that they will have more difficulty surviving confused communications, secrecy, and lies and distortions, even those that are presented for well-meaning reasons.

CHAPTER THIRTEEN

Young, Middle, and Late Adulthood

Adolescence ends at 17 or 18 or 19 or perhaps at 21 or 22. Old age begins at 60 or 62 or 65 or 70. From the end of adolescence to the beginning of old age is at least half, perhaps much more, of our normal life span. Yet we know relatively little about changes in reactions to death during that period. The first part of this chapter will discuss the adult years prior to old age; the second part will cover those issues that relate to the elderly.

Differences among adult age groups in their responses to death and dying arise from several factors. First, at different ages, we tend to die from different diseases, and the progress of the disease, including our capacity to resist the condition, also changes. Second, we are at different places in our own lives as we age, and this affects both our reactions to death and how we respond to the dying process: at 30 we have young children, while at 55 our children are likely to be independent; at 30 our careers are just beginning, while at 55 we can probably foresee the rest of our careers. Third, we tend to view death as less appropriate for younger persons; this can even be reflected in the kind of medical treatment provided. Fourth, as we become older, we gain more experience with death, dying, and grief, and these experiences affect our feelings and behavior.

THE ADULT YEARS:
THE MEANING OF DEATH/THE PROCESS OF DYING

Sometimes we treat the years from about ages 21 to 60 as a transition from youth to old age rather than as a part of the life-span developmental process. In recent years, books like *The Seasons of a Man's Life* (Levinson and Associates, 1978) remind us that growth and change are as much a part of these years as of the years of childhood or old age. The study of death and dying, like the rest of the behavioral sciences, lacks knowledge about the changes in attitudes toward death that occur during these years.

The Meaning of Death

It isn't that there are no studies of the meaning of death for people during these years—there are substantial numbers. The difficulty, rather, is the paucity of attention focused on the adult development of concepts and feelings about death and loss. Some research has established correlations of one or another variable with age; for example, it has been shown that fear of death diminishes with age, but nothing has been said about the development of this reduced fear of death. Most studies look only at the end point, the later years, and discuss only how the older person developed his or her views, not how these views were expressed at various adult ages. There is, to my knowledge, *no* study that has accomplished for people between 18 and 60 what Nagy (1948) or Bluebond-Langner (1977) accomplished for children.

Nevertheless, there is still a great deal that we can observe about the changing involvement with death of people in this age group, and there is one study that compares responses of three adult age groups (20–39, 40–59, and 60+) on a large variety of death-related issues (Kalish & Reynolds, 1981).

First, each year, as we grow older, an increasing number of our age peers die. At 30, I rarely heard of a friend dying from any cause other than accident or suicide—and even those occurrences were rare. Each death was unique and remembered. By the time I was 40, this was no longer the case. Not only did I learn of the occasional death of a friend my age, but obituaries frequently informed me of the deaths of celebrities my age or younger. Such accounts are commonplace for me at 55. A statistical analysis performed in Scotland provided interesting substantiation of my experiences. This investigator assumed that a man had 32 friends of exactly the same age and that as soon as one died, that person was replaced by another. Given these circumstances, a person between the ages of 35 and 44 would suffer the death of a friend at least once during that time period; during the next decade, he would lose 2.6 friends by death; and between ages 55 and 65, 5.6 friends would die (Bytheway, 1977). Because of the way I have interpreted the data, these figures are slight underestimates.

Additional data confirm this study. In the youngest of the adult age groups in the Los Angeles study, 25% of those interviewed did not know personally anyone who had died during the previous two years; only 8% knew eight or more such persons. For those in their forties and fifties, the figures were 17% and 14%, respectively; for those over 60, it was 10% and 22%. Other responses support these data: among the youngest adults, 42% had not attended any funerals during the previous two years and 70% had not visited anyone's grave except during a burial service; in the two older age groups, 29% (40–59) and 27% (60+) had not attended funerals, and 50% (40–59) and 43% (60+) had not visited graves (Kalish & Reynolds, 1981).

One more question is relevant. Only 1% of the youngest group of adults had ever told someone that he or she was going to die; 7% of the middle-aged respondents had performed that task (Kalish & Reynolds, 1981). The data suggest that each year we are more often reminded of our own finitude, since death rates rise geometrically and, presumably, the deaths of our friends and age peers rise accordingly.

Second, as I get older—from 30 to 40 and then to 50—my parents also get older, and I increasingly find my friends concerned about their elderly, ill, and dying parents. Stan's mother dies a few years after his father's death, and he at 55 and Suzanne at 47 talk about becoming middle-aged orphans. What does this mean? When at least one parent is alive, our own death "feels" less probable, because we "know" that parents die before their children can die. The death of our parents means not only the loss of a loved person but also the elimination of one psychological barricade protecting us from death.

Third, time left to accomplish things begins to run out. At 30, there is ample time to do everything I want; at 40, I still have 25 or 30 years of work left ahead, but I become aware that not all my friends are going to live that long, and I have a tinge of wondering about whether or not I will make it; by 50, I know that well over half my life has been lived and that I need to sort out what I want to do with the remaining time. One author views age 40 as the time when "a man knows more deeply than ever before that he is going to die" (Levinson and Associates, 1978, p. 205). By and large, during the following few years, a person will come to terms with mortality and will give increasing thought to how he or she as an individual will achieve immortality (Levinson and Associates, 1978).

Fourth, my obligations to others change. When my children are young, not only do I feel an obligation to help them along in their beginnings of life, but I also want to enjoy being involved in the process. As they and I get older, the urgency of these feelings diminishes. When they are grown and have established themselves in whatever way they have chosen, I can feel one part of my work has been accomplished. Three times as many older persons as young adults stated that they were *not* concerned that death would mean they could no longer care for their dependents (Kalish & Reynolds, 1981). Other obligations may, of course, develop through work, community participation, or caring for an ill spouse, but these also may seem less demanding as I reach 50 and then 60.

Fifth, research does show that middle-aged adults are less fearful of death and dying—including their own death and dying—than are younger adults. Just over one-fourth of the middle-aged study participants stated that they were afraid of death; just over one-half stated that they were not afraid. The comparable figures for young adults were 40% and 36%; half again as many younger adults are afraid and half again as many middle-aged adults are unafraid (Kalish & Reynolds, 1981). Another study compared three generations of women in the same families: mothers (average age 46) were significantly less afraid of death than their daughters (average age 21) (Kalish & Johnson, 1972).

Responses to two other questions supported the idea that younger adults are more afraid of death than the middle-aged. Fewer younger adults (62%)

than middle-aged people (75%) stated that they never dreamed about their own death, and fewer younger adults (53%) than middle-aged adults (65%) would accept death peacefully rather than fight it actively (Kalish & Reynolds, 1981).

All these findings suggest to me that younger people have more difficulty with and feel more anxiety about death—especially their *own* deaths—than older persons. However, at the same time, because death seems much less imminent, it is much less salient in their lives. That younger people view their own deaths as many more years off than do older people (Reynolds & Kalish, 1974a) is neither surprising nor "bad." Young adults have more to lose than older adults: they have not yet received the number of years of life, the experiences, and the relationships to which they feel entitled. They are less likely to die soon, but if they did, they would be deprived of more.

Causes of Death

As we move into the adult years, the causes of death shift slowly from the sudden and unexpected youthful deaths from accidents and suicide to the deaths from illness and, eventually, from chronic illness. Accidental deaths diminish in the 25–44 age group, while all other causes of death rise slowly; even suicidal deaths increase slightly, but deaths from disease increase at a much faster rate.

By middle age (45–64), heart problems are overwhelmingly the major cause of death for men, while cancer is the primary cause of death for women. The second most frequent killer is cancer for men and heart attacks for women. Accidents are third for men, and strokes rank third for women. For women, cirrhosis of the liver, accidents, diabetes, pulmonary diseases, and pneumonia/influenza are the next leading causes of death; for men, the sequence is stroke, cirrhosis, pulmonary disease, suicide, and diabetes (*Statistical Abstracts*, 1982–83).

The nature of accidental deaths and deaths from suicide also changes over the adult life span. Motor-vehicle deaths rise from childhood to the late teens and early twenties, then decrease before slowly rising again in late middle age. Deaths from falls, which most people tend to underestimate as a cause of death, are negligible for women but much higher for men until the mid-fifties, when the rate for both sexes rises rapidly (*Statistical Bulletin*, Metropolitan Life Insurance Company, July–September 1978). Suicide death rates increase rapidly from childhood into the late teens and early twenties, then remain fairly constant into the later years, at which time the suicide rate for White males spurts upward again but the rates for Black men and women and for White women drop off (Seiden, 1981).

When Adults Die

Since Chapters 7 and 8 describe the dying process of adults, there is no need to repeat those materials here. Instead, I will restrict this section to an examination of a number of concerns that appear to be specific to adults of various age groups.

First, as mentioned before, as one grows older, the causes of death and, consequently, the processes of dying change. When deaths from heart disease, stroke, and cancer replace deaths from accidents, homicides, and suicides, the time that the dying person has to plan for his or her own death increases. This permits spending time with family members, talking about one's own imminent death, winding up plans and projects, and making preparations for survivors.

What I die from determines to an appreciable extent the pain, discomfort, financial cost, awareness of self, and cognitive competence that I experience during the dying process. The person dying from cancer may have weeks, months, or sometimes years to continue working, being with people, completing old and even generating new tasks, traveling, or reading. In this case it isn't age itself that influences the dying process; rather, the causes of death typical of different ages lead to different dying processes.

Second, older people are at a unique point in their careers. By 50 or 55, most people can predict their future work lives reasonably well. Future promotions and work projects, for example, are rather predictable. At this time many people begin to look to sources outside work for satisfaction. It is not so much that people are planning for retirement, although that does occur in a preliminary fashion, but that the challenges of major new gains from work diminish. Certainly, this is not true for everyone. Some people, like women returning to the work force, enter new careers at this age. And, of course, others still find excitement and new opportunity in their careers. At this point, however, satisfaction from one's work usually comes from doing the job well, rather than from exploring new territory. Consequently, when people this age find they are dying, they feel that they are losing what they have, not what they might yet attain.

Third, the older I am when I die, the less likely I am to feel that I am dying "ahead of time." To die at 35 is to be cheated out of what I believe life promised me; if I die at 55, I will still feel cheated, but less so.

When Adults Grieve

As we enter our adult years, we find that our parents are growing older; when we are middle-aged, our parents are elderly. As this occurs, most of us begin to become concerned about our parents' health and ability to resist disease; when one parent dies, we become deeply concerned about the other parent. How we respond to these concerns is obviously a function of many factors, including the history of our relationship with our parents, but many middle-aged children begin to anticipate the dying processes and deaths of their parents.

The middle-aged and young adult children of elderly parents are often less tied emotionally to their parents than their parents are to them; the younger generation has other pressures, such as spouses and growing or just-grown children, that vie for attention, along with active careers and community involvement. Our society offers no clearly defined roles for adult children of dying parents, so each family develops its own ways of functioning. Therefore, when the death does come, the adult children are ready, having gone through a lengthy "anticipatory orphanhood" (Moss & Moss, 1983–84, p. 69). Nonetheless, the loss still has a profound effect on the survivors, and among other changes it produces, parental death leaves the child a little more aware that his or her own death is now a real possibility.

Not only do parents die as we get older, but people just a little older than we are also die. And eventually we become aware that many of the deaths of people we know or those described in newspapers are deaths of people younger than we. Thus we inevitably grieve not only for those we lose but also for the increased sense of personal vulnerability to death that each such loss produces.

The age of the adult has a great deal to do with the nature of the support system that develops during bereavement. A young adult is unlikely to have children who can be supportive, while a 40-year-old or 50-year-old may well have children who are old enough and mature enough to provide extremely meaningful support (young children can offer love, which is important but is not quite the same). A young adult whose spouse dies may well also receive support from parents, while this is much less likely to be the case for a 50-year-old. In fact, a recent study showed that elderly parents were the most important source of informal support for their recently widowed daughters, providing more valued help than adolescent and young adult children (Bankoff, 1983).

Age also appears to affect the ongoing patterns of reactions to the death during the period of recovery. In a comparison of younger widows (average age in the early fifties) with older widows (average age in the early seventies), the younger women responded with greater initial shock, confusion, death anxiety, and guilt, along with disbelief; overall, their intensity of response was greater. After 18 months, however, the younger women seemed to have recuperated more successfully and the older women displayed more grief, in some instances more grief than 18 months earlier (Sanders, 1980–81). These findings show the value of longitudinal research, since to have compared the two groups either right after the death or 18 months later would not have provided an adequate picture of the process.

Chapters 10 and 11 describe grief, mourning, and bereavement, and almost all of that discussion is relevant to adult losses. Some of the discussion is particularly germane to the deaths of spouses. However, one kind of death that is especially painful to adults is the loss of a child. Even the death of an infant or the cessation of a pregnancy is of great concern to the parents. And certainly the death of an adolescent or young adult child, most often through accidents or suicide, leads to deep upset and grief.

Parents become deeply depressed at the death of a child, whether it was sudden and unexpected or not, and the death, rather than bringing the mother and father together as many people assume, actually weakens the marital tie. Moreover, the child is frequently idealized, and the "child's real nature is lost" (Raphael, 1983, p. 274). These consequences can easily lead to problems with other children in the family, who not only have had to share the stress produced by the dying process and the death but who may recall their brother or sister more accurately and be less than delighted that their own inadequacies are not so easily forgotten (Raphael, 1983).

Another aspect of the grieving process is "Why me?", which is a familiar chord in the symphony of death. Parents become angry that their child was "selected" to die and may, for a brief period, be resentful of others whose children remain healthy. Parents also may blame themselves for the death, since it was they who permitted the child to take the car that evening, to go swimming where the tides were dangerous, to avoid going for a medical examination until the disease had progressed too far. So depression, guilt, and anger, the familiar triad of grief, develop their own course when a child dies.

When death occurs before birth. Sometimes parents grieve for an as-yet-unborn child. This occurs with miscarriages, medical abortions, and still-births. In each of these situations, the emphasis of caretakers tends to be on the health of the mother (Worden, 1982), ignoring for the time being her emotional concerns or the concerns of the father. Yet in each of these situations, the mother frequently has major emotional issues to deal with and not infrequently is never given an adequate opportunity to handle them.

Guilt, for example, is a common outcome of any of the above experiences. After a miscarriage or a stillbirth, the mother feels she has done something wrong, either in caring for herself or in having done something for which she is being punished. She may also blame her husband, who is perhaps busy blaming her or blaming himself or both (Worden, 1982). Depression, guilt, and anger are once again all familiar. And the advice to "have another baby" is often given too quickly and with too little attention to the need for grieving. Even though the baby was never alive, the anticipations of the mother and father may well have created the equivalent of a live person. Advising them to have another baby right away is comparable to the actions of the father who brought home a puppy identical to the one that had been killed so that his child would not find out about the death.

Medical abortions produce other issues. Although the abortion is requested by the mother and often by the father as well, it is virtually never a decision that pleases them. Rather, it is a decision that appears to be the least unpleasant of the various alternatives. The guilt, anger, and depression arising from a medical abortion not only reflect the loss but also represent the thought that a murder was committed. However, these feelings frequently occur around six weeks after the operation (Raphael, 1983), and the mother may not be fully aware of the bases for her intense feelings. The role of the father in an abortion is even less well defined; some fathers never know that the mother was pregnant, and others are not included in the decision-making process. It is probably better for all concerned, under most circumstances, if the father continues to support the mother emotionally during the entire process, including her recuperation.

I won't go into the religious and political ramifications of abortion, but even though numerous women have had more than one abortion, it is uncommon for a fetus to be aborted without causing the mother, and usually the father, considerable anguish. Since many people wish to forget both the abortion and the events leading up to it, they do not permit themselves adequate opportunity for grieving the loss (Worden, 1982).

Women, and men also, who lose babies before their birth are often in need of more than medical treatment and a tranquilizer. For a few, self-help groups are available (Wilson & Soule, 1981). For others, we might consider the advice given to social workers who serve these people:

- Help the parents build memories, through photographs, giving the baby a name, understanding the cause of death, even holding and/or seeing the baby.
- Permit them to talk about their feelings.
- Help find someone to participate with them in planning what to do: a trusted friend, a clergyman/clergywoman, or a funeral director.
- Refer them to self-help groups or to others who have recovered from the same experience.
- Recognize that mourning is likely to occur and may be lengthy.
- Work toward changing hospital policies to improve general staff and physician sensitivity (Stringham, Riley, & Ross, 1982).

Sudden infant death syndrome.   One particular kind of death can be especially cruel: the **sudden infant death syndrome,** also known as SIDS or crib death. This syndrome, widely discussed today, refers to an infant death that occurs without warning, without—at least at present—known cause and without any known history of health problems; it also occurs quickly, so that parents may leave their infant after an early evening feeding and return, four hours later or sometimes even ten minutes later, to find their baby dead.

It has been estimated that between 15 and 20% of all infant deaths are due to sudden infant death syndrome (Mortimer, 1983); the rate is at its highest between two and three months, and male infants are more susceptible than females (Mellins & Haddad, 1983).

Although it was once assumed that these infants were in perfect health before their death, it no longer is. A detailed history of SIDS infants indicates that many had had some form of cardiorespiratory or neurological difficulty. Nonetheless, many experts in the field attribute these deaths to environmental rather than genetic factors (Mellins & Haddad, 1983).

Although the cause has not been determined, many causes have been eliminated. Crib deaths are *not* caused by birth control pills or fluoridated water, since the condition was reported for many years before either of these technological developments; they are *not* the result of suffocating, vomiting, choking, breast feeding, or bottle feeding; sudden infant death is *not* a hereditary condition. And the fact that the deaths can occur in as brief a time as five minutes eliminates a host of other diseases (Szybist, n.d.).

Although sudden infant deaths do occur to the infants of parents of all ages and from all kinds of living conditions, there are some circumstances in which the deaths occur more frequently. For example, SIDS victims tend to have lower birth weights than average, to be born during the winter months, to be born to mothers having below-average education and income and having a history of smoking, narcotics use, or anemia; and to be born to Native American and Black American families (even when income is controlled). There is also a greater likelihood that these infants had brothers or sisters who were SIDS victims and that they themselves experienced slow growth after birth (Mellins & Haddad, 1983).

Since an apparently healthy child dies suddenly, the parents feel extremely guilty. The mother and father, under tremendous stress because of the death, sometimes turn to blame each other. Father blames mother for being careless, for not having noticed that the baby had a cold or that the blanket was over the child's head; mother blames father for not wanting to leave the television set to check on the baby, for not wishing to move out of the city to the cleaner air of the country. And each, of course, feels that he or she must have done something wrong or the baby would still be alive. Their speculations range from having bad genes to being an incompetent parent.

To make matters worse, other family members, friends, and neighbors are also likely to blame the parents, overtly or implicitly. "I knew she shouldn't have married him, his brother being retarded and all that." "I hear they use marijuana in the evening, and they are probably so out of it, they didn't hear the baby cry." "I wonder if she did let him suffocate—I heard her saying that she wasn't sure she wanted a third baby." Furthermore, especially in the past, the police, suspecting child abuse, sometimes questioned the parents as possible offenders rather than providing support to deeply grieving people (Halpern, 1972).

Occasionally either a babysitter, who might have been with the child at that time, or an older sibling, who had expressed some resentment of the baby, gets blamed. Since siblings almost always have mixed feelings about a new baby, they feel very guilty, even if they never came near the infant, and later absolution from their parents does not completely remove the guilt (Halpern, 1972).

Since newspapers and other media have been carrying accounts of crib deaths and since many local health and human service agencies provide support programs for these parents, the situation that confronted SIDS parents 15 years ago is no longer quite so drastic. Nonetheless, the death of a baby has still occurred, and many parents still feel "toxic." One mother stated that, for two years after her infant died, she was not able to hold a baby for fear that she would cause that baby's death also. A letter written to a crib-death research project exemplifies the guilt a parent may feel.

When I went to bed that night, I put her in bed with me because she was fussing. When I woke up and found her, I got out of bed and carried her around with me for I don't know how long before I realized that she was really gone. . . . I told everyone I had smothered her sometime during the night. The doctor, the nurses at the hospital, and the ambulance driver said she had never smothered. If I could only believe that.... I still can't convince myself that [a disease] was the cause of her death [Bergman, Pomery, & Beckwith, 1969, p. 103].

Crib deaths are only a modest statistic in the number of infant and child deaths that occur each year, but the levels of distress they cause are dramatic. Biomedical researchers are investigating the causes of SIDS, and perhaps they will find ways to prevent these deaths or at least reduce their likelihood. And the National Foundation for Sudden Infant Death (310 South Michigan Avenue, Chicago, Illinois 60604) serves as an advocate for the victims, both infants and parents, of sudden infant death syndrome.

DEATH IN THE LATER YEARS

Many of the trends described in the previous section continue into the later years. The inevitability of death comes closer and probably impinges more on day-to-day activities; it certainly impinges on future plans. Yet there are considerable individual differences in the reactions of older persons to death.

Older people are constantly reminded of death. It is difficult to ignore death when not only age peers but much younger persons die. The elderly are, of course, much more likely than the young to have lost a spouse, brother, or sister through death; they almost always have experienced the death of at least one parent; they have had more friends die; they attend more funerals; and they are more likely to visit grave sites (Kalish & Reynolds, 1981).

Coping with Death

Erik Erikson (1963) has described the two ego conflicts of the second half of life as *generativity versus stagnation* and *ego integrity versus despair*. In earlier years, because time seems unlimited, it is possible to use time freely and to plan a future. The meaningfulness of an activity, a relationship, education, work—all appear to extend into an indefinite future. As years pass and the indefinite future becomes less infinite, meaningfulness must be generated increasingly in terms of the present. The middle-aged person needs to remain capable of generating involvements and avoiding stagnation—especially in view of her or his diminishing fantasies about what the future can be. In later years, it is equally necessary to retain a good sense of self in the face of increased potential for despair: despair that so many things are still not done, so many hopes still unrealized—and so many things done that cannot be undone. Time may now seem too brief to begin again.

In some ways, this new awareness provides freedom rather than despair, but the older individual must be able to *see* it as freedom for it in fact to be freedom. Since long-range plans must sometimes be curtailed because of death, ill health, or diminishing access to power through work and relationships, the older person may devote himself or herself to more immediate concerns. When you can no longer build a new service program, increase your hardware-store sales, or put into effect your idea for improved office efficiency, you can focus on enjoying the sun, taking a walk, watching grandchildren and great-grandchildren grow up. Perhaps these things are as important anyway. Since everything we do will eventually not matter very much, we might as well do what brings us enjoyment and pleasure at the moment we do it. Our "immortality" will not endure very long by establishing a better sales program, so why not watch a flower grow?

These matters, obviously, are philosophical and there is no wand we can wave magically to make an older person see them as described. But at least the potential is there. Death, then, simultaneously gives freedom and takes freedom away.

Another way older people cope with death is by preparing for it. More older people than younger people have (1) made out a will, (2) made funeral arrangements, (3) paid for a cemetery plot, and (4) arranged for someone to handle their affairs (Kalish & Reynolds, 1981; Riley, 1968). The elderly are less likely to have life insurance than late-middle-aged persons. This is consistent with what we know about the realities they face: many older persons no longer have dependents who will require support after their death and the cost of the insurance is higher. Again, it is important to draw attention to the differences not only between age groups but within age groups. For example, the extent of a person's education also influences the preparations she or he makes for death; the better-educated elderly are more likely to make such plans (Riley, 1968).

Belief in some form of continuity after death is undoubtedly another method of coping with death. In a Florida study, 61% of older persons strongly believed in a life after death, and another 11% tended to believe (Wass, Christian, Myers, & Murphey, 1978–79); 64% of those over 60 in the Los Angeles study also believed in some sort of life after death (Kalish & Reynolds, 1981); even higher numbers have been found in earlier studies (Cantril, 1951). However, a larger proportion of older people wish there were life after death than believe there is (Wass et al., 1978–79).

Attitudes toward Death

As mentioned earlier, one of the more consistent research results in the area of death is that fear of death diminishes with age. Studies of diminishing fear of death with age have been conducted with a variety of populations and have utilized a variety of instruments (Bengtson et al., 1977; Feifel & Branscomb, 1973; Kalish & Johnson, 1972; Kalish & Reynolds, 1981; Kogan & Wallach, 1961; Martin & Wrightsman, 1965). And the proportion of older persons who state that they fear death remains amazingly similar from study to study. Even a study in India confirmed the findings (Sharma & Jain, 1969). As an example, in a group of alert, institutionalized elderly, 16% stated that they feared death (Kimsey, Roberts, & Logan, 1972). Five percent of one multiethnic population in Los Angeles County indicated that they were "very afraid" (Bengtson et al., 1977); the figure from a totally different multiethnic group in the same community was 10% who were either "afraid" or "terrified" (Kalish & Reynolds, 1981); 10% of a group of older community volunteers admitted that they feared death (Jeffers et al., 1961). Depending on the particular group surveyed, the wording of the questions, and the context, specific percentages will obviously vary, but the numbers are normally not far from those cited.

A well-known longitudinal study of older men, begun when the participants were in their early seventies and completed a decade later, provides additional substantiation. Among these men, who were studied intensely, "few were found to be overtly afraid of death, and those who were seemed to have attitudes formed early which were deeply characteristic of their entire lives" (Rosenfeld, 1978, p. 16). Many of these healthy older men were able to accept their own future death. Among those who did not wish to confront the idea of their own mortality, most used defense mechanisms such as humor and appropriate denial, and most had made concrete plans for their own death—for example, wills had been written, burial arrangements made. Perhaps the most significant finding of this study was that, at least for many of these men, the greatest challenge was not that of facing death but that of using the "bonus years," the years after retirement and after most of their age peers had died, to their own good advantage (Rosenfeld, 1978).

At the same time that older persons are less fearful and more accepting of their own deaths, they think more about death than younger persons (Kalish & Reynolds, 1981; Riley, 1968). At first appearance these two results may seem contradictory, but perhaps they are not. First, older people recognize that they have relatively little futurity. The deaths of age peers and younger people and the awareness that their lives are coming to a close make them think more about death. In turn, having had more death experiences and having been forced to think about death, they have also been required to work through some of their fears and anxieties.

Second, their futures are not as attractive as those of younger persons. Many older people have some chronic disease or physical handicap that they know is likely to worsen; the losses of friends, of work possibilities, and of perceived social value all conspire to reduce the value of life for them. This can lead to a disengagement from life and a greater willingness to accept death.

Third, most people in industrialized nations anticipate a life expectancy of 65 to 70 years. Many people appear to accept this fact as a given: if they face their deaths in advance of those ages, they feel deprived, but if they live longer, they feel they have received their just measure.

Fourth, some older people are ready to stop coping with the demands of the world. One 92-year-old man, functioning with minimal impairment and enjoying life, said that he was ready to die whenever his time came—although he denied that he was eager to die. He feared the changing social and political arena, and he was suspicious of his new neighbors; he felt no more meaning in life and was no longer interested in seeking new experiences, which finances and health made difficult anyway. For the next three years, he pursued only familiar routines, which he appeared to enjoy in a quiet way. Then he died easily and quietly.

This fourth point may find additional confirmation in the results of the study, mentioned earlier, that asked people of various ages whether they felt that death came too soon. Middle-aged persons were more likely than younger people to feel that death comes too soon. The number of people over 60 who agreed with this statement was small, as was the number of younger people who agreed (Riley, 1968). The wear and tear of life becomes too much, and death, though not actively sought, is essentially accepted when it occurs.

In some ways, death has very much the same meaning over the entire life span. But because views and feelings are inevitably influenced by situation and context, older people look at death from a position different from that of middle-aged or younger persons; children and young adolescents are in still a different position. And historical situations also affect age differences. People who were socialized to those views of death that prevailed in 1910 are likely to be different in their feelings and attitudes from those who were socialized in 1980.

Thus, while the ultimate meaning of death remains the same, perceptions of the meaning of death change as the individual grows older. It is possible, of course, that older people simply deny their fear of death more frequently than the nonelderly. I don't believe this is the case, but it is a hypothesis that cannot be tested adequately at this time. You will need to judge this for yourself.

When the Elderly Die

How does the dying process of older people differ from the dying process of the nonelderly? Primary, of course, is the issue of the causes of death. Among the elderly, heart disease is the major killer, although it has been diminishing in recent years. Cancer and stroke rank second and third for both men and women. Then come pulmonary diseases, pneumonia/influenza, accidents, atherosclerosis, and diabetes for men; for women the order is pneumonia/influenza, atherosclerosis, diabetes, accidents, pulmonary diseases. As people get older, the chances that death will be caused by chronic rather than acute conditions increase (*Statistical Abstracts*, 1982–83).

The dying process of people who suffer from chronic conditions, such as heart disease, stroke, and cancer, differs from the process of those suffering from acute conditions, in which the death occurs more rapidly. Financial costs differ; the nature of both the health care and the human care differs; the potential for continuing with a fairly normal life, at least for a period of time, is greater; the potential for contemplating death is of greater duration; the opportunity to see old friends or to visit new places may be greater. Many of the differences between generations in the dying process are not a function of age itself but of the conditions that tend to cause deaths at different ages.

There are, of course, numerous other bases for differences. First, the death of an elderly person is considered by the community to be less tragic than deaths in other age groups (for example, Kalish & Reynolds, 1981). Therefore, the social value of the remaining life of the older person diminishes, and he or she is likely to receive less attention and fewer life-sustaining measures than younger people. The investment of time, energy, money, and personal affect in the remaining time of a dying older person is often seen to produce little reward.

Second, because it is assumed that an older person will die soon of some illness—if not the present one—the impetus for keeping the person alive or even for providing optimum care is less.

Third, many older persons reside in long-term-care institutions during their dying process, especially during the early phases prior to hospitalization. This has obvious implications for the kinds of family contact that occur during this period and for the extent of professional medical attention.

Fourth, because more older persons than nonelderly are confused or comatose during the period leading up to death, they receive a different kind of care. Communication is more difficult or impossible. They are already functioning as nonpersons in many ways, and they may even engender resentment from those who are required to care for them, because the demanding nature of their illness is not compensated for by a reciprocal human relationship.

Fifth, an extremely high proportion of older persons, especially older women, enter the living-dying interval without a spouse to help in their care. Some of them also do not have children, brothers, or sisters who are capable of participating and willing to participate in their care. Consequently, they may die without the ongoing love and attention that are, at least potentially, available to those with families. They are also less likely to have an advocate to intercede on their behalf with health or social agency staff.

Sixth, an older person frequently has reviewed his or her life; this reminiscing over an extended period of time helps to integrate the person's entire life (Butler, 1968). When an older person realizes that the living-dying interval has begun, the pressure to review his or her life increases. On the one hand, doing so may make death easier; on the other hand, impending death may encourage the effort. Butler adds an important point qualifying his suggestion that reminiscing may make death more acceptable: "I do not intend to imply that a 'serene and dignified acceptance of death' is necessarily appropriate, noble, or to be valued. Those who die screaming may be expressing a rage that is as fitting as dignity" (Butler, 1968, p. 494).

All of the foregoing suggests that the conditions in which older people die are more isolated and lonely than those in which younger persons die. Sometimes we seem to justify the deaths of older people: we remind ourselves of how ill they were; we suggest that somehow they're to blame for their deaths; we insist that they had nothing more to live for anyway.

Although the elderly appear better able to cope with dying and death, they may still struggle to maintain life. Their struggle probably receives less support than the efforts of younger people. It may well be that one of the reasons some older people die sooner than expected is that, having lost support from others, they find themselves with less sense of being cared for and being cared about. "The terminally aged may be as helpless as a child, but they seldom arouse tenderness" (Weisman, 1972, p. 144). Eventually they tire and simply give up life.

Dying in Institutions and Retirement Communities

What happens to older people when they die in institutions or retirement communities? Although they are less likely to have access to their adult children in both settings, in the retirement communities, at least, they are very likely to receive support from friends who reside near them. And if the facility is church-related, there may be a sense of connection with their faith. Both settings serve constantly to remind older people of their mortality, because they frequently see other residents become ill and die.

Sometimes this constant exposure makes the elderly come to accept their own deaths more easily. For example, the author of one incisive study of a retirement community concluded that its residents accepted impending death in a matter-of-fact fashion and were not preoccupied with dying.

Many elderly persons (in the general community, as well as in retirement communities) are ready to die, but because they have an obligation to care for a husband or a sister, they feel useful to someone else, and this feeling makes their lives meaningful. A woman in her nineties stated "I'd like to live as old as I am useful. And after that, I'm willing to go" (Marshall, 1975); another, when asked how long she would like to live, answered "[Until] I'm no use to my sister any longer" (Marshall, 1975).

Nursing homes are, of course, very different from retirement communities. In fact, about their only similarity is a population of older persons, and even then, the average age in a nursing home is usually at least ten years older than in a retirement community. Although only about 5% of persons over age 65 are in any kind of long-term-care institution at any given time, a much higher percentage—probably around 25%—are in a nursing home at some time in their lives (Kastenbaum & Candy, 1973).

When an older person enters a nursing home, he or she and the staff are both aware that it is likely to be the person's last residence. In a way, then, the dying process begins there, regardless of the condition of the person's health. Residents may seek confirmation from the staff and from within themselves that they do indeed have a future—that is, that death is not near. Without this confirmation their feelings of hope wane. They find themselves bargaining for postponement of death—an endeavor for which the resident may or may not receive encouragement and support from the staff (Gustafson, 1973).

Several studies have examined the effects of relocation on the health and longevity of elderly nursing-home patients. Although the results have been contradictory, my own personal evaluation of the various results is that relocation offers advantages to the older person, both in life satisfaction and in life expectancy, *if* the relocation is to a more desirable residence and *if* the elderly person is properly prepared in advance for the move. To the extent that deaths do result from relocation, it is probably because those elderly people who are already in poor health and somewhat confused find the move highly stressful and leading to increased confusion because of the lack of familiarity with their new surroundings (Rowland, 1977).

When Dying Is All Right

There comes a time, especially for older persons, when dying is all right. To use the expression suggested by Marshall (1980), there comes a time when dying is "legitimated," a point at which death is neither too soon nor too late. Marshall proposes five situations in which death is considered preferable:

First, when one is unable to be active;

Second, when one is unable to be useful;

Third, when one becomes a burden because of physical infirmity or social dependency;

Fourth, when one loses one's mental faculties;

Fifth, when one has progressively deteriorating physical health and concomitant physical discomfort.

Each of us depends on our system of values to decide whether we would want to live in each of the five situations. Of course, a hypothetical decision might well be contradicted when a real decision has to be made. Although a person of any age might have to make these choices, they are more likely to fall to an older person.

Each of the five cases exemplifies a situation that runs counter to the general values of our society and its criteria for a full life. We place great stress in our society on autonomy and independence, on competence, comfort, activity and involvement, health, growth and the possibility of growth. When any one of these becomes impossible, the potential for enjoying the kind of life that we have been brought up to value diminishes greatly. Not all societies are concerned that the elderly must be cared for; not all societies believe that being useful is the criterion for a worthwhile life—but our society does. Another culture might consider death preferable to bringing intense shame to the family, to being captured in battle, to being entered by an evil spirit.

If you work with the elderly and want them to choose life, rather than death, when faced with any of the above five situations, you have three alternative approaches. First, you can try to help the older person believe that death is still worse than any of the situations. Second, you can try to help the older person believe that the situation itself really isn't so bad. And third, you can try to change the circumstances of the situation, if possible, so that the older person does, for example, remain active or useful.

BEREAVEMENT IN OLD AGE

Just over half of all women over age 54 are widows, and the proportion goes up to 70% among women over 75; widows outnumber widowers 6:1 among those 65 to 75, and the ratio is nearly 5:1 for those over 75 (Brotman, 1982). This leads to the development of a "society of widows"—that is, a group of primarily older women whose husbands have died and who develop friendships over a period of time. Relatively few of these women will remarry, although a substantial proportion of widowers, especially those who are young-old (under age 75), do remarry.

Since older widows and widowers are often frail and vulnerable to health problems, often exacerbated by the arduous process of having cared for their dying spouse, they have less recuperative power than younger widows. Many elderly widows and widowers report poor physical health, depression, or both. In one study, elderly widows and widowers were more depressed than those of the same age who were not recently bereaved, but the proportion of those who were pathologically depressed was only slightly higher than among the nonbereaved (Gallagher, Breckenridge, Thompson, & Peterson, 1983).

Who provides supports for the elderly bereaved? The husband or wife, of course, if the bereavement is due to the death of a parent, a brother or sister, or a child (keep in mind that people who live into their late eighties or older may well have children in their late sixties), and children or brothers and sisters if the death is that of a spouse.

Older people, having fewer years ahead of them, may decide to cherish the memories of the dead person, rather than attempting to find a replacement for the relationship (Raphael, 1983). This doesn't mean that they avoid new relationships but that they do seldom permit a new relationship to provide the role of spouse or brother or sister. When asked how long after the death of a spouse it should take before someone of their age group could appropriately go out on dates, a much higher proportion of older people responded "never" (Kalish & Reynolds, 1981).

The death of a pet has been mentioned as the first important death for many children. Ironically, it may be the last important cause for grieving for an elderly person. Many elderly people who live alone keep a pet, often an aging pet, for comfort and company, perhaps also for something alive they can touch. When the pet dies, the elderly person may not wish to develop another attachment or to go through the process of accustoming a pet to accept his or her lifestyle. It is one more important loss, and since it is not to be replaced, it is particularly painful.

In spite of the problems and the pain of bereavement in the later years, the elderly do an amazingly fine job of maintaining themselves, of handling their depression, and of continuing to be resources for others.

CARING
RELATIONSHIPS

"WE ARE ALL SURVIVORS
OF THE DEATHS
OF OTHERS."

John (1943–1983)

January 15, 1982

My friend John was having severe headaches which finally drove him to the physician, and he went in for some tests. A CAT scan revealed a tumor in his left temporal lobe. John and I have talked about this, and we noted that life takes on whole new hues once you are faced with your own mortality. He and his wife, Lin, have become closer and more solicitous of each other's needs. The tumor is apparently benign, but dying has been on his mind since anything is possible. He is really open, and it is fun to talk to him about it. (Letter to my parents)

July 24, 1982

John is feeling better, but has lost all the hair on one side of his head where the radiation got it. (Letter to my parents)

March 15, 1983

John went into the hospital briefly on Sunday. He woke up with one side of his body numb. . . . no evidence from the CAT scan that there was a return of the cancer to his brain, but there was some swelling in his brain. He can't drive now because he seems to be losing peripheral vision, especially on the left side. He puts up a front which seems very optimistic and yet somehow it does not seem "true." I have spoken to Lin . . . and she sees it too. At least they are willing to talk about it. I am worried that one day cancer will kill him, and it is painful for me to watch. (My journal)

March 30, 1983

This has been a weird week. John went to Seattle this week and found that the tumor in his brain is growing back. He has spent a lot of time not telling most of us. That would not be so bad but part of what he is doing is not being honest. The worse he feels, the bigger the lie. It leaves those of us who love him feeling ripped off, and we have to "pretend" a lot of things.

It is strange because he might be dead soon. We don't know how long he has. Surgery has been ruled out. There is a procedure with a catheter being inserted in an artery and threaded to the affected spot, and chemicals let in to deal with the growth. It *might* work, they say.

I have never had a friend die slowly before me. Some of what I feel is probably confusion and some is another realization of my own mortality. I have to separate what I feel for him and what I feel for *me!* I. Me. I do not want to lose a friend. I don't want to see him suffer. I. I. I. Am I speaking for John's needs or my own? (My journal)

April 7, 1983

John says they give him three or four months to live. He does not seem to be in any pain, but it is obvious that he is distracted, either by his own

260

knowledge or by symptoms or both. Occasional headaches ... vision is failing ... like tunnel vision ... especially on the left side.

I had lunch with him and he cooked a can of hash. The pan was always dangerously off center on the gas burner and when hash would fall off the left-hand side of the skillet he wouldn't see it. Several forkfuls went between the stove and the counter and hit the floor. His mental acuity and his vision both seem impaired. He seems forgetful at times. It's still John, with his warmth and caring, but not all there. He is using a drug that increases his appetite, so when he finished sharing the first can of hash, he cooked another for himself and finished it off.

He does not want surgery, which would buy time, but not much, and the trade-offs would include more drugs and more pain. He may fly to the Philippines to visit some faith healers there—it is his only hope, he thinks. He says he has no fear of death, of leaving "this body." He regrets not seeing his kids grow up. He says he is not afraid, and he does not seem afraid. He has dealt with this about a year now; perhaps the time has permitted him to deal with death. (Letter to my parents)

April 11, 1983

Had lunch with John's wife—he went into the hospital just before noon. She bears up well around him, but she needs a release and there are not currently any support groups in Fairbanks for this sort of grief/loss. This morning John fell. Seems the paralysis in his left side gets worse with pressure on the brain. Lin says that John was like a vegetable this morning, but he may be out of the hospital tomorrow.

I think they are all coming to Anchorage and would like to see you. They need to leave the kids with some good memories. This has been a tough two years for them and they need some uppers. (Letter to Laura)

April 13, 1983

John is doing much better today, and the four of them will go to Anchorage tomorrow.

"What do you say after you say hello?" To a dying man. You tell him you are sorry. You tell him you are aware of his problem, that you won't ignore him or it because he is a human being and part of your life. He and I talk about Buckminster Fuller and poetry. John still believes that he cannot stop learning in this lifetime because "if I don't get it this time around, it will be harder to learn next time." And you hug him and tell him by your actions that he is not poison.

Lin needs a lot of understanding. She has been carrying a heavy load and is very tired. Exhausted. They need, as a family, to have a good time together.

John does not always function well physically. If he controls the conversation, his mental acuity is incredible. Perhaps he doesn't want to bother talking about certain things that are not relevant just now. Remember that Hugh Mulligan said "What I am doing today is important because I am exchanging a day of my life for it." In John's case every hour is precious in the same way. (Letter to Laura)

April 15, 1983

I hope you were able to connect with John and his family. The Philippines? Apparently about 10 people from Fairbanks, diagnosed terminal cancer, made the trip. All were dead within two years. But the doctor says that he won't discourage the trip—it gives people the sense that they have done all they could.

I read the other day that if you spend too much time worrying about dying, you won't have time to live and then death has already won. It wins soon enough anyway. (Letter to Laura)

April 16, 1983

I'm glad you got to see John and Lin while they were down there. I don't recall if I mentioned it, but I'm trying to get the Fairbanks Memorial Hospital to reinstitute their "I Can Cope" group for the terminally ill and their families this month. I looked around Fairbanks for support groups for Lin and there was simply nothing available. I hope I have inspired the folks to get one going again. (Letter to Laura)

April 19, 1983

I spoke with John and Lin last night and they both sounded TERRIFIC! It was good to hear them so UP. I understand the antiswelling drug is in pretty high doses now. I wonder what happens when that stops working or gets too strong or whatever. Right now it does not seem to be affecting his mind too much. (Letter to Laura)

April 21, 1983

John seems to be doing quite well. I have seen him twice in the last two days and his spirits are up and his behavior is 100% better.

Sometimes, at a very cold level, we all seem to be saying: If you are going to die, would you get it over with so we can all return to normal. I am not sure if that is true, but we all feel fairly strong and seem to have a need to be practical. I think John needs to make a statement about his desire to live and then go with it. I sense that we sometimes stifle him. Looks like he won't be going to the Philippines. (My journal)

May 23, 1983

I just got a call from John. He is doing better lately. An organization he belongs to collected money to pay his way to a meeting in Washington, D.C. It is a real upper for John. He says he experiences occasional numbness in his left side, but nothing like it was last month. (My journal)

Labor Day 1983

On Saturday John had taken a dramatic turn and was incoherent and filled with a sort of terror like I have never seen. He did not recognize me and seemed barely able to recognize Lin. I think he could see, but it was largely unfocused and it seemed like he was blind. It was eerie. He seemed to be fighting a demon battle like he was not sure if he needed permission to die. He was not sure if it was safe to go. He asked several times if he could "leave." Then he would start talking about being afraid.

I suggested he go to the hospital, which was probably not the best thing for him but was best for the family. I have a sense that he wanted to get permission to die and then do it at home. I think the hospital represents a fight against death for him. When he got to the hospital, he became uncontrollable and had to be restrained for several hours. It took five people to get him down. I guess it was pretty wild. Lin says he had a grand mal seizure in their car on the way to the hospital. Jaina (age 11) seems pretty aware of what is going on, but Erik (age 7) is either denying it and trying to believe that things are normal or simply is not old enough to be very aware of what it all means.

I visited John that Sunday night and he was "all there" occasionally, but seemed very tired and faded in and out. He did not seem on the verge of death. He seemed to recognize people and was no longer in restraints. I think I am not dealing with it very well. I can't sleep and I find myself thinking about him. Lin and I both feel it is time for him to let go. I have prayed that he simply go quickly and painlessly. It is hard to see a friend suffer. It is incomprehensible the way that making a million dollars is incomprehensible. To grasp the fact requires a leap into another dimension. I can intellectualize it, but I can't "see" it. (My journal)

September 21, 1983
John continues to deteriorate and that has an impact. I have been helping Lin plan for the inevitable, which seems imminent. It makes me pensive.
Hmmm. I am mortal. (Letter to my parents)

September 26, 1983
Lin just called and said John is some worse. He does not really wake up any more and while he will momentarily recognize voices, he does not do much more than respond minimally. I sometimes think we are simply waiting out the disease. (Letter to Laura)

October 3, 1983
John died today. He died just before 2 P.M. I was there, with his wife Lin, and Claudia, the home health nurse who had visited the family daily for about three weeks.
Just after noon, when I arrived, Lin was sitting quietly at John's side, on the mattress on the floor. This was where he wished to die. And it was here that he lay today, gasping bravely for breath, a death rattle that foretold of pneumonia which would claim him in a matter of less than two hours.
He was virtually comatose, but at times his eyes would open and roll up,

and he would have a faraway look which I prayed would signal his recovery, a light comment, a chuckle. Instead he gazed, glazed, then dozed off again. The real ambiguity is that I also prayed for his painless and immediate death. His mouth dripped mucus. It was not John, but something like John. But this time there was no control. He had controlled all he could and was perhaps at peace now, knowing that, while he could not be in control, the love and caring of his family and friends ensured that the eventuality of his passing would be as he would want it.

His blood pressure dropped dramatically after the noon hour and he was near death. His left arm, on which he had lain for a while to help his breathing, seemed withered and blue. The blood pressure simply could not sustain life in his limbs.

Lin lay by his side as life ebbed. We changed his position so he could breathe, and drain his lungs, more easily. His breathing came in fits and starts. Long pauses punctuated labored gasps. Then, as Lin held him, he simply stopped breathing and, as Lin described it, "faded away." His arm became covered with goose bumps, his color faded, and with it his life.

She told me later she felt terror. SHE was out of control. He was going. That was it. She could not stop this passing as it unfolded before her. She wept openly and whispered silently over and over, "Damn it, damn it." There was a helplessness to it. "He left too soon," I said. All we could do was touch and wish hopelessly that this was not happening.

Claudia was good at what she did. Just minutes before John died, when it seemed so evident the spark of life was waning, she changed dressings, took life-sign readings, and labored patiently. When there is life, we do labor to sustain and nurture it. THAT is comforting. Then he was gone.

We grieved for a while and talked about the miracle of life. Then Lin drove to the school and picked up the kids. While she was gone, Claudia and I dressed John in his favorite shirt and sweatpants. When they returned, he appeared asleep, natural, in repose. He looked more at peace than perhaps anytime in several months. His last coherent conversation with me was at dinner a month ago. We spoke of Jung and he remarked that "we should talk a lot more about this." Conversations since then were gasps, regrets, brief and precious comments. "You look better." "It's terrific that you are here." "Including 'nothing,' what would you want to talk about now?" A squeeze of the hand and "Nothing, thanks." The energy for clear thought and speech went mostly to his family. I remember he apologized once for "embarrassing" me when he told his brother, who was on the phone long distance from Bar Harbor, Maine, "Phil is here, my best friend, talk to him." And we spoke. Later John said he was sorry to put that "burden" on me! He should waste breath on such things! Indeed, I always felt at the end that what he said, each word, was important because the words were to the point of being counted.

When the kids arrived, there were more tears. Jaina especially was keenly attuned to John's death. She cried, wept, and talked, quite articulately. Erik was subdued. He knew John was dead, but he could not articulate what must be, at his age, an imponderable fact of life ... the leaving of it. They talked about the cremation. They would put a couple of small gifts in the fire with John. Eeyore, a gift from Jaina to John when he first went into surgery in January 1982, would be one symbol. And as they spoke, the kids brought in treasures to share with John before he left home forever. Erik had a stuffed "mousekin," a fuzzy animal John had given him. Jaina brought in a music box with a dancing clown. It was, while not irreverent, a celebration that seemed to acknowledge the death of someone playful and the continuity he gave to the lives of his children. One of his last spoken thoughts, several days ago: "I'm going to miss the kids."

As the day dragged on, Lin, myself, Claudia, the kids (who drifted in and out ... Claudia remarked, " The beat goes on!") and friends, Lin's sister Brenda, and others came to see John, to wish him bon voyage. In the late afternoon the doctor came to pronounce John dead and speak with the family. Then others came, and after several hours of "death watch," I was glad, but not happy, to bid my friend a last farewell and depart. (My journal)

Philip H. Deisher

CHAPTER FOURTEEN

Roles and Relationships

We are all survivors of the deaths of others. We are all individuals who will someday die. Consequently, the insights we gain from those who work—or otherwise relate in a structured fashion—with the dying and the bereaved are insights we can readily apply to our own lives.

It is not an accident that you are reading this book. Either you have signed up for a course in which the book is used, or you were looking for a book on this topic, or the title caught your attention and you decided to look it over. Something brought you and the book together. Perhaps a close friend or family member has died recently or is extremely ill. Perhaps you have had occasion to believe that you were going to die in the foreseeable future. Perhaps you have been told of the sudden, unexpected death of a person you cared about. Perhaps you have wanted to know more about death and grief. Whether it is your death or the death of another or a general interest in death, you will understand that sensitivity is needed to relate in appropriate ways to the dying and the bereaved.

RELATIONSHIPS WITH THE DYING AND THE BEREAVED

Twenty years ago I might have written that it was almost impossible to find people who wished to work with dying persons and that it was difficult to find people who were sensitive to the needs of their dying relatives and close friends. That is no longer the case, but this does not mean that competence in relating to the dying and the bereaved is a familiar capacity.

Problems in Relating to the Dying and the Bereaved

In developing relationships, either personal or professional, with the dying and the bereaved, we are confronted with several sources of stress that may lead us to wish to withdraw and that are not found in most other personal or professional relationships. Some of these pertain primarily to the dying, others primarily to the bereaved, and some develop in both kinds of relationship.

First, the future of dying people is a particularly limited one; we are reluctant to invest a lot of our time and energy for individuals who will not be around to relate to or be productive in any fashion. Their social value becomes less. And many people desire to work only with individuals who have a potentially promising future. The dying are disengaging; others are disengaging from them. The impetus to care for and to care about them diminishes.

Second, dying people remind us that we also will not live forever. They remind us that we, like they, are transient, impermanent, subject to decay and death. Many of us don't like the reminder and don't want to work in a setting in which we are constantly reminded of our mortality.

Third, when we begin to think about our own mortality and transiency, we are also required thereby to consider the ephemeral quality of what we accomplish. The novel we write, the educational program we develop, the sales campaign we devise, the computer software we create, the fine wood cabinet we design—none of these will last forever.

Fourth, death is loss, and we don't like to have to encounter a series of losses. It is bad enough that we must suffer the pain from the inevitable losses of people we love; we don't want to add to our pain by developing new relationships with people we know are going to die.

Fifth, the dying remind us that we cannot truly control our environment. A girl just entering her teens suffered a serious epileptic seizure. Although she was eventually stabilized on medication, so that she had no more seizures, the event was always fresh in her memory as an example of the suddenness with which life can change, the absurdity of a condition within one's own body that comes unexpectedly, as if from nowhere, and has the potential for depriving life of some of its most basic satisfactions—even for depriving life of life, since a seizure at the wrong moment can lead to death. Each of us, at every moment, potentially has the seed of death within our body, and each of us, at every moment, confronts the potential for death from outside ourself. And we do not always have the power to control either the internal or the external environment from which this potential emanates. Neither, of course, are we necessarily without power, but working with people who are dying is a constant reminder that change, absurdity, and chance are always in our lives. It is easier to ignore dying and death and to pretend to ourselves that we are really in charge of everything.

Sixth, dying people often look peculiar, talk strangely, have an unpleasant odor, and are not able to offer some of the normal amenities of normal relationships. This is especially true during the later stages of some diseases.

Seventh, people who are grieving and, in fewer instances, dying often express a level of emotionality that we find difficult to handle. It is troublesome for me, whether functioning as your friend or as a professional who is trying to provide help and support, to be with you when you are so upset about events in your life and I am powerless to diminish your anguish to any appreciable extent. I then need to handle both your pain, which also pains me, and my powerlessness, which adds to my pain.

Motives for Developing Relationships with the Dying and the Grieving

In spite of the difficulties described above, a significant number of individuals make the conscious choice to devote at least a part of their working time to the dying. Innumerable others relate to the dying and the grieving because the relationships had been established much earlier and to ignore the suffering person would be totally inappropriate. Fortunately, those who find themselves in the latter situation usually conduct themselves very well and enrich the lives of their friends or colleagues or family members.

What of the former group, those who choose such experiences? Perhaps their own interests and experiences are sufficient to overcome the negative aspects of the task. Or, in some instances, they may even be attracted by the prospect of developing relationships under demanding and stressful conditions. In studying those staff members in hospitals who choose to work with the dying, one author (Vachon, 1978) has proposed a number of reasons for their decisions and suggested that each brings its own unique form of stress. Although the paper was written about health professionals, the reasons are also applicable to others who wish to be with the dying. The reasons

- Accident
- Desire to do the "in" thing
- Desire to affiliate with a charismatic leader
- Intellectual appeal
- Desire for mastery over pain and death
- A sense of "calling"
- Previous personal experience
- Suspicion that one might someday develop the disease one is treating

Guidelines for Caring Relationships

When all is said and done, the most important relationships for the dying and the grieving are going to be with the persons to whom they have been closest all along. You may never have a professional relationship as a help provider, but you are very likely to have many such personal relationships. However, whether your relationship is personal or professional, there are several things you can do to improve the quality of your time together as well as to reduce the tension that sometimes invades these occasions.

First, be more conscious of what is going on. Perhaps this is why you are reading this book right now. We have hundreds of years of experience in relating to dying persons, thousands of pages of writing, tens of thousands of experienced persons, and millions of personal experiences. There is no need, as Kastenbaum has succinctly phrased it, "to reinvent the square wheel."

Second, probe your own assumptions and expectations to try to understand how you developed your views. To what extent are you drawing from one or two personal experiences? To what extent are you biased by your own prejudices—for example, toward the elderly, toward physicians, toward funeral directors, toward cancer? To what extent are your psychological defenses propelling you toward your present beliefs: your own denial, your own fears and anxieties, your own projection?

Third, be honest with yourself about what you are willing to give to the dying or bereaved; otherwise, you will find it difficult to be honest with them. Are you offering an intimate relationship or an occasional visit? Will you really "keep in touch," or do you say that just as an excuse to get away? Do you actually want that person living with you during the living-dying interval, or do you find yourself resenting the guilt that pressed you to make the offer? So often, when we do things we don't want to do for someone, that person ends up suffering.

Fourth, try to understand your own feelings about death and dying. Your own anxieties and denial can limit your competence in relating to others, although the claim that no one can work with dying persons until his or her own death fears have been worked through is doubtful. That is like saying that no member of the clergy should ever doubt his or her religious beliefs or that no psychologist should ever practice until he or she has left all personal peculiarities behind. You can still provide good emotional support to a friend or family member even though you have strong anxieties about death or, for example, feel uneasy about embracing someone with cancer. Perhaps the best approach is to acknowledge your anxieties or discomfort to that person. We can't afford to postpone caring relationships until we have perfected our adjustment or our personal growth.

Fifth, be willing just to be there, without doing anything. Even be willing not to be there. Too many of us feel that unless we are doing something "positive," we aren't being effective. There are things you are not going to be able to do: you are not going to be able to take the pain of a loss away from other people. It is their pain, and they will suffer it. With both the dying and the grieving, your presence is sometimes more important than your "doing something." A close friend of mine who was mourning the death of her brother became angry with me and ordered me to leave her house; it was late at night, and I told her that I wasn't going to leave but would go into the den and sleep on the couch there. About one hour later, much calmed, she came in and woke me up; we had coffee together and talked for several hours more. In that situation I took a risk—that leaving her presence and not leaving the house was what would be most helpful to her. My behavior turned out to have been appropriate, although, obviously, it doesn't always work out that way. What my action "said" was, in effect, "I care for you and will respect your desire to have privacy from me, but I will continue to make myself available when you wish it." The suffering person is more capable of passing through the suffering because you care and you are being supportive, not because you are trying to take the pain away.

Sixth, be aware of your energy levels and avoid exhaustion and burnout. If you don't eat, sleep, or have any leisure for an extended period, you may find your ability to care for someone diminished. You need to know yourself, but since the stress of a close relationship to someone dying may alter your capabilities without your realizing it, you may also have to be alert to what your friends and family are telling you.

Seventh, don't try to impose your philosophy of dying or your notion of appropriate grieving on the person you are seeking to help. This does not mean that you cannot express your views, only that you should not try to persuade, exhort, or manipulate the other into doing what you view as the "proper thing." You may believe that meditation enriches the dying process or that one needs to accept death in order to die properly; the dying person may believe that meditation is something the hippies of the 1960s left behind and that accepting death is a fruitless intellectual exercise. The more you help others live their lives more richly and confront their deaths in their own way, the more you enhance their capacity to accept death *in their own way.* You may believe that crying and being surrounded by loving friends is the best road to healthy grieving; the grieving person may prefer to avoid tears and spend most of the time alone.

Eighth, be willing to understand the pain that the dying or grieving person is experiencing without taking on the pain as your own.

Tasks for the Caretaker

Psychologist Lawrence LeShan has described two kinds of roles played by people who relate to the dying. The first is that of a mechanic, who helps the person die, and the second is that of a gardener, who helps the person live in whatever time is left. Most of us see ourselves as gardeners, but it is easy to let the pressures of limited time and personal anxieties lead us to focusing on the mechanic's role, to the exclusion of the gardener's role.

If we are to help people live fully in the time they have remaining, we need to recognize their strengths and permit them to use these strengths. "It's not the patient's illness or dying that produces upset, but the insanity of those around him who deny reality" (LeShan, personal communication). The dying person receives so many mixed messages, finds so many people who are not responding with honesty (and eventually doesn't know who is being honest), that personal strength is dissipated just in handling the anxiety caused by these uncertainties.

Chaplain Walter Johnson, a Presbyterian clergyman serving at a hospital near San Francisco, described an equation that sums up LeShan's statements in a different way:

Truth minus love = brutality
Love minus truth = sentimentality
Truth plus love = healing relationship

Over and over again, dying and grieving persons indicate that they fear being abandoned. Thus, one of the most important aspects of a caring relationship is to reduce this fear. But this must be done in a realistic fashion. First, you need to be reasonably—not precisely, just reasonably—clear about the kind and amount of aid you are offering: daily visits? weekly visits? home care during the living-dying interval? Of course the nature of your help can change, but if it does, it must be explained clearly. Second, you should live up to your offer. Much as the dying person may wish to hear that you will visit frequently, it is more important to be able to count on whatever you have offered to do—even if it's less than might have been wished.

You can abandon a person by not being there physically. You can also be there physically but be far away psychologically. Of course, when you are suffering yourself, from depression and impending loss, you may spend some of your visiting time immersed in your own fantasies. Sick people understand that as well as healthy people. But the greater distress occurs

---

BOX 14-1. CARING FOR THOSE WE LOVE

Many more of us have the experience of caring for grieving persons we love than caring for dying persons we love, and the principles are very much the same. Although this topic will be brought up from other points of view in the next two chapters, at this point we will set out some guidelines proposed by one experienced and sensitive author:

1. Don't probe. Wait until you are invited to talk about these concerns. Be careful that you don't respond to your own anxieties, rather than to the grieving person's desires.
2. Don't be afraid to display your own feelings.
3. Don't pity the grieving person.
4. Don't be afraid of silence.
5. Don't be afraid of embarrassment—for example, of saying the wrong thing or expressing a shallow sentiment.
6. Don't be afraid to laugh with the grieving person.
7. Prepare well ahead of time if possible: perhaps read a book on grief or do some thinking about your own losses.
8. Protect the person from intruders during the initial stages of mourning, if this is appropriate considering your relationship to that person and his or her preferences.
9. Help with day-to-day tasks. As you do so, be prepared to deal with the grieving person's outpouring of anguish and anger, even though it may be, seemingly inappropriately, directed at you.
10. Permit the grieving person to express strong feelings or to maintain privacy.
11. Know what normal grieving is so that you can reassure the grieving person that he or she is normal, without implying that the feelings are trivial.
12. Be aware that your involvement with the grieving person may make others feel uncomfortable, since many people cannot accept open expression of emotions or discussion of death.
13. Be aware that things take time and that grief may seek expression months or years after the death.
14. Listen.
15. Listen.
16. Listen.

(Adapted from Kollar, 1982)

when you isolate yourself from the dying person by hiding behind a barrier of pretense. Usually a caring relationship is enhanced when both the dying (or grieving) person and the caretaking person can speak openly of the death or at least are both aware of the death and both know that the other is aware. In this way, each can make the decision to talk or to be silent, without concern that the "secret" might be exposed.

This does not require that you or anyone inform the dying person specifically that he or she is dying. And it certainly doesn't permit you or anyone to offer a timetable for death. Elisabeth Kübler-Ross (1974a) encourages letting the patient know that the condition is serious, then permitting the patient to digest this information and bring up the subjects of death and dying when he wishes. If someone believes you care and are open to talking about what is important, that person will bring up dying when he is ready.

Dying people—and, to a lesser extent, those who are grieving—are very vulnerable to others, and they are likely to be willing to pay a high price to keep from being abandoned. If they feel you might leave them if they tried to talk about death, they probably won't talk about death; if they feel you might leave them if they complained about hospital care or medical care, they will probably avoid such discussion. Your presence, as friend or hospital worker or physician, is more important than airing these ideas or grievances; dying people are in a good position to evaluate other people and then respond in terms of their own survival.

This includes bedside conversions, whether the debate concerns God, afterlife, politics, lifestyle changes, or the relative merits of community college or a university. The dying person, in order to keep you from leaving, might even totally distort her views. I've often wondered how many deathbed religious conversions were founded on a desire to have one's clergyman present and approving.

Of course, you can disagree with someone who is dying, even become angry with that person, as long as you make it clear that your disagreement or anger will not cause you to leave and remain away. There is no reason that you shouldn't offer your religious views or beliefs about life after death, as long as the price of your company is not agreement with your views.

The dying or the grieving person may wish to discuss his or her feelings, either about death or about any other topic. You can permit such discussion, but without causing the person to feel that your own needs are so tied up in "talking about death" that the conversation must be held *for you!* I've found dying people to be extremely solicitous of the feelings of those who visit them. If you want to talk about my dying, if that makes you happy and fulfills you, all right, I'll talk about it, although the truth is that I'm rather bored with talking about it.

All this means that your major task in communication is to be sensitive to what the dying or grieving person is saying to you, to be aware of symbolic language, of body language, and of attempts to find out what you know and how you feel. Sometimes a patient who complains about the physician or the hospital or family members and friends is expressing a deeply felt grievance; sometimes the same words are indirectly expressing a displaced anger about dying. Similarly, some patients will become angry with fate or with God, but others are expressing the message "I don't want to die!" And it isn't unusual for dying persons to become angry with those who care for them—like the classroom teacher who harangues the students who are attending class about excessive absences. After all, you are there and provide an available scapegoat. It's helpful to be sensitive to the possibility that these sorts of situations may arise.

Fortunately, dying and grieving people, behind their distress, anger, and frustration, are really caring people—at least as caring as anyone else—and they are likely to care for you. If you do something foolish, misinterpret the meaning of what they are saying, forget to arrive on time, or inadvertently make a silly statement, they are likely to be forgiving. If they realize that you care for them and that they can trust you, they will overlook all kinds of things they might not really like.

Nor do you have to be afraid of your own tears, if the experience touches you. The person who is dying can take care of you, or you can take care of each other. A caring relationship is not a one-way relationship—it is reciprocal, although each person gets something different. Chaplain Johnson, mentioned earlier, has offered some helpful words: "Don't cry for the future—cry for right now." There is enough pain and loss and fear happening at the moment to allow for many tears. And there is no need to be brave, put up a good front, or deny hope, when the tears are for the feelings and events of the moment. It hurts, physically and emotionally, right now. You can cry right now.

Don't expect people to follow a preestablished program to die in preestablished stages. Elisabeth Kübler-Ross herself has said "Patients do not necessarily follow a classical pattern from the stage of denial to . . . acceptance. Most of my patients have exhibited two or three stages simultaneously and these do not always occur in the same order" (1974a, pp. 25–26). The right way to die is the way the person wants to die, and if you are open and available, the person will probably let you know what that is. It's not your task to set up a stage time schedule or to be critical of people who don't die the way you want them to die.

Encouraging reminiscence.   It may also be helpful to encourage reminiscing. Ask the elderly widow to tell you about her husband, who has recently died. Ask the dying man to tell you about what it was like when he was young. Ask people to tell you about the things they are proud of, about the times they enjoyed, about the people they liked, about the good things that have happened in their lives.

David Oliver, a sociologist now teaching in Kansas City, tells of visiting an elderly woman in a San Antonio nursing home. He had asked to be introduced to someone who was cognitively alert, who had lived in San Antonio for many years, and who had very few visitors. Oliver told the woman that he had recently moved to San Antonio, that he liked the city, and that he wanted to know more about it: would she tell him what San Antonio was like when she was young? He assumed that 30 to 40 minutes would exhaust both the woman and him. It was over 90 minutes later when the woman began to tire and Dave removed his third 30-minute tape. It had been an exhilarating experience. As Dave left, he said "I'll be back in a couple of months and see you then." Her response was, "I don't think I'll be here then." Dave hesitated at the door, then turned and said "That's possible, but I hope you will be here, and if you are, I will see you in two months." When he returned, two months later, the woman had died, but she had left her legacy both in Dave's experiences and on his tapes.

Reminiscing with people they love may be very valuable for the dying. It can be an attempt to make sense out of their personal histories, to try to recall why they as individuals mattered or made a difference, to put events and situations into perspective. When this is shared with someone they love, the events take on even more importance. And when the person they talk with also shared the experience they are reliving, the significance can become still greater (Kübler-Ross, 1974a).

Some specific techniques.   There are probably no standard techniques in relating to the dying or the bereaved that can be counted on to work all the time. Nonetheless, there are some specific things a person can do that are likely to improve the level of satisfaction of both parties. These differ somewhat as a function of your role with the individual—whether you are a personal friend, a volunteer worker, a nurse or chaplain or physician.

For example, your opening greeting, especially if it is the first time you have met, is very important. People who are vulnerable to the moods and desires of others—and the dying or grieving person is vulnerable—notice many things that may slip by unnoticed in less emotionally invested interactions (Feigenberg, 1980). What are the appropriate qualities of a greeting? Warmth, sincerity, lack of being hurried, lack of pressure for "instant intimacy," displaying willingness to be guided by the other person regarding the rate at which the relationship will develop and the intensity that will evolve. Of course, you cannot establish all that in your opening greeting, but it is your beginning.

It is also important to sit down, especially when visiting someone who is bedridden or already seated. Sitting down means (1) you will probably be there a while, (2) you have given up the power and control that occur when you look down at someone as you speak, and (3) you are not likely to turn suddenly and leave.

And while you are sitting, don't sneak a quick or surreptitious look at your watch. Instead, state at the beginning that you can stay for only ten minutes or a couple of minutes or an hour or whatever. If you must keep careful track of time, place your watch where you can see it without bodily contortions or pretense.

Since you are sitting down, probably fairly close to the other person, don't be afraid to reach out and touch him or her, on the hand or the face or wherever seems appropriate. Even taking the person's hand in yours can be supportive. Touch is a powerful tool in building a caring relationship. However, be alert to nonverbal reactions to your touch, since not everyone responds positively to touch. Also be alert to your own reactions to touching, since not all well-intended persons who wish to help others are themselves comfortable with physical touching.

When you leave, make it clear that you are leaving and why. This needn't be an excuse. All you need to say is "Well, I guess it's time to be going on to other things" or "It's been delightful/exciting/enjoyable/stimulating/et-cetera being with you. Back to work for me now."

Sometimes the person you are visiting may doze off while you are there. This, of course, does not mean that your presence is boring but that the course of the illness or the medication or lack of sleep the night before has taken its toll. At this time you might simply sit for a while or read a magazine or book, since the dying or grieving person is likely to move in and out of awareness, and your silent presence is often comforting (Feigenberg, 1980). This is particularly true as the time of death nears.

One additional helpful technique is so obvious that people often ignore it: offering to assist with some practical task. This might mean that you will talk to the children about going to college, see that a favorite cousin gets the back issues of *National Geographic*, make certain that the wonderful floor nurse receives a gift of some sort, verify that the credit-card bills have been paid, or get the magazine subscriptions shifted to the grandchildren. These all seem like inconsequential matters when the issue of death is imminent, but these are the kinds of things that frequently prey on people's minds, and your taking responsibility may offer a sense of relief far disproportionate to the apparent significance of the task.

Dying and grieving people often will not ask favors of others, and so your offer may be rejected. Nonetheless, as the person you are visiting comes to trust you and to recognize your sincerity, he or she is increasingly likely to be honest in expressing personal needs. So don't hesitate to renew your offer from time to time. You might even suggest some of the things that you could do. Feed the cat? Empty the garbage? Pick up a suit at the cleaners?

CARING WHEN DEATH OCCURS

The approach of death, whether at the hospital or in the home, tends to alter the caring procedures. Even in institutions, the psychosocial takes precedence over the medical at that point (Glaser & Strauss, 1968). Rules are bent and even broken. Children too young to be permitted to visit are smuggled up the back stairs; forbidden food, drink, or tobacco is provided. The hospital, however, does have practical matters to attend to: seeking autopsy permission when appropriate; anticipating the removal of the body without disturbing the other patients in the room; preparing the death certificate; and establishing the **death watch.**

The Death Watch

At the end of the death trajectory, the hospital staff (or, if the patient is at home, whoever is responsible for care) becomes deeply involved with providing comfort, reducing pain, and offering the human companionship that may be more important than anything else (Glaser & Strauss, 1968). When the family is not present and the death occurs in the hospital, the person attending these last hours will often need to report to the family how the death occurred; the extent to which this person reports accurately or attempts to make the family feel better about the final moments of dying is never fully known. Often, of course, the death occurs when no one is in attendance: "She just slipped away quietly during the night."

During the death watch, if the patient is alert, he or she may want to see certain members of the family or make a final attempt to reconcile an ancient feud or confess some earlier transgression in a last attempt to assuage guilt. Similarly, family members may wish to come for a final reunion or to make peace. However, as Kübler-Ross (1969) and others have pointed out, these last hours may be used by the dying person to see only those individuals who seem very important at the time, and it is possible that a cousin or a close friend may appear, only to be told that the dying person has found it impossible to visit with everyone.

Among many families, the death watch is a respected tradition, and at least one family member or friend will be with the dying person at all times. At times, several people will arrive, and as death nears, many family members may wish to be in attendance. Although this may be a long-held and valued practice of these families, it is often contrary to hospital regulations and regarded as a threat to efficiency and decorum. The nursing staff will try to get most of the visitors to leave; if necessary they will complain that the behavior is disruptive to the other patients. Even if the dying person is apparently comatose, both family members and attending hospital staff can speak softly to the person, who may in fact be more aware of what is going on than is apparent (Munley, 1983).

Some people seem to make an assumption that there is value to being in a quiet, peaceful environment when death occurs. This may be a valid assumption, but I certainly don't know the evidence for it. Obviously, for people with limited energy, too much stimulation may hasten death, but for some people for whom death is at hand, a certain amount of chaos, noise, and excitement might be desirable.

Although some families will establish a round-the-clock vigil, this is impractical or impossible for others, and the hospital staff will often urge family members to return home to sleep or to get some relief from the tension of being at the hospital. In these situations, however, they are usually telephoned when death is imminent, so that they can be with their relative when death occurs.

The hospital staff faces a dilemma in these situations. If they telephone the family too soon and the patient recovers somewhat, the trip to the hospital, with all its attendant tensions, will have to be repeated. It is not unknown for a dying patient to rally three or four times and for the family to have rushed to the hospital for its farewells each time. As might be expected, the family members eventually become detached from the patient's death—a strange example of the boy who cried wolf. However, if the call is too late, the patient will be dead before the family arrives, and the family may feel guilty about having left the hospital or be angry with the staff for their poor timing.

At the Moment of Death

Attending a person at the moment of death can be very distressing. Not only are the attending person's feelings about death and loss stress-provoking, but the physical changes the body undergoes are also found upsetting (Glaser & Strauss, 1968). Therefore, it is important, even rewarding, to know that one's presence might have provided the deceased with comfort, with a feeling of not having been abandoned.

For the most part, neither fear nor pain appears to be present as death occurs. In our society, many, perhaps most, people are confused or comatose as they die, because of medication or of the effects of their illness. Some people still fight for life—they may feel they are leaving unfinished business, or, not reconciled to death, they do not want to die. Other deaths are, indeed, beautiful: the dying person has made peace with himself or herself and with others, has felt life to be fulfilling, and is ready for the release that comes with death.

And there may be visions. Lecturing in the early 1930s, Alfred Worcester (1961) noted the frequency of such reports both in earlier medical literature and in his own extensive experience as a physician:

> I found a patient propped up in bed, smoking a cigarette and reading the morning paper. He seemed to be normally convalescent after an appendectomy a week earlier. As I left his room the nurse stopped me to report that the patient had been talking to some visitor invisible to her, who he said was dressed in white. I went back to ask him about it. "Oh, it was only my sister," he answered casually and went on reading the newspaper. His sister had died previously, yet her presence seemed to him merely a natural fact. A few hours afterwards, without any other warning, his heart suddenly stopped beating [p. 54].

The patient was not a particularly religious man, nor was Dr. Worcester inclined to the mystical. The story is like many others reported by people during near-death experiences, on "successful" LSD trips, or during mystical or deeply religious experiences; it is also like incidents reported by persons who claim to have died and subsequently returned from death. Dr. Worcester did not presume to explain the cause, but the possibilities range wide— from signals of impending death within the body to an encounter with actual ghosts or spirits to a shortage of oxygen in the brain. Your interpretation of these events, and the intensity with which you adhere to it, will say a great deal about your concepts both of subjective reality and of death and immortality.

Once the death has been verified at the hospital, the family members may come by for a final time, or a particularly despondent spouse or parent or child may wish to remain in the room with the dead person for a while. When these final goodbyes are complete and the relatives and friends have departed, the most likely next step is to prepare the body—for now the "person" has become the "body"—for removal from the hospital room and, soon after, from the hospital. This is usually a rapidly accomplished, technical process, fulfilling hospital regulations, and without much sense for the feelings of the survivors (who, of course, are not there to observe) (Sudnow, 1967). The body is secretly hurried to the hospital morgue, often in a gurney or cart that appears just like other carts transporting patients but in fact has a false bottom that is hidden from the view of those who might inadvertently share an elevator or a hospital corridor with what is now a corpse (De-Spelder & Strickland, 1983). Caring for the dying has ended. Caring for the dead begins. Caring for the grieving begins or is intensified.

THE CARETAKING PROFESSIONS

A handful of vocational fields accomplish most of the work-related caretaking tasks for the dying, the dead, and the bereaved. For the dying, these fields are primarily health-related and include medicine, nursing, hospital administration, and long-term-care administration. A second group focus on mental health and spiritual well-being; these include social work, counseling, and the chaplaincy. For the dead, the comparable vocational fields are mortuary sciences and cemetery management. For the bereaved, the fields are primarily those concerned with mental health and spiritual well-being, such as social work, clinical psychotherapy and counseling, and the clergy.

The tasks of ministering to the dying, the dead, and the grieving are not equally divided among professionals in these various fields. Some physicians, some nurses, some social workers, some funeral directors, some clergy members spend time with a disproportionate number of dying and grieving persons. The others focus their energies on administrative tasks, planning and program development, or relating to people for whom death is not presently a salient concern.

For the most part, the discussion that formed the earlier sections of this chapter is just as relevant for the caretaking professionals as for people who have personal relationships with the dying or bereaved. However, some additional focus on four of these caretaking groups seems appropriate.

Physicians

In the eyes of the community, the most powerful and undoubtedly the most prominent member of the health care team is the physician. I once described today's physician as a contemporary priest: she or he is considered the gatekeeper to the rewards of today's religion (long and healthy life on earth), just as the traditional priest was the gatekeeper to the rewards of traditional religion (access to a life after death with God). Unfortunately, since each of us sees others die, we know that the new "priest" fails in keeping us alive forever; the traditional priest's promises of life everlasting could never be verified by those still alive (Kalish, 1980–81).

Most physicians appear to perceive their role as that of producing a cure so that a patient can return to normal activities or at least to near-normal activities. The fact that doctors cannot accomplish this for the dying patient is a source of conflict for many physicians. If they continue to treat a dying person, they are applying their costly skills and training to a situation that might better be handled by others; if they do not continue to treat the dying person, they then feel they have failed to fulfill the patient's expectations. Furthermore, if physicians identify with every dying patient, they are likely to suffer emotional exhaustion or else find themselves withdrawing psychologically; conversely, if they do not have any emotional involvement with dying patients, they may communicate an unfeeling quality at the very time that the patients need to relate to a health professional with feelings.

If physicians define their tasks as providing cure, improvement, or at least maintenance levels of functioning for a patient, then they are inevitably going to fail with each dying person; if, however, they define their task as assuaging physical and psychological suffering and increasing physical and psychological satisfactions, they may perceive themselves as succeeding, even if the patient is dying.

Too often physicians make impossible demands of themselves, then react maladaptively to the situation. Three frequent maladaptive responses are anger, denial, and depression/resignation (Garfield, 1978). A physician may actually exhibit anger toward a patient, usually in indirect ways, if the patient does not respond as the physician feels he or she should. The anger may take the form of avoiding the patient. This avoidance may, in turn, intensify a patient's fears of abandonment by significant persons. Or the anger may be manifest in a tense voice or a brittle touch. Physicians also displace their anger onto other hospital staff members, the patient's family, or even their own family and friends.

Physicians may use the mechanism of denial to avoid confronting the inevitability of the death of a particular patient. They may deny the death by turning their attention to other activities, more demanding patients, or personal obligations (Artiss & Levine, 1973); or denial may occur by a refusal to treat patients who cannot possibly recover—accomplished by transferring them to other facilities or to other health care professionals (Garfield, 1978).

Some physicians become depressed, and depression can be understood as anger turned inward. "I have known physicians who, for years, via a sheer act of will, fought off incipient depression only to succumb finally to the cumulative emotional impact of patient deaths" (Garfield, 1978, p. 107). Some such physicians turn to their informal social network of other physicians for understanding and support; others get the help they need from their spouses; relatively few seek professional help, usually from psychotherapists. Others respond by withdrawal, somatic problems, or chronic depressed behavior, which often interfere with their ability to work.

Physicians are human—a platitude that is ignored both by patients, who want them to perform miracles, and by the physicians themselves, who may unconsciously expect themselves to be able to perform the same miracles. Sometimes the frustration of their final inability to keep a person alive bursts through in angry humor—one example being the physician who became angry with the paperwork that confronted him. "The doctor agonized, 'Here a human died and I must fill out *cards*'" (Reynolds & Kalish, 1974b, p. 149).

Nurses

Nurses, more than any other vocational group, find themselves in constant interactions with both the dying and the survivors of the dying. Whereas other members of the hospital or long-term-care-facility staff can make brief appearances and then leave, the nurses (RNs, LVNs, and sometimes aides, although the last are not nurses) are expected to continue the health and mental health support services.

The patients themselves appear to recognize this. Studying both patients and staff in a Montreal hospital, one investigator found that the critically ill perceived nurses as being more sensitive to the emotional needs of the patients than were social workers, residents and interns, or the attending medical staff (Mount, Jones, & Patterson, 1974). In addition, the residents and interns also viewed the nurses as most attentive, while the attending staff saw them as equally attentive to themselves, and social workers saw them as second most attentive (to themselves). The nurses, of course, saw themselves as most attentive. Although this was only one hospital and the study was conducted over a decade ago, comparable results would probably be found at many hospitals and long-term-care facilities today.

If nurses are attentive to dying patients, it is in large part because they view their profession as the appropriate one to perform these human tasks. They could avoid the dying, and most certainly some of them do; they could turn the tasks over to aides, volunteers, or licensed vocational nurses, and most certainly some of them do (in nursing homes, where the RNs are few and are expected to provide most administrative and supervisory tasks, such delegation of responsibility is more common). Nonetheless, in spite of these opportunities to avoid the dying and the grieving, nurses appear to have accepted such care as part of their professional role.

In some ways, they pay a penalty for this form of nurturing. On occasion, they develop relationships with the dying patients that are so close that they end up grieving when the patient dies. They think and talk about the dead person, feel helpless because of their inability to have changed his or her life course, may cry or feel depressed, and may even express displaced anger, anxiety, or difficulty in concentrating. Even such symptoms as fatigue, headaches, insomnia, and appetite loss are not uncommon (Lerea & LiMauro, 1982). In fact, they develop the familiar symptoms that all grieving people encounter.

In my experience, it was the profession of nursing that recognized the importance of providing emotional and social services for dying persons while other health professionals were still debating whether dying patients had sufficient social value for a substantial investment of time, energy, and money.

But it appears that nurses view death differently than do physicians. At least in one study, which controlled carefully to see that adequate numbers of male nurses and female physicians were included, the nurses were more likely to see death as indicating peace, rest, and even victory, while physicians were more likely to associate death with coldness, being alone and unsafe, and abandonment (Campbell, Abernethy, & Waterhouse, 1983–84). Perhaps the more optimistic view of nurses permits them to spend more time with dying persons. Or perhaps the fact that their work requires them to spend more time with dying persons has led them to adopt the more optimistic outlook, since to do otherwise would make their daily endeavors much less rewarding.

Funeral Directors

Is the funeral director a mental health professional? Certainly not in the technical sense of the term, although he or she is a professional whose work involves mental health in a very direct fashion. First and foremost, the funeral director is a highly skilled person, part professional, part business executive, and part technician, whose task it is to remove the bodies of dead persons from the social milieu of the living. He or she is expected to do this in accordance with health regulations, business regulations and ethics, religious rituals and ceremonies, and personal sensitivity.

It is partly this mixture of roles that produces trouble for the funeral director. His role as a professional who works with the dead has simultaneously a taboo quality and a service orientation; his role as a business executive permits him to seek not just payment for services but financial profit for his organization. But some people feel that to earn money and make a profit from death is profane (physicians and clergy sometimes find the same reaction toward their dual roles as service providers and business executives), and they resent funeral directors, sometimes without realizing it, for their earning capacity.

Funeral directors appear to come under attack in three ways. First, they become a source of humor, which may well be a way in which people handle their anxiety concerning death.

The second basis for attack is financial. Half the respondents in a national survey stated that they perceived funeral directors as combining professional and business services, and fewer than one-fourth viewed them only as businesspersons or as having a lower status than businesspersons (Fulton, 1965). This uneasy position has made them the objects of frequent criticism for dubious financial practices. Since funeral directors are working with (or selling to) a highly vulnerable group of people, they are expected to be much more ethical and less profit-oriented than, for example, car repair services or the oil industry. Both these businesses have also come under criticism for exploiting the public, but the criticism directed toward them has been considerably less angry than that hurled at funeral directors. Again, much of this strong emotional attack undoubtedly arises from the association of the funeral director with death, a role that makes many people very uncomfortable. Nonetheless, there have been considerable attempts to document their exploitation (Federal Trade Commission, 1978; Harmer, 1963; Mitford, 1963). There is the suggestion that exploitation tends to come more from larger, more bureaucratic funeral homes than from those that are family-owned and run and integrated into the community (Pine, 1975).

Third, some individuals believe that funeral directors aid in the denial of the reality of death, partly through their tendency to avoid using words like *death* in their discussions with the bereaved and partly through their embalming practices, which prettify the body. However, because many of the major critics of these forms of death avoidance do not attend funerals, reject the idea of open-casket ceremonies, and prefer nontraditional services, it is difficult to know who is doing the denying—or whether these kinds of denial are necessarily inappropriate.

When people are asked directly to describe their reactions to a particular funeral that they helped to arrange, almost all express high regard for the funeral director. This is true for both clergy and members of their congregations (Kalish & Goldberg, 1978, 1979–80). Nonetheless, there are obviously enough incidents that anger people and enough desire for simpler, less costly funerals to lead to the development of memorial societies, in which arrangements are made at any time during a person's life for a funeral and burial (Fulton, 1965).

In recent years, some funeral directors have attempted to move into new territory and act as grief counselors as well. This attempt to extend their role, which represents a formalization of something they already did informally, has caused controversy, even within the profession, and little has been done to provide appropriate training to pursue this task. An alternative, proposed by the funeral directors themselves, is to have trained professionals in the community to work in liaison with funeral directors in providing mental health services and to encourage the formation of the Widow-to-Widow program or similar programs (Steele, 1975) (see Chapter 16).

Death Counselors

In the past decade or so, a small number of persons have become identified as **death counselors,** and they work, on either a paid or a volunteer basis, with persons who are dying, with those who are grieving, with people who care for the dying, and with professionals whose work brings them into frequent contact with death and the dying. They may do direct counseling, or they may do staff training or provide consultation to administrators and policy makers. Some have become involved with hospice programs.

One person who could be called a death counselor, although he might reject the title, is Dr. Loma Feigenberg, a Swedish oncologist on the staff of a Stockholm hospital, who shifted his attention some years ago from the medical care to the psychological care of cancer patients. Using a referral system within the hospital, he develops what he terms *friendship contracts* with critically and terminally ill cancer patients, and in so doing, he becomes their friend. As a matter of principle, Feigenberg will not serve as intermediary between the patient and his or her family members, since he believes that doing so would dilute his relationship with the patient. He offers the patients his time and energy for casual discussions, for counseling and therapy, for advocacy regarding medical treatment and pain management, and for whatever reasonable requests the patients make (Feigenberg, 1980).

These services are rarely provided in hospitals because they are costly and because it is highly unusual to find a physician and cancer specialist who is both qualified and willing to move into the role of counselor. However, there are numerous other models through which death counseling and similar services can be provided at lower cost and by nonphysicians, and this is taking place at various institutions around the country.

PERSONAL NEEDS OF CARETAKING PERSONS

It is only too easy to view caretakers, whether family members or professionals, solely in their caretaking capacity, rather than as individuals who have health problems, family concerns, financial pressures, and emotional stresses. Yet they are obviously human beings with all the problems of other human beings; it should also be obvious that caring for the dying or ministering to the grieving is a demanding, stress-inducing task, regardless of whether it is performed for love or money or a combination thereof.

One common outcome of intense work involvement in emotional settings is **burnout.** This term, widely used (and often misused) in recent years, describes a condition that occurs when a person becomes emotionally and, therefore, physically exhausted because of a role or relationship that requires an intense, ongoing emotional commitment. The result of burnout is that the individual withdraws emotionally to a point that permits recuperation. However, in withdrawing, he or she also reduces the level of commitment to the task, sometimes dropping it altogether and sometimes changing the involvement in the task to that of technical proficiency but without the ardor previously exhibited.

One author who is experienced both in nursing care and in academic endeavors (Vachon, 1983) has described a number of reasons which bring people to work with the dying but which might simultaneously make them susceptible to stress. Although Vachon was referring specifically to hospice workers, her statements would also be applicable to others working with the dying and the bereaved. Among these reasons were resolving past losses, relieving feelings of guilt, having a sense of special calling, proving that one can care for the dying better than others cared for one's own dying relatives, having a hidden agenda, wanting to make this work one's entire life, and having unrealistic expectations or fantasies regarding the tasks required by their role. Given the idealism commonly found among these individuals, and the reality of their work, it would be expected that tension might arise.

The term *burnout* implies that there was once fire and now the fire has gone out. If the flame was fed by the motives listed above, the dangers of its being extinguished would seem high. Caretakers need to be aware of the motives that lead them into their work, and they also need to take care of their own health and mental health needs (see Box 14-2). Otherwise, they are likely to become ineffective in their work and may actually do some harm to their patients or, more likely, to themselves.

BOX 14-2. WAYS TO REDUCE BURNOUT

1. Try to find others to take over some of your tasks, particularly those tasks that involve the dying person.
2. Get away for a few days every once in a while; do something you enjoy or be with people you enjoy.
3. Find ways to have fun.
4. Develop other interests, both on the job and away from it.
5. Become involved with an appropriate support group that meets on a regular basis. If you can't find one, start one.
6. Make certain to maintain the relationships that you have. Evaluate your informal support system and make use of it. Work to improve it.
7. Follow good health practices: exercise, nutrition, rest, and so forth.
8. Avoid drugs as much as possible; keep use of alcohol and tobacco to low levels or avoid altogether.
9. Use your sleeping time more effectively: take a hot bath or exercise lightly before going to bed; stretch your muscles in bed if you have trouble falling asleep.

At the beginning of this chapter, I described seven problems that occur in relating to the dying and the bereaved. All these contribute to burnout, many of them in ways that do not occur in other kinds of caring relationships, and at the same time, all the stresses common to these other relationships also occur in caring for the dying and the grieving.

Procedures for caring for the dying, the dead, and the grieving are part of the social customs of virtually every society that has ever existed. The procedures may differ immensely, and most certainly the nature and characteristics of the caretaker have differed immensely, but the tasks were carried out. There is a great deal of discussion today that the way we accomplish these tasks is inappropriate, perhaps insensitive, perhaps lacking in respect. Whether or not this judgment is valid, it is most certainly true that the concern regarding these matters is much greater today than two decades ago.

CHAPTER FIFTEEN

Health and Educational Programs

Facilities and programs that serve the dying and the grieving have increased greatly in number and improved greatly in quality over the past 15 years, and those of us who complain about their insufficiencies and inadequacies are comparing what exists now with what *could* exist, not with what *did* exist. Although developing categories is always hazardous because of overlapping goals and services, we will discuss these programs under three broad groupings: physical health care programs, educational programs, and, in the next chapter, emotional well-being programs.

MAINTAINING LIFE THROUGH MEDICAL TREATMENT

In writing a book like this, there is a tendency to ignore programs that attempt to keep people from dying, as opposed to those that are focused on the dying process. For the most part, this makes sense, since otherwise we would need to describe a wide array of frequently successful health treatments, and this is not a book on medicine. However, there are three medical programs that have been developed to maintain life yet frequently appear in death-related literature because they are sometimes brought into play in an effort to delay the time of death, although the inevitability of death is recognized. Two of these treatment programs, radiation treatment for cancer and kidney dialysis, are medically accepted; the third, called the Simonton approach, is highly controversial.

Radiation Treatment

One medically accepted procedure for critically ill cancer patients is radiation treatment. Sometimes the treatment is given in the hope of destroying enough cancer cells to permit a lengthy future life, with reasonable or even good health. In other instances, radiation is recommended in order to slow down the spread of the cancer, but it is recognized that dying can only be postponed.

Radiation treatment has significant side effects, ranging from extreme fatigue to vomiting to hair loss. One woman described her life with this procedure as "one week of post-treatment sickness, one week of slow recovery, and one week of health, before I have to take the next treatment." She finally chose to stop the treatment and lived an almost normal life for about as long as had been predicted with radiation therapy. Another woman became so embarrassed by her baldness that she refused to wear a wig and isolated herself from everyone she knew.

An obvious question emerges: has anyone attempted to develop psychological and social supports for people who are undergoing difficult treatments for life-threatening illnesses? Such support is not unknown, but it also is not routine. Family, friends, and neighbors assist, but relatively little psychosocial help is offered through the formal channels of health institutions, and psychotherapists and counselors in private practice have rarely had experience with such patients and may be resistant to treating them.

Kidney Dialysis

A second example of a medically accepted treatment for survival is machine dependency. Many individuals remain alive only because some kind of machine has been placed in their bodies (such as a pacemaker) or can be temporarily used as part of their bodies. Chronic hemodialysis, a treatment for kidney failure, is probably one of the more dramatic and most frequently discussed of all forms of such treatment. The patient normally goes to a center twice a week to be dialyzed: the blood is shunted from his or her body through a machine that cleanses it of impurities—the task that the kidneys normally accomplish—and then returns it to the body.

There is no question that these machines prolong life, since patients will die fairly soon if they do not arrive for their dialysis. The treatment includes some dietary and related restrictions and some care requirements; it also may have some severe side effects. However, the greatest difficulty in the treatment is probably learning to live with the dialyzer (Abram, 1977). An intense relationship between the person and the machine may develop, since the treatment demands some 30 hours a week of "intimacy." Some dialysis patients see themselves as having been brought back from the dead; many have fantasies of being part machine, part person (Abram, 1977).

A new procedure, continuous ambulatory peritoneal dialysis (CAPD), permits the dialysis patient to perform his or her own blood purifying and drastically reduces both cost and the need to visit dialysis centers, as well as allowing greater flexibility in diet. Patient acceptance is very high for this procedure, and the growth of centers that provide the instruments and instruction is rapid (Nolph & Van Stone, 1982).

Dialysis patients face other problems: failing health, deteriorating body image, loss of previous family status, sexual impotence, increasing dependence on others, and financial stress arising from job difficulties and treatment costs. Furthermore, deaths from cardiovascular and other medical problems are common (Abram, 1976). No wonder dialysis patients often talk about suicide: one study of nearly 3500 patients found that approximately 1 in 20 had died from some form of self-destructive behavior; these patients either committed suicide or decided to withdraw from the program and not follow medical requirements (Abram, Moore, & Westervelt, 1971).

Some people seem to do better on dialysis than others. Persons with a strong internal locus of control (who believe they control what goes on in their lives rather than being controlled by other persons or social forces) adapt more successfully to dialysis than those with external locus of control (Nolph & Van Stone, 1982).

Is life worth living if one is machine-dependent or debilitated by the side effects of various treatments? This is a value judgment, of course, that can be made only by each individual for himself or herself. Certainly the eagerness of many dialysis patients to receive transplants and the research evidence that those with successful transplants have a better sense of wellbeing than those continuing in dialysis suggest the difficulties of this way of life (Nolph & Van Stone, 1982). Greater understanding of the psychological stresses attached to these treatment procedures and more services to help patients and family members handle these stresses could undoubtedly reduce many of the problems.

The Simonton Approach

Another familiar health treatment program uses procedures developed by physician Carl Simonton. The highly controversial **Simonton approach,** which claims to be effective in healing cancer patients who have been deemed terminally ill by their physicians, combines imagery, relaxation, and psychotherapy as its major components (Simonton, Matthews-Simonton, & Creighton, 1978). This process requires that cancer patients accept responsibility for having cancer; that is, they are told that they have, perhaps unconsciously, caused their cancer and, therefore, they also have the power to get rid of the cancer. Part of the treatment is to develop visual imagery of the site of the cancer—to see it in the mind's eye in either literal or metaphoric terms—and then to visualize healthy cells attacking and destroying the cancerous cells. It is easy to see that this approach takes the control of the illness away from the physician and places it directly in the hands of the patient. It says, in effect, that whether you live or die is completely up to you; you have the power; use it. The treatment also includes relaxation techniques and appropriate traditional medical regimens.

Simonton and his followers have claimed an extremely high rate of success—especially considering that they work primarily with patients diagnosed as having terminal cancer. Of 159 patients whom they treated, 63 were alive an average of two years after treatment began, and those who died had lived over 20 months from the time treatment was initiated. The life expectancy of these patients had previously been approximately one year, so even those who died far outlived their prognoses. Equally important, the activity level of the patients was considerably greater than had been anticipated (Simonton et al., 1978).

The Simonton approach undoubtedly marshals whatever will to live exists, and the patient's belief that he or she has power or can succeed where his or her physician has failed may certainly reduce depression and promote health and well-being in a variety of ways. However, the emphasis on being responsible for one's own illness may induce immense guilt, anxiety, and stress for the patient who is not recovering or at least remaining stable, and these emotions could exacerbate the health problem and turn the last months of life into a period of depression and tension (Rosenbaum, 1978).

It seems possible to explain Simonton's results without depending on his specific techniques, at least until someone conducts research using both control groups and varied experimental conditions. Such an explanation might hypothesize that high psychological stress, perhaps loss-related stress, induces biochemical changes in the human body that encourage the growth and spread of cancerous cells. Patients in whom cancer is diagnosed feel powerless to do anything about it and also fear its outcome; these feelings increase stress and, thereby, increase the spread of the disease. Perhaps the stress-induced changes inhibit or interfere with the body's natural defenses, its immunological system, so that the individual is no longer as capable of destroying the destructive cells.

For many cancer patients, the Simonton approach enhances the sense of power and self-sufficiency—thus reducing feelings of psychological stress and perhaps restoring the body's defenses. Instead of concentrating on losses, people focus on what they have. In some fashion and for some persons, this process encourages the growth of healthy cells and thus blocks the spread of cancer. This oversimplified explanation does not contradict Simonton's models, but it does suggest that Simonton's specific techniques would not be necessary for success. Instead, a variety of self-healing approaches would be equally likely to lead to health. Another way of looking at it would be that the Simonton method has a powerful placebo effect (Holden, 1978).

In fact, many people have regained health by methods that do not fit the specific techniques. I personally know several people who have experienced such recovery. One woman reduced the size of a cancer-infested area by 50% during a three-month period; the only change in her life during that period had been a deep devotion to meditation and relaxation exercises. Although she eventually died from the cancer, she outlived the predictions of her life expectancy by many months. A middle-aged man I know visited a faith healer, who was also a personal friend; after several sessions over a period of weeks, his diagnosed cancer disappeared altogether. These two examples could be explained by the model described in the previous paragraphs.

An illness, of course, exists in a body that has a history and that contains a brain, and it is not at all far-fetched to assume that the history and the brain activities will influence other parts of the body in ways we cannot presently understand. There are still several basic questions that must be asked about the effectiveness of Simonton's techniques and comparable healing programs:

- Do they work? True, many people claim to have been cured by these programs, but is there any systematic research conducted by anyone who was not an advocate in the first place?
- If they do work, why do they work? Does taking responsibility for one's own illness cause these techniques to work? Are we responsible for our own cancers? Do the visual imagery techniques really lead to the death of cancer cells? If so, by what process?
- If Simonton's method does work, are its techniques the only ones that would work, or would meditation or prayer or faith healing or psychotherapy work just as well? Or better? Or better for some persons?
- If these healing programs do work, can they be used for people dying of other causes, such as heart attacks, strokes, and respiratory diseases?
- Are there any hazardous side effects?

PHYSICAL HEALTH CARE PROGRAMS

Most deaths in the United States and Canada occur in hospitals; a smaller number occur in other institutions, such as nursing homes and other long-term-care facilities, mental hospitals, and—in increasing numbers—hospices. These facilities, though providing certain basic services in common, tend to differ in essential purpose, staffing, day-to-day non-health-related procedures, and expectations of the dying person.

Hospitals

Patients come to hospitals to be treated, cured, and sent home. While there, they normally remain in their beds or, at the very least, in their rooms. Their contacts with other patients, except for roommates, range from slight to none; their contacts with most staff members are numerous, brief, and task-related, although a great deal of warmth and support may be packed into those contacts.

When death occurs, it usually occurs after a relatively brief time. The other patients are seldom disturbed, except for an occasional roommate; staff members are seldom upset, although with the death of a child or of someone else who, for whatever reason, had made a special impact on the staff, grieving is not uncommon. The greatest emotional impact on the hospital staff often arises in their contacts with grieving family members, with whom they have varying kinds of relationships during the dying process and after the death.

One author has described three common types of dying processes, or trajectories, that occur in hospitals: (1) lingering processes, which might also mean that the patient has come into the hospital on a number of previous occasions, (2) a rapid decline leading to an expected death, as would be found with a patient who had a history of heart attacks of increasing severity, and (3) a sudden and unexpected decline leading quickly to death, as in a death from suicide or an automobile accident or from an initial heart attack in a seemingly healthy nonelderly person (Benoliel, 1979). Each of these types of death tends to occur in different types of units and to lead to different kinds of staff activity (Benoliel, 1979).

Some deaths, of course, take place on the intensive care unit (ICU), where the patients are critically ill and are presumed to have the potential for recovery. Here they are carefully monitored and given all possible life-sustaining procedures. These are the people who die "hooked up to all manner of life-prolonging apparatus" (Benoliel, 1979, p. 150). The duration of life on an ICU may be very brief, measured in minutes or an hour or two, or may continue over several days and occasionally longer. The death may occur on that unit, or the ICU staff may determine that the patient is not going to recover, and the staff will have him or her moved to another ward for the final hours.

With the patient who is facing a lingering dying process, as is often the case with cancer, there is general understanding of the prognosis. The hospital stay may be brief or lengthy, but the emphasis is on care, not cure, although at earlier times during previous visits, there might have been extensive treatment. The patient may arrive from a nursing home, his or her own home, or the home of relatives. Staff members find these patients emotionally most easy to care for when they are comatose and require only physical care; patients who are alert and capable of social interactions can be unsettling for the staff, since they are now human beings and their physical and emotional suffering will affect the staff (Benoliel, 1979).

Dying in a Hospital versus Dying at Home

Where do people die? Some die in their own homes, either because their deaths occur suddenly and unexpectedly or because they had planned to spend their last days and weeks at home. Others die in the community, again because their deaths occur without warning, from an accident or an unexpected coronary, for example. Many die in long-term-care institutions. A very few die in hospices or under a hospice-care program. But most people in the United States, Canada, England, and most European nations die in hospitals (Hinton, 1979; Lerner, 1970).

As health care has become more effective and health care institutions have become more efficient, increasing numbers of people have sought the best facilities possible to help them recover from their illnesses. Even when their conditions are no longer remediable, they tend to remain in hospitals, where professional staff is readily available, where medical equipment is at hand, and where the technology of medicine is at its best.

Hospitals offer other advantages for dying persons and their families. The demands of caring for someone at home often include physical space, which may be in short supply; access to someone who will operate medical equipment, administer medicine, or monitor health conditions; and people to render care 24 hours a day. When any of these is unavailable at home, some form of hospital or institutional care may be necessary.

In addition, we have become accustomed to giving medical care priority over personal or spiritual care. The hospital is presumably the most effective and efficient place for the physical body to receive care, although it may not offer an optimum environment for retaining autonomy or for enjoying intimate personal relationships. Thus, although most people will state that they would prefer to die at home (Kalish & Reynolds, 1981), the assumption is often made that the hospital is the "proper" place to die.

What factors determine where a person dies?

First, and perhaps most obvious, is the condition that is leading to death. Some conditions require hospital treatment in order to reduce pain and discomfort or avoid contagion; other conditions do not require medical or professional care or else lead so quickly to death that there is no opportunity for such care. And some diseases lead to such repugnant changes in appearance or odors that family members who have a low tolerance for them would have great difficulty dealing with the unpleasant circumstances.

A second factor is the availability of caretakers outside an institution or hospital and their attitudes toward caring for a dying person. In a British study, only 25% of persons who lived alone died in their own homes; 59% died in hospitals. Conversely, 47% of those with living spouses and 49% of those who lived with younger relatives (regardless of whether they were with a spouse) died at home; the comparable figures for hospital deaths were 46% and 41%, respectively. Since married men are more likely to die at home than married women, it would appear that wives are more likely to care for dying husbands than the converse (Cartwright et al., 1973). It isn't enough, however, to have a spouse or live with younger relatives; these people must be willing to undergo the demanding routines often required in the care of dying persons.

Finances are a third factor. In some situations, hospital care is less expensive; in other situations, home care is. When insurance or Medicare or Medicaid will cover most hospital bills but relatively few incurred at home, the dying may choose hospital care to avoid immense financial costs. Sometimes, because family members provide care at home or the person doesn't need extra care at home, considerable money is saved by remaining home. The determination of financial cost is largely a function of what expenses will be covered by private insurance or governmental health care programs.

Fourth is the competence of the available institutions. If a particular hospital is well reputed or the patient or family members have had good prior experiences with it, they are more likely to trust its care.

A fifth possible factor is age, insofar as older people are more likely to die in nursing homes and other nonhospital institutions, while younger people are most likely to die in hospitals (most probably because of the kinds of conditions that cause their deaths).

Over and above all demographic factors are personal preferences. Some individuals greatly prefer being at home, where they have familiar surroundings, fewer restrictive rules and regulations, greater autonomy, more access to family and friends, and more opportunity for individual choice. Others are concerned about limited space in the home, about disturbing or burdening the lives of family members, or about altering the nature of previous role relationships (for example, being cared for by their children) and will choose a hospital or other institution.

People are also concerned about whether returning home may mean that emergency treatment will not be available when necessary or that ongoing treatment may be curtailed—thus increasing distress or reducing probable life expectancy. For many dying persons, the opportunity to die at home is well worth the loss of a few days of life; others will remain in the hospital in order to hold onto life as long as possible.

Since a hospital or other institution is still perceived as the "natural" place to die, many people don't even consider the alternative of dying at home. The physician is often the appropriate person to propose this alternative, but he or she may be reluctant to interfere in family dynamics. This seems to be an issue that the dying person and his or her family should be able to resolve, although the former may fear to bring the matter up, dreading rejection or—even worse—irritated acceptance if his or her preference is to die at home. It is useful to have an understanding in advance.

Long-Term-Care Facilities

In settings where patients reside for longer periods, such as nursing homes, Veterans Administration hospitals, and general-hospital units for the chronically ill, the death of one patient may have a profound effect on other patients and on the staff members as well. These patients are well known to one another and have developed some close friendships; they are definite and real human beings to the staff, who may also have come to know their family members as well. Death is more personal and often more difficult to accept, especially when it is the death of a child or a nonelderly person. With the elderly, especially the confused or deteriorated elderly, both staff members and other residents appear much less affected.

Several factors, however, make death in long-term-care facilities easier on the staff than death in a hospital. First, as indicated above, most of those who die are elderly, not infrequently in their eighties and nineties, and they had come to the facility with the expectation that they would die there, not that they would be treated and released. Second, their close family members have already experienced some separation and have had time to anticipate and prepare for the death, so that reactions of family members are less likely to upset the staff. Third, many of the deaths occur to those who have already become nonpersons of sorts, either because of serious losses in cognitive capacities or because they had become depressed and isolated from contacts with others.

Some of the larger institutions have special wards set aside for patients who are extremely ill and expected to die shortly. One such facility was referred to by both patients and staff as "Death Valley" (Kastenbaum, 1967a); another was alternately called "the morgue" and "the dumping ground" (Reynolds & Kalish, 1974b). Patients who are transferred to these wards without adequate explanation may assume, sometimes incorrectly, that the transfer signifies that they are terminally ill. When one patient returned from "Death Valley" to his previous ward in a geriatric hospital, several of his wardmates were astounded to see him—literally viewing him as someone returned from the dead.

Hospice: A Concept of Care

In reaction to the cure-centered, often impersonal approach of the general hospital, an innovative and humanistic program for the care of the terminally ill patient was launched in England in 1967 and spread rapidly throughout Europe and North America. Referred to as **hospice,** a term originally designating a waiting place for travelers, including those who were ill or dying, during the Middle Ages, this new form of hospice combines institutional care and home care for terminally ill persons and adds a dimension of its own.

The first of the modern hospices, established by Cicely Saunders, a British physician, is St. Christopher's, just outside London, and it is still a model for all other hospices, both in its basic philosophy and in the nature of its services. However, as the movement has grown, it has inevitably generated many alternatives to the original model. St. Christopher's Hospice provides both inpatient and outpatient services, as well as working with family members. It is not connected with any other health facility in England, nor is it a formal part of the British National Health Service, although there is constant interchange between the two.

Hospices offer a variety of services. For the most part, they provide health and personal care for dying persons and emotional support for them and their families. They also arrange for these services to be brought to the patient's home, through a system of professional and volunteer service providers, and they help the family take care of the dying person through both technical instruction and personal support. When the patient eventually needs some form of institutional care, he or she will usually either go directly to the inpatient service of the hospice, if one exists, or go to a local hospital that is in accord with hospice philosophy and that permits the hospice to continue providing some services. Many hospices also offer support services for the bereaved after the death.

But hospice is also a concept of care, a philosophy. According to one pioneer in the field, "The primary message that must be conveyed to the dying patient is that he/she is unique, and that his/her needs are special and will be met in an individual way" (Buckingham, 1982–83, p. 164). In the hospital, treatment is for a disease or other health condition, and the psychological and social needs of the individual may sometimes have to be ignored in order to get him or her back to health; once recovery is impossible and death is foreseeable, then full attention can be given to the patient's personal and unique concerns, which should take top priority (Koff, 1980).

Other principles that are part of the hospice philosophy include the following:

1. Patients and their family members must be seen as a unit, and "nothing

we do as caregivers should serve to separate someone who is dying from his or her family" (Woodson, 1978, p. 378).

2. The program needs to begin from the moment of admission. For example, at St. Christopher's, patients are greeted as they enter and are personally guided, usually with their family members, to their beds.

3. All possible efforts are extended to maintain patients in their own or their families' homes as long as they wish, while giving these persons the assurance that they have priority in entering the inpatient service when they are ready.

4. The family members, assisted by volunteers and trained staff, are taught how to provide medical care at home and how to help the patient and one another through psychological and social stress.

5. Pain must be truly controlled, not just reduced, to the extent possible. By understanding the nature of pain, the extent to which it is physical, psychological, social, or spiritual, and by treating it before it begins, the role of pain in the dying process can be greatly diminished. These measures will also reduce stress and feelings of tension, both of which make people more susceptible to pain. Since the usual approach is to wait until the patient is in pain before administering the medication, the pain can become intense before the medication takes effect; however, many patients can become pain-free by a proper pain-management program that requires knowledge of both the biochemical impact of drugs and the psychosocial state of the patient (Woodson, 1978).

6. Hospice care emphasizes the alleviation of symptoms and does not attempt to cure the condition. If the condition can be cured, the person should not be in the hospice program.

7. People should be permitted to die in their own way, using the rituals they wish, denying or accepting death as they wish, expressing their feelings as they wish (Koff, 1980).

Because of extensive home health and home care programs and use of volunteers, a hospice can handle a large number of patients during the course of a year. St. Christopher's, with about 70 beds, cares for between 600 and 700 inpatients each year while serving an additional 300 to 400 patients in its home care program. The average stay for the inpatients is around three weeks; the home care patients have a median of 34 days of care, although some have been maintained on this status for a year and more (Munley, 1983).

Hospices in the United States and Canada have not followed the St. Christopher's model exactly. For example, the first hospice to provide inpatient services did so in a wing of the Royal Victoria Hospital in Montreal, Quebec, and was completely under the auspices of the hospital, though functioning with considerable autonomy.

One author (Davidson, 1979) has outlined four hospice-care models. The first of these, the hospital-based unit, follows the design of the Royal Victoria program, outlined above. It has the advantages of avoiding the need for a new physical plant or organizational structure, and it offers the full array of hospital services for those patients who may find some of these services adding to their comfort. It also builds on an already-existing, financed organizational and programmatic base. The disadvantages accrue from the risk of being too closely integrated with a facility operating on the traditional medical model, which may contradict hospice philosophy in some basic ways. Not so much by intent as by osmosis, the traditional medical procedures may be reintroduced into the hospice program.

The second model is limited to home care services. These hospice programs may be under the auspices of some local health coordinating body or may be privately owned and operated. They may work out arrangements with one or several local inpatient facilities, so that their staff and volunteers can continue to serve the patients after they are hospitalized, or they may have only informal connections with other facilities.

The third model consists of both inpatient and outpatient services but is free-standing—that is, not under the auspices of a larger institution. A modification of this model is operated in connection with a long-term-care facility or a religious order but not with a hospital.

The last model is termed a wholly voluntary program. These are self-help groups, organized by the residents of a community to provide outpatient care through both professional and recently trained volunteers. Although the services they provide are modest, the financial costs to the community and to the recipients are also very modest. These programs may exist in areas that have not been able to develop one of the other programs or where other health agencies are functioning in ways that make hospices unnecessary. It seems likely that many such operations eventually evolve into one of the other three models.

Perhaps the most innovative aspect of the hospice movement is the change in attitude it has effected. The attitude toward a dying person has changed from "There is nothing more we can do to help" to "We need to provide the best human care possible." Although some health care professionals have always espoused this latter view, hospitals and other institutions have not always incorporated it into practice.

Although studies of hospices are now in progress, few have been completed. One study has compared a small number (34) of cancer patients at St. Christopher's with a similar number of comparable patients who died elsewhere. The results are illuminating:

1. The hospice patients were more mobile.
2. The hospice patients rated their physical pain as less severe, and this was not due to more drug-caused confusion.
3. Spouses of hospice patients reported less anxiety and fewer somatic symptoms.
4. Spouses of hospice patients spent more time visiting; more time talking to staff, other patients, and other visitors; and more time helping care for the patient.
5. Because patients at the hospice perceived physicians and nurses as less busy, they found them more accessible.

6. Very few hospice patients were reported by their families as upset by the deaths of other patients

7. Seventy-eight percent of the patients' families regarded St. Christopher's as being like a family; 11% of the matched nonhospice families felt that way about the institutions where their dying family members were (Parkes, 1975).

Another investigation compared the emotional state, attitudes toward illness, and opinions of care of cancer patients in a hospice and in two other settings: an acute hospital and a long-term-care facility. Hospice patients were found to be less anxious and less depressed; the general open-awareness context of the hospice received substantial approval; and the hospice staff and treatment program were better received than those of the other institutions (Hinton, 1979).

In a study in the United States, a group of home care hospice patients were contrasted with a control group lacking hospice support. The former were significantly better off on measures of anxiety, depression, hostility, and the satisfaction of family members (Lack & Buckingham, 1978). However, Parkes (1980) has warned that home care, in comparison with hospital care, may increase stress on dying persons who are anxious or who feel guilty about burdening family members, as well as on the family members themselves.

And not all studies indicate that hospices are fully successful. One extensive study has shown that hospice patients and nonhospice patients did *not* differ in the extent to which they experienced pain, depression, or anxiety, but both the patients and their family members were more satisfied with the care and the staff involvement when the dying person was in the hospice (Wales, Kane, & Bernstein, 1983). Nonetheless, the majority of the studies do show broad social, psychological, and physical advantages for hospice patients.

There are some limitations to hospices. First, many health professionals oppose segregating the dying from other patients. They believe that this kind of labeling is harmful: being in a *place for the dying* exacts a toll of unnecessary anxiety. Second, hospice care is not appropriate for everyone: some deaths do not permit hospice care; some health conditions require equipment or treatment not available in hospices; some persons will find the program unsuited to their personal needs.

The advantage of the hospice program is not that it solves the problem of where to die but that it offers another significant choice, which itself includes alternative models. The National Hospice Organization is located at 1901 North Fort Myer Drive, Suite 402, Arlington, Virginia 22209.

DEATH EDUCATION

Historically, education was provided through family members and other members of the community who had expert knowledge of a particular matter. Removing education to the formal classroom is a fairly recent development. In the same fashion, education involving death-related concerns also took place in the home and from community specialists, such as the clergy. Now it has also moved into more formal settings. As with education in general, it would appear that the home and informal community resources were no longer sufficient for educating people about death.

The goals of death education are numerous. One expert (Knott, 1979) has designated three broad categories of goals: first, to receive information, including knowledge of research findings and clinical observations; most of the material in this book would fall into this category. The second goal is to improve one's understanding of personally held values, including such issues as belief in life after death or the meaning of death itself. And third is the goal of improving coping behavior—that is, one's ability to function effectively in the face of the stresses and demands that surround death, dying, grief, and caring relationships.

Contents of Death Education Programs

Death education is simply what its name implies: an educational process in which a learner receives some form of understanding about death. The student of death education may be (1) personally concerned because of some early experience in life that has never been completely resolved, (2) personally concerned because of some present experience, such as the illness or death of a family member, (3) involved with death or dying because of work or because of a volunteer service project, or (4) interested in learning more about death and dying to understand better what death means or to develop a more satisfying philosophy of death.

Death education can take a variety of forms:

- A credit course in a graduate or undergraduate college program.
- A special project in a high school class.
- A seminar in a professional school: medical, nursing, seminary, social work, mortuary sciences.
- A series, for example, of Tuesday evening lectures in a Presbyterian church; a series of Sunday morning preservice discussions in a Unitarian church; a discussion group for the recently bereaved in a Catholic church.
- A single presentation at a senior center.
- A book, magazine article, newspaper story, or television or radio program or series.
- A weekend university-sponsored continuing education workshop taken for credit.
- An informal discussion with the physician-father of one of the pupils in a fifth-grade class.
- An in-service program for nurses, chaplains, funeral directors, journalists, physicians, hospital aides, nursing-home administrators, mental health professionals, clergy.
- What you are doing right now.

Death education programs are just as varied in format, length, interest, numbers of students, cost, and everything else as any other kind of education. They are also just as helpful, disturbing, growth-producing, anxiety-creating, and generally productive as any other educational program, although the nature of the topics covered is likely to make them a little more upsetting than a course on nutrition or one on nursing-home cost accounting.

The format of a particular educational program is as varied as the format of any topic covered in educational programs. Thus, a discussion of death on *Mister Rogers' Neighborhood* (Sharapan, 1977) is just as much death education as a credit university course; a class period discussing death themes in Melville's novels or in Hesse or Kafka is just as much death education as a class period spent discussing improved hospice programming. Educational needs are served by consciousness raising as much as by learning facts.

Some people believe that proper death education must be directed toward reducing death anxieties and improving sensitivity to the feelings of persons undergoing death-related experiences; others seem to think that only an increase in factual knowledge is appropriate death education. The answer, I feel, does not lie in between but encompasses both. If you are reading this book in conjunction with a course, you may be using class time to discuss feelings and experiences about death and dying and reading time to increase your information on the topics. In any event, both learning information through reading and listening and learning new feelings and attitudes through planned experiences are educational.

Death education programs may be oriented toward a variety of topics or disciplines: medicine, nursing, or general health care; theology, religion, or pastoral care; fiction, drama, or poetry; psychology, psychiatry, or psychotherapy; sociology, anthropology, or social work; art, music, or dance; history, philosophy, or ethics; or any combination of the above.

Furthermore, death education can focus on death, the process of dying, grief and bereavement, or caring relationships (the four major components of this book) or equally on all of these. Since most death education has been directed toward persons who work with the dying and the bereaved, it has emphasized the process of dying and caring relationships, rather than the meaning of death or the nature of grief. This emphasis may have been taken too far: "For some in fact, the dying process is taken to be identical to the whole concern with death" (Kastenbaum, 1977, p. 90).

In an article titled "We Covered Death Today," Kastenbaum (1977) expresses an additional concern about death education: "One can deny death by accepting its commonalities and correlates with safer, more familiar experience. Death becomes a course title and number. It is a topic on the syllabus. It is a certain time or space allotment in the media. In effect, death is set alongside everything else that reassures us through its ongoing, routine nature. This tamed version of death education makes one think of a Disneyworld attraction as contrasted with the tang and danger of a true adventure" (1977, p. 91).

Evaluation of Death Education Programs

Does death education work? This can only be answered, of course, in terms of what we want it to accomplish. We can evaluate a particular death education program on the basis of whether the participants (1) learned factual information, (2) became more aware of their own feelings about their own dying and death, (3) became better able to develop relationships with the dying and the grieving, (4) reduced their personal death fears and anxieties, (5) were better able to understand death themes in literature, music, or art, (6) had greater appreciation of philosophic treatments of death, or (7) were more capable of developing death education or counseling programs themselves.

Several studies have looked at changes in death attitudes as a result of participation in death education programs. In one typical study, 39 students from university health education classes were selected to receive the death education instructional materials and 40 to receive regular health education materials. Two death attitude scales were administered to all students both before and after the courses. The experimental group changed more in the expected direction—that is, toward favorable death attitudes—than the control group. The conclusion, therefore, was reached that the death education course had changed death attitudes (Watts, 1977). A more cautious interpretation could be that the students in the class learned what attitudes were considered "better" and responded in terms of those attitudes.

In a later study, involving a larger number of students, death attitudes of students in a death education class were compared with those of students in an introductory psychology class. This time, the death education students displayed less fear of the death and dying of others (based on the scales from Collett & Lester, 1969), but did not show significant changes in attitudes toward their own deaths or dying. In addition, a number of other measurements of death attitudes showed some small differences with no discernible meaningful pattern (Leviton & Fretz, 1978–79). In a third study comparing two eight-hour workshops, one using an experiential approach and the other a didactic approach, some slight additional changes seemed to be produced by the experiential approach. These changes were indicated on one of the two scales administered; the other gave no advantage to the experiential approach (Durlak, 1978–79).

One death educator compared two groups of students, both of which were signed up for a death education course but only one of which had taken the course in its entirety; the other had completed only a small part of it. The former group responded significantly more favorably to 23 out of 30 death-related questions, while the latter responded significantly more favorably to only one statement. This study is especially interesting because the statements dealt with coping with death—for example, "I can express my fears about dying," "I feel prepared to face my death," "I can communicate with the dying," and "I can tell someone, before I or they die, how much I love them" (Bugen, 1980–81).

A final study is worthy of note because of the honesty of the investigators.

Once again, college students in a death education course were compared with a control group; it found that the only significant difference in changes between the two groups was that the students taking the course thought a great deal more about their deaths than those who didn't take the course (Knott & Prull, 1976).

To return to the seven criteria for evaluating a death education program, outlined at the beginning of this section: (1) it seems obvious that participants will learn factual information; (2) it appears likely that they become more aware of their own feelings, although the evidence is not strong; (3) there is no information on whether they become better able to develop relationships with the dying and the grieving, although they may claim they have done so; (4) there is some evidence that, at least for the short term, they reduce their death fears and anxieties, although we need to accept their statement to this effect at face value; (5) they probably could learn to be better able to understand death themes in the arts, although there doesn't appear to be any research on this issue; (6) they may expand their appreciation of philosophies of death, although again evidence is lacking; and (7) they probably become more capable of developing death education or counseling programs themselves—it would be surprising if this were not the case.

It is probably best to assume that death education can provide useful information, encourage a form of consciousness raising, improve insight into one's own feelings and values, sensitize people to what others are thinking and feeling, and provide a useful framework for thinking about death, the process of dying, and grief. To expect a single course to reduce fears and anxieties to an appreciable extent is probably asking too much of a relatively brief experience.

CHAPTER SIXTEEN

Providing for
Emotional Well-Being

The stress that accompanies dying and loss through death is intense. This is true for the person who is dying, for family members and friends, and for people who work with the dying and the bereaved. At one time or another, people in all these categories may need emotional support for themselves.

Most such support definitely comes from sources other than mental-health professionals. People who are concerned about dying or who are grieving are likely to visit their pastor, talk to their friends and relatives, or try to develop a relationship with their physician or another health professional that provides what they wish. Contacts with mental health agencies for these concerns are rare, although a few persons have developed a specialty in death counseling and receive some support in their endeavors.

Crisis intervention centers and community mental health centers undoubtedly receive calls and visits from people for whom death or grieving is a major issue, but there is no good record of the frequency with which this occurs nor of the adequacy of their staff counselors in handling these matters. We can only assume that people seeking such help encounter professionals whose competence in providing help and support is extremely variable.

Other mental health resources include private counselors and psychotherapists who provide individual and group sessions, volunteer self-help groups, and volunteer individual interventions.

Caring for the dying and the grieving has benefits well beyond the immediate situation. It also prevents more serious occurrences from arising later. Thus, the counselor who improves the personal well-being of a dying older woman may be simultaneously improving the well-being of her husband, who is taking care of her; the nurse who directs a teenage child to a local support group after his father's death is not only helping the teenager cope with his present situation more effectively but laying the groundwork for a more successful recovery from grief a year or two later.

PROVIDING EMOTIONAL WELL-BEING FOR THE DYING

The best way to provide emotional well-being for the dying is to find ways to make their present lives as satisfying as possible. Accomplishing this is usually the task of the family members, close friends, and health professionals. And to supplement the kinds of care that family members and health professionals can offer, we also have the option of psychotherapy or counseling.

Caring for Persons You Love

One of the most demanding, and often one of the most rewarding, relationships that you can enter is that of caring for someone you love who is dying. Most dying people receive a lot of physical and psychological care from family members. According to a British study described earlier (Cartwright et al., 1973), married persons received most of their help from spouses (30%) and from children (31%); those widowed or divorced received their support from children (40%) and children-in-law (16%); persons who had never married obtained help from brothers and sisters (24%) and other relatives and in-laws (31%). The nature of the help received is shown in Table 16-1.

The person who provides the greatest amount of care is in a unique situation. Such caring is often a full-time job, and demands—ranging from changing the dying person's bedding to giving a bath to sitting silently and holding hands to talking about funerals and cemeteries—may be made around the clock. As the person's condition worsens, the demands for attention and involvement increase. At this point, some people hire caretakers at home or transfer the dying to an acute hospital or long-term-care facility; others, who want the dying to be able to die at home, face tasks that are continual, difficult, and emotionally draining.

The major caretaker may come to resent his or her involvement, feeling that others in the family are not helping enough or that the sacrifices made to provide the care—such as leaving a job, relocating from another community, or requiring younger children to become self-sufficient—are high prices to pay. Given that some tension and resentment might enter the relationship, the caretaker may end up feeling angry and then guilty over the anger and over the feeling that he or she could have done better.

However, the caretaker, more than any other person, can feel, after the death has occurred, "I did everything I could have done." He or she becomes a kind of gatekeeper to the dying person and to information about the dying person. When the person's condition becomes truly incapacitating, those who wish to visit must make arrangements through this caretaker; friends who want to send their regards or check to see how everything is do so through the caretaker.

One issue is usually overlooked: who is taking care of the caretaker? Is there enough sustenance from the caretaking role to provide the caretaker with a sense of well-being? Are there others in his or her life who can provide the emotional support that is needed to endure both the physical fatigue and the emotional pain? Are there others also offering help to the dying person? (Table 16-1 would indicate that there often are.) Will there be material rewards after the death has occurred? If the illness is lengthy, is there a way for the caretaker to leave for an evening, a day, a two-week trip?

TABLE 16-1.
Nature of Help Given Dying Persons by Family and Other Roles

	Percentage of Spouses	Percentage of Daughters	Percentage of Sons	Percentage of Other Relatives	Percentage of Friends, Neighbors, Others
Personal care	80	62	44	47	33
Nursing care	61	39	14	18	9
Night care	55	34	31	24	21
Social care	61	52	39	33	26
Financial care	n.a.	6	15	3	—
Housework	22[a]	50[a]	21	35	44
Total Number	289	341	218	553	441

SOURCE: From *Life before Death,* by A. Cartwright, L. Hockey, and J. L. Anderson. Copyright 1973 by Routledge and Kegan Paul. Reprinted by permission.
NOTES: Based on 785 deaths in England.
Examples of personal care are washing, bathing, and taking the dying to the bathroom.
Examples of nursing care include giving medicines and injections and massaging the patient.
Examples of social care are reading to and writing letters for the dying.
[a]Not including persons who had previously done housework.

It's important, as we turn more and more attention to caring for persons who are dying and those who are grieving, that we don't ignore or turn into "villains" those who, either as professionals or as family members, are doing their best to provide physical and emotional care and support.

Anthony Antonelli had 26 years of happy marriage, but his wife developed bone cancer in her late forties and, after a few months of treatment, was declared to be beyond the possibility of cure. Tony decided, to his wife's relief, that she would remain at home as long as possible, although he knew that his income plus their health insurance would not cover their costs indefinitely.

Tony's work schedule as a high school principal had always been fairly demanding, but the addition of his new caring role turned it into a nightmare. He left for work by 7:30 in the morning, having already prepared breakfast and lunch for his wife; he came home between 4:30 and 5:30 P.M. to prepare dinner, did some housecleaning, and then either left for an evening meeting or else completed the paperwork from the day. He also made certain that he and his wife shared a leisurely meal and had ample time to talk about the day, which meant he was rarely in bed before midnight. Weekends were only slightly more relaxing.

After following this program for several weeks, Tony hired a local service to bring lunch to his wife, who could no longer get out of bed, and to do some of the housecleaning. And at about the same time, he and his wife became grandparents for the second time, but with both grandchildren over 2000 miles away, contacts were limited to brief telephone conversations.

His social life, of course, was reduced virtually to zero; his involvement was seven days a week, without respite; and his sleep was rarely undisturbed. Initially it was his own unease that woke him, but as time went on, his wife's suffering caused her to be restless, which, in turn, kept him awake much of the night. Five months after his routine began, Tony suddenly became aware that he was contemplating his wife's coming death not as a source of pain but as a source of relief.

Tony Antonelli had many advantages over other people his age who have confronted similar situations: he had a good income, substantial savings, reasonable health insurance, a stimulating job where he could spend time with people he liked, colleagues who understood his situation, good personal health, and no young children who required attention. Yet when his wife did die, some 13 months later, after a few days in the hospital, he returned directly from the cemetery to his home and remained there, grieving, sleeping, and staring blankly at the television set, for nearly two weeks before he emerged.

Psychotherapy and Counseling with the Dying

We could make the case that all psychotherapy involves death-related issues. That is, dealing with our own feelings about loss, finitude, mortality, immortality, death, and dying is an ongoing process that is never fully resolved, although its priority ebbs and flows across time. Therefore, a patient's concern with mortality is one factor in any psychotherapeutic relationship.

More to the present point is the use of psychotherapy with dying persons. A dying person will enter therapy for a variety of reasons, any one of which may be particularly stressful. First, since dying is really a phase of living, persons who are dying still have most or all of their usual conflicts and anxieties. Of course, some may have receded in importance because dying has taken precedence: anxieties about work and achievement *may* diminish; conflicts with grown children *may* be resolved; financial problems *may* now seem unimportant. Conversely, any one of these sources of stress may actually increase in importance and intensity because impending death places a boundary on the opportunity to resolve the problem.

Second, there are significant stresses imposed on many dying persons by their physical suffering, the losses already experienced, and the anticipation of additional losses.

Third, a dying person's will to live may have so diminished that he or she is failing more rapidly than necessary.

Fourth, fear of death may be limiting the individual's ability to make good use of the time remaining. Stress may derive less from the idea of loss of self than from unfinished tasks and unresolved relationships—leading to a sense of despair that forms a cloud over everything else in the patient's life.

LeShan, whose writing on this topic dates back nearly 30 years, has emphasized that most psychotherapy with dying persons should focus neither on mental pathology nor on preparation for death. Instead, the therapeutic issues are finding areas of personal strength and preparing for remaining life (LeShan, 1969b).

Patients who lack the will to live, who feel despair, may have long histories of such feelings, which often incorporate low self-esteem. The physical pain and discomfort of dying, the loss of supportive persons, and the recognition of finitude often conspire to intensify despair. If the meaning of life was questionable when the person was healthy and involved with work, community, activities, accomplishments, family, and friends, it is likely to be even more dubious when these supports (and distractions) are no longer available.

Those persons who were not fully engaged each day of their lives, but spent most days planning for a nebulous future, now find that they will not have that future and that they have wasted what they did have—time. "'I always lived as if there were only tomorrow and yesterday. Today didn't exist'" (LeShan, 1969b, pp. 38–39).

However, even individuals who have maintained the will to live and who have lived fully in the present may need to reexamine their values and bases for meaning as they face death. Most of us put considerable value on long-term relationships, the development of competence in our work, and effective interactions with our physical and social environments, and psychotherapy has traditionally focused on enabling people to accomplish these goals more successfully. For the dying person, however, external accomplishments are often impossible, and the focus often needs to be on internal and personal growth (LeShan, 1969b). It becomes the process and satisfaction of growing, not the notion "I have grown to a preestablished point," that is of therapeutic value.

The very fact that therapy is taking place provides some sense of potential growth. "There can be great value ... in ... someone's believing in him enough to ... work to help him toward greater self-understanding and inner growth at a time when he cannot 'repay' by a long period of adequate functioning. ... Life no longer ... seems to have the quality of something that is fading away, but takes on new meaning and validity" (LeShan & LeShan, 1961, p. 318). If the dying person can understand that the worth of a person's life is not in accomplishments but in one's humanity and self, then not having reached the achievement goals established years earlier will seem less important, and the dying person can get on with the task of living in whatever time is left. The reduced stress and anxiety and the increased desire for inner growth may even serve to mobilize the life force and reverse the downhill path of the illness (LeShan, 1969a).

Family Therapy with Dying Persons

One family therapist (Bowen, 1978) reports that psychotherapy at the time of death must consider the same issues that are important in therapeutic efforts not directly or immediately focused on death-related matters. The total family constellation, the family's general level of adjustment to life, and the importance and meaning of the dying person to the family and of the individual family members to the dying person are significant concerns for anyone working with families or individuals during the dying process or shortly after the death.

Treating all deaths in the same way without considering the ability of the family to adapt in times of severe emotional crisis, and aiming the therapy largely at the encouragement of overt expressions of grief, may miss the deeper emotional process involved in confronting death and one's own mortality. Bowen (1978) states that an overwhelming majority of dying persons who seek therapy do so either in an effort to cope with their pain without upsetting their families or because they are lonely and feel cut off from the world. In either instance, a session or two usually shows that the family structure has made it impossible for the dying to talk about their deaths. The family will have rules, usually covert, that are essentially automatic responses people use to protect themselves from being affected by other persons' anxiety.

Generally families seek therapy as a result of problems that are ostensibly independent of their need to deal with the death of a relative. Therapists who are conscientious about history-taking will occasionally uncover severe anxiety about death that has become displaced into an apparently unrelated dysfunction. When this occurs, families attempt to refrain from talking about death and, thereby, from having to deal with its harsh and painful consequences, with the fear of their own mortality, and with the need to cope with severe upset while maintaining a semblance of tranquility purportedly for the sake of the dying person. These dynamics are often directly responsible for the emotional dysfunction, regardless of the form it takes.

The following is an example of such a case:

> The young couple had entered marital therapy with the expressed goal of improving their sexual relationship. They were essentially newlyweds, married about a year. As the therapy progressed, it became clear, as it often does in such situations, that the couple's problem had little to do with their sexual adequacy. Rather, there appeared to be an underlying resentment between them that had become concretized as mutual sexual dissatisfaction.
>
> On taking the initial history, the therapist discovered that both spouses had experienced the death of a parent in their childhood and that, in the wife's case, the death had made her responsible for her surviving parent, who had never remarried and "was always sick with something or other."
>
> The initial sessions were difficult, and such progress as there was seemed unusually slow. When the therapist evaluated the course of the work, she decided to approach the problem differently, and at the next session she asked the young wife why she thought that the couple could not solve this problem themselves. The wife answered without hesitation: "Because then I would be taking care of him [the husband], and I had to take care of my mother all my life, and I am not taking care of my husband." The therapist asked the wife how she thought that participating in problem resolution would mean taking care of her husband, and again she answered easily: "Because he ignores everything and pretends that if he does it long enough, whatever is bothering him will go away." The husband reacted at this point with a weak denial. The wife reaffirmed her earlier statement and added, "Like with your father." There was a period of silence, which ended when the therapist asked the wife what she meant. The wife answered, this time in tears: "Because the poor old man is dying, and he knows that he is dying, and everybody pretends that he is not dying, and they don't even talk to him." The husband

interjected: "We just don't want to upset him, that's all." The wife's tears turned into sobbing. After she quieted, the therapist suggested that perhaps it was the husband's father who required therapy, not they, and that if they were freed of the worry of dealing with the father's death, their relationship might improve of its own accord. The therapist added that it was very difficult to make love when there was a dying man in bed with them and all three pretended that he wasn't dying—in fact, that he wasn't even there. (The resemblance to the "horse on the dining room table" metaphor is worth noting.)

This suggestion seemed eminently reasonable to the husband. He was convinced that it would make his wife feel better if "the old man has someone to talk to, and it probably wouldn't hurt him, either." The wife thought that this conclusion displayed a remarkable callousness on the part of the husband, commented that "your father doesn't need therapy—he's not the one that is impotent," and started to cry again. This was the first time during the therapy that the issue of impotence had surfaced. No one said anything for a long time. After a while, the husband said: "I'm not really impotent, you know. I just get this idea that I'm going to hurt you, and I can't."

This session presented a number of breakthroughs, the most important of which was the clue that the young couple were dealing with severe anxiety about the imminent death of the father by developing a pattern of sexual dysfunction. Further exploration was conducted about the relationship between the husband's impotence and his inability to talk to his father about the older man's death. This issue took on considerable importance, since the young man had been reared by his father but had poor relations with his father's extended family; he was assuming that these family members would drop their contacts with him altogether after his father's death, which had been his experience with his mother's family after she had died. The additional exploration and some reality orientation about their ability to cope with life stresses permitted the young couple to progress rapidly.

During the ensuing weeks, the therapist was able to encourage the young couple to look realistically at their anxiety about the father's death and eventually to ask the father to help with that anxiety. This worked well, since it allowed the young people to establish contact with the father in a way that was not overly stressful for these particular individuals, given their family history; and it meant opening a dialogue with the dying man about his dying. As the dialogue proceeded, the couple's death anxiety (which had concretized as sexual dysfunction) diminished. The husband's potency returned, and the wife's responsiveness increased. The presenting problem—that is, the young couple's poor sexual relationship—was not mentioned again after the "breakthrough" session.

Approximately two months after the session described above, the therapist received the following letter from the father:

Dear——:

This isn't exactly a thank you letter. Yet I think that someone ought to tell you thank you. I was very lonely before my kids started talking to you, and I was afraid that when I died I would leave two immature, helpless young people behind, who were so scared of death that they would avoid the responsibility of living. Now, I know that you understand about responsibility, because those kids of mine are assuming responsibility for themselves and each other, and leaving me free to concentrate on dying. I always wanted this special tombstone, and my son is driving me to look at the place where they make them. And my daughter-in-law, bless her heart, is making him a fine wife. So I guess that I have a lot to be grateful for, even though I won't live to see my grandchildren, like I always wanted. I know that I have done a good job, and that they are going to be all right, the kids, that is. Thank you, Ms. ———, I want you to know that with my kids around me, dying has turned out to be a lot easier than a lot of living I've had to do. God Bless You. [From the records of Toni C. Mehler.]

Limitations to Psychotherapy

There are numerous difficulties in providing psychotherapy to dying persons, the most obvious one being that the traditional 50-minute hour in the therapist's office may be impossible, either because the patient cannot get there or because sitting for nearly an hour (contrary to stereotypes, most psychotherapists do not have couches in their offices) is uncomfortable. However, there is no sacred rule that psychotherapy must be performed for 50-minute sessions sitting in offices; perhaps 20 minutes by a hospital bed would be just as significant.

Other difficulties may arise from a psychotherapist's social and psychological beliefs. As mentioned in the previous chapter, a psychotherapist may perceive a dying person's social value to be reduced. A second source of difficulty in treating the dying may be that the therapist is reminded and upset by the specter of his or her own death. Third, some therapists, particularly psychoanalysts, are reluctant to begin therapy with a patient who will not be able to continue in the relationship for an extended period. Fourth, to the extent that a psychotherapist maintains a pathology model of psychotherapy, work with dying persons may be counterproductive: the dying person may have neither the time nor the energy to deal with a lifetime of memories, events, and relationships that have contributed to an emotional pathology. Rather, dying persons may need to focus on the meaning of the past, to become involved in the meaning of the present, and to cope with a limited future.

A caring relationship does not have to offer formal psychotherapy in order to have a psychotherapeutic effect. Or, putting it another way, much of the psychotherapeutic effect of any relationship occurs because of its human caring qualities. Thus, the concerned physician, the attentive nurse, the interested chaplain may all contribute to a substantial therapeutic effect, even though their procedures are much different from that of the psychotherapist.

Evaluating Death Psychotherapy and Counseling

Studies of counseling with the dying themselves are extremely rare, but one that was conducted with 120 terminally ill cancer patients did find that participation in therapy improved life satisfaction (Linn & Linn, 1981). In addition, a handful of studies have been conducted with persons not facing imminent death, and these have had mixed results, so that one study of using psychotherapy to reduce the death anxiety of nurses found no results (Testa, 1981), while another, also with nurses, showed favorable results (White, Gilner, Handal, & Napoli, 1983–84). A recent study of group desensitization therapy found that it was also successful in reducing death anxiety (Peal, Handal, & Gilner, 1981–82). These inconsistencies may be a function of the instruments used to measure death anxiety or some other inadequacy of the research design or procedures, or they may represent the inability of the therapy program to elicit any meaningful change.

These interventions were conducted in group sessions, so that there was no indication of the effects of one-to-one forms of counseling and therapy. In addition, they involved persons who were available to participate in the research, not individuals who were indicated to have need for counseling or therapy. Nonetheless, they do provide a beginning.

Use of LSD

An additional treatment program geared to provide emotional support is the use of LSD (lysergic acid diethylamide) in conjunction with extensive personal support during the LSD experience. Although very few people have been treated in this fashion, and it is difficult to ascertain whether there are any formal programs presently in existence, the use of LSD with the dying has created considerable interest both in the media and among persons who continue to seek better ways of enabling people to die appropriately.

The LSD is administered only under careful supervision, and a professional psychotherapist or comparable person is available to the patient throughout the experience. In addition, there is ample preliminary discussion concerning what might happen and some subsequent discussion of what did occur. Therefore, it is possible that the positive effects of LSD are due not so much to its direct chemical action as to the extensive caring relationships surrounding its administration.

How does LSD help patients in the living-dying interval? Dying patients report that, through their psychedelic experiences, they experience "the importance of accepting, surrendering, and relinquishing" (Grof & Halifax, 1977, p. 52), as well as a sense of unity or oneness with the infinite or the cosmos. The boundaries of the self and of consciousness become blurred, and transpersonal experiences, such as out-of-body experiences or space and time travel, are not uncommon. "In the extreme form the individual consciousness seems to encompass the totality of existence and identify with that of the universal mind" (Grof & Halifax, 1977, p. 56).

If you look back at these past few sentences, you will realize that LSD seems to have the effect of reducing the distinctions between life and death, between this world and other worlds, between body and spirit. It may, in fact, enable some people to face their own deaths more peacefully because they have the sense of having already experienced what death may be, and the experiences have not been distressing. Death becomes not an end, not extinction, but a shift to a form or level of being that is not altogether different from what has already been experienced (Grof & Halifax, 1977).

LSD appears also to reduce pain, perhaps by increasing a sense of well-being and relaxation or perhaps through some more direct biochemical means. Both the reduction in pain and the improved sense of well-being permit the living-dying interval to be more fulfilling—more open to the enjoyment of the company of other people and to the accomplishment of final tasks. It must be emphasized that LSD does not reduce pain, as some drugs do, by clouding consciousness and reducing awareness. Rather, it improves awareness and permits the cognitive powers of the individual to be more active and alert. Use of the drug does not encourage hiding from death or denying it but allows patients to cope with their dying more effectively (Pahnke, 1969). It should be mentioned, of course, that LSD is not given on a continuing basis; one or two experiences appear to have a very powerful effect.

Although some research has supported the usefulness of LSD with dying persons (for example, Grof, Pahnke, Kurland, & Goodman, 1971), none of the studies has guarded adequately against the placebo effect. It's very likely true that this treatment procedure works, but as Dr. Cicely Saunders remarked to me nearly two decades ago, quality care programs such as are provided by well-functioning hospices produce comparable effects without the expensive and elaborate procedures required when using LSD.

PSYCHOTHERAPY AND COUNSELING WITH THE BEREAVED

Bereaved persons suffer their grief not only during the period shortly following a death but from early in the living-dying interval until years, even decades, after the death. Since virtually all adults eventually suffer significant losses, all psychotherapy, in a sense, includes psychotherapy for the bereaved. However, we can differentiate four stages of bereavement, each of which calls for somewhat different kinds of therapeutic support.

The first stage occurs during the living-dying interval. Emotional stress is high and, often, unrelenting; the demands of caretaking may lead to fatigue, poor diet, and lack of recreation and social relationships. A good, relaxed dinner, a weekend away, or a movie may be more valuable than any kind of psychotherapy at this point. Psychotherapy might be helpful in enabling the individual to improve the relationship with the dying person, if there are still tensions; to handle his or her feelings of guilt and any unresolved, distressing aspects of the relationship; to deal with impending loss and possible loneliness; to be able to take responsibility as required and turn over responsibility to others as appropriate; to recognize his or her own limitations and to accept them; and to begin an engagement in what life will be after the death occurs. Over and above all else, these people who have begun to grieve but are not yet technically bereaved may need someone to whom they can express feelings of anger, frustration, fear, and hope.

Psychotherapy during the second stage, at the time of death, is most likely to be a kind of crisis intervention; there may also be an understanding that the therapeutic relationship will need to continue for some time. Feelings are likely to be intense; moods will come and go quickly; depression will be constant, underlying all else. Psychotherapy can offer catharsis, an opportunity to reminisce and simultaneously to begin to become future-oriented, a time to explore what the loss means and is likely to mean, and to continue work begun in the first stage.

For some bereaved persons, the third stage, during the weeks following the death, is still filled with acute grief and intense mourning; others display little grief. For the latter, therapy might be used to help them begin active mourning, to permit the expression of feelings, although some of these individuals have worked through their loss in ways that are not evident to others. Probably those who need therapy the most are those who have neither grieved overtly nor worked through their feelings of grief in other ways: those who insist on being "brave" and "going on as though nothing ever happened."

And, finally, psychotherapy may be called for to help individuals who, even years after the loss, have not successfully completed their grieving. This includes more people than is normally assumed. One psychiatrist has developed what he terms **re-grief therapy** to work with such persons. The goals of re-grief therapy are to help the individual understand why he has not finished grieving and then to "complete it in the present, to experience and to express the emotions generated by his loss" (Volkan, Cilluffo, & Sarvay, 1975, p. 191). For some reason, the bereaved individual is unable to let go of the person who has died, and Volkan and his associates focus the psychotherapy both on "letting go" and on differentiating the therapy client from the person who has died, since there is a tendency to obscure the distinctions between the self and the dead person (Volkan, 1970). Sometimes this identification is accomplished by keeping some possession or other object associated with the dead person to form a linkage. The linking object has intense emotional connotations for the therapy client, and the client must deal with these feelings (Volkan et al., 1975). This is not the only form of psychotherapy appropriate for people who have not overcome their grief, but it is the only one I know of that has been developed specifically for this one task.

Another therapeutic approach to facilitate expression of grief is to have the client talk directly to a fantasized image of the dead person. This can be done in the therapy session, where it may be particularly powerful, or at home or anywhere, for that matter. The client will turn to an empty chair, perhaps visualize the dead person, and say what he or she had not said while the person was still alive. This may include expressions of love, of anger, of desire for absolution of guilt, of sadness at the loss of the relationship. Talking *to* instead of talking *about* is very likely to elicit strong feelings.

There are times, especially at the start of grieving, just after death has occurred or around the time of the funeral, when the intensity of sorrow is so great that many persons resort to tranquilizers and alcohol. Physicians are likely to prescribe tranquilizers fairly freely at that time. Respondents in the

Los Angeles study were very likely to expect others to take tranquilizers during a wake or funeral (40–50% of the Blacks, Mexican Americans, and Whites) and fairly likely to expect others to drink during those occasions (20–40% of the same three ethnic communities) (Kalish & Reynolds, 1981). Confirming these results was a study of widows and widowers: about one-third had used tranquilizers in the years since their spouse's death and nearly one-third had used sleeping medicine; there was no indication of the extent of overlap (Bornstein et al., 1973).

Some people have expressed concern that frequent use of tranquilizers will impede the normal grieving process, and there is some controversy about whether they should be used at all at this point. It appears that our feelings, especially our loss-connected feelings, catch up with us one way or another, at one time or another. When they are not permitted expression at the time they initially occur, they may return to haunt us later. For most of us, our psychological processes of denial and repression serve to protect us from emotional pain, and perhaps the use of drugs is indeed unnecessary for most grieving persons.

SELF-HELP GROUPS

One familiar source of social and emotional support for troubled persons (and for those who are not troubled) is the self-help group, directed either by an outside professional or by a group member. Widows have used this kind of program, and the results from one research study have shown it to be quite effective. Some 70 widows who responded to a request in a local newspaper participated in a group program for seven weeks. Three kinds of groups had been established: self-help, confidant (where women were encouraged to develop a confidant relationship with another woman in the group), and conciousness-raising, and each woman was assigned randomly to one group. After the program, the women in all three groups, compared with control-group participants, indicated higher self-esteem, greater optimism concerning their future physical health, and more ability to feel and express the intensity of their grief. They also found themselves less predisposed to remarry. A follow-up, conducted several months later, showed that most of these changes had endured. This project suggests that such groups can be very helpful—an important finding because, although the costs in money and time were modest, the results showed the process to be valuable (Barrett, 1978a). Similar results were found in a Canadian study (Vachon, 1983).

Numerous self-help groups involved with dying and grief have developed around the country. Many of these are strictly local, such as a group of heart-attack patients and their spouses that was formed on the West Coast. Others, however, have national linkages. Three major national self-help groups are Make Today Count (for dying persons), The Compassionate Friends (for grieving parents), and THEOS (for widows) (Klass, 1982).

Although these groups are called self-help groups, it has been pointed out that their members provide help, support, encouragement, and information for one another and receive their help in large part from one another (Klass & Shinners, 1982–83). In fact, through his experiences in sitting in with many Compassionate Friends groups as a professional, Klass (1982) reported that he found that his own participation diminished over time. The more he learned about self-help groups, the more he realized that the participants received much more help from those with whom they shared experiences than from the insights of the professionals.

Self-help groups have become familiar in the mental health field, with their origins in Alcoholics Anonymous and their more recent history having found expression in drug addiction, gambling, health problems, women's consciousness raising, and other concerns. Some mental health professionals are concerned that nonprofessionals, no matter how well intended, will have a tendency to uncover serious emotional problems among the participants through their discussions and then not be able to—in effect—put the person back together again. Once again, Klass' experience differed: he found that the support of the other group members prevented the emergence of pathological behavior resulting from the interactions in the group more effectively than the intervention of the professional. At least in his experience, no one left the group seriously disturbed (Klass & Shinners, 1982–83).

This does not mean that participation in death-related self-help groups never leads to serious disturbance or even to pathology. We know that participation in group therapy or individual therapy with the most astute of psychotherapists will occasionally create serious emotional disturbance. The findings do suggest, however, that such participation is extremely low-risk and that the potential rewards are substantial. Caution, of course, is necessary in the selection of the group, especially if it has a designated leader.

Other Volunteer Groups

Similar to self-help groups, but using a somewhat different service model, are groups that provide support for emotional well-being through programs that have been planned, developed, and directed by professionals, often in association with a service agency, but that use volunteers for the personal services. Sometimes the volunteers are limited to persons who have experienced the same kinds of concerns that those in need of service are experiencing; sometimes this is not a requirement of the program.

There are many examples of this model. Shanti, with its headquarters in San Francisco, developed a program for providing support services to the dying and the bereaved. Founded by Dr. Charles Garfield in the early 1970s, Shanti provided in-service training for its many volunteers, although a high proportion of them were in the helping professions. Persons wanting a friend, a visitor, or an informal counselor would contact Shanti, either directly or through someone else, and would request help (Garfield & Clark, 1978).

A similar program was developed in Toronto, Ontario, to minister to the needs of adults with close relatives who had committed suicide. Here the support services were administered by volunteers under the supervision of professionals from the University of Toronto (Rogers, Sheldon, Barwick, Letofsky, & Lancee, 1982). In this program, all members of the family met with two volunteers for a designated period of weeks. When asked later which of their needs had been met most effectively, the participants stated that the greatest help had been in getting the suicide into perspective and being able to express their feelings without being judged (Rogers et al., 1982).

A final example, also from Toronto, is a volunteer-based, University of Toronto-directed program for recent widows. This used the model of having the widow meet individually (although later in small groups) with another woman who had been widowed for some time. And again, the volunteers functioned under the supervision of professionals. In a well-executed evaluation of the program, it was obvious that the widows who received the volunteer help were coping with their grief more effectively than those who did not receive such support and that this was especially true for those women who had experienced an initial high level of distress at the time of death (Vachon, Lyall, Rogers, Freedman-Letofsky, & Freeman, 1980).

These organizations have to struggle to continue to function, sometimes because they cannot find adequate funds and at other times because of inadequate leadership or planning. The organizations come and go—perhaps aided by newspaper coverage or harmed by the loss of the individual who worked hardest. Nonetheless, the dynamic quality of such groups is certainly a very healthy sign. They display a willingness of people to take time to help others, and they also indicate the ability of those who are dying or who have suffered the loss of someone else to do something for themselves. Rather than sitting back passively waiting for someone else to plan and develop a program, the people who are closest to a problem are developing the program themselves, and the caregivers receive payment in personal satisfaction.

To provide a better understanding of the nature of these groups, we will discuss two of them in greater detail.

Make Today Count

Orville Kelly's experiences as he coped with his diagnosed cancer and limited life expectancy persuaded him to reach out to others who were living with the same sword of Damocles overhead. Thus in mid-1973 a group of 18 people met—the group included patients, family members of patients, and professionals—and launched Make Today Count in order to meet with others with whom they could talk and share their problems. The meeting was described by the wire services and carried to newspapers all over the country, and Orville Kelly and Make Today Count became the focal point for a national organization. Kelly died of his cancer in 1980, having outlived his prognosis, but his death did not halt the organization, and today there are chapters all over the country.

The purpose of the organization is to bring together people who are either suffering from cancer or closely related to someone who is. They meet, exchange experiences, provide social and emotional support, offer encouragement, and try to make each day matter. The psychological difficulties suffered by cancer patients are not always recognized. "Many patients experience deep emotional problems centering on loss of sex appeal or rejection after a scarring operation for certain types of cancer, or on loss of hair or disfigurement from radiation therapy" (Kelly, 1978, p. 65). These, of course, are only two of many such problems. "It isn't possible to solve all of these problems, but bringing them out in the open and discussing them seems to help. Just knowing that others face some of the same problems relieves the anxieties of many patients and family members" (Kelly, 1978, p. 65).

Make Today Count is an example of an organization begun not by professional caretakers or professional organizers but by those individuals most affected. Chapters are fairly autonomous, and funding needs are minimal, since there are no paid local leaders and national office expenses are extremely modest; local programming requires only that people get together to serve their own purposes. Individual chapters are begun by members of the clergy and physicians, as well as by patients and family members, and meetings are usually held in homes and churches. The national headquarters is located at 210 Burlington Building, Burlington, Iowa 52601.

Compassionate Friends

Like Make Today Count, Compassionate Friends is an informal operation with over 380 chapters throughout the United States. Chapters also exist in Canada, as well as in England, where the organization began in 1969. Chapters are begun by bereaved parents; finances are minimal—voluntary contributions, rather than dues, cover costs; meetings are held in public buildings and churches; work at both local and national levels is accomplished mostly by volunteers. The major difference between the two organizations is their membership: participants in Make Today Count are themselves facing death or facing the death of someone they love; participants in Compassionate Friends are parents who have already experienced the death of a child.

The aims of Compassionate Friends are to (1) offer support and friendship to sorrowing parents, (2) listen with understanding and provide "telephone friends," (3) come together with others once a month, (4) offer information about the process of grieving, and (5) provide contact and friendship with other bereaved parents who have lived through the experience and are finding hope and strength in their lives. Perhaps the group's orientation is best expressed in a statement from its brochure: "Many bereaved parents do have the need for more understanding, more hope, more knowledge, or more comfort than the people around them provide. Sometimes a conversation, a book, or a professional presentation may assist healing and give new insight and understanding about a particular question or concern. In trying to help bereaved parents cope with their loss, Compassionate Friends does not focus morbidly on death and thus only rekindle unhappy feelings. We do acknowledge the pain that is a part of loving. We have loved, therefore, we grieve. We are willing to share someone's sorrow."

For more information, write Compassionate Friends, National Headquarters, P.O. Box 1347, Oak Brook, Illinois 60521.

A recent study of participants in Compassionate Friends programs indicates that the organization also offers prevention against emotional problems in the future. Of parents whose child had died within the preceding 18 months, those who were more involved in helping other people whose children had also died were likely to be less depressed a year later than those who were members of the group but expended little effort; they also became less preoccupied with the death that had occurred (Videka-Sherman, 1982).

WHAT DO THE DYING AND GRIEVING WANT?

Interestingly enough, we almost never ask people who are suffering from a particular condition or status what it is that they would like. The tendency is for observers or experts to make that determination. There are, however, two good ways to learn what people want: first, we can ask them, although we need to do so in ways that will elicit what they *really* want, not what they think we want them to want; and second, we can watch what they do.

In one study, 60 terminally ill cancer patients were asked about the kinds of services they wanted. They mentioned help with (1) financial problems, which arose frequently from high medical costs and reduced income, (2) illness-related matters, such as concern about pain, loss of strength and energy, long confinements to home and hospital, and trouble with medical tests and procedures, (3) changes in social and sexual relationships, (4) difficulties at the hospital, including erratic nursing attention, inadequate information about their condition, and impersonal treatment, and (5) handling emotional problems, including anxiety, depression, hostility, and suicidal ideation (Koenig, 1968).

It's likely that many of the things that these terminal cancer patients said they wanted, nearly 20 years ago, would appear on a comparable list developed today. Certainly financial problems would be no fewer today and are probably not dealt with much more effectively, and it is questionable whether dying patients are now better informed about changes in social and sexual relationships or whether their attention from the nursing staff has improved. So, as stated at the beginning of the chapter, in spite of significant advances in care of the dying, there is still much to do.

What do the dying and the grieving actually do? They go to hospices, and the success of these programs is certainly an indication of what the dying want. They initiate and maintain self-help groups, which is another clue. And they, as well as the rest of us, attend workshops and seminars, read books and articles, and talk to people about their concerns. So even though there aren't a lot of what we would call "hard" research data, there is ample information around to enable us to develop new programs and facilities and to improve those already in existence.

Epilogue

DEATH:
BEGINNING, MIDDLE, END, OR PART OF THE CYCLE

In *A Christmas Carol*, Dickens wrote of Christmas Past, Christmas Present, and Christmas Yet-to-Come. Perhaps each of us consists of past, present, and yet-to-come. Our past is our memories, for without memories we are nothing. Our present is our meanings, including relationships and tasks, for without these our present is simply empty movement through time and space. Our future is time and hope, for without time there is no future, and without hope time has little value.

When we read of death, think of death, or experience death or grief, we immerse ourselves even more deeply in the past, present, and yet-to-come. In confronting death, we can enrich ourselves by our memories. This, of course, implies that our lives have been lived in such fashion as to produce memories that are enriching. We can also enrich ourselves with our meanings—knowing that we have had meaning and that we still have meaning. And we can enrich ourselves with time, even when there is little time—but when all is said and done, time is all that any of us ever has.

Death can be a beginning: for the survivors, the beginning of new responsibilities, new anguish and pain, new opportunities; for the dead person, the beginning of what we can only speculate on. And death can be a middle, a transition from one state or status to another state or status, both for the survivors and for the dead person. And death can be an end, an end of relationships, an end of experiencing, an end of hopes, but also an end of distress, an end of frustration and depression, an end of misery.

Perhaps, then, death is part of a cycle, or part of many cycles. It is part of the life cycle for the dead person, and it is a different part of the life cycle for the survivors. It is also part of the evolutionary cycle. And as the words of the old folk song remind us, it is part of the cycle of all that is in the world.

Where have all the flowers gone?
    Long time passing—
Where have all the flowers gone?
    Long time ago—
Where have all the flowers gone?
    Gone to young girls, every one.
When will they ever learn?
When will they ever learn?

Where have all the young girls gone?
    Long time passing—
Where have all the young girls gone?
    Long time ago—
Where have all the young girls gone?
    Gone to young men, every one.
When will they ever learn?
When will they ever learn?

Where have all the young men gone?
    Long time passing—
Where have all the young men gone?
    Long time ago—
Where have all the young men gone?
    Gone to soldiers, every one.
When will they ever learn?
When will they ever learn?

Where have all the soldiers gone?
    Long time passing—
Where have all the soldiers gone?
    Long time ago—
Where have all the soldiers gone?
    Gone to graveyards, every one.
When will they ever learn?
When will they ever learn?

Where have all the graveyards gone?
    Long time passing—
Where have all the graveyards gone?
    Long time ago—
Where have all the graveyards gone?
    Gone to flowers, every one.
When will they ever learn?
When will they ever learn?

References

Abram, H. S. (1976). *The choice between dialysis and transplant: Psychosocial consid-erations.* Presentation at the Institute of Society, Ethics, and Life Sciences, Hastings Center, New York.

Abram, H. S. (1977). Survival by machine: The psychological stress of chronic hemo-dialysis. In R. H. Moos (Ed.), *Coping with physical illness.* New York: Plenum Press.

Abram, H. S., Moore, G. L., & Westervelt, F. B. (1971). Suicidal behavior in chronic dialysis patients. *American Journal of Psychiatry, 127,* 1199–1204.

Achté, K. A., & Vauhkonen, M.-L. (1971). Cancer and the psyche. *Omega, 2,* 46–56.

Aday, R. H. (1984–85). Belief in afterlife and death anxiety: Correlates and compari-sons. *Omega, 15,* 67–75.

Alexander, I. E., & Adlerstein, A. M. (1960). Studies in the psychology of death. In H. P. David & J. C. Brenglemann (Eds.), *Perspectives in personality research.* New York: Springer.

Alexander, I. E., Colley, R. S., & Adlerstein, A. M. (1957). Is death a matter of indiffer-ence? *Journal of Psychology, 43,* 277–283.

Amenta, M. M., & Weiner, A. W. (1981). Death anxiety and general anxiety in hospice workers. *Psychological Reports, 49,* 962.

American Council of Life Insurance. (1983). *1983 life insurance fact book.* Washing-ton, DC: Author.

Appleton, W. S. (1975). The blame of dying young. *American Journal of Psycho-analysis, 35,* 377–381.

Argyle, M., & Beit-Hallahmi, B. (1975). *The social psychology of religion.* London: Routledge & Kegan Paul.

Ariès, P. (1974). *Western attitudes toward death: From the Middle Ages to the present* (P. M. Ranum, Trans.). Baltimore: Johns Hopkins University Press.

Ariès, P. (1981). *The hour of our death* (H. Weaver, Trans.). New York: Knopf.

Aronow, E., Rauchway, A., Peller, M., & DeVito, A. (1980–81). The value of the self in relation to fear of death. *Omega, 11,* 37–44.

Artiss, K., & Levine, A. (1973). Doctor-patient relations in severe illness. *New England Journal of Medicine, 288,* 1210–1214.

Augustine, M. J., & Kalish, R. A. (1975). Religion, transcendence, and appropriate death. *Journal of Transpersonal Psychology, 7,* 1–13.

Averill, J. R. (1968). Grief: Its nature and significance. *Psychological Bulletin, 70,* 721–748.

Ball, J. F. (1976–77). Widow's grief: The impact of age and mode of death. *Omega, 7,* 307–333.

Bankoff, E. A. (1983). Aged parents and their widowed daughters: A support relationship. *Journal of Gerontology, 38,* 226–230.

Barber, T. X. (1961). Death by suggestion. *Psychosomatic Medicine, 23,* 153–155.

Barrett, C. J. (1978a). Effectiveness of widows' groups in facilitating change. *Journal of Consulting and Clinical Psychology, 46,* 20–31.

Barrett, C. J. (1978b). *Strategies for preventing the stresses of widowhood.* Presentation at the Southwestern Psychological Association, New Orleans. Cited in a working document prepared by R. L. Taylor.

Barrett, C. J., & Schneweis, K. M. (1980–81). An empirical search for stages of widowhood. *Omega, 11,* 97–104.

Becker, E. (1973). *The denial of death.* New York: Free Press.

Bellah, R. N. (1969). Transcendence on contemporary piety. In D. Cutler (Ed.), *The religious situation.* Boston: Beacon.

Bellah, R. N. (1970). *Beyond belief.* New York: Harper & Row.

Bendiksen, R., & Fulton, R. (1975). Death and the child: An anterospective of the childhood bereavement and later behavior disorder hypothesis. *Omega, 6,* 45–59.

Bengtson, V. L., Cuellar, J. B., & Ragan, P. K. (1977). Stratum contrasts and similarities in attitudes toward death. *Journal of Gerontology, 32,* 76–88.

Benoliel, J. Q. (1979). Dying in an institution. In H. Wass (Ed.), *Dying: Facing the facts.* New York: McGraw-Hill.

Bequaert, L. H. (1976). *Single women: Alone and together.* Boston: Beacon Press.

Bergman, A. B., Pomery, M. A., & Beckwith, B. (1969, December). The psychiatric toll of the sudden infant death syndrome. *GP,* 99–105.

Bertman, S. L. (1979–80). The arts: A source of comfort and insight for children who are learning about death. *Omega, 10,* 147–162.

Binger, C. M., Ablin, A. R., Feuerstein, R. C., Kushner, J. H., Zoger, S., & Mikkelsen, C. (1969). Childhood leukemia: Emotional impact on patient and family. *New England Journal of Medicine, 280,* 414–418.

Blauner, R. (1966). Death and social structure. *Psychiatry, 29,* 378–394.

Blazer, J. A. (1973). The relationship between meaning in life and fear of death. *Psychology, 10,* 33–34.

Bluebond-Langner, M. (1977). Meanings of death to children. In H. Feifel (Ed.), *New meanings of death.* New York: McGraw-Hill.

Bornstein, P. E., & Clayton, P. J. (1972). The anniversary reaction. *Diseases of the Nervous System, 33,* 470-472.

Bornstein, P. E., Clayton, P. J., Halikas, J. A., Maurice, W. L., & Robins, E. (1973). The depression of widowhood after thirteen months. *British Journal of Psychiatry, 122,* 561–566.

Bowen, M. (1978). *Family therapy in clinical practice.* New York: Jason Aronson.

Bowlby, J. (1961). Childhood mourning and its implications for psychiatry. *American Journal of Psychiatry, 118,* 481–498.

Brent, S. B. (1977–78). Puns, metaphors, and misunderstandings in a two-year-old's conception of death. *Omega, 8,* 285–293.

Bromberg, W., & Schilder, P. (1933). Death and dying. *Psychoanalytic Review, 20,* 133–185.

Brotman, H. B. (1982). *Every ninth American.* Washington, DC: U.S. Government Printing Office.

Brown, G. (1982). Early loss and depression. In C. M. Parkes & J. Stevenson-Hinde (Eds.), *The place of attachment in human behavior.* New York: Basic Books.

Bryer, K. B. (1979). The Amish way of death. *American Psychologist, 34,* 255–261.

Buckingham, R. W. (1982–83). Hospice care in the United States: The process begins. *Omega, 13,* 159–171.

Bugen, L. A. (1977). Human grief: A model for prediction and intervention. *American Journal of Orthopsychiatry, 47,* 196–206.

Bugen, L. A. (1980–81). Coping: Effects of death education. *Omega, 11,* 175–183.

Bulka, R. P. (1974). Death in life—Talmudic and logotherapeutic affirmations. *Humanitas, 10*(1), 33–41.

Bunch, J., & Barraclough, B. (1971). The influence of parental death anniversaries upon suicide dates. *British Journal of Psychiatry, 118,* 621–626.

Butler, R. N. (1968). The life review: An interpretation of reminiscence in the aged. In B. L. Neugarten (Ed.), *Middle age and aging.* Chicago: University of Chicago Press. (Reprinted from *Psychiatry,* 1963)

Bytheway, W. R. (1977). Aspects of old age in age-specific mortality rates. In J. P. Carse & A. B. Dallery (Eds.), *Death and society.* New York: Harcourt Brace Jovanovich.

Cain, A. C., & Cain, B. S. (1964). On replacing a child. *Journal of the American Academy of Child Psychiatry, 3,* 443–456.

Cain, A. C., Erickson, M. E., Fast, I., & Vaughan, R. A. (1964). Children's disturbed reactions to their mother's miscarriage. *Psychosomatic Medicine, 26,* 58–66.

Cain, A. C., Fast, I., & Erickson, M. E. (1964). Children's disturbed reactions to the death of a sibling. *American Journal of Orthopsychiatry, 34,* 741–752.

Campbell, T. W., Abernethy, V., & Waterhouse, G. J. (1983–84). Do death attitudes of nurses and physicians differ? *Omega, 14,* 34–49.

Cannon, W. B. (1942). Voodoo death. *American Anthropologist, 44,* 169–181.

Cantril, H. (Ed.). (1951). *Public opinion: 1935–1946.* Princeton: Princeton University Press.

Carey, R. G. (1979–80). Weathering widowhood: Problems and adjustments of the widowed during the first year. *Omega, 10,* 135–145.

Carlin, J. E. (1977). The life of the malformed child. In E. M. Pattison (Ed.), *The experience of dying.* Englewood Cliffs, NJ: Prentice-Hall.

Cartwright, A., Hockey, L., & Anderson, J. L. (1973). *Life before death.* London: Routledge & Kegan Paul.

Castaneda, C. (1972). *A separate reality: Further conversations with Don Juan.* New York: Pocket Books.

Choron, J. (1963). *Death and Western thought.* New York: Collier.

Choron, J. (1964) *Modern man and mortality.* New York: Macmillan.

Clayton, P. J., Halikas, J. A., & Maurice, W. L. (1972). The depression of widowhood. *British Journal of Psychiatry, 120,* 71–77.

Cochrane, A. L. (1936). A little widow is a dangerous thing. *International Journal of Psychoanalysis, 17,* 494–509.

Collett, L. J., & Lester, D. (1969). The fear of death and the fear of dying. *Journal of Psychology, 72,* 179–181.

Comfort, A. (1969). Longer life by 1990? *New Scientist, 11,* 549–551.

Conte, H. R., Weiner, M. B., & Plutchik, R. (1982). Measuring death anxiety: Conceptual, psychometic, and factor-analytic aspects. *Journal of Personality and Social Psychology, 43*, 775–785.

Coolidge, F. L., & Fish, C. E. (1983–84). Dreams of the dying. *Omega, 14*, 1–8.

Corcos, A., & Krupka, L. (1983–84). How death came to mankind: Myths and legends. *Omega, 14*, 187–199.

Cross, F. L. (Ed.). (1958). *Oxford dictionary of the Christian church.* London: Oxford University Press.

Davidson, G. W. (1979). Hospice care for the dying. In H. Wass (Ed.), *Dying: Facing the facts.* New York: McGraw-Hill.

Derogatis, L., Abeloff, M., & Melisaratos, N. (1979). Psychological coping mechanisms and survival time in metastatic breast cancer. *Journal of the American Medical Association, 242*(4), 1504–1508.

DeSpelder, L. A., & Strickland, A. L. (1983). *The last dance: Encountering death and dying.* Palo Alto, CA: Mayfield.

Dickstein, L. S. (1972). Death concern: Measurement and correlates. *Psychological Reports, 30*, 563–571.

Diggory, J. C., & Rothman, D. Z. (1961). Values destroyed by death. *Journal of Abnormal and Social Psychology, 63*, 205–210.

Doka, K. J. (1981–82). The social organization of terminal care in two pediatric hospitals. *Omega, 12*, 345–354.

Dore, R. P. (1958). *City life in Japan.* Berkeley and Los Angeles: University of California Press.

Dublin, L. E. (1951). *Factbook on man from birth to death.* New York: Macmillan.

Durlak, J. A. (1972). Relationship between individual attitudes toward life and death. *Journal of Consulting and Clinical Psychology, 38*, 463.

Durlak, J. A. (1973). Relationship between attitudes toward life and death among elderly women. *Developmental Psychology, 8*, 146.

Durlak, J. A. (1978–79). Comparison between experiential and didactic methods of death education. *Omega, 9*, 57–66.

Durlak, J. A., & Kass, R. A. (1981–82). Clarifying the measurement of death attitudes: A factor analytic evaluation of fifteen self-report death scales. *Omega, 12*, 129–141.

Easson, W. M. (1974). Management of the dying child. *Journal of Clinical Child Psychology, 3*(2), 25–27.

Eliot, T. D. (1933). A step toward the social psychology of bereavement. *Journal of Abnormal and Social Psychology, 27*, 380–390.

Eliot, T. D. (1947). Attutudes toward euthanasia. *Research Studies, State College of Washington, 15*, 131–134.

Eliot, T. D. (1955). Bereavement: Inevitable but not insurmountable. In H. Becker & R. Hill (Eds.), *Family, marriage, and parenthood.* Boston: Heath.

Engel, G. (1977, November). Emotional stress and sudden death. *Psychology Today*, pp. 114, 118, 153–154.

Erikson, E. (1963). *Childhood and society* (2nd ed.). New York: Norton.

Ettinger, R. C. W. (1966). *The prospect of immortality.* New York: McFadden.

Federal Trade Commission, Bureau of Consumer Protection. (1978). *Funeral industry practices.* Washington, DC: Author.

Feifel, H. (1959). Attitudes toward death in some normal and mentally ill populations. In H. Feifel (Ed.), *The meaning of death.* New York: McGraw-Hill.

Feifel, H. (1963). Death. In N. L. Farberow (Ed.), *Taboo Topics.* New York: Atherton.

Feifel, H., & Branscomb, A. B. (1973). Who's afraid of death? *Journal of Abnormal Psychology, 81,* 282–288.

Feifel, H., & Nagy, V. T. (1981). Another look at fear of death. *Journal of Consulting and Clinical Psychology, 49,* 278–286.

Feifel, H., & Nagy, V. T. (in preparation). *Coping styles and strategies in dealing with old age, illness, and death.*

Feigenberg, L. (1980). *Terminal care: Friendship contracts with dying cancer patients.* New York: Brunner/Mazel.

Feldman, M. J., & Hersen, M. (1967). Attitudes toward death in nightmare subjects. *Journal of Abnormal Psychology, 72,* 421–425.

Felner, R. D., Ginter, M. A., Boike, M. F., & Cowan, E. L. (1981). Parental death or divorce and the school adjustment of young children. *American Journal of Community Psychology, 9,* 181–191.

Fenichel, O. (1945). *The psychoanalytic theory of neuroses.* New York: Norton.

Fitchett, G. (1980). It's time to bury the stage theory of death and dying. *Oncology Nurse Exchange, 2*(3), no page numbers.

Florian, V., & Har-Even, D. (1983–84). Fear of personal death: The effects of sex and religious belief. *Omega, 14,* 83–91.

Frankl, V. E. (1963). *Man's search for meaning: An introduction to logotherapy.* New York: Washington Square Press.

Frazer, J. G., & Gaster, T. H. (1959). *The new Golden Bough.* New York: S. G. Phillips.

Freud, S. (1959a). Thoughts for the times on war and death (J. Riviere, Trans.). In *Collected papers* (Vol. 4). New York: Basic Books. (Originally published, 1915.)

Freud, S. (1959b). Mourning and melancholia (J. Riviere, Trans.). In *Collected papers* (Vol. 4). New York: Basic Books. (Originally published, 1917.)

Fulton, R. (1965). The sacred and the secular: Attitudes of the American public toward death, funerals, and funeral directors. In R. Fulton (Ed.), *Death and identity.* New York: Wiley.

Fulton, R. (1979). Death and the funeral in contemporary society. In H. Wass (Ed.), *Dying: Facing the facts.* New York: McGraw-Hill.

Fulton, R., & Fulton, J. (1971). A psychosocial aspect of terminal care: Anticipatory grief. *Omega, 2,* 91–100.

Gallagher, D. E., Breckenridge, J. N., Thompson, L. W., & Peterson, J. A. (1983). Effects of bereavement on indicators of mental health in elderly widows and widowers. *Journal of Gerontology, 38,* 565–571.

Garfield, C. A. (1977). Ego functioning, fear of death, and altered states of consciousness. In C. A. Garfield (Ed.), *Rediscovery of the body.* New York: Dell.

Garfield, C. A. (1978). Elements of psychosocial oncology: Doctor-patient relationships in terminal illness. In C. A. Garfield (Ed.), *Psychosocial care of the dying patient.* New York: McGraw-Hill.

Garfield, C. A. (1979). The dying patient's concern with "life after death." In R. Kastenbaum (Ed.), *Between life and death.* New York: Springer.

Garfield, C. A., & Clark, R. O. (1978). The SHANTI project: A community model of psychosocial support for patients and families facing life-threatening illness. In C. A. Garfield (Ed.), *Psychosocial care of the dying patient.* New York: McGraw-Hill.

Geer, J. H. (1965). The development of a scale to measure fear. *Behavior Research and Therapy, 3,* 45–53.

Glaser, B. G., & Strauss, A. L. (1964). The social loss of dying patients. *American Journal of Nursing, 64,* 119–121.

Glaser, B. G., & Strauss, A. L. (1965). *Awareness of dying.* Chicago: Aldine.

Glaser, B. G., & Strauss, A. L. (1968). *Time for dying.* Chicago: Aldine.

Glick, I. O., Weiss, R. S., & Parkes, C. M. (1974). *The first year of bereavement.* New York: Wiley.

Glock, C. Y., & Stark, R. (1965). *Religion and society in tension.* Chicago: Rand McNally.

Golding, S. L., Atwood, G. E., & Goodman, R. A. (1966). Anxiety and two cognitive forms of resistance to the idea of death. *Psychological Reports, 18,* 359–364.

Gordon, A. K., & Klass, D. (1979). *They need to know: How to teach children about death.* Englewood Cliffs, NJ: Prentice-Hall.

Gorer, G. (1967). *Death, grief, and mourning.* New York: Anchor Books.

Gosselin, J.-Y., Perez, E., & Gagnon, A. (1981). The physician and the terminally ill patient. *Psychiatric Journal of the University of Ottawa, 6,* 252–256.

Gottlieb, C. (1959). Modern art and death. In H. Feifel (Ed.), *The meaning of death.* New York: McGraw-Hill.

Greeley, A. M. (1975). *Sociology of the paranormal: A reconnaissance.* Beverly Hills, CA: Sage.

Grof, S., & Halifax, J. (1977). *The human encounter with death.* New York: Dutton.

Grof, S., Pahnke, W. N., Kurland, A. A., & Goodman, L. E. (1971). *LSD-assisted psychotherapy in patients with terminal cancer.* Presentation at the Fifth Symposium of the Foundation of Thanatology, New York. (Mimeograph)

Gustafson, E. (1973). Dying: The career of the nursing-home patient. *Journal of Health and Social Behavior, 13,* 226–235.

Habenstein, R. W., & Lamers, W. M. (1974). *Funeral customs the world over* (2nd ed.). Milwaukee: Bulfin.

Hackett, T. P., & Weisman, A. D. (1961). "Hexing" in modern medicine. *Proceedings of the Third World Congress of Psychiatry,* 1249–1252.

Hall, G. S. (1915). Thanatophobia and immortality. *American Journal of Psychology, 26,* 550–613.

Halpern, W. I. (1972). Some psychiatric sequelae to crib death. *American Journal of Psychiatry, 129*(4), 58–62.

Handal, P. J. (1969). The relationship between subjective life expectancy, death anxiety, and general anxiety. *Journal of Clinical Psychology, 25,* 39–42.

Harmer, R. M. (1963). *The high cost of dying.* New York: Crowell-Collier.

Harrison, A. A., & Moore, M. (1982–83). Birth dates and death dates: A closer look. *Omega, 13,* 117–125.

Haug, M. (1978). Aging and the right to terminate medical treatment. *Journal of Gerontology, 33,* 586–591.

Hilgard, J. R., & Newman, M. F. (1959). Anniversaries in mental illness. *Psychiatry, 22,* 113–121.

Hilgard, J. R., & Newman, M. F. (1961). Evidence for functional genesis in mental illness: Schizophrenia, depressive psychosis, and psychoneurosis. *Journal of Nervous and Mental Disease, 132,* 3–16.

Hinton, J. M. (1963). The physical and mental distress of the dying. *Quarterly Journal of Medicine, 32,* 1–21.

Hinton, J. M. (1972). *Dying* (2nd ed.). Baltimore: Penguin Books.

Hinton, J. M. (1979, January 6). Comparison of places and policies for terminal care. *Lancet, 8106,* 29–32.

Hinton, J. M. (1980). Whom do patients tell? *British Medical Journal, 281,* 1328–1330.

Hodges, D. M. (1981). Using art and poetry with terminally ill children in the hospital. *The Arts in Psychotherapy, 8,* 55–59.

Hoelter, J. W., & Hoelter, J. A. (1980–81). On the interrelationships among exposure to death and dying, fear of death, and anxiety. *Omega, 11,* 241–254.

Holden, C. (1978). Cancer and the mind: How are they connected? *Science, 200,* 1363–1369.

Huber, P. S. (1972). Death and society among the Anggor of New Guinea. *Omega, 3,* 233–243.

Hyland, J. M. (1978). *The role of denial in the patient with cancer.* Presentation at the Forum for Death Education and Counseling, Washington, DC.

Jackson, E. N. (1965). *Telling a child about death.* New York: Channel Press.

Jacobs, S., & Ostfeld, A. (1977). An epidemiological review of the mortality of bereavement. *Psychosomatic Medicine, 39,* 344–357.

Jankofsky, K. P. (1981–82). From lion to lamb: Exemplary deaths in chronicles of the Middle English period. *Omega, 12,* 209–226.

Jeffers, F. C., Nichols, C. R., & Eisdorfer, C. (1961). Attitudes of older persons toward death: A preliminary study. *Journal of Gerontology, 16,* 53–56.

Jeffers, F. C., & Verwoerdt, A. (1970). Factors associated with frequency of death thoughts in elderly community volunteers. In E. Palmore (Ed.), *Normal aging.* Durham, NC: Duke University Press.

Jones, B. (1967). *Design for death.* Indianapolis: Bobbs-Merrill.

Jones, E. (1952). *The life and work of Sigmund Freud.* New York: Basic Books.

Jorgenson, D. E., & Neubecker, R. C. (1980–81). Euthanasia: A national survey of attitudes toward voluntary termination of life. *Omega, 11,* 281–292.

Jung, C. G. (1959). The soul and death. In H. Feifel (Ed.), *The meaning of death.* New York: McGraw-Hill. (Originally published, 1934)

Kalish, R. A. (1963). An approach to the study of death attitudes. *American Behavioral Scientist, 6,* 68–70.

Kalish, R. A. (1963). A continuum of subjectively perceived death. *Gerontologist, 6,* 73–76.

Kalish, R. A. (1969). Experiences of persons reprieved from death. In A. H. Kutscher (Ed.), *Death and bereavement.* Springfield, IL: Charles C Thomas.

Kalish, R. A. (1970). Non-medical interventions in life and death. *Social Science and Medicine, 4,* 655–665.

Kalish, R. A. (1972). Special memorial . . . . *Gerontologist, 12,* 324.

Kalish, R. A. (1980–81). Death educator as deacon. *Omega, 11,* 75–85.

Kalish, R. A. (1982, November). Death and survivorship: The final transition. *Annals of the American Academy of Political and Social Science, 464,* 163–173.

Kalish, R. A., & Goldberg, H. (1978). Clergy attitudes toward funeral directors. *Death Education, 2,* 247–260.

Kalish, R. A., & Goldberg, H. (1979–80). Community attitudes toward funeral directors. *Omega, 10,* 335–346.

Kalish, R. A., & Johnson, A. I. (1972). Value similarities and differences in three generations of women. *Journal of Marriage and the Family, 34,* 49–54.

Kalish, R. A., & Reynolds, D. K. (1981). *Death and ethnicity: A psychocultural study* (2nd printing). Farmingdale, NY: Baywood. (Originally published by University of Southern California Press, 1976)

Kalish, R. A., Reynolds, D. K., & Farberow, N. L. (1974). Community attitudes toward suicide. *Community Mental Health Journal, 10,* 301–308.

Kass, L. R. (1971). Death as an event: A commentary on Robert Morison. *Science, 173,* 698–702.

Kastenbaum, R. J. (1967a). Multiple perspectives on a geriatric "Death Valley." *Community Mental Health Journal, 3,* 21–29.

Kastenbaum, R. J. (1967b). The child's understanding of death: How does it develop? In E. A. Grollman (Ed.), *Explaining death to children.* Boston: Beacon Press.

Kastenbaum, R. J. (1969). Death and bereavement in later life. In A. H. Kutscher (Ed.), *Death and bereavement.* Springfield, IL: Charles C Thomas.

Kastenbaum, R. J. (1975). Is death a life crisis? On the confrontation with death in theory and practice. In N. Datan & L. H. Ginsberg (Eds.), *Life-span developmental psychology: Normative life crises.* New York: Academic Press.

Kastenbaum, R. J. (1977). We covered death today. *Death Education, 1,* 86–92.

Kastenbaum, R. J. (1981). *Death, society, and human experience* (2nd ed.). St. Louis: Mosby.

Kastenbaum, R. J. (1982). New fantasies in the American death system. *Death Education, 6,* 156–166.

Kastenbaum, R. J., & Aisenberg, R. B. (1972). *The psychology of death.* New York: Springer.

Kastenbaum, R. J., & Briscoe, L. (1975). The street corner: Laboratory for the study of life-threatening behavior. *Omega, 6,* 33–44.

Kastenbaum, R. J., & Candy, S. E. (1973). The 4% fallacy: A methodological and empirical critique of extended care facility population statistics. *Aging and Human Development, 4,* 15–22.

Kastenbaum, R. J., & Kastenbaum, B. S. (1971). Hope, survival, and the caring environment. In E. Palmore & F. C. Jeffers (Eds.), *Prediction of life span.* Lexington, MA: Heath.

Keith, P. M. (1979). Life changes and perceptions of life and death among older men and women. *Journal of Gerontology, 6,* 870–878.

Kelly, O. E. (1978). Living with a life-threatening illness. In C. A. Garfield (Ed.), *Psychosocial care of the dying patient.* New York: McGraw-Hill.

Kimsey, L. R., Roberts, J. L., & Logan, D. L. (1972). Death, dying and denial in the aged. *American Journal of Psychiatry, 129,* 161–166.

Klass, D. (1981–82). Elisabeth Kübler-Ross and the tradition of the private sphere: An analysis of symbols. *Omega, 12,* 241–267.

Klass, D. (1982). Self-help groups for the bereaved: Theory, theology, and practice. *Journal of Religion and Health, 21,* 307–324.

Klass, D., & Shinners, B. (1982–83). Professional roles in a self-help group for the bereaved. *Omega, 13,* 361–375.

Klein, M. (1948). A contribution to the theory of anxiety and guilt. *International Journal of Psychoanalysis, 29,* 114–123.

Knott, J. E. (1979). Death education for all. In H. Wass (Ed.), *Dying: Facing the facts.* New York: McGraw-Hill.

Knott, J. E., & Prull, R. W. (1976). Death education: Accountable to whom? For what? *Omega, 7,* 177–181.

Knudtson, A. L. (1967). The definition and value of a new human life. *Social Science and Medicine, 1,* 7–29.

Koenig, R. R. (1968). Fatal illness: A survey of social service needs. *Social Work, 13,* 85–90.

Koenig, R. R. (1969). Anticipating death from cancer—physician and patient attitudes. *Michigan Medicine, 68,* 899–905.

Koestenbaum, P. (1971). *The vitality of death.* Westport, CT: Greenwood.

Koff, T. H. (1980). *Hospice: A caring community*. Cambridge, MA: Winthrop.

Kogan, N., & Wallach, M. (1961). Age changes in values and attitudes. *Journal of Gerontology, 16*, 272–280.

Kollar, N. (1982). *Songs of suffering*. Minneapolis: Winston Press.

Kroeber, A. L. (1948). *Anthropology* (2nd ed.). New York: Harcourt Brace Jovanovich.

Kübler-Ross, E. (1969). *On death and dying*. New York: Macmillan.

Kübler-Ross, E. (1974a). *Questions and answers on death and dying*. New York: Macmillan.

Kübler-Ross, E. (1974b, Summer). The languages of dying. *Journal of Clinical Child Psychology, 3*, 22–24.

Kübler-Ross, E. (1975). Introduction. In E. Kübler-Ross (Ed.), *Death: The final stage of growth*. Englewood Cliffs, NJ: Prentice-Hall.

Kunz, P. R., & Summers, J. (1979–80). A time to die: A study of the relationship of birthdays to time of death. *Omega, 10*, 281–290.

Lachman, S. J. (1982–83). A psychophysiological interpretation of voodoo illness and voodoo death. *Omega, 13*, 354–360.

Lack, S. A., & Buckingham, R. W. (1978). *The first American hospice: Three years of home care*. New Haven, CT: Hospice, Inc.

Langer, W. L. (1964). The black death. *Scientific American, 210*, 114–121.

Leaf, A. (1973). Getting old. *Scientific American, 229*, 44–53.

Lepp, I. (1968). *Death and its mysteries*. New York: Macmillan.

Lerea, L. E., & LiMauro, B. F. (1982). Grief among healthcare workers: A comparative study. *Journal of Gerontology, 37*, 604–608.

Lerner, M. (1970). When, why, and where people die. In O. G. Brim, H. E. Freeman, S. Levine, & N. A. Scotch (Eds.), *The dying patient*. New York: Russell Sage Foundation.

LeShan, L. (1969a). Mobilizing the life force. *Annals of the New York Academy of Sciences, 164*, 847–861.

LeShan, L. (1969b). Psychotherapy and the dying patient. In L. Pearson (Ed.), *Death and dying*. Cleveland, OH: Case Western Reserve University Press.

LeShan, L., & LeShan, E. (1961). Psychotherapy and the patient with a limited life span. *Psychiatry, 24*, 318–323.

Lester, D. (1967). Experimental and correlational studies of the fear of death. *Psychological Bulletin, 67*, 27–36.

Lester, G., & Lester, D. (1971). *Suicide: The gamble with death*. Englewood Cliffs, NJ: Prentice-Hall.

Levinson, D. J. (1978). *The seasons of a man's life*. New York: Knopf.

Leviton, D., & Fretz, B. (1978–79). Effects of death education on fear of death and attitudes towards death and life. *Omega, 3*, 267–277.

Lifton, R. J. (1967). *Death in life: Survivors of Hiroshima*. New York: Random House.

Lifton, R. J. (1977). The sense of immortality: On death and the continuity of life. In H. Feifel (Ed.), *New meanings of death*. New York: McGraw-Hill.

Lifton, R. J., & Olson, E. (1974). *Living and dying*. New York: Praeger.

Lindemann, E. (1965). Symptomatology and management of acute grief. In R. Fulton (Ed.), *Death and identity*. New York: Wiley. (Reprinted from *American Journal of Psychiatry*, 1944, *101*, 141–148)

Linn, B. S., & Linn, M. W. (1981). Late stage cancer patients: Age differences in their psychophysical status and response to counseling. *Journal of Gerontology, 36*, 689–692.

The longest war. (1979, June 11). *Newsweek*, p. 100.

Lopata, H. Z. (1973). *Widowhood in an American city*. Cambridge, MA: Schenkman.

Lopata, H. Z. (1979). *Women as widows: Support systems.* New York: Elsevier/North-Holland.

Lundahl, C. R. (1981). Directions in near-death research. *Death Education, 5,* 135–142.

Maddison, D., & Viola, A. (1968). The health of widows in the year following bereavement. *Journal of Psychosomatic Research, 12,* 297–306.

Maizler, J. S., Solomon, J. P., & Almquist, E. (1983). Psychogenic mortality syndrome: Choosing to die by the institutionalized elderly. *Death Education, 6,* 353–364.

Mandelbaum, D. G. (1959). Social uses of funeral rites. In H. Feifel (Ed.), *The meaning of death.* New York: McGraw-Hill.

Markusen, E., & Fulton, R. (1971). Childhood bereavement and behavioral disorders: A critical review. *Omega, 2,* 107–117.

Marris, P. (1975). *Loss and change.* New York: Anchor Books.

Marshall, V. W. (1975). Socialization for impending death in a retirement village. *American Journal of Sociology, 80,* 1124–1144.

Marshall, V. W. (1980). *Last chapters: A sociology of aging and dying.* Monterey, CA: Brooks/Cole.

Marshall, V. W. (1982). Death and dying. In D. J. Mangen & W. A. Peterson (Eds.), *Research instruments in social gerontology.* Vol. 1: *Clinical and social psychology.* Minneapolis: University of Minnesota Press.

Martin, D. S., & Wrightsman, L. (1965). The relationship between religious behavior and concern about death. *Journal of Social Psychology, 65,* 317–323.

Maslow, A. H. (1970a). *Motivation and personality* (2nd ed.). New York: Harper & Row.

Maslow, A. H. (1970b). *Religions, values, and peak experiences.* New York: Viking Press.

Maurer, A. (1961). The child's knowledge of non-existence. *Journal of Existential Psychiatry, 2,* 193–212.

Maurer, A. (1966). Maturation of concepts of death. *British Journal of Medical Psychology, 39,* 35–51.

May, H. J., & Breme, F. J. (1982–83). SIDS Family Adjustment Scale: A method of assessing family adjustment to sudden infant death syndrome. *Omega, 13,* 59–74.

Mazess, R. B., & Forman, S. H. (1979). Longevity and age by exaggeration in Vilcabamba, Ecuador. *Journal of Gerontology, 34,* 94–98.

Mbiti, J. S. (1970). *African religions and philosophy.* Garden City, N.Y.: Anchor Books.

McDonald, R. T. (1981). The effect of death education on specific attitudes toward death in college students. *Death Education, 5,* 59–65.

McMordie, W. R. (1981). Religiosity and fear of death: Strength of belief system. *Psychological Reports, 49,* 921–922.

McNeil, J. N. (1983). Young mothers' communication about death with their children. *Death Education, 4,* 323–339.

Medvedev, Z. A. (1974). Caucasus and Altay longevity: A biological or social problem? *Gerontologist, 14,* 381–387.

Mellins, R. B., & Haddad, G. G. (1983). Sudden infant death syndrome. In R. E. Behrman & V. C. Vaughn, III (Eds.), *Textbook of pediatrics* (12th ed.). Philadelphia: Saunders.

Menig-Peterson, C., & McCabe, A. (1977–78). Children talk about death. *Omega, 8,* 305–317.

Meyers, D. W. (1977). *The California State Bar Journal, 52,* 326–331; 381–383.

Mitchell, M. E. (1967). *The child's attitude to death.* New York: Schocken Books.

Mitford, J. (1963). *The American way of death.* New York: Simon & Schuster.

Monk, M. (1975). Epidemiology. In S. Perlin (Ed.), *A handbook for the study of suicide.* New York: Oxford University Press.

Moody, R. A., Jr. (1976). *Life after life.* New York: Bantam Books.

Morgan, S. A., Buchanan, D., & Abram, H. S. (1976). Psychosocial aspects of hyaline membrane disease. *Psychosomatics, 17*(3), 147–150.

Morrissey, J. R. (1963). A note on interviews with children facing imminent death. *Social Casework, 44,* 343–345.

Mortimer, E. A. (1983). Preventive pediatrics and epidemiology. In R. E. Behrman & V. C. Vaughn, III (Eds.), *Textbook of pediatrics* (12th ed.). Philadelphia: Saunders.

Moss, L. M., & Hamilton, D. F. (1957). Psychotherapy of the suicidal patient. In E. S. Shneidman & N. L. Farberow (Eds.), *Clues to suicide.* New York: McGraw-Hill.

Moss, M. S., & Moss, S. Z. (1980). The image of the deceased spouse in remarriage of elderly widow(er)s. *Journal of Gerontological Social Work, 3,* 59–69.

Moss, M. S., & Moss, S. Z. (1983–84). The impact of parental death on middle aged children. *Omega, 14,* 65–75.

Mount, B. M., Jones, A., & Patterson, A. (1974). Death and dying: Attitudes in a teaching hospital. *Urology, 4,* 741–747.

Munley, A. (1983). *The hospice alternative: A new context for death and dying.* New York: Basic Books.

Myers, J. E., Wass, H., & Murphey, M. (1980). Ethnic differences in death anxiety among the elderly. *Death Education, 4,* 237–244.

Nagy, M. H. (1948). The child's theories concerning death. *Journal of Genetic Psychology, 73,* 3–27.

National Council on the Aging. (1975). *The myth and reality of aging in America.* Washington, DC: Author.

Natterson, J. M., & Knudson, A. G. (1960). Observations concerning fear of death in fatally ill children and their mothers. *Psychosomatic Medicine, 22,* 456–465.

Nehrke, M. F., Bellucci, G., & Gabriel, S. J. (1977–78). Death anxiety, locus of control, and life satisfaction in the elderly: Toward a definition of ego-integrity. *Omega, 8,* 359–568.

Nehrke, M. F., Hulicka, I. M., Turner, R. R., Morganti, J. B., Whitbourne, S. K., & Cohen, S. H. (1981, November). *Factor analysis of death anxiety.* Paper presented at the 34th Annual Gerontological Society of America meeting, Toronto, Ontario.

Nelson, L. D., & Nelson, C. C. (1973). *Religion and death anxiety.* Presentation at the annual meeting of the Society for the Scientific Study of Religion, San Francisco.

Nelson, L. D., & Nelson, C. C. (1975). A factor analytic inquiry into the multidimensionality of death anxiety. *Omega, 6,* 171–178.

Nolph, K. D., & Van Stone, J. (1982). Dialysis. In H. C. Gonick (Ed.), *Current nephrology* (Vol. 5). New York: Wiley.

Noss, J. B. (1969). *Man's religions* (4th ed.). New York: Macmillan.

Noyes, R. (1982–83). The human experience of death or, what can we learn from near-death experiences? *Omega, 13,* 251–259.

Noyes, R., & Kletti, R. (1972). The experience of dying from falls. *Omega, 3,* 45–52.

Noyes, R., & Kletti, R. (1976). Depersonalization in the face of life-threatening danger: An interpretation. *Omega, 7,* 103–114.

Noyes, R., & Slymen, D. J. (1978–79). The subjective response to life-threatening danger. *Omega, 9,* 313–321.

Nuckols, R. (1973). Widows study. JSAS *Catalog of Selected Documents in Psychology, 3,* 9. Cited in a working document prepared by R. L. Taylor.

Osis, K., & Haraldsson, E. (1977). *At the hour of death.* New York: Avon Books.

Osler, W. (1904). *Science and immortality.* Boston: Houghton Mifflin.

Ostheimer, J. M. (1980). The polls: Changing attitudes toward euthanasia. *Public Opinion Quarterly, 44,* 123–128.

Owen, G., Fulton R., & Markusen, E. (1982–83). Death at a distance: A study of family survivors. *Omega, 13,* 191–226.

Pahnke, W. A. (1969). The psychedelic mystical experience in the human encounter with death. *Harvard Theological Review, 62,* 1–32.

Parkes, C. M. (1964). The effects of bereavement on physical and mental health—a study of the medical records of widows. *British Medical Journal, 2,* 274–279.

Parkes, C. M. (1972). *Bereavement.* New York: International Universities Press.

Parkes, C. M. (1975). Determinants of outcome following bereavement. *Omega, 6,* 303–323.

Parkes, C. M. (1980). Terminal care: Evaluation of an advisory domiciliary service at St. Christopher's Hospice. *Postgraduate Medical Journal, 56,* 685–689.

Parkes, C. M. (in press). Research: Bereavement. *Omega.*

Parkes, C. M., Benjamin, B., & Fitzgerald, R. G. (1969). Broken heart: A statistical study of increased mortality among widowers. *British Medical Journal, 1,* 740–743.

Parkes, C. M., & Brown, R. (1972). Health after bereavement: A controlled study of young Boston widows and widowers. *Psychosomatic Medicine, 34,* 449–461.

Parkes, C. M., & Weiss, R. S. (1983). *Recovery from bereavement.* New York: Basic Books.

Parsons, T., & Lidz, V. (1967). Death in American society. In E. S. Shneidman (Ed.), *Essays in self-destruction.* New York: Science House.

Pattison, E. M. (1977). The dying experience—restrospective analysis. In E. M. Pattison (Ed.), *The experience of dying.* Englewood Cliffs, NJ: Prentice-Hall.

Paulay, D. (1977–78). Slow death: One survivor's experience. *Omega, 8,* 173–179.

Peal, R., Handal, P. J., & Gilner, F. H. (1981–82). A group desensitization procedure for the reduction of death anxiety. *Omega, 12,* 61–70.

Peck, M. (1982). Youth suicide. *Death Education, 6,* 29–47.

Perlin, S., & Schmidt, C. W., Jr. (1975). Psychiatry. In S. Perlin (Ed.), *A handbook for the study of suicide.* New York: Oxford University Press.

Phillips, D. P., & Feldman, K. A. (1973). A dip in deaths before ceremonial occasions: Some new relationships between social integration and mortality. *American Sociological Review, 38,* 678–696.

Pinder, M. M., & Hayslip, B. (1981). Cognitive, attitudinal, and affective aspects of death and dying in adulthood: Implications for care providers. *Educational Gerontology, 6,* 107–123.

Pine, V. R. (1974). The social context of disaster. In V. R. Pine (Ed.), *Responding to disaster.* Milwaukee: Bulfin.

Pine, V. R. (1975). *Caretaker of the dead: The American funeral director.* New York: Irvington.

Pollak, J. M. (1979–80). Correlates of death anxiety: A review of empirical studies. *Omega, 10,* 97–121.

Portz, A. (1972). The child's sense of death. In A. Godin (Ed.), *Death and presence.* Brussels, Belgium: Lumen Vitae Press.

Raether, H. C., & Slater, R. C. (1974). *The funeral: Facing death as an experience of life.* Milwaukee: National Funeral Directors Association.

Raether, H. C., & Slater, R. C. (1977). Immediate postdeath activities in the United States. In H. Feifel (Ed.), *New meanings of death.* New York: McGraw-Hill.

Ramsey, P. (1975). The indignity of 'death with dignity.' In P. Steinfels & R. M. Veatch (Eds.), *Death inside out.* New York: Harper & Row.

Raphael, B. (1983). *The anatomy of bereavement.* New York: Basic Books.

Rees, W. D. & Lutkins, S. G. (1967). Mortality of bereavement. *British Medical Journal, 4,* 13–16.

Reilly, T. P., Hasazi, J. E., & Bond, L. A. (1983). Children's conceptions of death and personal mortality. *Journal of Pediatric Psychology, 8,* 21–31.

Reynolds, D. K., & Farberow, N. L. (1976). *Suicide: Inside and out.* Berkeley and Los Angeles: University of California Press.

Reynolds, D. K., & Kalish, R. A. (1974a). Anticipation of futurity as a function of ethnicity and age. *Journal of Gerontology, 29,* 224–231.

Reynolds, D. K., & Kalish, R. A. (1974b). The social ecology of dying: Observations of wards for the terminally ill. *Hospital and Community Psychiatry, 25*(3), 147–152.

Reynolds, D. K., & Kalish, R. A. (1976). Death rates, attitudes, and the ethnic press. *Ethnicity, 3,* 305–316.

Rhudick, R. J., & Dibner, A. S. (1961). Age, personality, and health correlates of death concern in normal aged individuals. *Journal of Gerontology, 16,* 44–49.

Ribble, M. A. (1943). *The rights of infants: Early psychological needs and their satisfaction.* New York: Columbia University Press.

Richmond, J. B., & Waisman, H. A. (1955). Psychologic aspects of management of children with malignant diseases. *American Journal of the Diseases of Children, 89,* 42–47.

Richter, C. P. (1959). The phenomenon of unexplained sudden death in animals and man. In H. Feifel (Ed.), *The meaning of death.* New York: McGraw-Hill.

Riley, J. W., Jr. (1968). Unpublished research data. In M. Riley, A. Foner, & Associates (Eds.), *Aging and society.* Vol. 1: *An inventory of research findings.* New York: Russell Sage Foundation.

Riley, J. W., Jr. (1970). What people think about death. In O. G. Brim, H. E. Freeman, S. Levine, & N. A. Scotch (Eds.), *The dying patient.* New York: Russell Sage Foundation.

Ring, K., & Franklin, S. (1981–82). Do suicide survivors report near-death experiences? *Omega, 12,* 191–208.

Rodabough, T. (1981–82). Funeral roles: Ritualized expectations. *Omega, 12,* 227–240.

Rodman, M., & Rodman, W. (1983–84). The hundred days of Sara Mata: Explaining unnatural death in Vanuata. *Omega, 14,* 135–144.

Rogers, J., Sheldon, A., Barwick, C., Letofsky, K., & Lancee, W. (1982). Help for families of suicide: Survivors Support Program. *Canadian Journal of Psychiatry, 27,* 444–449.

Rosen, D. (1975). Suicide survivors: A follow-up study of persons who survived jumps from the Golden Gate and San Francisco Bay bridges. *Western Journal of Medicine, 122,* 289–294.

Rosenbaum, E. H. (1978). Oncology/hematology and psychosocial support of the cancer patient. In C. A. Garfield (Ed.), *Psychosocial care of the dying patient.* New York: McGraw-Hill.

Rosenfeld, A. H. (1978). *New views on older lives.* Washington, DC: U.S. Government Printing Office.

Rosenheim, E., & Muchnik, B. (1984-85). Death concerns in differential levels of consciousness as functions of defense strategy and religious belief. *Omega, 15,* 15–24.

Rosenzweig, S., & Bray, D. (1943). Sibling deaths in the anamneses of schizophrenic patients. *Archives of Neurology and Psychiatry, 49,* 71–92.

Rowland, K. F. (1977). Environmental events predicting death for the elderly. *Psychological Bulletin, 84,* 349–372.

Ryan, J. (1983–84). Silent barter. *Omega, 14,* 145–154.

Sabom, M. B., & Kreutziger, S. (1977). The experience of near death. *Death Education, 1,* 195–203.

Sainsbury, P. (1975). Community psychology. In S. Perlin (Ed.), *A handbook for the study of suicide.* New York: Oxford University Press.

Sanders, C. M. (1980–81). Comparison of younger and older spouses in bereavement outcome. *Omega, 11,* 217–232.

Sanders, C. M. (1982–83). Effects of sudden vs. chronic illness death on bereavement outcome. *Omega, 13,* 227–241.

Schmitt, R. L. (1982–83). Symbolic immortality in ordinary contexts: Impediments to the nuclear era. *Omega, 13,* 95–116.

Schoenberg, J., & Stichman, J. (1974). *How to survive your husband's heart attack.* New York: McKay.

Schulz, R. (1978). *The psychology of death, dying, and bereavement.* Reading, MA: Addison-Wesley.

Schulz, R., & Aderman, D. (1974). Clinical research and the stages of dying. *Omega, 5,* 137–143.

Scott, C. A. (1896). Old age and death. *American Journal of Psychology, 8,* 54–122.

Searles, H. F. (1961). Schizophrenia and the inevitability of death. *Psychiatric Quarterly, 35,* 631–655.

Seiden, R. H. (1981). Mellowing with age: Factors influencing the nonwhite suicide rate. *Aging and Human Development, 13,* 265–284.

Seligman, M. E. P. (1975). *Helplessness: On depression, development, and death.* San Francisco: W. H. Freeman.

Shaffer, T. L. (1970). *Death, property, and lawyers.* New York: Dunellen.

Shaffer, T. L., & Rodes, R. E., Jr. (1977). Law for those who are to die. In H. Feifel (Ed.), *New meanings of death.* New York: McGraw-Hill.

Sharapan, H. (1977). "Mister Rogers' Neighborhood": Dealing with death on children's television series. *Death Education, 1,* 131–136.

Sharma, K. L., & Jain, U. C. (1969). Religiosity and fear of death in young and retired persons. *Indian Journal of Gerontology, 1,* 110–114.

Shneidman, E. S. (1970, August). The enemy. *Psychology Today,* pp. 37–41.

Shneidman, E. S. (1971a, June). You and death. *Psychology Today,* pp. 43ff.

Shneidman, E. S. (1971b). On the deromanticization of death. *American Journal of Psychotherapy, 25,* 4–17.

Shneidman, E. S. (1973). *Deaths of man.* New York: Quadrangle/New York Times.

Shneidman, E. S., & Farberow, N. (Eds.). (1961). *The cry for help.* New York: McGraw-Hill.

Shoor, M., & Speed, M. H., (1963). Death, delinquency, and the mourning process. *Psychiatry Quarterly, 37,* 540–548.

Simmons, L. W. (1945). *The role of the aged in primitive society.* New Haven, CT: Yale University Press.

Simonton, O. C., Matthews-Simonton, S., & Creighton, J. (1978). *Getting well again.* Los Angeles: Tarcher.

Simpson, M. A. (1979). *The facts of death.* Englewood Cliffs, NJ: Prentice-Hall.

Smith, J. Q. (1975). The life and death of a schizophrenic. *Psychotherapy: Theory, Research, and Practice, 12,* 2–7.

Smith, R. J., Sherman, M. F., & Sherman, N. C. (1982–83). The elderly's reactions toward the dying: The effects of perceived age similarity. *Omega, 13,* 319–331.

Spinetta, J. J., Rigler, D., & Karon, M. (1973). Anxiety in the dying child. *Pediatrics, 52,* 841–844.

Statistical Abstract of Funeral Service Facts and Figures (1983). Published by the National Funeral Directors Association.

Statistical abstracts of the United States (103rd ed.). (1982–83). Washington, DC: U.S. Department of Commerce.

Steele, D. W. (1975). *The funeral director's guide to designing and implementing programs for the widowed.* Milwaukee: National Funeral Directors Association.

Stein, Z., & Susser, M. (1969). Widowhood and mental illness. *British Journal of Preventive Social Medicine, 23,* 106–110.

Stekel, W. (1949). *Conditions of nervous anxiety and their treatment.* New York: Liveright.

Stillion, J., & Wass, H. (1979). Children and death. In H. Wass (Ed.), *Dying: Facing the facts.* New York: McGraw-Hill.

Strassman, H. D., Thaler, M., & Schein, E. H. (1956). A prisoner of war syndrome: Apathy as a reaction to severe stress. *American Journal of Psychiatry, 112,* 998–1003.

Stringham, J. G., Riley, J. H., & Ross, A. (1982). Silent birth: Mourning a stillborn baby. *Social Work, 27,* 322–327.

Sudnow, D. (1967). *Passing on: The social organization of dying.* Englewood Cliffs, NJ: Prentice-Hall.

Swenson, W. M. (1961). Attitudes toward death in an aged population. *Journal of Gerontology, 16,* 49–52.

Szybist, C. (n.d.). *The subsequent child.* New York: National Foundation for Sudden Infant Death.

Telban, S. G. (1981). Death anxiety and knowledge about death. *Psychological Reports, 49,* 648.

Templer, D. I. (1972). Death anxiety in religiously very involved persons. *Psychological Reports, 31,* 361–362.

Templer, D. I., Ruff, C., & Frank, C. (1971). Death anxiety: Age, sex, and parental resemblance in diverse populations. *Developmental Psychology, 4,* 108.

Testa, J. A. (1981). Group systematic desensitization and implosive therapy for death anxiety. *Psychological Reports, 48,* 376–378.

Thielicke, H. (1970). *Death and life.* Philadelphia: Fortress Press.

Tillich, P. (1959). *The theology of culture.* New York: Oxford University Press.

Tobin, D. & Treloar, D. (1979). *A survey of responses to death in Victorian high school students.* Unpublished. Cited in Raphael, 1983.

Toch, R. (1977). Cancer in the school age child. In E. M. Pattison (Ed.), *The experience of dying.* Englewood Cliffs, NJ: Prentice-Hall.

Tramill, J. L. et al. (1982). A proposed relationship between the unidimensional short form of the TMAS and the DAS: The effects of embedding vs. separate administration. *Bulletin of the Psychonomic Society, 19,* 209–211.

Trent, C., Glass, J. C., Jr., & McGee, A. Y. (1981). The impact of a workshop on death and dying on death anxiety, life satisfaction, and locus of control among middle-aged and older adults. *Death Education, 5,* 157–173.

Vachon, M. L. S. (1978). Motivation and stress experienced by staff working with the terminally ill. *Death Education, 2,* 113–122.

Vachon, M. L. S. (1983). Bereavement programmes and interventions in palliative care. In *Proceedings, 13th International Cancer Congress.* New York: Alan R. Liss.

Vachon, M.L.S., Lyall, W.A.L., Rogers, J., Freedman-Letofsky, K., & Freeman, S.J.J. (1980). A controlled study of self-help intervention for widows. *American Journal of Psychiatry, 137,* 1380–1384.

Vachon, M. L. S., Sheldon, A. R., Lancee, W. J., Lyall, W. A. L., Rogers, J., & Freeman, S. J. J. (1982). Correlates of enduring distress patterns following bereavement: Social network, life situation, and personality. *Psychological Medicine, 12,* 783–788.

Van Arsdale, P. W., & Radetsky, C. L. (1983–84). Life and death in New Guinea. *Omega, 14,* 155–169.

Vargo, M. E., & Batsel, W. M. (1981). Relationship between death anxiety & components of the self-actualization process. *Psychological Reports, 48,* 89–90.

Veatch, R. M. (1976). *Death, dying, and the biological revolution.* New Haven, CT: Yale University Press.

Veatch, R. M. (1979). Defining death anew. In H. Wass (Ed.), *Dying: Facing the facts.* New York: McGraw-Hill.

Veatch, R. M. (1982). When should the patient know? In A. E. Doudera & J. D. Peters (Eds.), *Legal and ethical aspects of treating critically and terminally ill patients.* Ann Arbor, Michigan: AUPHA Press.

Volkan, V. D. (1970). Typical findings in pathological grief. *Psychiatric Quarterly, 44,* 231–250.

Volkan, V. D., Cilluffo, A. F., & Sarvay, T. L., Jr. (1975). Re-grief therapy and the function of the linking object as a key to stimulate emotionality. In P. Olsen (Ed.), *Emotional flooding.* New York: Behavioral Publications.

Volkart, E. H., & Michael, S. T. (1957). Bereavement and mental health. In A. H. Leighton, J. A. Clausen, & R. N. Wilson (Eds.), *Explorations in social psychiatry.* New York: Basic Books.

Waechter, E. H. (1971). Children's awareness of fatal illness. *American Journal of Nursing, 71,* 1168–1172.

Wahl, C. W. (1959). The fear of death. In H. Feifel (Ed.), *The meaning of death.* New York: McGraw-Hill.

Wales, J., Kane, R., & Bernstein, L. (1983, November). *Who benefits? Randomized trial data.* Paper presented at the 36th annual meeting of the Gerontological Society of America, San Francisco.

Ward, R. A. (1980). Age and acceptance of euthanasia. *Journal of Gerontology, 35,* 421–431.

Wass, H., Christian, M., Myers, J., & Murphey, M. (1978–79). Similarities and dissimilarities in attitudes toward death in a population of older persons. *Omega, 9,* 337–354.

Wass, H., & Sisler, H. (1978). *Death concerns and views on various aspects of dying among elderly persons.* Paper presented at the International Symposium on the Dying Human, Tel Aviv, Israel.

Watt, N. F., & Nicholi, A. (1979). Early death of a parent as an etiological factor in schizophrenia. *American Journal of Orthopsychiatry, 49,* 465–473.

Watts, A. W. (1957). *The way of Zen.* New York: Pantheon.

Watts, P. R. (1977). Evaluation of death attitude change resulting from a death education instructional unit. *Death Education, 1,* 187–193.

Weisman, A. D. (1972). *On dying and denying.* New York: Behavioral Publications.

Weisman, A. D. (1977). The psychiatrist and the inexorable. In H. Feifel (Ed.), *New meanings of death.* New York: McGraw-Hill.

Weisman, A. D., & Hackett, T. P. (1961). Predilection to death: Death and dying as a psychiatric problem. *Psychosomatic Medicine, 23,* 232–256.

Weisman, A. D., & Worden, J. W. (1975). Psychosocial analysis of cancer deaths. *Omega, 6,* 61–75.

Weiss, R. S. (1975). *Marital separation.* New York: Basic Books.

White, P. D., Gilner, F. H., Handal, P. J., & Napoli, J. G. (1983–84). A behavioral intervention for death anxiety in nurses. *Omega, 14,* 33–42.

Wilson, A. L., & Soule, D. J. (1981). The role of a self-help group in working with parents of a stillborn baby. *Death Education, 5,* 175–186.

Wittkowski, J. (1981, July). *Attitudes toward death and dying in older persons and their dependence on life satisfaction and death-related experiences.* Paper presented at the 12th International Congress of Gerontology, Hamburg, Germany.

Wolfenstein, M. (1977). *Disaster: A psychological essay* (2nd ed.). New York: Free Press.

Woodruff, D. S. (1977). *Can you live to be 100?* New York: Chatham Square Press.

Woodson, R. (1978). Hospice care in terminal illness. In C. A. Garfield (Ed.), *Psychosocial care of the dying patient.* New York: McGraw-Hill.

Worcester, A. (1961). *The care of the aged, the dying and the dead* (2nd ed.). Springfield, IL: Charles C Thomas.

Worden, J. W. (1982). *Grief counseling and grief therapy.* New York: Springer.

Young, M., Benjamin, B., & Wallis, C. (1963). The mortality of widowers. *Lancet, 2,* 454–456.

Zeligs, R. (1974). *Children's experience with death.* Springfield, IL: Charles C Thomas.

Zinker, J. C., & Fink, S. L. (1966). The possibility of psychological growth in a dying person. *Journal of General Psychology, 74,* 185–199.

Name Index

Abeloff, M., 129
Abernathy, V., 281
Ablin, A. R., 198, 231
Abram, H. S., 125, 286, 287
Achté, K. A., 151
Aday, R. H., 109, 112
Aderman, D., 135
Adlerstein, A. M., 18, 91, 99
Aisenberg, R. B., 19, 45, 93
Alexander, I. E., 17, 18, 91, 99
Almquist, E., 17
Amenta, M. M., 106
American Council of Life Insurance, 155–157
Anderson, J. L., 151, 291, 302, 303
Appleton, W. S., 49
Argyle, M., 60
Ariès, P., 20, 39, 44, 76
Aronow, E., 110
Artiss, K., 279
Atwood, G. E., 99
Augustine, M. J., 56
Averill, J. R., 182, 184, 211

Ball, J. F., 198
Bankoff, E. A., 246
Barber, T. X., 172
Barraclough, B., 199
Barrett, C. J., 208, 312
Batsel, W. M., 110

Becker, E., 94, 95, 96, 97, 228
Beckwith, B., 250
Beit-Hallahmi, B., 60
Bellah, R., 58
Belluci, G., 109
Bendiksen, R., 194
Bengtson, V. L., 82, 251
Benjamin, B., 186
Benoliel, J. Q., 290
Bequaert, L. H., 206
Bergman, A. B., 250
Bernstein, L., 296
Bertman, S. L., 22
Binger, C. M., 198, 231
Blauner, R., 69, 79
Blazer, J. A., 111
Bluebond-Langner, M., 227, 232, 242
Boike, M. F., 235
Bond, L. A., 225
Bornstein, P. E., 189, 199, 312
Bowen, M., 14, 305, 306
Bowlby, J., 171, 186, 190, 234
Branscomb, A. B., 92, 106, 251
Breckenridge, J. N., 257
Brent, S. B., 229
Briscoe, L., 104
Bromberg, W., 12, 90
Brotman, H. B., 206, 256
Brown, G., 194
Brown, R., 188

Subject Index

Abortion, 247–248
Acceptance, 133–134
Adolescents, 237–240
  causes of death, 239
  and death, 237–239
  dying, 239
  grieving, 178–180, 239–240
Adulthood (young and middle),
  241–250
Adults:
  causes of death in, 244
  and death, 241–244
  dying, 244–245
  grieving, 245–250
  as parents, 246–250
Aging processes, intervening in, 37
Alcohol, 311–312
Altered states of consciousness (see
  Near-death experiences)
Alzheimer's disease, 31
Amish, 112–113
Anger, 96, 133, 190–193
Annihilation, 66
Anniversary reactions, 199–200
Anticipatory bereavement/grief,
  197–199
Arts, the, 20–22
Atomic bomb, 168–169
Attitudes toward death, 87–92 (see
  also Death anxiety/fear)
  in adolescents, 237–239

Attitudes toward death (continued)
  in adults, 241–244
  changes in, 299–300
  in children, 225–230
  death as punishment/reward, 49
  death education, 299–300
  defined, 87–88
  dislike, 90
  in the elderly, 251–253
  euthanasia, 166–167
  factors in, 88–89, 106–107
  fear, 43
  of health professionals, 279–280
  "healthy-minded," 97–98
  and immortality, 47, 60
  learning of, 94–98
  limited finitude, 55
  longevity, 49
  as loss, 50, 51
  measurement of, 16–17, 88–89, 91,
    106–108
  "morbid-minded," 97–98
  after near-death experiences, 76
  religious, 111–113
  unconscious, 90–92, 98
Avoidance, 98–99
Awareness of death, 5–23
Awareness of dying:
  in children, 222, 223, 229–233
  closed awareness, 145–146
  contexts, 145–149